A Poet At Court:

Antonio Hurtado de Mendoza

A POET AT COURT:
ANTONIO HURTADO
DE MENDOZA

(1586-1644)

By

Gareth A. Davies

The Dolphin Book Co. Ltd.
Oxford, *1971*

PRINTED IN SPAIN

DEPÓSITO LEGAL: V. 2.775 - 1971

ARTES GRÁFICAS SOLER, S. A. - JÁVEA, 28 - VALENCIA (8) - 1971

Vn dia es siempre Maestro de otro;
contra lo que se escriue oy, estara
lo que mañana se sabe mas.

ANTONIO DE MENDOZA in the prologue
to *Querer por solo querer* (1623)

CONTENTS

ABBREVIATIONS

AHN	Archivo Histórico Nacional, Madrid.
BAE	*Biblioteca de Autores Españoles.*
BH	*Bulletin Hispanique.*
BHS	*Bulletin of Hispanic Studies.*
BM	British Museum Library, London.
BNM	Biblioteca Nacional, Madrid.
BNP	Bibliothèque Nationale, Paris.
Bol.Ac.Esp.	*Boletín de la Real Academia Española.*
Clás.Cast.	Clásicos Castellanos.
d.	died.
ed.	edited.
edn.	edition.
FC	*El Fénix castellano, D. Antonio de Mendoça* ... (Lisboa, Miguel Manescal, 1690).
GOC	Baltasar Gracián, *Obras completas,* ed. Arturo del Hoyo (Madrid, 1960).
Hisp.Am.Cat.	A. Rodríguez-Moñino and María Brey Mariño, *Catálogo de los manuscritos poéticos castellanos* ... *de The Hispanic Society of America* (New York, 1965-6), 3 vols.
His	*Hispania,* Madrid.
HisL	*Hispania* (Stanford, California, and now Lawrence, Kansas).
Hisp.Soc.Am.	Hispanic Society of America.
HR	*Hispanic Review.*
JHI	*Journal of the History of Ideas.*
La Barrera	Cayetano Alberto de la Barrera y Leirado, *Catálogo bibliográfico y biográfico del teatro antiguo español* (Madrid, 1860).
MLN	*Modern Language Notes.*
MLR	*Modern Language Review.*
MPh	*Modern Philology.*
MOP	Antonio Hurtado de Mendoza, *Obras poéticas,* ed. R. Benítez Claros (Madrid, 1947-8), 3 vols.
NBAE	*Nueva Biblioteca de Autores Españoles.*
Nicolás Antonio	Nicolás Antonio, *Bibliotheca Hispana Nova* (ed. Matriti, 1783-8), 2 vols.
n.p.	no place.
Pérez Pastor	Cristóbal Pérez Pastor, *Bibliografía madrileña* (Madrid, 1891-1907), 3 vols.
PMLA	*Publications of the Modern Language Association of America.*

PMS	Bibliothèque Nationale, Paris, *MS Espagnol* No. 418, *Palacio de las Musas y Musas de Palacio, en las poesias de D. Antonio Hurtado de Mendoza* ...
QOCP	Francisco de Quevedo y Villegas, *Obras completas: Obras en prosa,* ed. Luis Astrana Marín, 2nd edn. (Madrid, 1941).
QOCV	Francisco Quevedo y Villegas, *Obras completas. I. Poesía original,* ed. J. M. Blecua (Barcelona, 1963).
Real Ac.Esp.	Real Academia Española.
RFE	*Revista de Filología Española.*
RH	*Revue Hispanique.*
RPh	*Romance Philology.*
RR	*Romanic Review.*

PREFACE

N o apology is needed for publishing a study of the life and work of Antonio de Mendoza. [1] He was, in his period, and for some time afterwards, accounted a major literary figure. One does not have to look far for proof of the high esteem in which he was held, nor of the central position he occupied in the literary life of his times. He was also a highly significant figure, since he epitomizes clearly an attitude only fitfully expressed in the work of his contemporaries, namely the conviction that a palace poetry was, and should strive to remain, a superior form of art. In consequence Mendoza's view of the *poeta de bien* (as he might have termed his own ideal image) opens up an obscured perspective, enabling us to see more clearly how a court poet understood his function, what his aesthetic criteria and preferences were, and in what literary tradition he stood.

What is surely puzzling is the way that Antonio de Mendoza's literary contribution has been laid on one side, and forgotten. The explanation lies in part with the more general neglect suffered by a number of important poets in this period, a situation to which Luis Rosales drew attention as long ago as 1943, in the introduction to the second volume of the anthology *Poesía heroica del imperio*. The "unjustified and long-maintained oblivion" to which Sr. Rosales referred could certainly be extended to contain not only Mendoza, but the Counts of Salinas, and Villamediana, the Prince of Esquilache, and later Gabriel Bocángel, Pedro de Quirós, and Antonio de Solís. Rosales was probably right in attributing such neglect to the selection of poets and poems made for the *Biblioteca de Autores Españoles* in the middle of the last century, a selection which reflected criteria that tended to exclude, or to minimize the value of, the work of poets such as those mentioned. The fact that the critics' preferences were for the established orthodoxy of Italianate poetry meant that the poems in the pithy Castilian metres were given less than their due attention. Furthermore, since these metres and their

---

[1] For ease of bibliographical reference I have retained the poet's full name in the title of this book. In the text, however, I normally use the form by which he was known to his contemporaries, plain Antonio de Mendoza.

accompanying poetic forms were primarily those preferred by the court poet, the neglect inevitably affected not so much individuals, as a whole tradition, that of the palace. Paradoxically, the successful attempt by Dámaso Alonso and others in the late twenties to rehabilitate Luis de Góngora, a great poet who had suffered most perhaps from the dogmatic Philistinism of nineteenth-century criticism, did not lead to the rehabilitation of the minor figures in the poetry of the early seventeenth, for Góngora, once restored to his rightful eminence, cast a shadow which obscured the reputation of many of his contemporaries, including Antonio de Mendoza.

However, it would be unfair to lay too large a portion of the blame at the door of the architects of the *Biblioteca de Autores,* for other principal reasons for neglect have been the unsatisfactory state of our knowledge of the texts of these poets, and the shirking of the laborious and dusty duty of publishing their poems. Over twenty-five years after Rosales's cry of protest, the works of Esquilache still need to be printed in a modern edition; Villamediana has only now at last achieved a comparatively complete edition of his *Obras* (edited by Juan Manuel Rozas, for Editorial Castalia, Madrid, 1969); whilst Salinas's work is still inadequately represented even in the anthologies, so that one has to go to the manuscripts in search of much rich and valuable material. To some extent, therefore, that Antonio de Mendoza is the subject of this book reflects the simple fact that only with the publication of the *Obras poéticas* (edited by Rafael Benítez Claros in three volumes, in the *Biblioteca Selecta de Clásicos Españoles,* Madrid, 1947-48) did it become possible even to begin studying the poet's work in earnest. Even so the difficulty of the editor's task is shown by the existence of two large collections of Mendoza's work, one in Paris, another in New York, that were not available for consultation in making this edition. And to make both editor's and critic's task more unenviable, the main source of the Benítez Claros edition, *El Fénix castellano* (Lisbon, 1690), is full of printer's errors, which are often further confounded rather than dispersed by the consultation of other sources.

The present writer's interest in Mendoza stems from an original curiosity as to why Baltasar Gracián, author of the *Agudeza y arte de ingenio* and a perceptive critic of Spanish seventeenth-century poetry, expressed wholehearted admiration for a poet that modern critics have hardly found to their taste. No proper answer to this question could be given without attempting to estimate Mendoza in the light of seventeenth-century views on the nature of poetry, nor could it be done on the basis of a purely literary appraisal, since Mendoza was the product of a palace society, in which poetry was both an artistic and a social expression. For these reasons therefore, I have presented him in a twofold setting, that of the contemporary literary phenomenon of *concettismo,* and that of a social tradition based on courtly values and pursuits. The first of these two aims, while inevitably following paths already taken by others, at least has the merit of presenting a complex European movement within an individual cultural form, thus bringing to a wider audience's attention those aspects of *concettismo* that Spain shared with other countries, as well as certain aspects that were more particularly Spanish. In pursuing the second aim I profited from the work carried out (sometimes uncritically) by T.F. Crane in his *Italian Social Customs of the Sixteenth Century and their Influence on the Literatures of Europe* (New Haven, Conn., 1920), but was responsive also to some of the aspects of court society explored so fascinatingly in John Stevens's *Music & Poetry in the Early Tudor Court* (London, 1961), and in Edward John Mawby Buxton's *Elizabethan Taste* (London, 1963): here again a study of these things in a Spanish palace setting, it seemed to me, would not only illumine Antonio de Mendoza's career, but make a modest contribution to the wider understanding of the role of palace society in the arts during that period.

In the footnotes English renderings have been given of the Spanish quotations, both prose and poetry, in the body of the text, mainly with the intention of making this study more readily accessible to readers outside the Spanish field. But in addition the great difficulty of interpreting texts which are often highly allusive and obscure justifies any attempt to make sense of the meaning in a different language. The versions I have made are literal, tentative, and apologetic. In most cases, too, where the main text gives a Spanish source in an English version, I have added the Spanish original in the footnote. The main exception to this practice has been the chapter on Mendoza's interludes, where I have at times included snatches of quotation in English when giving an account of the plot.

Quotations from the poems have usually been given in the Benítez Claros text, though sometimes an alternative source has been preferred where that version seemed better. Where doubts have occurred about the accuracy of the text quoted, I have included, alongside the quotation, an alternative reading where available, or a tentative emendation. In such cases the translation in the footnote gives what seems to me the most likely interpretation. In the case of Mendoza's interludes and plays I have borne in mind that the texts should be readily available to the reader for further consultation. Thus, *Querer por solo querer* and the bulk of Mendoza's other *comedias* are quoted in the *Fénix castellano* edition. In the case of plays not included in that collection, I have used the text of other seventeenth-century collections and *sueltas*, with the exception of *Cada loco con su tema*, where I quote the text of the *Biblioteca de Autores* volume that included three of Mendoza's plays. The interludes refer to the texts printed by Emilio Cotarelo in his collection of *entremeses* in two volumes of the *Nueva Biblioteca de Autores Españoles*. I have decided against complete textual consistency in the provision of quotations. To modernize would mean in some cases getting away from new texts in forms close to their originals; to retain seventeenth-century spellings and punctuation everywhere, on the other hand, would make it more difficult for the reader to seek out certain texts for fuller consultation.

My thanks are due to a host of institutions and people. To the University of Leeds, and Dartmouth College, New Hampshire, U.S.A., for the provision of leisure and a congenial environment; to the Brotherton and Baker Libraries at those institutions, as well as to the British Museum Library, the Bodleian Library, the National Libraries in Paris and Madrid, the Library of the Ateneo, Madrid, and the King's Library in Copenhagen, for much patience and advice. Likewise, to the public archives: the Archivo Histórico Nacional, the Archivo de Simancas, the Archivo de Protocolos, the Archivo de Palacio; and to the private collections of the Real Academia de la Historia, and the Hispanic Society of America (whose trustees kindly gave permission for the publication of some of their manuscript material). Among individuals I single out Professors Arthur Terry, E.M. Wilson, and John E. Varey, who read the whole book in typescript, and offered their criticisms and comments; and Professor Keith Whinnom and Mr. Jack Sage, who gave expert assistance in the formulation of Chapters VI and VIII respectively.

I would thank also, for help both specific and intangible, Professor R.F. Brown and my colleagues in the Spanish Department in the University of Leeds, Professors Juan López-Morillas, P.E. Russell, and Norman Shergold, Mrs. Margaret Borland, Mrs. Christine Challis, and Mrs. Martha de Narváez, Miss Carole Adams, Dr. Colin Smith, Mr. Victor Dixon, Mr. Harold Hall, Mr. Dan Rogers and Sr. Luis Rosales. In conclusion, some specific debts: to the secretaries and clerical staff of the departmental office for typing a presentable final draft; to Mr. J.L. Gili, my publisher, for his kindness, efficiency, and attention to detail; to my printers, Artes Gráficas Soler, for their cheerful acceptance of unreasonable requests; to my wife for her supervision of the proofs and the index, as well as for her unstinting encouragement. I record here too my appreciation of certain generous awards: a Laming Travelling Fellowship at the Queen's College, Oxford, which enabled me to spend a year working in Spain; the research grants given to me from time to time by the Cassel Trust; and now the provision by the University of Leeds of a handsome loan towards the cost of publication of this book.

University of Leeds   G. A. D.

October 1970

Diego Hurtado de Mendoza, another ambassador in Rome, but more famed as poet, historian and bibliophile. Indeed Antonio's literary predilections were in all likelihood affected by a knowledge of his distinguished ancestor's work.

Antonio Hurtado de Mendoza y de la Rea was born in Castro Urdiales in the province of Santander, being baptized in the Church of Saint Mary on the 11th of December 1586. [3] "That famous Hurtado of the Muses" (as Lope de Vega called him) [4] must later, however, have wished that his own branch of the family tree had been more richly endowed, for he was the son of a mere *segundón,* the title *Señor de Salcedo* being the prerogative of his paternal uncle, Diego Hurtado de Salcedo y Mendoza, and later of that Don Francisco who petitioned his King in 1642. Like other members of his family Antonio de Mendoza oriented himself genealogically by the House of Salcedo, which he described in a letter to the Count-Duke of Olivares as "possessing great authority in all that region, and the only one to have vassals." [5]

Not until 1608 do we hear again with any certainty of the future poet, by which time indeed he had begun to write verse, for, now a page in the service of the Count of Saldaña (second son of the favourite, the Duke of Lerma), he penned some lines in celebration of the publication of a volume by another dependant of Saldaña, Luis Vélez de Guevara (author later of *El diablo cojuelo*), who celebrated the administration of the oath to the Crown Prince in his *Elogio del juramento del Serenissimo Príncipe Don Phelipe Domingo, Quarto deste nombre.* [6] But what of the blank years that precede 1608? Circumstantial evidence (along with the firm knowledge that at a later date Antonio enjoyed such ducal patronage) points to his having been in the service of Juan Hurtado de Mendoza, sixth Duke of the Infantado, step-father to Luisa de Mendoza, the seventh

---

[3] For details, see Gareth Alban Davies, "Antonio Hurtado de Mendoza: Biographical Notes," *BHS*, XXXIV (1957), 79-88. A copy of the *partida de bautismo* is given in AHN Calatrava, *Pruebas de Caballeros, legajo* 1255: *Hurtado de Mendoza y de la Rea, Antonio,* 1623.

[4] Lope de Vega, *Laurel de Apolo,* Silva 3, in *Colección escogida de obras no dramáticas,* in *BAE*, XXXVIII, p. 198: "Aquel famoso Hurtado de las Musas."

[5] See Antonio Hurtado de Mendoza, *Discursos,* ed. the Marquis of Alcedo (Madrid, 1911), p. 128: "La [casa] de Salcedo es de gran autoridad en toda aquella tierra, y la que sólo tiene vasallos."

[6] For both poem and complimentary verses, see Joaquín Entrambasaguas, "Un olvidado poema de Vélez de Guevara," *Revista de Bibliografía Nacional,* II (1941), 91-176.

Duchess, wife of the Count of Saldaña. It would have been natural for the Duke to have taken a distant cousin into his service as a page, and this connexion may well explain his later transference to the court of the Duke Don Juan's son-in-law, perhaps on the latter's marriage in 1603. [7]

Saldaña's court was no ordinary one. Celebrated for his harumscarum pranks, the Count was also a keen patron of the arts, and a bad poet. [8] As beneficiary of a most considerable marriage dowry, he could even afford to keep salaried poets, the most eminent at this time being Luis Vélez; although Lope de Vega's warm praise of Saldaña's patronage in the dedication of the epic *Jerusalén conquistada* in 1608 may suggest that the beneficence extended to him also. [9] It may be assumed that Saldaña encouraged a young poet like Mendoza, but we must think of Luis Vélez and Lope de Vega as those best equipped to help him. Lope was to be a lifelong friend of the poet, their friendship perhaps already established, for the surmise that Antonio was the Don Hurtado de Mendoza who stood as godparent at the baptism of Lope's illegitimate child by Micaela de Luján in 1607 is strengthened by Lope's overt acknowledgement of the generosity of Saldaña's patronage in the following year. [10]

[7] See discussion in "Biographical Notes," pp. 79-80. A memory of being in a kinsman's service may be preserved in Mendoza's *Los empeños del mentir*, where Marcelo is described as a "criado antigo de los que / llamamos despues parientes" (*FC*, p. 274). If the attribution however of a poem in Hisp. Soc. Am. *MS HC*: 371/224 (*Varias Poësias a diferentes asumps*. Compuestas Por el Discreto de Palacio D.n Antonio Mendoza), ff. 27-28, is correct, the young poet may have seen service in the household of Felipe de Cardona y Borja Ruiz, Admiral of Aragon. Mendoza, in addressing a letter to "don Phelipe de Cardona, Primogenito del Almirante de Aragón" says he has "veinte años." Circumstantial evidence favours this connexion: two Valencian poems (*MOP*, II, 40-44) would tally with the Admiral's home in Valencia, an immature play like *Celos sin saber de quien* (located in Zaragoza) could reflect the family's Aragonese connexions. However, the attribution of the poems in the Hisp. Soc. Am. MS is fraught with problems, not least that many pieces indicate a poet of the mid-seventeenth century rather than earlier (see my forthcoming "A new Manuscript of Poems attributed to Antonio Hurtado de Mendoza"). Furthermore the *MOP* Valencian poems seem incontrovertibly linked to one of the royal *jornadas*, probably that of 1632 (see Martin Hume, *The Court of Philip IV*, new ed., London, no date, p. 256 et seq.).

[8] On Saldaña's court, see Emilio Cotarelo, "Luis Vélez de Guevara y sus obras dramáticas," *Bol. Ac. Esp.*, III (1916), 621-652, IV (1917), 137-171, 269-308, and 414-444. See also Note 11 below.

[9] See Lope de Vega, *Ierusalén conquistada, epopeya trágica* (Madrid, 1609), prologue: "La afición que Vuestra Excelencia tiene a las letras mayormente a las de este género, el amparo que hace a los que las profesan, siendo su Mecenas y bienhechor..." Narciso Alonso Cortés (in *Noticias de una corte literaria*, Valladolid, 1906, p. 47) wrongly identified our Don Antonio as the student from Castro Urdiales who studied in the University of Valladolid in 1608 and 1609: this was the poet's cousin, Juan Antonio, Saldaña thereby losing an attributed merit as Maecenas (see my "Biographical Notes," p. 81).

[10] The godparents of Lope's child were Jerónima de Burgos and a certain D. Hurtado de Mendoza. Joaquín de Entrambasaguas (*Vida de Lope de Vega*, Madrid, 1942, p. 178)

Luis Vélez's connexion with Don Antonio at this time is more certain: Antonio's senior by some seven years, he may well have served as the younger man's poetic mentor, the main objection to this interpretation being the palpable inferiority of Luis Vélez's lyric verse alongside that of his supposed pupil — but such a situation is not unknown.

Luis Vélez's panegyrists on the publication of his *Elogio del juramento* include a number of names to be associated with Antonio de Mendoza during his later career: not only Lope de Vega but Quevedo, whose friendship with Mendoza may well have originated in this period, although he appears to have broken his association with this group by 1611; Pedro Soto de Rojas, the Granadine poet who, through his friendship with Olivares, may have helped forge the link with the man whom Antonio de Mendoza was to serve over long years; Salas Barbadillo, author of numerous *vignettes* of Spanish life, and later Mendoza's panegyrist in the *Coronas del Parnaso* (1635); and García de Salcedo Coronel, poet, and author of a famous commentary on the works of Góngora. [11]

Antonio de Mendoza spent more than ten years in Saldaña's service but we know little of his activities, and his occasional commendatory verses to volumes by other authors afford our infrequent glimpses of him during that time. He did belong, however, to that tumultous, ill-starred academy, under Saldaña's patronage, which Lope mentioned several times in his letters to the Duke of Sessa. [12] Lope had been elected at the opening session in November 1611, and despite his doubts about its survival, it continued, though on an unsteady course, until a very stormy meeting in the spring of 1612 when two of the academicians, Luis Vélez and Pedro Soto de Rojas "bit each other poetically" in open session. Lope's account

---

proposed the identification. The main objection is Don Antonio's age, then just over twenty. But the unrespectable circumstances of the baptism may even strengthen the case for identification with such a young person.

[11] Some of Luis Vélez's poems are included in BNM *MS* 3700, "Poesías diversas". In the early part of this collection poems by Luis Vélez alternate with others by Saldaña, Lope de Vega, Góngora, Antonio de Mendoza, and the Count of Lemos, Lerma's son-in-law. The MS shows Saldaña's poetry to have been conventional and dull. The date of these poems (and of the association they reflect) may be hinted at by a poem (f. 38) about a Lerma *fiesta* of October 1613 (sic), whilst the inclusion of Mendoza's "No corras arroyo vfano" (f. 82v) and Quevedo's "Don Repollo" (f. 126) suggests material available for use in Arias Pérez's *Primavera y flor* (1621) — see pp. 194-195 here. In Vélez's *Elogio*, Góngora's commentator, if the identification is correct, is called Francisco Coronel y Salcedo.

[12] Lope de Vega, *Epistolario*, ed. Agustín de Amezúa (Madrid, 1935-43), III, Letters 64, 65, 70, 76, 82, 86.

of the occasion helps us to identify some of the permanent figures in the Saldaña group. Few names are mentioned, and a number of poets (some like Mendoza later to be celebrated) may remain hidden beneath the anonymity of "others of a lesser hierarchy," the words used by Lope to round off his list of those who attended one of the academy sessions. However, casting our minds back to the *Elogio del juramento,* at least three names are permanently associated with this clique: Lope de Vega, Pedro Soto de Rojas, and Luis Vélez. By this time Quevedo, Salas Barbadillo and Salcedo Coronel's names no longer occur, but Cervantes emerges as an associate of the Saldaña group, and here probably he made Mendoza's acquaintance, for in 1614 in his *Viage del Parnaso* he includes him among the travellers. [13] Another literary figure who may not only have known Mendoza in the Saldaña group but have had influence on him was Vicente Espinel, author and part-protagonist of the picaresque novel *Marcos de Obregón* (1618). [14] At this earlier moment, however, Espinel's reputation was as poet and musician — he had invented and popularized the epigrammatic *espinela* form, and was famed as guitarist and composer.

A passage from *Los empeños del mentir,* written in the thirties, may well re-create something of Mendoza's situation and spirit in this earlier period of his life. [15] The man who is speaking, an "anciano hidalgo," looks back upon a heritage in which distinction of lineage was accompanied by a modicum of wealth, and upon a youth spent in Madrid in the temper of these airs, which in flowering poison, form the green bonds of sweet, tender years. These were the years of youthful pleasures and frivolities (whatever the moral snake in the grass), years spent also writing verse with a "sprightly pen." But they were also, we may presume, years of seeking wider

[13] Miguel de Cervantes, *Obras completas,* ed. Aguilar (Madrid, 1962), p. 71. One of the four poets given the task of supporting Apollo's temple, were it to collapse, is the Count of Saldaña, also celebrated by Cervantes in an ode (pp. 55-56) as an "honra y amparo dulce de mi pluma."

[14] For Espinel's association with Saldaña's academy, see George Haley, *Vicente Espinel and Marcos de Obregón. A Life and its Literary Representation* (Providence, R. I., 1959), p. 44. Cervantes in the *Viaje del Parnaso* (1614) referred to Espinel as the one "que en la guitarra / tiene la prima y en el raro estilo" (*Obras completas,* ed. Aguilar, Madrid, 1962, p. 71).

[15] See *FC,* p. 259: "Crieme en Madrid, al temple / destos ayres, que en venenos / floridos, son verdes lazos / de los dulces años tiernos. (The imagistic catalyst here is the classical "latet anguis in herba") ... De airosa pluma indiciado / horas entreguè a los versos," cf. also *Cada loco* (*BAE,* XLV, p. 464).

patronage. This desire is implicit in the sonnet addressed by Antonio de Mendoza to the Count of Tendilla, when a volume of Diego Hurtado de Mendoza's works (dedicated to the Count) was published in Madrid: but the flattering comparison drawn between the Count and Don Diego is a reminder too that Don Antonio could regard both the Count and the illustrious humanist as kinsmen. [16] A poem written for Lope de Vega's *Pastores de Belén* two years later may have helped bring Mendoza's name to the notice of a wider audience. The poem is, for all we know, the earliest of Mendoza's successful compositions:

> Estas lágrimas de Dios
> En su niñez soberana
> Belardo, ¿qué lira humana
> Las cantara como vos?
> Diversa acción de los dos,
> Pues que Dios llora en el suelo,
> Y vuestro piadoso celo
> Cantando tal gracia encierra,
> Que Dios las baja a la tierra,
> Y vos las subís al cielo. [17]

In 1613 another member of the Hurtado de Mendoza family, the Marquis of Cañete, received Don Antonio's attentions in one of the dedicatory poems to Gabriel Pérez del Barrio's *Dirección de secretarios*. [18] The book's title might seem to have been significant for one whose later career would be that of royal secretary, but Don Antonio's poem only breathes the hope that he may, like the author, deserve the bounty of such a generous Maecenas:

> Pues de un claro varón no es menos digna [hazaña]
> Que domar al rebelde, honrar al sabio,
> Premiar la pluma, que regir la espada.

---

[16] See *MOP*, II, 178. The volume was entitled *Obras del insigne cavallero Don Diego de Mendoza, embaxador del Emperador Carlos Quinto en Roma* (Madrid, 1610).

[17] See *MOP*, II, 179: *These tears of God shed in His sovereign childhood, what human lyre, Belardo* [=Lope], *could sing them like you? Diverse action by both of you, since God weeps in heaven, and your pious zeal holds such grace in song that God brings down His tears to earth whilst you take yours up to heaven.*

[18] See *MOP*, II, 181: *For it is no less noble* [a deed] *in a man of renown to honour the sage than to tame the rebel, to acknowledge the pen than to wield the sword* (the reference is to the Marquis's part in the Morisco revolt of 1568-71). Pérez del Barrio in a continuation of the *Dirección de secretarios*, his *Secretario y consejero de señores y ministros...* (Madrid, 1667) fails to mention Mendoza, even though he frequently relates anecdotes about other royal secretaries.

The continued existence of the Saldaña group is perhaps suggested by other names associated with this volume: Lope de Vega, Cervantes, Vicente Espinel, and Soto de Rojas. Yet whatever hopes Mendoza may have entertained of getting advancement elsewhere, he still remained in Saldaña's service, and his future was bound up with the destinies of the Sandovales, the royal favourite's family. The way in which literary patronage and political power was associated is implicit in the continued viability of the Saldaña group, and the predictable way in which the principal names occur together. Thus in 1617 on the occasion of the translation of the image of *Nuestra Señora del Sagrario* to a chapel specially built for her in Toledo by the Archbishop, Cardinal Bernardo Sandoval y Rojas (kinsman of the favourite), Lope de Vega, Cervantes, Soto de Rojas, Vicente Espinel and Mendoza all made their poetic contribution, thus emphasizing their common awareness that the Cardinal had already established himself as something of a literary patron. [19] Appropriately the theme of one of Mendoza's poems was the glory of the Sandovales: he had evidently hitched his wagon to their star.

In 1617 Philip III attended the festivities arranged in his honour by the favourite at the inauguration of the collegiate church at the Duke of Lerma's ancestral home. This brilliant and varied occasion included the performance of two plays, one *El caballero del sol* by Luis Vélez, the other by an unknown author but presented by Lerma's son-in-law, the Count of Lemos. [20] The audience also applauded a minor event in the *fiesta*, an interlude by Mendoza, in all probability his *El ingenioso entremés del examinador Miser Palomo*, first printed at Valencia in 1618. This piece may well have been Mendoza's first venture into the theatre, and significantly it occurred

[19] See Pedro de Herrera, *Descripción de la Capilla de N.ª Sra del Sagrario, que erigió en la Sta Iglesia de Toledo el Illmo Sor Cardenal D Bernardo de Sandoual y Rojas...* (Madrid, 1617), Mendoza's contributions being on f. 60ᵛ and f. 100. See also Haley, p. 44 and p. 51. In his sonnet, which celebrates the ashes of the Sandovales buried in the Cathedral, Don Antonio emphasized the dynasty's glories: "Cenizas lumbre a España, al mundo gloria" (*MOP*, II, 184). BNM *MS* 2802 adds a title: "Soneto al Tumulo del cardenal de Toledo, Don Berdo de Rojas y Sandobal." But the description is wrong (or ambiguous), the title of the competition being: "Vn soneto con muestras de estimacion y tristeza, atando la magestad del edificio a vn epitafio deuido a los huessos de los padres y hermanos del Cardenal que están en las vrnas" (Herrera, f. 100).

[20] See Cotarelo on Luis Vélez, *Bol. Ac. Esp.*, III (1916), 652, and Norman D. Shergold, *A History of the Spanish Stage from Medieval Times until the end of the Seventeenth Century* (Oxford, 1967), pp. 255-257, and p. 224 here.

not in one of the public *corrales,* but on a private, and royal occasion. For the author the *fiesta* probably represented more than literary success: it marked his first public accolade, since he was invited to accompany his master in the entry into the *juego de cañas,* an acknowledgement, we are informed, of his "quality and good wit." [21] In a later play, *Cada loco con su tema,* Mendoza may have borne this period in mind: Don Luis de Peralta, recalling his youth, avers that he then wrote verses with discretion and skill,

> Ni pesados en las burlas
> Ni en las veras descorteses,
> Sin hacer ofensa á nadie. [22]

He goes on to say that he had thus won public esteem. If these words also apply to Mendoza himself, they probably gloss over the sharp edge of his satirical interludes, but they do help to recapture the time when he was moving towards the esteem of a wider public.

During this second decade of the century we continue to catch an occasional view of the circle of *ingenios* that Mendoza probably cultivated. After the demise of Saldaña's academy, its place was soon taken by another: [23] by mid-April 1612 *El Parnaso* had begun to meet in the house of Francisco de Silva, brother to the Duke of Pastrana, "light of the Muses and Mars's greatest trophy" Soto de Rojas called him. [24] *Parnassus* came to be known by a different name, the *Academia Selvaje,* in honour of its president don Francisco, and its known members included both Lope de Vega and Soto de Rojas. [25] The case for Mendoza's continuing association

---

[21] Pedro de Herrera, *Translacion del Santissimo Sacramento a la Iglesia Colegial de San Pedro de la villa de Lerma; con la Solenidad, y Fiestas, que tuuo para celebrarla el Excellentissimo Señor don Francisco Gomez de Sandoual y Roxas* (Madrid, 1618), f. 67: "don Antonio de Mendoça, criado del Conde de Saldaña, que le sacó por compañero, demonstracion propia de tan gran Principe, supuesta la calidad y buenas partes de ingenio de don Antonio." See also p. 207 here for consideration of the occasion.

[22] See BAE, XLV, p. 464: *Neither heavy-handed when in jest, nor discourteous when dead serious, nor ever giving anyone offence.* A conscious attitude may be reflected in subsequent words: "Que no es donaire el que agravia, / Ni agudeza la que ofende."

[23] Two recent studies have thrown light on the academies, an important, but neglected, aspect of Spanish literary life: José Sánchez, *Academias literarias del Siglo de Oro español* (Madrid, 1961), and Willard F. King, *Prosa novelística y academias literarias en el siglo XVII* (Madrid, 1963).

[24] "aquel lucido ingenio, ... mayor trofeo de Marte." In King, p. 48, Note. She examines the evidence (pp. 47-61) for the changing character and identity of these groups. Sánchez (pp. 36-116) follows the same course, including more abundant material, but applying a less severe critical judgment.

[25] Sánchez, pp. 100-112; King, pp. 48-49.

with this group is strengthened by his certain connexion with an academy that succeeded *Parnassus* (which had come to an end with the departure of its martial patron for war-service in Lombardy in 1614). The new academy, which attained both greater renown and longevity, was founded through the efforts of a rich young poet, Francisco de Medrano, who in later years, after retirement from the poetic fray, recalled the remarkable success of his enterprise, that came to be known as the *Academia de Madrid*. [26] Medrano affirmed that by 1622 he could count Spain's most eminent men of letters among his friends: it is a fair presumption that the list, which included Mendoza's name, referred to acquaintances made at the academy meetings held in Medrano's house.

The argument for Mendoza's active participation is strengthened by other evidence: Juan de Arguijo's letter to Lope de Vega, published in the latter's *La Filomena* (1621), referred to the opening of a new academy, an imaginary meeting on the Parnassan slopes being described, with both Antonio de Mendoza and Luis Vélez de Guevara present; [27] Don Antonio's part in an attack on Ruiz de Alarcón's supposed plagiarism ("a subject on which the best geniuses of the Court wrote," according to the poem's title in one of the manuscripts) proves that the *décima* figured among those read in the *Academia de Madrid* in 1623, when the Mexican dramatist was censured for some offence given by his verses describing a *fiesta* on the occasion of the Prince of Wales's court visit. [28]

Medrano's testimony also suggests that Luis Vélez was an academy member around 1621 to 1622, and proof of his continued association with Mendoza is afforded by other sources. However, the *fiesta* at Lerma in 1617 fairly marks the end of the long period during which both served the Count of Saldaña, since after 1618 Luis Vélez was in the service of the Duke of Peñafiel, son to the Duke of Osuna, but still linked by marriage to the Sandoval family. [29]

---

[26] Sánchez, esp. pp. 49-97, who quotes Medrano's own ref. to Mendoza in the *Favores de las Musas* (1631), but the association with the actual academy must remain a presumption (p. 52); cf. King, pp. 50-51.

[27] In King, p. 52, Note.

[28] *MOP*, II, 198. *PMS* (p. 285) gives the title as: "A un Poeta Corcobado que se valio de trabajos agenos — y era D. Iuan de Alarcón, el tal a cuyo asumpto esscrivieron los mejores Ingenios de la Corte." See also Luis Fernández-Guerra, *D. Juan de Alarcón y Mendoza* (Madrid, 1871), p. 394 *et seq.*, and Sánchez, pp. 53-54.

[29] For this episode in Luis Vélez's life, see Cotarelo, *Bol. Ac. Esp.*, IV (1917), 138-143.

Mendoza for his part remained with Saldaña and by that same year had merited the description of "gentleman," and no longer page. [30] The description "gentleman" occurs also in a document dated 14 March 1619, which throws some light on the poet's income during his early career at court. [31] It is a *carta de poder* reaffirming the poet's right to a salary of six hundred ducats a year, payable to him as a charge on the property of Don Sancho Díaz de Zurbano, "Viceroy of the Kingdoms of Peru." The income had originally been granted to the poet's father as remuneration for the administration of Don Sancho's estate, but by a document issued in Quito on 15 March 1613, the right was transferred to the son, who was to be responsible for pursuing the employer's application for membership of one of the military orders. If Don Antonio did not succeed within the year, the salary would be terminated; but in the case of success the poet would receive the money for a further three. The four years are now up, but the poet has evidently remained unpaid, and seeks by means of the *poder* to give his cousin Juan Antonio Hurtado de Mendoza living in Castro Urdiales, the right to distrain on Don Sancho's income in that region. The document is interesting for two reasons. Firstly, it shows the poet's direct connexion with someone in Peru, to which may be added the sentimental relation with the poet's famous kinsman and homonym, Antonio Hurtado de Mendoza, Viceroy of New Spain and of Peru (d. 1552): this may throw some light on the poet's interest in the *indiano* theme in one of his plays, *Cada loco con su tema,* for Luis de Peralta there is a Peruvian. Secondly, his present experience in expediting an application for membership of one of the orders may have given the poet an expertise in these matters that would prepare him for certain of the court duties he would later pursue. [32]

That March 1619 should still find Don Antonio at Saldaña's court, his interests tied up with those of the Sandoval family, is a fact of some significance, since already the storm-clouds were gathering around the House of Lerma. The events which led to the triumph of the new favourite, the Count of Olivares, on the accession of

[30] See title-page of the printed edn. of the *Miser Palomo* interlude (Valencia, 1618).

[31] See Pérez Pastor, III, 388-389; "yo Don Antonio Hurtado de Mendoza residente en esta corte, xentil hombre de camara del señor Conde de Saldaña."

[32] See pp. 35-36 here.

Philip IV, are too well-known to require enumeration here. That accession sealed the fate of the principal members of the Sandoval family. Lerma himself had successfully gained immunity from arraignment by securing his own appointment as Cardinal, though his wealth was considerably reduced. His eldest son, the Duke of Uceda, was imprisoned. The Count of Saldaña was stripped of his palace appointment and exiled to Flanders. The Sandovales' allies also suffered. The great Duke of Osuna, viceroy of Naples, was disgraced and imprisoned, his fall probably spelling disaster for the advancement of Luis Vélez de Guevara, who was in the service of Osuna's heir. [33] This emphasizes what might have happened to Mendoza had he remained with Saldaña, or with any of the other political managers of Philip III. But whereas Luis Vélez was destined to remain unimportant and poor for the rest of his life, [34] Mendoza, having seen the way the tide was running, had been quick (or lucky) enough to ally himself with the Olivares faction, and get carried into royal favour on the new King's accession.

Mendoza may already in 1619 have realized that it was time to move. In any case the events of that summer would probably have hastened that decision, for Saldaña's wife died in August of that year, and owing to the peculiar conditions of the marriage settlement, control of the estate reverted to the House of the Infantado. [35] Though his own son was to become Duke of the Infantado, the Count himself could benefit nothing, and he became once more only the *segundón* of the House of Sandoval. But we do not know when precisely Mendoza left Saldaña's court, and we next see the poet entering the new King's service as "assistant of the robe," taking the oath at the hands of Philip IV's *sumiller de corps*, the Count of Olivares, two months after Philip III's death in March 1621. [36] Mendoza, having long served a suspect family, reappears as the *protégé* of the new royal favourite. The close ties which bound both men together in the years which followed make it likely that Mendoza's appointment was Olivares's personal gift. But when, and in what circumstances,

[33] For a full account, see Martin Hume, also Gregorio Marañón, *El Conde-Duque de Olivares,* revised edition (Madrid, 1945).

[34] See pp. 56-57 here.

[35] See Cotarelo on Luis Vélez, loc. cit., 139-140, which outlines this aspect of Saldaña's history.

[36] See "Biographical Notes," p. 82. The date was 23 May.

had the two become intimate? Mendoza's dependence on the Sandovales would have found him in a weak position at the critical stage of the political game, and it must be assumed that Mendoza won the Count's favour when the latter revealed himself as the ablest conspirator about the royal throne. Olivares associated himself with the forces of opposition to Lerma, led by the Duke of Uceda, [37] and it would have been relatively easy for Mendoza to make the acquaintance of a man who belonged to the circle of his master's brother. However, we must not rule out the possibility that the association had begun not in the corrupt atmosphere of intrigue, but in the rather healthier atmosphere of the Parnassan slopes. Olivares, himself no mean scholar, was interested in the arts, and a practiser of poetry. Furthermore, it is not unlikely that Olivares, after his definitive return to court in 1615, had occasion to meet and admire Antonio de Mendoza at some of the academy sessions, for we know that the future *privado* had been associated with Saldaña's academy. [38] The two men were united also by their age — Olivares being less than one year younger than Mendoza — and by ambition.

Finally, in attempting to trace the smooth transition effected by Mendoza from the service of a suspect family to that of a new court régime, attention should be paid to the continuing influence of the Duke of the Infantado, who was an important palace figure in the latter days of the Lerma ascendancy. [39] Don Antonio may already have enjoyed the Duke's favour: certainly he would do so during the new régime, on the occasion of his first marriage in 1623; and in the following year he would praise the Duke as an "autorizada y venerable persona." [40] Don Antonio's easy passage into royal favour may have reflected not only Olivares's good offices, but the continuing regard of a noble who had managed to maintain his position under two monarchs and two favourites.

---

[37] Marañón, pp. 30-45.

[38] See Sánchez, p. 45. For Olivares's artistic interests, see Marañón, pp. 143-166.

[39] See Pietro Gritti's report for 1615-19, in Barozzi and Berchet, *Relazioni degli stati europei ... Ambasciatori Veneti*, Series 1, vol. I (*Spagna*), Venice, 1856, p. 531.

[40] Praise of the Duke is from the poet's *Vexamen que había de dar en Maese Rodrigo de Sevilla a unos grados en que avía de asistir el Rey Phelipe 4o, en Março de 1624, y no se dio. Compúsolo don Antonio [Hurtado] de Mendoza*, in Homero Serís, *Nuevo ensayo de una biblioteca española de libros raros y curiosos* (New York, 1964), pp. 212-216.

Mendoza did not have to wait long for promotion: in August 1621 he became an aide in the royal chamber. [41] Chances of further advancement were strengthened as a consequence of the great festival held in the spring palace at Aranjuez to celebrate the King's birthday in 1622. At the suggestion of the Countess of Olivares Mendoza wrote two glowing accounts of the occasion, one in prose and another in verse. [42] The poetic account in fact formed part of an equally splendid entertainment, a spectacle play *Querer por solo querer* in which Mendoza at the behest of the King celebrated the Queen's birthday in that same year. [43] The play, which made pleasing remarks about the royal patrons and the King's favourite, may by its success have helped the poet's appointment to a royal secretaryship in March 1623. [44] The extent to which he now identified himself as Olivares's creature is suggested in the dedication of the printed version of *Querer por solo querer* in 1623, a text which I quote in its entirety, not only because of its obsequious tone, but because of its elegance of expression:

A la Reyna nuestra señora.

Señora. Aviendose Permitido à los ojos de V. Magestad esta Comedia, licencia tiene de llegar à sus pies. Escriuiose, para celebrar sus años; esto le ganò el credito, que deuiera perder por mia. Ha sido buscada por fiesta

---

[41] See "Biographical Notes," p. 82. Significantly the oath of office was made to the *mayordomo mayor*, the Duke of the Infantado.

[42] *Fiesta que se hizo en Aranjuez a los años del Rey Nuestro Señor D. Felipe IIII. Escrita por D. Antonio de Mendoça* (Madrid, 1623). In the foreword, dedicated to the Countess of Olivares, Mendoza wrote: "Vuesa Excelencia, señora, me mandó escribir esta relación..." The vol. included both the prose account and one in verse (see *MOP*, I, 1-41). The poetic account is part of *Querer por solo querer* (cf. also *FC*, pp. 387-389). These problems are discussed in my "A Chronology of Antonio de Mendoza's Plays," to appear in *BHS*. The *Fiesta* is also discussed by Shergold (pp. 268-270). The Count of Villamediana's play, also given on this occasion, was later published: *Comedia de la Gloria de Niquea, y descripción de Aranjuez* (n.p., no date). According to the title-page the play was performed on 8 April 1622, but this must refer to the date originally planned. BNM MS 9395, f. 15, contains a contemporary ref. to the *Fiesta*, which mentions that "dos comedias de las damas... costaron mas de 30.000 d[ucado]s."

[43] The question of the early performances of *Querer* is puzzling (see "A Chronology..."), but Shergold (p. 270) is probably right in claiming that it was first performed, in Aranjuez, for the Queen's birthday — whether it was actually given on that day, 9 July 1622, seems less certain, since the Aranjuez season was earlier in the year. See also ch. X.

[44] I here correct a conclusion wrongly drawn in my "Biographical Notes," p. 83. See also "A Chronology," whose conclusions likewise vindicate La Barrera's original claim (*Catálogo*, pp. 246-250) that the Secretaryship was a token of appreciation. The appointment is mentioned in *Noticias de Madrid (1621-27)*, ed. A. González Palencia (Madrid, 1942), p. 42, which qualifies it as "sin exercicio;" and in *Cartas de Andrés de Almansa y Mendoza, 1621-26*, in *Colección de libros españoles raros y curiosos*, XVII (Madrid, 1886), p. 177. La Barrera also mentioned the post of *ayuda de cámara* in this context, but, as was seen, Mendoza was appointed one in August 1621.

de V. Magestad, que en la estimacion; que le da su nombre, le perdonan, auerla escrito yo. Fiòme este cuidado Doña Maria de Guzman, creyendo, que hechura de su Padre acertaria, à servir à V. Magestad mejor con la obligacion, que otros con el ingenio. Iusto fue el engaño, no le culpo, ni à los que dessea[n] leerla, si merecio ser oida de V. Magestad, y tendra dos aplausos (sin deuerle ninguno) siendo V. Magestad aora segunda vez su dueño.

Criado de V. Magestad.
Don Antonio de Mendoça. [45]

The dedication makes it clear that María, daughter of Olivares, had originally prompted Mendoza to write the play for the Queen's birthday: a reference to María was therefore quite appropriate. What seems excessive is that the poet should make it an excuse to fawn in public before the royal favourite.

However, the poet's subsequent career would owe a great deal to such subservience, for as one of the Venetian ambassadors to the Spanish court in the sixteen-twenties observed it was Olivares's method to bind his confidants and favourites to himself by a sense of gratitude and obligation to their master: "Ho osservato, che ... sono tutti soggetti non solo confidenti del conte d'Olivares, ma avassallatti in tutto al suo volere, per aver da lui sentito il vantaggio della loro fortuna, ed il beneficio della loro promozione." [46] It was doubtless necessary too for the gratitude, from time to time, to be made clear to the master.

Antonio de Mendoza's marriage to Luisa Briceño de la Cueva in 1623 must be accounted a social success. [47] Lope de Vega acclaimed

---

[45] *Querer por solo querer, comedia que representaron las Señoras meninas, a los años de la Reyna Nuestra Senora. Escriuiola D. Antonio de Mendoça* (Madrid, 1623), ¶ 2. Sir Richard Fanshawe eventually published anonymously his brilliant trans. of the play, *Querer Por Solo Querer: To Love only for Love Sake: A Dramatick Romance. Represented at Aranjuez before the King and Queen of Spain, To celebrate The Birth-day of that King, By the Meninas...* (London, 1671). I quote Fanshawe's version of Mendoza's dedication: "To the Queen of Spain. Madam, This Comedy having been admitted to Your Majesties Eyes, hath leave to throw itself at Your Feet: It was written to Celebrate the Birth-Day of the King; this gained it that Credit, which it ought to have lost for being mine: It hath been sought at the *Festival* of Your Majesty; for, in virtue of that Esteem which Your Name gives it, / *verso* Men pardon it, the having been penn'd by me. To this Task I was emboldened by D. Maria de Gusman, believing that a Creature of her Father would happen to Serve Your Majesty better with his Obligation, than Others with their Wit; the mistake was just, I do not blame it, nor those who desire to read it, since it had the Honour to be heard by Your Majesty; and it will gain *two* Plaudits (without deserving *one*) Your Majesty being now the *second* time its Patroness. Your Majesties Servant, Don Antonio de Mendoza" (f. A2r+v).

[46] Barozzi and Berchet, I, 639-640: report of Alvise Mocenigo III, for 1626-31.

[47] For Doña Luisa's marriage, ancestry etc., see "Biographical Notes," p. 83. The basic documents are a *poder,* dated Madrid, 25 July 1623, granting authority to solemnize

her arrival in Madrid that summer by dedicating to her his play
El vellocino de oro, whose performance at the *fiesta* of Aranjuez
in the preceding year her husband had so vividly described. [48] But
for all the ballyhoo in favour of Doña Luisa, Don Antonio was really
the lucky man, for the marriage had been generously arranged
through Don Juan, Duke of the Infantado, who considered the lady
his kinswoman, a link perhaps best established via her paternal
grandfather, Jerónimo Briceño de Mendoza, *corregidor* in Laredo and
other places in Vizcaya. Doña Luisa was a native of Almería but
had close ties with the principal families of other cities in southern
Spain, her nobility being most patent in the descent from the House
of Alburquerque. The marriage was celebrated by proxy in July
1623, the witnesses to the contract revealing the strength now of
Don Antonio's connexions; among them were the Count-Duke
of Olivares, and Juan Alfonso Enríquez de Cabrera, Admiral of
Castile, Duke of Medina de Ríoseco, and future rival to the present
favourite. The Admiral's presence signifies Mendoza's friendship with
the House of Medina de Ríoseco, also attested in his poetry.

In addition to the publication of his *Querer por solo querer,*
other events of 1623 show the strength of his position at court. He
had received along with his royal secretaryship four accountancies
for Crown rents and taxes that he could afterwards farm out at a
profit; and we now hear of his connexion with the Inquisition, for
he carried the tassels of its standard in the solemn procession of
Corpus Christi. Two years later he became Secretary of the Holy
Office. [49] The greatest honour fell to him however in September 1623

---

the marriage by proxy (Archivo de Protocolos, No. 2034, *Escribano Santiago Fernández,*
1623, ff. 345-346), a text given in my art.; also AHN *Inquisición, legajo* 1185, No. 20:
Hurtado de Mendoza Rea, Antonio, y su mujer Briceño de la Cueva y Figueroa, Luisa,
1620 (it should read 1625), and AHN *Alcántara, Pruebas de Caballeros, legajo* 934:
Mendoza Briceño, Jerónimo de, 1628 — the applicant, a child approximately three years
old, was a son of the poet and Doña Luisa. The child's mother was then still alive.

[48] See Lope de Vega, *Parte decinueve, y la mejor parte de las comedias...* (Madrid,
1625), ff. 216ᵛ-217. The dates of the volume's *aprobaciones* are 16 and 22 June 1622.
For the original edn. of 1623, see Rennert and Castro, p. 292. The dedication refers to
Doña Luisa as "muger de don Antonio Hurtado de Mendoça, Cauallero del Abito de
Calatraua:" the volume presumably appeared after Mendoza was granted that title in
September 1623 — see below. The *relaciones* of the *Fiesta de Aranjuez* are discussed
on pp. 224-225, and in "A Chronology". Lope's dedication refers to them as something
already in existence, but not yet perhaps available to the public: "... como las relaciones
del señor don Antonio tendran advertida [a.V.M.?] (f. 216ᵛ)."

[49] For the Inquisition appointments see "Biographical Notes," p. 85. The four accountancies (*escribanías de rentas*) are mentioned in Pérez Pastor, III, 389, in *Noticias de
Madrid,* p. 49, and in Almansa y Mendoza, p. 167: they had been the privilege of
the Count of Villamediana, assassinated after the *Fiesta de Aranjuez.* The *merced* was

when he received the habit of the military order of Calatrava at the hands of the Count-Duke. Contemporary chroniclers insist that this was no ordinary investiture, and one of them notes that Don Antonio may now be regarded not just as Olivares's friend, but as his favourite and confidant. [50] Certainly for Mendoza the investiture must have symbolized the triumph of the *arriviste*. In less than five years he had risen from comparative obscurity to be not only royal secretary but an intimate associate of the power behind the throne. His poetry reveals the extent to which that triumph was due to assiduous blandishment. Mendoza, well attuned to Olivares's attitudes, did not allow him to overlook the extent of the poet's friendship and patronage: one sonnet proclaims that nothing on earth would make Mendoza ungrateful to his master, another epistolary poem to the Count-Duke's son-in-law declares his loyalty to both, and intimates that his crest bears the picture of a slave. [51]

Antonio de Mendoza's actual activities as royal secretary in the years which followed form a minor tracery around the main outline of Olivares's rule. He attended to the disbursement of the King's private purse, accompanied his monarch to Andalusia in 1624 and to Aragon in 1625. [52] It was probably in Zaragoza in January 1626

---

transferred to Mendoza on 22 October 1622 (see Pastor), but the news was only made public in March 1623. In July 1632 we catch a glimpse of the poet taking part in the procession at an *auto-da-fe* in Madrid (see *Relacion del auto de la fe, que se celebro en Madrid Domingo a quatro de Iulio de M.DC.XXXII*, Madrid, 1632, f. 7v). The "Secretario de la General Inquisicion" walked on the right of Josef González, representative of the "Consejos de la Camara y Real de Castilla:" such conjunction, followed throughout, accorded distinction to the Holy Office of the *Tribunal de Toledo* and the *Consejo de la Suprema Inquisición*, and symbolized the co-operation between civil and ecclesiastical power. I am grateful to Prof. E. M. Wilson for this reference.

[50] Almansa y Mendoza (p. 219) notes how Olivares "con grande ostentacion, dio el [hábito] de Calatrava a D. Antonio de Mendoza, de la Cámara de su Majestad, y su valido, justamente, por su calidad, su ingenio, agrado y buenas partes, pues pocas veces se hallan hombres de ánimo igual." The context on the whole supports the interpretation that the poet is the *valido* of Olivares, rather than of the King. The *Noticias de Madrid* record only one other case for the period 1621-27 of Olivares investing a supplicant for a habit, the Marquis of Toral, Duke of Medina de las Torres, in December 1622 (p. 43): he was the favourite's son-in-law.

[51] *MOP*, III, 232 ("sólo a mí no podrás hacerme ingrato"), and *MOP*, I, 195, where he signs off: "y tuyo pone / un esclavo por empresa", cf. also similar terms in a letter to the Count-Duke, *MOP*, I, 186.

[52] The royal secretary's daily duties are reflected in the Archivo de Palacio, *Cuentas del Secretario de la Cámara*, legajo 6764 (1621-38). For the Andalusian royal progress, see *Noticias de Madrid*, p. 118. For Mendoza's participation, see Diego Pérez, *Relación de las fiestas que el Marqués del Carpio hizo al Rey Nuestro Señor* (Sevilla, 1624), f. 2, and Ignacio Aguilera, "Sobre tres romances atribuidos a Quevedo," *Boletín de la Biblioteca de Menéndez y Pelayo*, XXI (1945), 497. The *vejamen* by the poet on the occasion of the granting of degrees at Seville in March 1624 (see note 40) would have been made during this *jornada*. For the Aragonese progress of 1625-26, see Almansa y Mendoza, p. 319.

that he was promoted to the office of his senior, Antonio de Losa, deposed for a trivial offence. [53] One piece of evidence suggests that Mendoza realized that what power he had lay not in his secretarial office but in his special relationship with the King's favourite. The occasion was a letter addressed to Olivares from Aranjuez in May 1627 in which Mendoza tried to dissuade Olivares from allowing Juan de Vera y Figueroa, Count de la Roca (author of a widely-read book El Embajador [1620] and an old Sevillian acquaintance of the favourite), to be his biographer. [54] Mendoza resorted to calumny and innuendo in order to blacken Roca's name in the eyes of a friend, but the most significant aspect of this venomous letter is what is left unexpressed, that Mendoza probably vented spite on Juan de Vera because of an unwillingness to see someone else engaged on a labour of pietas that the poet had probably himself coveted. The limitations to Mendoza's influence with Olivares are indicated by the favourite's refusal to take the hint: Juan de Vera's Fragmentos históricos de la vida de D. Gaspar de Guzmán were published, at least in manuscript form, in 1628, though it may be surmised that the fact the work was not actually printed at that time was the result of Mendoza's tactic of dissuasion.

By 1631 Mendoza's first wife was dead, and the poet sought permission from the Order of Calatrava (in which he now held the encomienda of Zorita de los Canes) to marry Clara Ocón Coalla de Pineda. [55] Like Doña Luisa she had close connexions with Southern Spain; her descent was if anything more noble; she was young, beautiful, and brought him a goodly dowry. In a poem addressed to Anarda, Mendoza has left us a self-portrait sketched, in rather pompous style, at this time of life when, as he puts it, his marriage

---

[53] Almansa y Mendoza, p. 319.

[54] The episode is dealt with in my "Una carta inédita de Antonio Hurtado de Mendoza al Conde-Duque de Olivares," His, XIX (1959), 82-91.

[55] See "Biographical Notes," pp. 85-86. The relevant documents are AHN Calatrava, Pruebas de Caballeros (Casamientos), legajo 17, No. 500: Ocón Coalla Pineda, Clara, 1631; and AHN Alcántara, Pruebas de Caballeros, legajo 1082: Ocón y Coalla, José Antonio de, 1633. The latter, baptized in Madrid on 1 November 1632, was the son of the poet and Doña Clara. Mendoza refers more than once to his wife's beauty: of her picture he says (MOP, III, 223) "este admirable, celestial y esquivo / rostro," and devotion as well as appreciation are expressed in a poem sent to her from the Cuenca region: "que si es clara la verdad, / es más clara la hermosura" (MOP, II, 165-167). The Commandership of Zorita de los Canes was not a wealthy one: in 1659 it produced 500 ducats, whereas the Encomienda of Calatrava was worth 10,500 (see "Commanderies de l'Ordre de Calatrava et leur valeur" in François Bertaut's Voyage d'Espagne, RH, XLVII [1919], 270-271). For a history of Zorita's connexion with the Order, see Francisco Layna Serrano, Castillos de Guadalajara (Madrid, 1933), pp. 353-389.

bed, already cold, had been occupied by a new and lovely consort.
Above all we see a vain and fussy man, with great pride in his
lineage:

> En el peinado volumen
> del copete y del bigote
> no hay pelo sin obediencia
> no hay penacho con desorden.
>
> En la edad mentida siempre
> apagado ya lo joven,
> aun las hojas centellean
> aun no caducan las flores.
>
> En la calidad, que es trato
> que no importa, tiene el hombre
> harta sangre para hidalgo,
> y harto riesgo para Conde. [56]

The most revealing passage however is that in which he tells
of the place which he has established for himself at court. We hear
a hint of envy of the titled nobility who are his superiors, and the
satisfaction he feels at having become a "minister's truthful shaft,"
a man with a reputation for brilliant conversation whose thoughts
and expressions are culled by even the most famous of preachers,
Hortensio Paravicino. [57] The poem hints at aspects of a man's life
generally hidden from the biographer. His sense of personal triumph
must have lain more in the aura of respect surrounding him than in
the overt proofs of success, and to understand his position clearly
we must consider not only his status as man of letters at court (the
subject of our next chapter), but also the rather obscure duties which
fell to him, or which he made his own.

In 1632 there appeared Mendoza's *Convocación de las Cortes
de Castilla, y Iuramento del Principe nuestro señor, Don Baltasar*

---

[56] *MOP*, II, 348-352: *In the well-groomed ranks of forelock and moustache not one
hair shows disobedience, not one plume unruliness. In years that always tell lies, youth
has already faded, but the leaves still glint, the flowers have not been shed. As for
quality — style of address being that which does not count — the man has more than
blood enough for an* hidalgo, *and enough daring to be a Count.*

[57] *MOP*, II, 350: "Ya tenebrosa, ya tierna / su pluma, que fué virote, / veraz flecha
de ministro... Tan crespos sus pensamientos / que el Hortensio en sus sermones / los
pide para misterios /o los toma para voces."

Carlos, Primero deste nombre.[58] This volume whose title clearly echoes Luis Vélez's *Elogio del juramento* of 1608, sought to give a colourful account of the administering of the oath to the young prince on 22 February 1632. It was not Mendoza's only attempt to record this ceremony, and another brief work indicates more clearly in what manner he interpreted the duty he was undertaking.[59] His prime purpose was to place the ceremony in a historical perspective and to lay down a firm procedure that might hold for all times. From this we deduce that the poet hoped to arrogate to himself the post of official chronicler on state ceremonies, and adviser on protocol, important duties in a society dominated by rules of etiquette.[60] These relations of 1632 were not indeed the first of that kind which Mendoza had penned. In 1629 he had written one called "The Manner in which the King holds a Council of State in his room," which amounted to a statement by a court public relations officer, informing the public what procedure was adopted at meetings of this kind.[61] We are told who the most important people present were, how the room was arranged, what was the order of precedence, what rules of etiquette were observed. The author alluded to the ridiculous position of the courtier who every day had to ask himself what was going on, since established procedures had not been laid down. Mendoza's purpose was evidently to enlighten him, and to bring some order into the prevailing chaos. Undertakings of this kind indicate why Mendoza was referred to as the "Discreto de Palacio," a title deserved too on a different count, as certain items

---

[58] The first edition was printed in Madrid by the Imprenta del Reino. A second came from the same press in 1665; a copy of this is bound into BNM *MS 7467*. A continued interest in court etiquette is reflected by a further edition, *Ceremonial que se observa en España para el juramento de príncipe hereditario ó convocacion de las Cortes de Castilla...*, Madrid, 1789 (copy in National Library of Scotland, *pressmark* G. 10. f. 19).

[59] See *Discursos*, pp. 26-34, "Forma que se guarda en tener las Cortes, y el Juramento que se hizo al príncipe nuestro señor y se ha hecho para siempre [sic] con todos los que hubiesen de suceder en esta real corona."

[60] The demand for such knowledge is clear from the extant copies of the *Etiquetas* setting out the duties, order of precedence, etc., even the salaries of court officers (see John E. Varey, "L'Auditoire du *Salón Dorado* de l'*Alcázar* de Madrid au XVIIᵉ siècle," in *Dramaturgie et Société. Rapports entre l'œuvre théâtrale, son interprétation et son public aux XVIᵉ et XVIIᵉ siècles*, ed. Jean Jacquot, Élie Konigson and Marcel Oddon, Paris, 1968, pp. 81-85). Mendoza's contribution to court etiquette may be regarded as the extension of such regulation into the field of periodic ceremonial, cf. his "Cómo el Príncipe Nuestro Señor tomó el Toisón" (pp. 37-43), 24 October 1638. See also Varey's "La mayordomía mayor y los festejos palaciegos del siglo XVII," *Anales del Instituto de Estudios Madrileños*, IV (1969), pp. 145-168.

[61] *Discursos*, pp. 18-21. The reference originally was to a Council meeting of 23 January 1629. Mendoza's main charge is that "nunca se ajusta ni se sabe el modo con que se hizo ayer, ni hay nada decidido ni asentado en casos semejantes" (p. 20).

of evidence make plain. [62] He was consulted by the Marchioness of Villahermosa about the choice of husband, and in reply proposed a number of candidates, making appropriate comment on their nobility, fortune and character. [63] In another place, a poem, he reminded a client of "money for gloves," a payment still due to him for information given in connexion with an application for membership of one of the military orders. [64] There probably were other similar occasions when Mendoza's knowledge of genealogy and the state of family fortunes was put to good use. Perhaps his usefulness in this domain owed more than a little to the specialized knowledge he had of the rights and prerogatives of the nobility, a knowledge attested by his discourse on the grandees and titled nobility of Spain into which was intercalated, rather haphazardly, a brief excursus on the tutelage of princes. [65] The main body of the work is a review of the customs that had prevailed in Spain in respect of the granting of titles. The principal theme, that a title was not hereditary but an honour granted to the individual that has deserved it, may be regarded as a timely contribution to Olivares's long, and eventually fruitless, attempt to become a grandee. [66] The argument has further significance. Olivares, in his choice of key subordinates, showed preference for the "gentes de condición mediocre" over the "primeras Casas de España," a preference that may well be reflected in Mendoza's own advancement. [67] The present thesis gave historical basis to a nobility of merit as against one of blood, whilst at the

---

[62] Cotarelo, *El Conde de Villamediana*, p. 115, Note, makes ref. to this title. It occurs too in the title of Hisp. Soc. Am. *MS HC*: 371/224, an eighteenth-century manuscript.

[63] *Discursos*, pp. 163-171. The poet had no compunction about proposing members of his own family as suitable matches.

[64] *MOP*, II, 18. The *décima*, a sharp rebuke doubtless well publicized, was addressed to Antonio de Moscoso, Marquis of Villanueva del Fresno. The latter who had succeeded in becoming the *valido* of Philip IV's brothers, Fernando and Carlos, was no friend of Olivares (see Marañón, pp. 247, 335-336 and 444). *Dar para guantes*, a nice euphemism, often involved quite large sums of money (see Baltasar Gracián, *El Criticón*, ed. M. Romera-Navarro, Philadelphia, 1938-40, I, 234).

[65] Real Academia de la Historia *MS* 12-2-2, B-101, *Discurso sobre los Grandes y Títulos de Castilla*. The work consists of 32 folios, the intercalation on tutelage being on ff. 18v-24v.

[66] See Marañón, esp. pp. 89-105.

[67] This quotation from a shrewd contemporary observer, Vittorio Siri, is in Marañón, p. 91. That Doña Clara at least, aspired to a family title is clear from a *memorial*, dated 28 September 1644, presented just after her husband's death, requesting a title of Marquis or Count (see AHN *Títulos del Reino, Sección de Consejos Suprimidos, legajo* 4735, No. 21). There appears to have been an earlier approach in November 1643.

same time it might serve to strengthen any claim to a title that the poet himself would wish to make.

Mendoza's position as confidant to the royal favourite demands attention despite the difficulty of reaching any certain conclusions regarding it. Certainly he had the ear of both King and *privado*, and at the time of the disturbances in Vizcaya in 1631-4 over the imposition of the salt-tax, he proposed to the Count-Duke what lines of action to follow. [68] But the affair of the proposed biography of Olivares in 1627 suggests the limits to Mendoza's power. Despite his close connexion with both King and *privado* and the fact that he was one of that inner ring of bureaucrats so powerfully dominated in the sixteen-thirties by the Protonotary, Jerónimo de Villanueva, there is no sign that the poet played an important role in shaping the policy which resulted in the secession of Portugal and the revolt of the Catalans at the end of that decade. [69] During these years mention is twice made of an appointment for Mendoza as ambassador abroad: in 1634 to Genoa, and in 1637 to replace the Count de la Roca in Venice. [70] But nothing came of these hopes, and once more the poet's only success was in the field of public relations — his pamphlet giving account of the military successes of the Infante-Cardenal in Picardy and by the Marquis of Leganés in Italy in 1636, significant campaigns in the never-ending deadlock of the Thirty Years War, was received with public acclaim, the work's success, interestingly enough, being attributed by a chronicler to Mendoza's public reputation. [71] One last sop to his pride came in January 1637

---

[68] See *Discursos*, pp. 139-148, "Al Conde-Duque cuando las alteraciones de Vizcaya, escribióle Don Antonio de Mendoza." Another *Discurso* (pp. 127-135) also seems to bear on the revolt, though this is far from clear.

[69] On Villanueva, see J. H. Elliott, *The Revolt of the Catalans: A Study in the Decline of Spain (1598-1640)*, Cambridge, 1963, *passim*. In a letter to me (27 January 1964) Mr. Elliott expressed his doubts whether Mendoza had influence on general policy. "If he had, I think he would have made his way into the *Junta de Ejecución*, like José González, another of Olivares' men."

[70] See "Biographical Notes," pp. 86-87. In January 1637 it was reported that "tiene grandisimos deseos de salir con esta ocasión de Palacio" (see *La corte y monarquia de España en los años de 1636 y 1637*, ed. A. Rodríguez Villa, Madrid, 1886, p. 80). Santa Coloma, subsequently Viceroy of Catalonia, was offered the appointment in May 1637 but refused it (see Elliott, pp. 328-329). The poet may however have spent part of the summer of 1634 in Italy and elsewhere, for *Los empeños del mentir*, apart from a number of other Italian refs., contains a vivid account of the march of imperial forces northwards from Italy to join the other Hapsburg army before closing with the enemy at Nördlingen (see *FC*, pp. 274-278 and my "A Chronology"). See also my "A New Manuscript," concerning a poem supposed to have been written by Mendoza in Italy.

[71] See "Biographical Notes," p. 87. The title may have been *Relación de los efetos de las armas de España en el año de MDCXXXVIII* (see Nicolás Antonio, I, 131): unless

with his invention of *papel sellado,* government-stamped paper. This, the predecessor of stamp duty, consisted of sheets of paper, duly stamped at different prices, that were henceforth necessary for all official documents. The invention, attributed also (but probably wrongly) to Father Salazar, the Count-Duke's Jesuit confessor, produced an outcry of protest, especially from the Church, which considered itself unduly penalized. [72] Mendoza may have foreseen the furore which this form of taxation created; he can hardly have realized the melancholy immortality which his invention ensured him.

Mendoza's uncertainty during the years 1634 to 1637 may well explain the frustration conveyed in a letter sent about 1635 to an unknown person. Beginning as a serious discourse on the duties of a royal secretary, it assumes the form of a personal revelation. [73] Having gained and kept the confidence of both King and royal favourite, Mendoza claims he has received far less remuneration than his predecessors in office. Even the minimum acknowledgement has not been granted him. Furthermore, his difficulties have been exacerbated by domestic trouble. His fortune and estate have suffered so that he is reduced to a poverty unsurpassed even by the lowliest of servants, his health is bad with no sign of improvement, and to crown his present misery he must put up with the "excess of reason of a young wife, very noble, very domineering, very rich, and who sees everything fail in my hands." [74]

Naturally the delicate position of a man who sought to serve two masters, his King and the royal favourite, must in the late sixteen-thirties have produced its own tensions and uncertainties. The disastrous policies pursued by Olivares and his supporters made it increasingly difficult for the favourite to command the support of

---

a quite different work, the title should read 1636 and not 1638. In 1635 a pamphlet appeared entitled *Declaracion de Don Phelipe quarto, Rey de las Españas, al rompimiento de la guerra que sin denunciarla ha echo Luys, Rey de Francia* (see J. M. Jover, *1635: Historia de una polémica y semblanza de una generación,* Madrid, 1949, pp. 505-511). Judging by the text's undue optimism, adulatory tone, and prolixity, Jover affirmed the "muy probable posibilidad" that Mendoza was the author (p. 365, Note). The argument seems flimsy. Indeed the *Declaración*'s lack of pungency and elegance affords good reason for questioning the attribution to Mendoza.

[72] See "Biographical Notes," p. 87.

[73] *Discursos,* pp. 61-69, "Papel del Mismo don Antonio de Mendoza, en el que discurre sobre los principios del oficio de secretario de Cámara."

[74] Ibid., p. 67: "obligado a sufrir el destemple de la demasiada razón de una mujer de pocos años, muy noble, muy autorizada, muy rica y que en mi poder lo ve mal logrado todo."

all the parties at court. [75] Mendoza's own dilemma is reflected in the fact that the Admiral of Castile, with whose family the poet had long enjoyed friendly intimacy, had by this time emerged, as did the young Duke of the Infantado (Mendoza's kinsman), as one of the favourite's enemies. [76] And as support grew among the nobility for a plan to oust the Count-Duke, Mendoza must increasingly have played the role of soothing mediator between King and favourite. His poetic role from the beginning had patently been to remind the monarch of his favourite's aims: a sonnet had proclaimed it was the *privado's* duty to "show off his King to effect in all things," and to build up the monarch's glory by means of the favourite's unselfish efforts. [77] By 1637 that task had become more difficult, but no signs appear that the poet wished to resolve his dilemma by rejecting the master to whom he had sworn eternal loyalty. A sonnet written approximately in that year still proclaims that he has been a witness now of sixteen years of "perfect reigning" by Olivares, and in June 1639 Mendoza's name was associated with the plan to give the Count-Duke proper recognition for the services he had rendered Spain. [78] This train of events was in fact a further consequence of the disastrous relations between Olivares and the Admiral of Castile. The latter had been instrumental in raising the siege of Fuenterrabía in September 1638, but got no thanks for it. Olivares rather made himself appear as the one chiefly responsible for the victory, and his supporters tried subsequently to fortify that impression by assiduous attempts to reward the Count-Duke officially, attempts which he of course magnanimously resisted. Presumably as a further outcome of the tactics of Olivares's supporters, Mendoza indited a curious document which sought to persuade Olivares of the appropriateness of receiving his country's homage: Mendoza appeared as the favourite's unswervingly loyal servant, and his actions in the matter may have been partly guided by the favourite himself. [79]

---

[75] See Elliott, e.g. p. 313, and pp. 453-454.

[76] Elliott, pp. 217-218, Marañón, pp. 91 and 94, and Donald L. Shaw, "Olivares y el Almirante de Castilla (1638)," *His*, XXVII (1967), 352-353.

[77] *MOP*, III, 230: "Lucir su Rey en todo, es de un valido, / lucimiento mayor / ... que en tus fatigas fabrica su gloria."

[78] *MOP*, III, 235, *Discursos*, pp. 103-109, "Biographical Notes," p. 88, and Donald L. Shaw, art. cit. See also Shaw's edn. of Virgilio Malvezzi's *Historia de los primeros años del reinado de Felipe IV* (London, 1968).

[79] "Discurso de don Antonio de Mendoza, secretario de cámara de Felipe IV, en que persuade al Conde-Duque se deje premiar de su Majestad," incomplete text in *Discursos*, pp. 103-109. That Mendoza was an official mediator is shown by Joseph Pellicer y Tovar,

One more distinction awaited the poet. In November 1641, "in consideration for his services" the King granted him the Secretaryship of Justice, left vacant through the death of Francisco Gómez de Asprilla. [80] It meant however relinquishing his post with the Inquisition. Lack of evidence prevents a proper understanding of such a move, though one detail may be significant: the official notice mentions that the new appointment was due to his Majesty's personal satisfaction with Mendoza's services. As the future of Olivares's régime became increasingly uncertain, his creature Mendoza at least had the satisfaction of knowing that he could move safely within the shadow of the King's throne.

Yet by the very end of the thirties, even the routine of palace life was threatened by the disturbing political situation. [81] War with France, the attempted French invasion of Catalonia in 1639, the cession of Portugal in December 1640, these events dulled the glory of the Spanish Parnassus and of King Apollo. By 1642 the unsuccessful campaigns pursued in Catalonia by Olivares's government prompted the King to move nearer to the front. So it was that the court took up residence in Zaragoza, the new Secretary of Justice probably accompanying the royal party. Meanwhile Olivares's career reached its final crisis. As the political and military situation worsened, the royal favourite's unpopularity increased. His strength was further weakened by what proved an unfortunate personal decision: in January 1642 he legitimized his bastard son, an action which provoked other members of the Guzmán family to show disaffection. [82] In particular, Luis de Haro, the favourite's nephew, who till that moment stood as his heir, began to plot against the *privado,* and indeed was eventually to succeed him as Minister. Olivares's fall, so long postponed, came in January 1643. His immediate entourage followed him into exile at the monastery of Loeches. Mendoza, despite

Avisos históricos (1639-44), in *Semanario erudito,* XXXI (Madrid, 1790), p. 28, 7 June 1639, who relates that a meeting of the Cortes, after consultation with the King, drafted a message which was handed to Don Antonio: the *Discurso* may have been an outcome of that note.

[80] See *decreto,* 21 November 1641, in Pérez Pastor, III, 389. The King adds "en consideracion de sus servicios y de la satisfacion con que me hallo de su persona." See also Archivo de Simancas, *Quitación de Cortes: Antonio Hurtado de Mendoza,* 24 November 1641, which refers also to his "Auilidad, fidelidad y buenas partes."

[81] For these events, see Elliot, *passim.* Also his *Imperial Spain 1469-1716* (London, 1963), *passim.*

[82] See Marañón, esp. pp. 293-294, Elliott, pp. 528-529. For Olivares's fall, see Marañón, p. 349 *et seq.*

his previous protestations of loyalty to the former favourite, continued in the royal service, and in July was granted an increase of salary. [83] Presumably the poet's apparent willingness to sacrifice principle to self-advantage underlay the public quarrel in Zaragoza between Mendoza and Enrique Felípez de Guzmán, Olivares's newly legitimized heir, in September of that year. That the incident aroused the interest of contemporary chroniclers suggests that for them at least it was a sign of the Guzmanes' anger at the poet's betrayal. [84] And it confirms the view that Mendoza now formed part of the political realignment occasioned by the fall of the Count-Duke.

But if Mendoza's survival of the palace revolution was shortlived, it was not — a comforting thought — because he had played the wrong card in the political game: death was what eventually removed him from office. When he died in Zaragoza on 22 September 1644, far from the capital where he had served his King for more than twenty years, José Pellicer, the chronicler, recalled how for many years Mendoza had enjoyed the esteem of all who had to do with him. [85] Certainly his steady promotion from being an aide in the royal chamber to the post of Secretary of Justice reflects a continuing regard for his qualities. Yet it is difficult not to avoid the conclusion that whatever talents he had as servant of both King and favourite, his advancement was in great part due to his uncanny gift for sensing, in the midst of the periodic storms in Spanish political life, which course would best suit his private ends. It is a matter for argument to what extent his prestige as poet was due to his position and influence at court, and to what extent to his artistic talent. But it is to the nature of his palace reputation that we turn next.

---

[83] Archivo de Simancas, *Quitación de Cortes*, 8°: *Antonio Hurtado de Mendoza*, at Zaragoza, 24 July 1643.

[84] See *Avisos históricos*, XXXIII, p. 73. The poet's words and subsequent action are significant: " 'ni soy vos, ni quiero ser vos,' con lo qual se salió de la sala y se lo fue a contar a S[u] M[ajestad]," cf. account in *Cartas de algunos padres de la Compañia de Jesús* (1634-48), in *Memorial histórico español* (Madrid, 1851-1918), XVII, p. 237.

[85] *Avisos históricos*, XXXIII, p. 232, *aviso* dated 20 September 1644. But see AHN *Inquisición*: *Consejo Supremo*: *Personal, juramentos prestados por empleados*, Book I (No. 1338: 1574-1635), f. 130ᵛ, marginal note opposite Mendoza's oath as Secretary of the Supreme Council on 9 March 1627: "murio en Zaragoza en 22 de S[eptiembr]e de 1644." A *décima*, probably written at this time, sums up, with cruel irony, a contemporary's view of the poet: *Al sepulchro de d. Ant[oni]o de Mendoza.* "Yace en esta sepultura, / sin sauer como, ni quando, / el que sin andar tentando / siempre hallo la coyuntura. / Represento su figura, / con ser tan mala, harto bien, / Viuio de ten y mas ten, / y tanto en flaqueças dio, / que al fin de flaco murio, / requiescat in pace. Amen." (See Hisp. Soc. Am. *MS B* 2505, f. 8, and ch. XIII, Note 1 here.)

II

THE POET'S REPUTATION

THOUGH it would be too much to claim that Mendoza's reputation was already made when he entered Philip IV's service in 1621, it must not be forgotten that this man of thirty-five years had been a poet for at least fifteen, and had moved in a society which had given him every opportunity to improve, as well as to display, his talents. On two occasions his wit in the theatre had won him regard: at the *fiesta* of Lerma in 1617, and in Toledo, sometime between 1618 and 1621, when Tirso de Molina (to whose *El vergonzoso en palacio* Mendoza had provided festive accompaniment in the shape of some interludes) spoke highly of the poet's qualities, claiming that his wit and conceits matched his gentleness and nobility. [1] His first experiments with the longer *comedia* form were also undertaken possibly during the years 1619-22, when his interludes were already enjoying considerable public success. [2] But for all this, Mendoza was perhaps equally appreciated for his poems — his reputation as a ballad writer is reflected in the inclusion of five of them in Pedro Arias Pérez's first edition of the *Primavera y flor de los mejores romances* in 1621; success in a different style is attested by Lope de Vega in 1620, when he described Mendoza as the best contemporary exponent of the epigrammatic *décima*. [3]

Nevertheless, the court made Mendoza, and his entry must have represented a watershed in his literary career. Many years later, the exile Jewish poet Antonio Enríquez Gómez, recalling the splendour of Spain's Parnassus during the early part of Philip IV's reign,

---

[1] Tirso's play, along with the interludes, was performed at one of the Toledan *cigarrales* (country houses): "Antonio de Mendoza, cuyos sales y concetos igualan a su apacibilidad y nobleza" (*Comedias de Tirso de Molina*, ed. Emilio Cotarelo, vol. I, in *NBAE*, IV [Madrid, 1906], pp. xxviii-xxix). For Tirso's residence at Toledo in 1618-20, ibid., pp. xxi-xxii. The *Cigarrales*, in which the Mendoza reference occurs, appeared in 1621.

[2] See "A Chronology."

[3] Lope's remark is found in his *Justa poética y alabanzas justas* (part of the San Isidro celebrations of 1620), in *Obras escogidas*, II (Madrid, 1946), p. 1583. Had Mendoza taken part in the competition, "Apolo dice que fueran, / de las primeras del mundo, / sus décimas las primeras."

commented how in an age of very brilliant poets "D. Antonio de
Mendoza, Apollo's secretary, carried the palace by storm."[4] At the
height of his career the secretary's fame had even reached Peru
where in 1632 he was described as the "gallant of the pen" and a
"valiant spirit who had put envy to shame."[5] How had such
a reputation been accomplished at a court already famed for its
devotion to the arts? This is the question I seek to answer.

Mendoza served as sounding-board to palace events. When some
occasion, public or private, called for celebration, he it was who
made the appropriate utterance, usually in poetry, but sometimes
in prose. The christening of a royal princess, for instance, inspired
a *loa* in which the poet gave what purported to be an eyewitness
account of the proceedings:

> Ya va el acompañamiento;
> los alcaldes van pasando,
> columnas de la justicia,
> y tiesos reyes de mármol. [6]

A more celebrated occasion, the baptism in 1629 of a long-await-
ed heir to the throne, Prince Baltasar Carlos, called forth a more
stiffly patriotic poem. Sometimes poetry spun its gossamer even
into the web of intrigue, as we see from a beautiful little poem
dedicated to the birthday of the future Queen of Hungary, the
Infanta María, who at the age of twenty-eight was to become wife
of Ferdinand, son of the Emperor of Germany. The alliance, it was
believed, would reunite the interests and policies of the two halves
of the House of Hapsburg, bringing nearer a successful outcome to
the long-drawn-out struggle in Germany against the Protestant
princes and forming a powerful bastion against France's plans for
expansion. In the poem, however, the exigencies of *Realpolitik* have
ceded, if only for a while, to the nobler conquests of love:

---

[4] Antonio Enríquez Gómez, *Sansón Nazareno. Poema heroico* (Ruán, 1656), Prologue:
"D. Antonio de Mendoza, Secretario de Apolo, se lleuó el Palacio."

[5] Two plays were presented to the city by the *pulperos* as part of some celebrations
in Lima: "Vna fue del galan de la plumilla... aquel valiente espiritu que vltraje se à
hecho de la embidia" (Rodrigo de Carvajal y Robles, *Fiestas de Lima por el nacimiento
del Príncipe Baltasar Carlos* [Lima, 1632], ed. Francisco López Estrada, Sevilla, 1950,
Silva V, lines 82 and 86-87). I am grateful to Prof. E. M. Wilson for drawing my attention to this reference.

[6] *MOP*, III, 57-63: *And now the* cortège *goes by: the mayors, pillars of justice, and
stiff-necked marble kings.* The *loa* in reality was played in the usual way as an introduction
to a *comedia*, probably performed at the palace.

Si goza su invicto padre
ya del Norte, y del Danubio
victorias tantas, María
de Fernando es mayor triunfo. [7]

While it may be assumed that compositions such as these sprang from the poet's own desire to celebrate, there were others that were the product of commissions. In 1632 he was called to give an account of the summoning of the Cortes to administer the oath to the Crown Prince; in 1636 his gifts were used to praise the exploits of the imperial armies in Picardy and on the Italian front, an encomium whose splendid language helped to make it a best-seller. Much earlier in his career a commission had come from a different quarter, when the Countess of Olivares in 1622 asked him to write a description of the *fiesta* of Aranjuez, whilst in the same year his spectacle play *Querer por solo querer* was part of the celebration of the Queen's birthday. [8] Mendoza saw fit also to treat more intimate aspects of his monarchs' life; King Philip's recovery from an illness, or his prowess as a huntsman, a "Mars dressed as Apollo"; or again Queen Isabel's churching after a successful pregnancy. [9] Yet even these occasions may be construed as muted fanfares to the imperial drama.

Such duties of poet laureate were only part of his work, for his help was regularly sought to spice and season the trivial moment, or to preserve the fragrance of a passing mood or event. The Duke of Medina de las Torres, when asked to decide some point of gallantry, turned to Mendoza to frame the reply. The Marchioness of Mirallo ate an oyster, and found two pearls inside: it was left to Mendoza to embroider the significance of the event. [10] On Amariles's birthday the poet sought to record in delicate hues the moment when Nise, accompanied by four "peasant girls," leaves the forest glade for the *fiesta,* to be pursued eagerly by four youths:

---

[7] *MOP*, I, 149-150 and 153-154: *If his unvanquished father now enjoys so many victories in the North and on the Danube, María is a greater triumph for Ferdinand.* The year was 1628. For the match and its background, see C. V. Wedgwood, *The Thirty Years War*, esp. pp. 208-209.

[8] For these commissions, see pp. 34-35, p. 37, and pp. 29-30 here.

[9] *MOP*, I, 155-156 (the year was 1636), II, 30-32 ("Marte de Apolo vestido"), and I, 151-152.

[10] *MOP*, I, 221-227, and III, 126-127.

Imitan sus lazos
las aguas sonoras
que en confuso enredo
los prados coronan.

The début at court of Doña María Manrique was likewise couched in idyllic unreality: having left her cruel mother's hut, she, "the divine shepherd lassie" is now assured of the attentions of courtly shepherds. [11] On these occasions the intention was possibly more social than lyrical, and in consequence where now Mendoza seems most trivial, he may have appeared to his contemporaries as most profoundly relevant. Bourciez in his study of St. Gelais, a French court poet of the first half of the sixteenth century, has alluded to the modern critic's difficulty: "Essayez d'attraper au vol un papillon, il vous restera entre les doigts un peu de poussière brillante. On pourrait en dire autant de ces vers menus et futiles, mais dont la futilité fait le charme, improvisés et semés au hasard, sans les préoccupations qu'a l'artiste et le penseur." [12] So also was it with Antonio de Mendoza. Considered from a literary standpoint alone, the charge of banality must stick, yet the very abundance of "futile" verse must also have contributed to his palace reputation.

Within the court Mendoza had a coterie whose friendship and patronage he enjoyed in a special degree. As we saw, the Count-Duke was the object of the poet's most assiduous attentions, as well as being the connecting line with most of those in the inner group, for they were for the most part members of the Guzmán family, or at the very least the favourite's close associates. After Olivares, Mendoza's most important patron may well have been the *privado*'s son-in-law, Ramiro Felipe Núñez de Guzmán, Duke of Medina de las Torres. He had married María de Guzmán, the Count-Duke's daughter, probably the Amariles celebrated in a number of the poet's pieces. [13] The Duke commissioned Mendoza to write, on the occasion of the marriage, a panegyric of himself and the Guzmán family, he

---

[11] *MOP*, I, 260-262: *Their hunters' snares are imitated by the sounding waters, which in a confused entanglement crown the meadows*, and *MOP*, III, 11-13: "la divina zagaleja."

[12] Édouard Bourciez, *Les Moeurs polies et la littérature de cour sous Henri II* (Paris, 1886), pp. 308-309.

[13] For the Duke and his marriage, see Marañón, esp. pp. 273-282. The marriage took place in October 1622, María died in childbirth in 1626. *MOP*, I, 218-221 has a poem from the Duke to the Countess of Cantillana, but composed in fact by Mendoza.

being a rather obscure member of the same house as his future father-in-law. Mendoza celebrated the union too with a rather dutiful epithalamium expressing the wish that the marriage prove fruitful. Another poem, intended mainly as an account of the King's journey out of Madrid, casts light on the poet's views of the nobility as well as revealing a presumption that the Duke, like the Count of Olivares, shared Mendoza's own prejudice against the grandees and the upstart nobles:

> Que hoy acomodan bonete
> muchos que (¡oh siglos traidores!)
> ni era empezada su cuna,
> ni amanecido su nombre.

And Mendoza concludes an impassioned invocation of the true aristocracy of a past era with these words:

> Cubra modesto silencio
> del tiempo las sinrazones,
> y cierren ya negras llaves
> estas iras, y estas voces. [14]

At one time too Mendoza seems to have been on good terms with the Count-Duke's illegitimate son, on whose behalf he wrote amatory or complimentary verses to Ana María de Velasco, a practice he may well have repeated for others on different occasions, perhaps receiving as remuneration, "something to buy gloves". [15] And membership of this inner ring brought stranger poetic duties in its train, as when, on the occasion of the birth of a royal princess in 1623, Mendoza was prompted to write a news-letter in verse to the Duke of Béjar, describing a *fiesta* given by the Count-Duke's brother-in-law, the Marquis of Alcañices. [16] Even the strange amatory duties of Lope de Vega as the Duke of Sessa's secretary are recalled when

---

[14] *MOP*, I, 268-273, 250-254, and 186-195: *For today there put straight the bonnet many (oh, traitorous centuries!) whose cradle was not yet begun, nor had their name yet seen first light* [The grandees had the right to remain with head covered in the King's presence] ... *Let a modest silence cover over time's stupidities, and black keys at once shut up these voices of anger.*

[15] *MOP*, II, 263-264. The bastard is here called Julián de Guzmán, on whom see Marañón, p. 283 *et seq.* The lady may have been the same as the María de Velasco who was Julián's *madrina* at his christening in 1613 (Marañón, p. 288).

[16] In Martin Hume, p. 145 and Note.

Mendoza in another poem gives a report on the mistress situation during his correspondent's absence from Madrid. [17]

The House of Medina Sidonia was the major branch of the Guzmán family. Mendoza may have made the acquaintance of some of its members on the King's journey to Andalusia in 1624. [18] But the evidence of a close connexion relates to 1636, when the poet celebrated the birthday of Ana de Guzmán, the ninth Duke's first wife, drawing attention also to the virtues of other members of the family. In the same year he celebrated the birth of a second son, a third poem praised the beauty of one of their children, whilst across a veil of ambiguous reference we perhaps catch now and again a hint of an even closer association between the poet and one of the ladies of this family. [19] The Duke of Medina de Ríoseco, Admiral of Castile, was, it will be recalled, a witness to the legal ceremony attendant on the poet's first marriage. The extent of Mendoza's friendship with the Admiral, whose family was allied through marriage with that of the Infantado, may only be traced in faint, and sometimes uncertain, outline in the poems. During the Admiral's exile from court in the years 1626-29 after a quarrel with Olivares, Mendoza may have maintained contact with his friend: this at least is a feasible interpretation of a poem sent to the Admiral "being exiled in Ríoseco". [20] And if another set of poems is authentic, the Admiral and Mendoza, at the very end of the latter's career, were both actively in touch with Luis de Ulloa, the so-called "poet of Toro" (not far from Ríoseco), who was favoured by the Duke of Medina de las Torres, and is particularly associated with the period spent by the favourite in Toro after the latter's fall from power. [21]

---

[17] See Lope's *Epistolario, passim.* The Mendoza poem, if authentic, is in Hisp. Soc. Am. *MS HC:* 371/224, ff. 27-28. It is a verse letter sent to Felipe de Cardona, eldest son of the Admiral of Aragon.

[18] See King's visit to the Duke in Pedro Espinosa, *El bosque de Doña Ana,* in *Obras,* ed. Francisco Rodríguez Marín (Madrid, 1909), pp. 199-221.

[19] *MOP,* III, 76-80, 184, and 136-138. The first and last poems refer also to the beautiful Leónida, presumably a daughter of the house. Other poems addressed to Anarda (the Duchess's pseudonym) may also indicate the latter. Leónida, a less common name, is found in a poem attributed to Mendoza (Hisp. Soc. Am. *MS HC:* 371/224, f. 95): there she and Fenisa compete for the favours of an "Adonis de la Montaña." See also *MOP,* I, 159-162, another "Leónida" poem.

[20] The attribution of this poem (see Hisp. Soc. Am. *MS HC:* 371/224, ff. 65v-68) is uncertain. It also gives information about women in whom the recipient has an interest.

[21] See Hisp. Soc. Am. *MS HC:* 371/224, ff. 79v-81. For Ulloa, see Marañón, pp. 277, 381 and 384. Olivares's period in Toro began in June 1643, an unpropitious period for a friendly relationship between Ulloa (a protégé of the fallen favourite) and two adherents now of the opposition.

However, in only one extensive poem can we be sure that Mendoza is the poet, and the Admiral's family the subject: these are the *redondillas* addressed by him to the fountain in the gardens at Medina, whose beauty was only surpassed by that of its owner, Filis. [22] But it is exceptional for the poem's title to betray the lady's identity, a point that underlines how so often the Celindas and Lisardas of the love-poems conceal the poet's patronesses. We can never therefore gauge with accuracy the strength of Mendoza's attachment to particular families, though we may conclude that in general his poetic reputation depended on an adroit loyalty to his patrons.

At court Mendoza also enjoyed a reputation as a playwright. Many of his early plays were probably first performed before Their Majesties at the palace, but after the brilliant success of his *Querer por solo querer* in 1622, Mendoza's court duties appear to have left him little time and energy to devote to the theatre. About 1629, however, he resumed writing plays, and between that year and 1635 the palace audience saw several of his *comedias,* among them his best known, *El marido hace mujer,* and *Los empeños del mentir:* indeed, on the testimony of Pérez de Montalbán in his *Para todos* (1632), that success was repeated outside the palace in the public *corrales,* a view confirmed by what Gracián was later to say about the former of these plays, *El marido hace mujer.* [23]

Two other forms of participation in the theatre doubtless added lustre to Mendoza's reputation, while at the same time their effect on his audience must have been the greater for the eminence that he had attained in court life. Firstly, his works of collaboration: in July 1625, with Quevedo and Mateo Montero, a play put together as part of the entertainment given by Olivares's son-in-law in celebration of the Queen's birthday; in 1631, this time in collaboration with Quevedo only, another play, *Quien más miente, medra más,* performed at a *fiesta* on St. John's Eve, sponsored by the Count-Duke, and held in the gardens of the favourite's brother-in-law, the Count of Monterrey. [24] Though this play has not survived, its effect

---

[22] *MOP*, II, 224-230. A prefatory *décima* shows that the Duchess requested the poet, "a servant of hers," to write on this subject. The poem is discussed on pp. 128-129 here.

[23] For the order of these plays, see my "A Chronology." Gracián declared of *El marido* in the *Agudeza*: "su donosísima y siete veces repetida con el mismo agrado, comedia" (*GOC*, p. 381).

[24] See *Noticias de Madrid*, p. 122, with ref. to 9 July 1625; the play was performed by the *ayudas de cámara.* For *Quien más miente,* see *Relación de la fiesta que hizo a*

may be gauged by the loud praise given it by the contemporary
chronicler. Secondly, the poet's fondness for writing *loas,* witty
introductions to palace plays and festivals, is probably a measure
of his success in that minor genre, and with his audience. [25] In them
he displayed his talent for apt comment, above all for honeyed flattery
of his royal patrons, and of the *privado.* And such ceremonial of
blandishment was thought appropriate to other theatrical occasions
too: not only great spectacles like *Querer por solo querer,* but also
his stock *comedias.* If such activities sought to add brightness to the
royal crown, they must also have suffused Mendoza with a reflected
glory.

Mendoza's relationship with other men of letters is important: it
further reveals the regard in which he was held, and has a bearing
on the significance of his position in the development of Spanish
poetry during that period. Furthermore, though his eminence at
court may have made him the object of interested adulation, there
can be no doubt that both the most renowned, and the most forgotten, of his fellow writers declared their admiration for him.

For Lope de Vega, it will be recalled, Mendoza was "that famous
Hurtado of the Muses," a regard which was reciprocated, since the
palace poet declared of Lope, from the theatre boards, that "he is
my friend," and referred to him elsewhere as "king of the stage." [26]
From Lope's side, affection went beyond tokens of respect or mere
flattery. There certainly was something of the latter in Lope's dedication of his *Vellocino de oro* to Don Antonio's first wife, for he
claims that he looked on her husband as his mentor — the truth, if
anything, was the very reverse. [27] Elsewhere, however, we meet with

---

sus *Magestades y Altezas el Conde-Duque la noche de San Juan de este año de 1631,* in
Casiano Pellicer, *Tratado histórico sobre el origen y progresos de la comedia y del histrionismo en España* (Madrid, 1804), Part II, pp. 167-190. The play, as well as its possible
relation to *Los empeños del mentir,* is discussed in "A Chronology."

[25] See *MOP,* III, 17-62. Mendoza defines the *loa* succinctly (p. 31) as "la vanguardia
de toda fiesta." The political significance of Mendoza's drama is discussed on p. 301.

[26] See *El galán sin dama,* where one of the characters claims to be a "great poet,"
and having said of Lope "Es mi amigo," affirms that the passage of time would more
easily reincarnate a Plautus, Virgil or Tasso than a Lope (in *El mejor de los mejores
libro que ha salido de Comedias nuevas,* Alcalá, 1651, p. 185). See also *MOP,* III, 32,
where Lope is the "Rey del tablado."

[27] *Parte decinueve,* f. 216ᵛ: Lope ranges himself among "los que le tenemos por
maestro."

Lope's sincere admiration. A letter in verse to "Antonio, bright honour of the Tagus Academy" (the reference presumably is to the palace at Aranjuez) is very significant. The poem's style is obscure, but the praise given Mendoza's "ingenio clarissimo" is unequivocal, and its appearance in *La Circe con otras rimas y prosas* of 1624 reflects how timely was Lope's counsel that his friend should pursue a policy of singing the praises of both king and royal favourite. [28] A letter sent to Mendoza by Lope in 1628 gives a clearer indication of the relation, in those later years, between the two poets. Mendoza had given Lope the manuscript of his unfinished poem, *The Life of the Virgin.* His friend now returns it, with an accompanying letter praising the poem's elegant style and sublime conceits. [29] The letter's tone reveals friendship. That Lope should previously have expressed the wish to see the poem argues frankness and confidence. Yet a certain reserve and respect in Lope's words suggest the feeling that he was writing to a man above him in station. Not unexpectedly Mendoza's final tribute to his life-long friend was made at the time of Lope's death in 1635. The first of the two *décimas* he wrote suggests Mendoza's appreciation of Lope's human qualities, as well as of his literary ones:

> Tu ingenio, que celestial
> se mide, se cifra, o suma,
> de alma, que sobró a tu pluma,
> te fabrica lo inmortal. [30]

Quevedo's relation with Mendoza is less easily decipherable. They may have known each other as early as 1608, but it is the twenties that primarily brought their names together. Both formed part of the King's retinue during the royal journey to Andalusia in 1624, but neither saw fit to comment on the other's presence. [31] The collaborations of 1625 and 1631 suggest, however, that they were

---

[28] Lope de Vega, *La Circe con otras Rimas y Prosas* (Madrid, 1624), ff. 150-155ᵛ: "Antonio, claro honor del Academia / del Tajo." Mendoza, who wrote the volume's *censura,* paid back the compliment in similar coin: Lope's works are "sin duda mas admirables en ser buenas, que en ser tantas."

[29] Lope de Vega, *Epistolario,* IV, 130-132: "no he visto en la lengua castellana cosa tan bien escrita y se auentaja a todas las deste género" (p. 130).

[30] *MOP,* II, 108-109: *Your genius, which when summed and totalled measures as divine, builds your immortality with that portion of soul left over from your pen.*

[31] *QOCP,* p. 1714 *et seq.* For the earlier connexions between the two poets, see present study, p. 20.

on terms of easy friendship. A letter, undated, which Quevedo addressed to his friend indicates a deeper relationship. In it Quevedo dwelt on the comforts of a Stoic philosophy, with its supreme disdain for the rigours of this life. Perhaps Mendoza was only by accident the recipient of this Stoic exercise, but possibly too it was intended to console him at a moment of crisis in his life. The final paragraph reads:

> This was written to you, Don Antonio, so that with like courage, despising the fears of death, our friend, you should transfer those fears to the travails of this life; and that, philosophically, you should not permit your spirit to be conquered, or bowed down, by the dread opinion [concerning death] which prevails. [32]

It could not be said that Mendoza was an avowed Stoic, but certain of his poems echo that philosophy, albeit in a subdued tone. We may quote as an example some lines from Mendoza's poem to the ruins of Sagunto, the Roman site near Valencia, where he reflects on what now remains of human effort, concluding that the fame achieved by constancy in virtue is proof against the ravages of time:

> Mas de tus fuertes varones
> los hechos grandes no quedan
> en memorias, que se fían
> a necedades de piedra,
> sino en la inmortal noticia
> de los hombres, que a la excelsa
> constante virtud el tiempo
> no bate ninguna almena. [33]

However, the two poets' intimacy is attested not so much by a common philosophic viewpoint, as by a common poetic practice. Certain poems share the same point of departure, and may reflect

---

[32] *QOCP*, pp. 1812-17, quot. on p. 1817: "Esto escrito a vuesa merced, señor don Antonio, para que con igual ánimo, despreciando los miedos de la muerte amiga, los pase a los trabajos del vivir; y filósofo, no deje vencer ni doblar el espíritu, de la opinión común y espantosa." The editor, without giving reasons, dates this letter 1632. All that can be said is that the death of Quevedo's friend, Don Diego, which prompted most of the reflexions in the letter (see p. 1816), could also explain Don Antonio's sense of loss: Don Diego has not been identified.

[33] *MOP*, II, 42-44: *But the great deeds of your [Sagunto's] powerful men are enshrined not in memories entrusted to stone follies, but in the immortal knowledge of mankind, for time does not batter down any battlement in constant virtue's lofty fabric.* The last two lines represent the *PMS* text, pp. 105-109.

participation at the same poetic academy. [34] More importantly, the
similarity of their burlesque poems, and of some of their *conceptista*
devices, hints at an association from which an almost common style
has emerged. This may help to explain the confusion that has
reigned over the correct attribution of certain poems. [35]

There is evidence that Mendoza maintained his friendship with
Quevedo up till the time of his death, since he offered Don Francisco
some official backing when the latter was seeking to publish his
Vida de San Pablo and *Vida de Marco Bruto* in 1644. [36] Signs such
as these of a continuing friendship between the two poets make
it necessary to speculate on one of Mendoza's *discursos,* in which
he sought to persuade the Count-Duke that an anonymous and
widely read libel should be seen as less harmful or offensive than
appeared at first sight. Mendoza argued that there were malcontents
in any age, and that any government must suffer its bad, as well as
its good, fortune. He reminded Olivares too how fickle public opinion
is: "La costumbre del pueblo es no medir nada con juicio: por un
accidente sin culpa se enoja, por una acción acertada se templa." [37]

The *discurso's* extraordinarily flattering tone, even for Mendoza,
suggests an ulterior motive, and though the poet does not make the
point openly, his aim was evidently to play down the seriousness
of the offence committed by the author of the libel, presumably in
the hope that it be judged less severely by the authorities. The
exact date of the *discurso* remains unknown, though a reference
to "Our Lord the Prince" might suggest that Baltasar Carlos, born
in 1629, was now more than a small child; whilst the poet's feverish
attempt to justify policy may reflect the political confusion of the
middle or late thirties. The attempt to link this *discurso* and an
incident in Quevedo's life is purely speculative. After a period
of thirteen and more years during which Don Francisco staunchly

---

[34] See for instance the sonnet beginning "Estas son, y serán ya las postreras" (*MOP*,
II, 189), whose opening line is identical with a Quevedo sonnet (*QOCV*, p. 512). Mendoza's poem first appeared in *Querer por solo querer*. Ignacio Aguilera ("Sobre tres
romances atribuidos a Quevedo," *Boletín de la Biblioteca de Menéndez Pelayo*, XXI
[1945], 495-496) suggests that both sonnets were first written for the *Academia de
Madrid*.

[35] See *QOCV*, p. cxxiii. See also Asensio, pp. 113-114.

[36] See James O. Crosby, "Dos contratos desconocidos para la publicación de tres obras
de Quevedo," in his *En torno a la poesía de Quevedo* (Madrid, 1967), pp. 229-235.

[37] *Discursos*, pp. 73-100, the quot. is on p. 79: "It is the custom of the people to
fail to measure anything with good judgment: it gets annoyed on account of some blame-
less accident, and is put in good mood by an action that proves to be right."

supported the Olivares régime — a fact that may help to explain his continuing relationship with Mendoza — he began to attack the *privado,* and at some time in the mid-thirties published anonymously a satire entitled *La Isla de los Monopontos* in which, under a thin disguise, he pilloried the régime, as well as the Spanish tradition which he saw as having produced it. [38] The satire, which circulated widely in manuscript, is thought to have been an important factor in the incarceration of Quevedo by the authorities from December 1639 to June 1643. [39] Though Marañón has argued that the principal reasons were different, there can be no doubt that popular opinion attributed Quevedo's imprisonment to the satires he had written against the government. And in the circumstances it is at least plausible that Mendoza, as an old friend, came to Quevedo's aid by pleading his cause before Olivares at the time that proceedings against Don Francisco were under consideration.

Mendoza, like Quevedo, did not approve of the highfalutin Gongorine style. But his poetry demonstrates how difficult it was, by the sixteen-twenties, to escape Góngora's influence. The question of the direct relation between the two poets is a mystery. There was certainly abundance of occasion for Góngora and Mendoza to have known each other, since at the end of Philip III's reign, and the beginning of the next, Góngora was actively associated with the court, and served as chaplain in the royal chapel. A letter of July 1617 alludes to the modest success which Don Luis's search for favour and applause at court had brought him. [40] His subsequent correspondence reveals his continuing attempts to exploit those good beginnings. Góngora and Mendoza, who probably were both members of the Selvaje and Madrid Academies, were engaged on identical voyages of exploration into court life at this time.

---

[38] Quevedo's relation with the Olivares régime is discussed by Marañón (pp. 126-137). *La isla* was only published after Quevedo's death, when in a modified form it was incorporated in *La hora de todos* (1650) — see text in *QOCP*, pp. 307-312. The title to Mendoza's *discurso* specifies that the libel was an "impresso," but the heading may have been added later; one cannot therefore conclude that the work referred to cannot have been *La isla* because the latter only circulated in manuscript.

[39] See e.g. Julián Juderías, *Don Francisco de Quevedo y Villegas: la época, el hombre, las doctrinas* (Madrid, 1922), p. 163.

[40] Luis de Góngora, *Obras poéticas*, ed. R. Foulché-Delbosc (New York, 1921), III, 161. In a sonnet (ibid., II, 380) dated 1623, which he dedicated to the Count-Duke, Góngora announced his imminent return to Córdoba. For the details here of Góngora's life, see Miguel Artigas, *Don Luis de Góngora: Biografía y estudio crítico* (Madrid, 1925), *passim*, and his correspondence in vol. III of *Obras poéticas*.

Furthermore, to continue Góngora's metaphor, both had at least one "good pilot" in common, the Count of Olivares. [41] Góngora was on good terms with his fellow-Andalusian and co-devotee of poetry: it will be recalled also that the Chacón manuscript of Góngora's poems was dedicated to the man who by that time had become the power behind the throne. [42] Despite the occasions, intimacies, and aims which presumably therefore joined Mendoza and Góngora, the evidence of direct contact is minimal. There was a tradition that Góngora had called Mendoza "el Asseado lego" ("the immaculate layman"), but it is a story purveyed long after the death of both poets, and its validity is further weakened by Mendoza's proneness to refer to himself as a "pulido lego" ("polished layman"). [43] Even were Góngora's phrase a parody of Mendoza's flattering self-description, it lacks the Cordobese's accustomed venom. There is a possible further reference to some association between the two poets in a poem, attributed to Mendoza, in which the author alludes to Góngora's participation in a hunting trip:

> Caminito del lugar
> volavamos cuya moza
> sobre el trenzado vn doblon
> pidio prestado a Gongora. [44]

The allusion may have been to some other Góngora, but there would be added piquancy if Don Luis were the man involved, as he was both cleric and allegedly mean. The identification with Góngora is strengthened by one of the poet's letters, which refers in July 1619 to an invitation received from the Admiral (presumably that of Castile). [45] The Hispanic Society text also refers to the host as "the great Admiral," but the two occasions can hardly have been the same one: Mendoza's poem complains of snow in the mountains,

---

[41] See letter quoted (III, 161): "con buenos pilotos he començado a tentar modestamente el aplauso de palacio i el fauor de mis protectores."

[42] See *Obras poéticas*, I, IX *et seq.*

[43] Mendoza was given his nickname by Góngora according to the anonymous *A la Majestad Catolica de Carlos II, nuestro señor, rendida consagra a sus reales pies estas vasallas voces desde su retiro, la Comedia* (1681), in E. Cotarelo, *Bibliografía de las controversias sobre la licitud del teatro en España* (Madrid, 1904), p. 43: "D. Antonio de Mendoza, á quien Góngora llamó el Asseado Lego."

[44] See Hisp. Soc. Am. *MS HC*: 371/224, ff. 62ᵛ-65ᵛ, the quot. on f. 62ᵛ: *We sped on our way to the village whose wench tried to borrow a doubloon from Góngora on the strength of her tresses.*

[45] In Artigas, pp. 302-303.

whereas Góngora's letter refers at another point to the intense July heat. However, Góngora's words at least establish a relationship with the Admiral, and thus with a coterie to which Mendoza belonged. There is in Mendoza's poem a lively picture of poetic entertainment on safari:

> el chocolate la Cena
> la musica, la parola
> y el desorden hicieron
> sazonada pepitoria.
> ....
> sin restaña se sangrava
> la vena de nuestras Coplas. [46]

If among "our *copıas*" were included some by Luis de Góngora, we catch an intriguing glimpse of his attempts to curry favour with an aristocratic audience at court. Mendoza we see contented in the element that favoured his genius. The available evidence, however, only permits us to talk of a parallel rather than a relationship between the two writers: but it is an instructive parallel, for like ambition led to different conclusions; in Góngora's case to frustration and disappointment, in Mendoza's to brilliant success. In discussing Mendoza's literary reputation in another chapter I shall comment on factors in court taste that may have a bearing on the court's preference for a Mendoza over a Góngora. [47]

Baltasar Gracián's case admits no doubt. Time and time again, the *Agudeza y arte de ingenio* attests its author's enthusiasm for Mendoza. Though there is no sign of a close friendship, they knew each other, for Gracián repeated in the *Agudeza* some verses recited to him by Mendoza in the corridors of the royal palace. [48] Gracián's expression of faith, in the sixteen-forties, that the passage of time would see Mendoza increasingly get the respect he deserved, was not fulfilled: by the time that the Second Part of the *Criticón* appeared in 1653 Gracián could only sorrow that this "royal lute"

---

[46] Hisp. Soc. Am. *MS HC*: 371/224, f. 63: *The chocolate drink, the supper, the music, the chatter and the confusion made a well-seasoned* pot-pourri... *The vein of our verses was bled unstaunched.*

[47] See pp. 183-185 here.

[48] *GOC*, p. 255. The stanza, which does not appear in *MOP*, runs: "A más de las de sus soles, / tiene Anarda dos beldades, / que son: la razón que dice, / y la sinrazón que hace."

should now lie abandoned. [49] Presumably, it was with the intention of awakening more interest in a neglected poet that Gracián, in the following year, included a large number of Mendoza's poems in the *Poesías varias de grandes ingenios españoles.* [50] This was the last tribute he paid to the memory of "el conceptuoso Mendoza".

Though Luis Vélez de Guevara does not rank, like Góngora or Gracián, among Mendoza's outstanding contemporaries, the relationship between them throws an interesting light on Mendoza's success. In the early years of the century both had been members of the Count of Saldaña's household, Luis Vélez having perhaps served the young Antonio as an instructor in the art of poetry. Both too were casting about for patronage. The brilliant career that might have lain ahead of Luis Vélez is suggested by the words of a fellow-poet Pedro Soto de Rojas in 1608 on the occasion of the publication of Luis Vélez's account of the administration of the oath to the future Philip IV:

> De un poderoso Rey tienes ayuda
> Lauro, sube a las salas de la vida
> Sin temor de fortuna, tiempo, ò muerte. [51]

Fortune did not choose to favour the fulfilment of the present promise. It was Antandro rather than Lauro who would win royal favour. The success of the one, and the failure of the other, lay in the way that the Sandovales' power was broken, and the future of the young Olivares settled. The relations between the two poets after Olivares's accession to power are naturally coloured by the events of the past. By 1625 Lauro, possibly with Mendoza's help, had obtained a palace appointment. [52] Nevertheless, his situation remained parlous, and his dependence on the royal secretary is accompanied by a sense of inferiority. He turns to Mendoza as intercessor

---

[49] *GOC*, p. 454. See *El Criticón*, ed. Romera-Navarro, II, 137: this "laúd real," said Gracián, "despedía gran resplandor de sí y de muchas piedras preciosas de que estava todo él esmaltado."

[50] I accept Romera-Navarro's arguments in favour of Gracián's considerable responsibility for this collection (see "La antología de Alfay," in *Estudios sobre Gracián*, Austin, Texas, 1950, 103-128).

[51] Pedro Soto de Rojas, *Obras*, ed. A. Gallego Morell (Madrid, 1950), p. 497: *You have, Lauro, the support of a powerful King, ascend to the halls of life without fear of fortune, time, or death.*

[52] For this period in Luis Vélez's life, see Francisco Rodríguez Marín, "Cinco poesías autobiográficas de Luis Vélez de Guevara," *Revista de Archivos, Bibliotecas y Museos,* tercera época, XIX (July-December 1908), 62-78.

when he needs money from the royal purse to finance himself on the King's journey to Aragon in that same year; on another occasion a request for money is accompanied by a shocking servility, if not indeed an ambiguous sarcasm:

> el criado conoced,
> que ha sido vuestro criado. [53]

The extent to which Luis Vélez could practise a jovial self-abasement is suggested by a note sent by him to the King, indicating a willingness to undertake any duties in the royal presence, including in Mendoza's absence the role of "*luminare minus*" and "poetic lieutenant". [54] Luis Vélez certainly felt tremendous admiration for his friend. In the *Diablo cojuelo* (1641), for instance, he called Mendoza "the supreme genius of La Montaña, and most eminent master of the lyric style, alongside whose divine music the bounty which fortune gave him seems small." [55] The envy adumbrated in the reference to Mendoza's good fortune reminds us of the occasions for tension in their relationship, and on at least one occasion that envy exploded into anger. Mendoza had made sport with the poor reception given one of Luis Vélez's *comedias*. The latter, in reply, made play with some of his own most popular lines, addressing them to Mendoza:

> Escollo armado de hiedra,
> Yo te conocí servicio;
> Ejemplo de lo que vale
> La mierda de los validos. [56]

The barb held the poison of a lifetime's frustration.

Mention must be made of one literary rivalry during Mendoza's palace career, that with Jerónimo de Villaizán. By the end of the

---

[53] In *MOP*, I, 322-323, two *décimas*: *recognize the servant who has been your servant* (or *[you] the servant recognize*[?]). Mendoza's reply follows.

[54] Marín, ibid.: "puede un Vélez / ser su luminare minus, / ... y su poeta teniente."

[55] Luis Vélez de Guevara, *El diablo cojuelo*, ed. Clás. Cast. (Madrid, 1941), pp. 249-250: "soberano ingenio montañés, y dueño eminentísimo del estilo lírico, a cuya divina música vendrán estrechos todo los agasajos de su fortuna."

[56] For this episode, see Cotarelo, *El Conde de Villamediana*, p. 115, Note: *Rock clothed in ivy, I knew you as one of the servants: an example of the worth of the shit of royal favourites [servicio* also meant "chamber-pot"]. For the original verse and its popularity, see Edward M. Wilson and Jack Sage, *Poesías líricas en las obras dramáticas de Calderón* (London, 1964), pp. 60-62.

twenties Don Jerónimo, then about twenty-five years old, was beginning to enjoy success at the palace, and a 1632 collection of plays, including Villaizán's *Sufrir más por querer más,* specifically mentioned that *comedia*'s success at the palace, adding that the King had given instructions for the time being for it not to be shown anywhere else. [57] About 1630 too Salas Barbadillo, in a sour appraisal of the *comedias de tramoyas,* exempted from stricture those put on at the royal palace, singled out Antonio de Mendoza as the outstanding exponent of the genre, but had a good word for some others, including Jerónimo de Villaizán. [58]

Significantly Salas accorded these dramatists success because they demonstrated an art befitting the royal court, and it is possibly for this reason in part that Gracián in his *Agudeza y arte de ingenio* would associate the names of "el conceptuoso Villaizán," and "el sentencioso Mendoza," meting out to them praise for their "sprightliness of verse, pregnancy of style, profundity of conceit, gravity of *sententiae,* and inventiveness of plot." [59] Gracián singled out two plays, Villaizán's *Ofender con las finezas,* and Mendoza's *El marido hace mujer,* both of them represented at the royal palace in the same period, Villaizán's in February 1632 with a repeat performance in November 1633; and Mendoza's sometime before the end of April 1633. [60] Gracián may have recalled thus something of the circumstances in which the public associated the two dramatists and their qualities. And it is understandable therefore that some people then took the view that Villaizán, consciously or unconsciously, was contending with Antonio de Mendoza for the favour of the palace audience. One cannot dispute that Don Antonio himself felt that his prestige was being challenged by the younger man, since in a poem directed, probably in 1632 or 1633, to an unknown Maruja, he made this rather jaundiced comment:

---

[57] The account here is mainly based on Victor Dixon, "Apuntes sobre la vida y obra de Jerónimo de Villaizán y Garcés," *Hispanófila,* XIII (1961), 5-22. Though *Sufrir más* (according to *Comedias de diferentes autores,* Part XXV, Zaragoza, 1632, f. 146v) scored such success in royal performance, the Royal Chamber accounts have not recorded it: but they do mention a later performance in October 1637 (see Norman D. Shergold and John E. Varey, "Some Palace Performances of Seventeenth-Century Plays," *BHS,* XL [1963], 238).

[58] Alonso de Salas Barbadillo, *Coronas del Parnaso y platos de las Musas* (Madrid, 1635), f. 34. The *privilegio* was actually given in October 1630.

[59] *GOC,* p. 441: "bizarría del verso, preñez de estilo, profundidad de concepto, gravedad de sentencias, invención de enredo."

[60] "Some Palace Performances," p. 232 and p. 229.

Cuando os bastaba mi pluma,
que fué la gala, y solaz
de Palacio, antes que fuese
en ti Apolo Villayzan. [61]

Furthermore, Don Antonio in some hard-hitting verses lampooned
Villaizán, accusing him of outrageous plagiarism as well as of
incredible conceit and presumption. [62] Mendoza, rather mysteriously,
also called him a *poeta de ayuda,* which could be interpreted as a
play on *ayuda de cámara,* thus indicating "poetic aide," and the
author may (or may not) have wanted to suggest that Villaizán helped
the King with his versifying. Certainly Villaizán enjoyed, in Lope
de Vega's description, "el voto singular del Sol Felipe," a power
that Lope in the same poem set against the envy — presumably that
of Antonio de Mendoza and others — which Villaizán had to suffer.
But Lope's remarks are taken from his Elegy to this "Spanish Te-
rence," a poem published in 1633 to commemorate Villaizán's passing, and the only known reference to the poet's ultimate fate. [63]
We may judge therefore that however harmful Villaizán could have
proved to Don Antonio's fame at court, the challenge was short-lived,
and the survivor lived on long enough to regain what prestige he
may have lost.

These relationships — sometimes stormy, more often friendly —
with other men of letters were an important contribution to Mendoza's standing, and were frequently a product of the rumbustious
atmosphere of the poetic academies. We turn now to the role which
the academies played in the life of a poet at court.

"In no other century has Spain known so many princes who write
poetry with wit and elegance, learning and a pure style." [64] Lope's

---

[61] MOP, II, 77: *When for you [Maruja] there sufficed my pen, which was the orna-
ment and solace of the Palace before Villaizán became Apollo in thee [= Palacio]."* The
ref. in the poem (p. 77) to Montalbán's *Para todos* (Madrid, 1632) dates it as of that
year, or just later. That the ref. to Villaizán would be irrelevant after 1633 is made
plain below.

[62] MOP, II, 18-22. There may also be further word-play on *ayuda,* = clyster, in this
passage.

[63] The text of Lope's rare *Elegía en la muerte del licenciado Don Gerónimo de Villaizán...* (Madrid, 1633) is given in Frank M. Inserni, *Vida y obra de Jerónimo de Villaizán*
(Barcelona, 1960), pp. 18-24.

[64] Lope de Vega, second part of his *Rimas,* quot. in Sánchez, *Academias literarias,*
p. 27: "En ningun siglo ha conocido España tantos principes que con tal gracia y primor, erudición y puro estilo escriban versos."

words are a fair comment on Philip IV's court. One can cite, as practisers of the poetic art, the Counts of Lemos, Salinas, Villamediana, Saldaña, Roca, the Prince of Esquilache, the Count-Duke, and even the King himself. The growth of court life during the reigns of Philip III and IV had brought about a situation in which many of the aristocracy, including titled nobility, delighted in their devotion to poetry, possibly finding in it also an occasion to veneer amorousness with a lyric sweetness. But another type of poet had multiplied too; the shiftless, feckless *ingenio* who trusted that his poetic gift would bring him the patronage he needed to keep the wolf from the door. Within the exclusiveness of court life the academies (an important feature of Madrid's literary life in the early seventeenth century) provided a common meeting ground for two very different sorts, whose paths in real life might not have otherwise crossed.

The *ingenios* themselves took pride in the noble patronage they enjoyed. Álvaro Cubillo de Aragón referred to the "received custom" of having some lord preside over the academy sessions; a report on Saldaña's academy gave an assurance that "there would be no lack of grandees;" and in the case of the *Academia de Madrid*, its founder, Medrano, proudly recounted the occasion when the young Philip IV had attended. [65] Such groups had presumably first afforded the young Mendoza a foothold in court life; in the twenties, when he was already established at court, the *Academia de Madrid* reveals the milieu in which he now often worked. After Medrano's retirement from the presidency, the King continued his patronage. The noble patrons were also still there, now including the Count-Duke's brother-in-law, the Marquis of Alcañices, as well as the Dukes of Medinaceli, Lerma and Híjar. [66] Even closer links with the royal *entourage* are suggested by the academy's present meeting-place, the house of Francisco de Mendoza, secretary to the Count of Monterrey, the latter being the Countess Olivares's brother. [67]

---

[65] In Sánchez, p. 23 ("por costumbre recibida"), and p. 38 ("no faltarán grandes"). Also Willard King, p. 54.

[66] Jacinto Aguilar y Prado, *Compendio histórico de diversos escritos* (Pamplona, 1629), ff. 45-60, an "Epítome de algvnos papeles escritos en diferentes asvmtos en la illustre Academia de Madrid," referring to meetings in 1625 and 1626. The King heard a *discurso* by the author on 18 August 1625.

[67] See Willard King, p. 57. "Mendoza's academy," begun in 1623, continued apparently until 1637.

We need not associate Mendoza's name exclusively with this academy: [68] he may well have patronized others. What is important is that they provided a focus of creative activity, where courtly ideals were pursued with intensity. What were these sessions like? In 1624 Manuel Faria y Sousa took a poor view of them: the poets who attended were no better than wasps buzzing in the air to no purpose at all. [69] In 1655 Antonio López de Vega similarly questioned the academies' usefulness, but at least gave a detailed picture of what went on in those years; debates on poetry, recitations of sonnets or *romances,* the reading of *comedias* followed by a critical discussion, or an appraisal of some play actually seen in the theatre. [70] Such activities had probably been the order of the day in earlier decades too, as had been the poetic competition, and the satirical *vejamen* which often commented on the character and habits of the members. In 1630 Jacinto Polo de Medina, at that time in close contact with the Madrid court, had in his *Academias del jardín* evoked, in a fictitious setting, the atmosphere of these literary sessions. [71] A more flattering picture than that of either López de Vega or Faria y Sousa, it shows poets of talent vying with each other in displaying their art and uttering their pastoral laments. Polo was not the only one to see good in the academies. In 1635 Pellicer y Tovar wrote a very eulogistic description of the *Academia de Madrid:* it was for him "the seminary of the learned, the workshop of the well-spoken, the college of the wise." [72] We may consider therefore that Mendoza by his presence at these gatherings both contributed to, and acquired more of, that elegance, and urbane tolerance which Juan de Zabaleta later noted in the life of the academies. [73] Two more points should be made concerning them; that, as Juan de Arguijo observed, the spirit of emulation which the sessions fostered was

---

[68] See p. 25.

[69] Manuel Faria y Sousa, *Noches claras* (Madrid, 1624), p. 323. Sánchez (p. 20) suggests however that Faria, who also criticized the academy poets in his *Divinas y humanas flores* (1624), may have resented his failure to be admitted to membership anywhere.

[70] Antonio López de Vega, *Paradoxas racionales,* ed. Erasmo Buceta (Madrid, 1935), p. 26. López's criticism had been voiced too in his earlier *Heraclito i Democrito de nvestro siglo* (Madrid, 1641), p. 47.

[71] In Salvador Jacinto Polo de Medina, *Obras escogidas,* ed. José María de Cossío (Madrid, 1931), *passim.*

[72] In Sánchez, p. 81: "Este es el seminario de los entendidos, el taller de los bien hablados, el colegio de los discretos." The occasion was a meeting of the *Academia de Madrid.*

[73] In King, p. 96.

such as to nurture genius; and that the academies were an important means by which the poet in this period achieved eminence — Pérez de Montalbán could give himself no higher praise than that he had written verses for "all the Academies and Competitions of Spain." [74]

The central position occupied by the Madrid Academy in court circles may well have made it a natural outlet for the talents of the "discreto de Palacio," and what we know of his participation in the special academies of the late sixteen-thirties may reflect the part that he played at unrecorded academy meetings. Willard F. King has argued that the first of these occasions was not a completely new phenomenon, but merely a special (and public) meeting of Francisco de Mendoza's *Academia de Madrid:* the argument may be equally applied to the other *certámenes* discussed below. [75] These public contests in any case evoke convincingly the prestige then enjoyed by Mendoza in this poetry-loving court.

The first extraordinary academy, organized as it happens by Antonio de Mendoza, was held on 20 February 1637 to celebrate the conferring on the King of Hungary of the title King of the Romans, an occasion graced by Philip's presence. The type of subject popular in academy competitions is reflected here: "Why is Judas represented with a red beard?"; "Why are palace maids called *mondongas* if they do not sell *mondongo* (tripe)?" It was not only the venue, the royal salon, that lent special dignity to the occasion, but the setting: Cosme Lotti, the Italian stage engineer, had devised and assembled the *décor.* At the appropriate moment, Mount Parnassus swung into view, and Apollo, accompanying himself on his lyre, sang melodious verses, after which he listened to the poets' recitation of their own compositions. The President on this occasion was Luis Vélez, but Mendoza acted as one of the judges, and earned from Jerónimo Cáncer, one of the poets, a compliment for his wit. [76] He was indeed "el grande Mendoça,"

---

[74] Arguijo in King, p. 52, Montalbán on p. 97.

[75] King, p. 93.

[76] The sources used here are Alfred Morel-Fatio, "Académie burlesque célébrée par les poètes de Madrid au Buen Retiro en 1637," in *L'Espagne au XVIe et au XVIIe siècle. Documents historiques et littéraires* (Bonn, 1878), pp. 602-676; *Academia burlesca en buen retiro a la Majestad de Philippo IV el Grande,* in *Libros Raros de Poesía de los siglos XVI y XVII* (Valencia, 1942); E. Cotarelo, *Rojas Zorrilla,* p. 46 et seq.; Rodríguez Villa, *La corte y monarquía de España,* p. 103; and *Sumario y compendio de lo sucedido en España, Italia, Flandes, Francia y otras partes. Desde febrero de 637 hasta el de 638,* an *impreso* (n.p., no date), f. 4v in Real Academia de la Historia, *Papeles variados de Jesuitas,*

who had so liberally sprinkled about the salt of his wit in the service of his King. [77]

The continuing esteem that Mendoza enjoyed is attested in two extraordinary academies of the following year, one held in February, the other in November. The latter represents Mendoza's last recorded public appearance as palace poet, but the earlier session (for which the poet wrote some *redondillas,* read by Luis Vélez's son Juan) is more valuable for having preserved one of our rare glimpses of the man as seen by a contemporary. [78] Rojas Zorrilla had been entrusted with composing that most entertaining item of academy fare, the *vejamen.* From it we may judge the ease with which Mendoza occupies the position of mediator between the King and the public at large: Don Antonio has been able to assure Rojas of the enjoyment which His Majesty had derived from his *vejamen* of the previous year. And it is Rojas in that same satirical news-letter who conveys with felicity a graphic moment from Mendoza's life: "He was crossing to his coach from one of the boxes of the theatre *corral,* moving with so polished a tread that everyone realized that he was walking on the feet of his own verses." [79] This seems an appropriate exit for such a "pulido lego." Some years of his literary career still remained, and in one sense a taste for his poetry appears to have increased. [80] Yet after 1638 he cannot have dominated the glittering palace scene with such ease, for during the closing years of his career the literary life of the court was itself diminished, and with that court's removal to Zaragoza the public reputation of a palace favourite must also have suffered an eclipse.

CXIX, No. 17; Antonio de León Pinelo, *Annales o historia de Madrid...,* BNM MS 1764, f. 313v; Jerónimo de Cáncer y Velasco, *Obras varias* (Madrid, 1651), f. 31v. Mendoza's *mondongas* poem (*MOP*, III, 81-84) shows every sign of improvisation: he also contributed an "Enigma del guardainfante" (*MOP*, II, 140-142), a riddle poem interpreted by members of the company (Morel-Fatio, pp. 620-623).

[77] Cáncer's verse is quoted in Morel-Fatio, p. 632.

[78] For the February meeting, see Cotarelo, *Rojas Zorrilla,* p. 46 *et seq.,* and *MOP*, III, 134-136. Some *décimas* (*MOP*, III, 167-168) were written for a competition celebrating the King's marksmanship in the hunt in mid-January 1638: they may have been part of the February celebrations (cf. *MOP*, III, 248), or a separate occasion. For the November meeting, see Rafael Benítez Claros, "Una curiosa *jinojepa* del siglo XVII," *Revista de Bibliografía Nacional,* VII (1946), 355-358. Mendoza was one of the judges.

[79] Cotarelo, p. 59: "...desde un aposento del corral atravesaba a su coche, pisando tan pulido, que todos entendieron que iba sobre los pies de sus consonantes."

[80] See pp. 192-193 here.

III

MENDOZA AND *CONCEPTISMO*

"DON Antonio de Mendoza, whose works the more they are sought after, the more will they gain applause and success." Baltasar Gracián's unbounded admiration for "Mendoza, el conceptuoso" occasioned this patently inaccurate prophecy. [1] How could the great critic of Spanish *conceptismo* have been so wrong? Indeed, was his judgment at fault?: a conclusion to which we may be led by a glance at Mendoza's poems, and a perusal of the instances where Gracián, in his *Agudeza y arte de ingenio* (1642 and 1648), has singled out the poet for praise. For example Mendoza's subtlety in "conceitful arguments" is acknowledged in some verses from the *Life of the Virgin:*

> Que si salió a ser vencida
> Eva sin pecado, es cierto
> que la que nació a vencelle,
> que se concibió con menos. [2]

But Gracián's praise, here and elsewhere, is for a device which we would not readily recognize as "conceitful," and we may wonder whether a subsequent critique has not misunderstood the *concepto.* Furthermore the reader's probable failure to share Gracián's enthusiasm for the verses quoted suggests that the poet may have been the victim of a radical change of taste. Both these conclusions receive apparent confirmation from Gracián's habit of praising other poets too in what we would now think of as their moments of infelicity.

Such a practical difficulty in appreciating Mendoza suggests the need to define more accurately the phenomenon of *conceptismo,* a

---

[1] *Agudeza,* in *GOC*, p. 454: "Antonio de Mendoza, cuyas obras cuanto más se desean han de lograr más aplauso y lucimiento." And p. 277.

[2] *GOC*, p. 413: *For if Eve being without sin contrived to be conquered, it is a sure thing that she who was born to conquer sin was conceived with less of it.* The text differs in detail from that in *MOP*, I, 51.

Spanish version of a characteristic European vogue in the early part of the seventeenth century. The fault in part lies with some of the Spanish poets themselves, for *conceptista* writing was in favour at a time when Góngora's great experiments with *culterano* verse caused many poets and critics to align themselves as the supporters, or the enemies, of Don Luis and the "new poetry." Such strong partisanship, accompanied on the one side by vociferous attacks on *culto* poetry, made it easy for later critics to assume that the opponents were supporters of a distinct movement, characterized by a devotion to a different style of poetry, that of the *conceptistas*. [3] More recently, however, attention has been drawn to the misleading nature of this view. The term *culto*, for instance, though it accurately describes the learned nature of Góngora's poetry and the attempt to introduce a Latinized vocabulary and syntax into the vernacular, embraces only certain aspects, and as a term either of abuse or praise fails to refer to other fundamental features of the verse, for instance that poet's incredible metaphorical virtuosity. And of course such virtuosity is found too in some of Góngora's opponents, for instance in Quevedo, generally regarded as a *conceptista*. In a desire to establish a more precise nomenclature A. A. Parker advocated the restriction of the term *culterano* to the strictly *culto* features of Gongorine poetry and sought to reserve *conceptista* for that use of metaphor which, for Alexander A. Parker, was the essence of *conceptismo*. "Góngora," he rightly remarked, "was as conceptist as Quevedo, or even more so." And as further confirmation of this opinion, he pointed to the fact that Gracián in the *Agudeza y arte de ingenio,* a compendium of the *conceptista* art, quoted from Góngora more frequently than from any other Spanish poet. [4]

It was right to attempt to close the gap between *culterano* and *conceptista*. Yet the latter term still needs further definition, since the metaphorical virtuosity which A. A. Parker distinguished as an essential feature of *conceptista* practice in Góngora and Quevedo does not merit much attention from Gracián, the latter frequently

---

[3] See e.g. M. Menéndez Pelayo, *Historia de las ideas estéticas en España* (Santander, 1946-1947), II, 325: "Nada más opuesto entre sí que la escuela de Góngora y la escuela de Quevedo, el culteranismo y el conceptismo."

[4] Alexander A. Parker, "La *agudeza* en algunos sonetos de Quevedo: contribución al estudio del conceptismo," in *Estudios dedicados a Menéndez Pidal,* III (Madrid, 1952), 345-360, quot. on p. 345. Lucien Paul Thomas long ago drew attention to the unreality of the rigid distinction (*Góngora et le Gongorisme considérés dans leurs rapports avec le Marinisme,* Paris, 1911, p. 4).

using Góngora's work to illustrate a stylistic feature that is quite different. For instance the sonnet "Mientras por competir con tu cabello" gets praise for its high sentence, whilst of its last line "en tierra, en humo, en polvo, en sombra, en nada" the critic says: "The rhetorical gradation serves as material for heightening the sententious pondering." [5] Gracián here has wandered far from the metaphoric process, yet regards himself as being evidently still in the field of the conceit, one *concepto* being "la agudeza sentenciosa."

An explanation of the conceit may be sought on theoretical grounds, or in terms of its use. The theoretical approach is dangerous to the extent that the theorists whose views we discuss and evaluate were in their own day attempting to give a reasoned ground to an already existing practice. For this reason Gracián's *Agudeza*, like the work of Tesauro or Pellegrini, must be treated with some circumspection. However, one may accept as fundamental their notion that the *concettista* (whose work in Italy in the late sixteenth century, and later elsewhere, was reshaping the poetry of a number of European countries) was "one who discovers and expresses the universal · analogies binding the universe together." [6] Through the exercise of his *ingenium* therefore the conceptist poet teased out of nature some resemblance or connexion hitherto ignored. At its highest pinnacle the poet might mystically intuit God's purpose, so that the *concetto* could be regarded in Tesauro's words as a "Symbolical Witticism, lightly hinted at by the Divine Mind: elegantly revealed by the mind of man." [7] But in any case the poet through the conceit attempted an *inventio novi*, which would get from his audience the appropriate response to the "marvellous." [8]

But the conceit (however sincere the poet concerning his task of uncovering God's hidden meanings) necessarily found expression

---

[5] *GOC*, p. 379: "Sirve la retórica gradación de materia al realce de la ponderación sentenciosa."

[6] Joseph A. Mazzeo, "A Critique of some Modern Theories of Metaphysical Poetry," *MPh*, L (1952-1953), 88. See also his "Metaphysical Poetry and the Poetic of Correspondence," *JHI*, XIV (1953), 221-234, and his "Universal Analogy and the Culture of the Renaissance," *JHI*, XV (1954), 299-304.

[7] In Mario Praz, "The Flaming Heart: Richard Crashaw and the Baroque," in *The Flaming Heart: Essays on Crashaw, Machiavelli, and Other Studies in the Relations between Italian and English Literature from Chaucer to T. S. Eliot* (New York, 1958), quot. from Tesauro's discussion of "preachable conceits" on p. 210. See also p. 206 *et seq.*, and Mazzeo's "Poetic of Correspondence," pp. 230-231.

[8] See Mazzeo, "A Seventeenth-Century Theory of Metaphysical Poetry," *RR*, XLII (1951), 245-255, and Ernst Curtius, *European Literature and the Latin Middle Ages,* trans. Willard R. Trask (London, 1953), pp. 296-297.

in forms and connexions which *concettista* and public shared. Furthermore, it was the product of a period in which the perception of order and relatedness was regarded as a fundamental principle of art, and the enjoyment of the "similarness" of the two terms of comparison a privilege to which the reader had full entitlement. [9] In this context too the discovery of the universal analogy and the elucidation of its features did no more than satisfy what was already a pre-existing aesthetic taste.

The great originality of Gracián's *Agudeza,* as Curtius stressed, lay in the attempt to bring *arte* (order) into practices largely disregarded by an older criticism. [10] Gracián's approach was flexible and empirical; he refused to be over-theoretical about the origin and nature of the conceit. Indeed, his definition was deliberately vague: "What beauty is for the eyes, and harmony for the ears, that is what the conceit is for the understanding." [11] And he acknowledged that the conceit could only be known broadly ("a bulto") rather than with precision. [12] However, he recognized the general principle at work, seeing in much of the poetry of his age a process which appealed to the intellective faculty's sense of order and relatedness in the same way that music or painting satisfied the sensorial side of human perception. The taste for the conceit therefore might be satisfied in innumerable ways, since theoretically there was no limit to the experiences from which the mind could extrapolate the *concepto;* but in practice, as I have suggested, the patterns of order out of which the conceit emerged would tend to be determined by the literary and stylistic vogues of the period.

What follows here is not another attempt to discover the origins of the conceit, but rather an endeavour to enumerate some of the influences and habits of mind that caused the *concepto* in Spain to emerge, and to follow certain forms of expression. In this I shall sometimes take the hint from Gracián's comments, but more frequently look to the literary and cultural profile of the early seventeenth century.

---

[9] See Rosemond Tuve, *Elizabethan and Metaphysical Imagery: Renaissance Poetic and Twentieth-Century Critics* (Chicago, 1947), esp. pp. 122-123.

[10] Curtius, pp. 297-301.

[11] *GOC*, p. 237: "lo que es para los ojos la hermosura, y para los oídos la consonancia, eso es para el entendimiento el concepto."

[12] *GOC*, p. 13.

The emblematist's art accompanied the *concepto,* but did not of itself create it. Mario Praz's view that the origin of the conceit lay in the emblem has been criticized by J. A. Mazzeo, who pointed out that for the *concettista* theorists at least, the emblem was only one incidental feature of the much larger phenomenon. [13] But Mazzeo's objections fail to do justice to the pragmatic side of Praz's case, for the latter pointed to the close connexion between the emblem and the epigram which accompanied and illustrated it. [14] The important thing here is the coincidence of two forms that separately and together helped to shape the vogue for the conceit: the emblem, as we shall see, gave the reader a thorough training in the perception of relatedness and the elucidation of its meaning, whilst the epigram disciplined the taste for brevity and concision as prime characteristics of the conceit. Furthermore, Mazzeo seems unfair to Praz in stating that "the vast bulk of the creations of the school of wit do not seem to be related to the emblem literature in any intrinsic way." [15] In the first place one is looking for a significant connexion, rather than any large-scale participation of emblematists in the writing of poetry, or any obvious and extensive use by the poets of emblematic material. Secondly, Mazzeo in asserting that emblem and conceit are only found together at a late date and in minor authors such as Francis Quarles overlooks the fact that, in Spain at least, the conceit as a conscious literary exercise emerged with the *Conceptos espirituales* (1600), whose author was Gracián's "el divino Ledesma," who as both poet and emblematist subtly conjoined the two arts. [16]

Spain participated in the vogue for emblematic literature even though native productions were few, the main exponents being Sebastián de Covarrubias, author of the *Emblemas morales* (1610), and Alonso de Ledesma. Covarrubias provides some basis for thinking that there were technical reasons why Spanish printers did not produce such books in large numbers for the Spanish market, but the demand could be met by texts from abroad, including some

---

[13] See Mario Praz, *Studies in Sevententh-Century Imagery,* I (London, 1939), esp. p. 18 *et seq.,* and Mazzeo, "A Critique," pp. 91-96.

[14] Praz, I, 18. See also his *The Flaming Heart,* p. 207 *et seq.*

[15] "A Critique," p. 94.

[16] "A Critique," p. 94. See *GOC,* p. 395 and *passim.* On Ledesma, see also Praz, I, 126-127 and his *The Flaming Heart,* p. 214.

multilingual ones. [17] Faria y Sousa in his *Noches claras* (1624) alluded to the contemporary liking for emblems, hieroglyphs, enigmas and devices, [18] and later in the century Gracián's use of Alciati's emblems in the *Criticón*, as well as his praise in the *Agudeza* for the "profound" Italian emblematist, reflect the continuing vogue. [19] Evidence from literature suggests the occasional direct inspiration of emblematic material: Lope de Vega in one play drew directly on Covarrubias; [20] Góngora's *Cupidillo* ballads drew on a commonplace in a number of emblem books of love, the emblem of Cupid upsetting the beehives and getting stung by the bees; [21] Bartolomé Leonardo Argensola's sonnet meditating on the opposing claims of Democritus and Heraclitus (the philosopher who laughed and the one who wept) reveals his debt to the visual inspiration of Alciati's famous emblem. [22] In a rather different way, Quevedo used a visual emblematic technique in the *Epístola censoria*, as he pictured his sorrow at Spain's plight:

> Ya sumergirse miro mis mejillas,
> la vista por dos urnas derramada
> sobre las aras de las dos Castillas. [23]

---

[17] Sebastián de Covarrubias Orozco, *Emblemas morales* (Madrid, 1610), dedication to the Duke of Lerma: "pareciome serian a proposito vnas emblemas morales, hallando entonces quien dibuxasse mis pensamientos, pero no quien supiesse abrir en estampa sus figuras, hasta agora que unos oficiales estrangeros me las abrieron en madera." See Praz's *Studies*, II (London, 1947) for a bibliography of this literature. Ledesma published *Amoris divini emblemata* (Antwerp, 1615). See also Karl Ludwig Selig's studies, "La teoria dell' emblema in Ispagna: i testi fondamentali," *Convivium*, XXIII (1955), 409-421, "Addenda to Praz, *Bibliography of Emblem Books*," *MLN*, LXX (1955), 599-601, and "The Spanish translations of Alciato's *Emblemata*," *MLN*, LXX (1955), 354-359.

[18] Manuel Faria y Sousa, *Noches claras* (Madrid, 1624), p. 349.

[19] *GOC*, pp. 327-328 and *passim*.

[20] See Duncan Moir, "Lope de Vega's *Fuenteovejuna* and the *Emblemas morales* of Sebastián de Covarrubias Horozco (with a few remarks on *El villano en su rincón*)," in the forthcoming *Estudios y ensayos sobre el teatro antiguo hispánico, y otros ensayos. Homenaje a William L. Fichter*, ed. A. D. Kossoff (Brown University Press).

[21] *Obras completas*, Nos. I-V of *Romances atribuibles* (ed. 1951, pp. 249-257), cf. emblems reproduced in Praz, *Studies*, I, 118-119, and Gracián's *Agudeza*, in *GOC*, p. 285, which quotes Alciati's epigraph with a paraphrase by "un antiguo español," in fact another version of the latter part of Romance III, "Por los jardines de Chipre." See also Lope's treatment of the theme in *Poesías líricas*, Clás. Cast., I (Madrid, 1946), 188. The chorus runs: "Abejitas me pican, madre; ¿que haré que el dolor es grande?" For the more general relevance of the emblem to Góngora, see Hector Ciocchini, *Góngora y la tradición de los emblemas* (Bahía Blanca, Cuadernos del Sur, 1960).

[22] The sonnet "De los dos sabios son estos retratos" is discussed by Gracián, *GOC*, p. 341. For a discussion of the "two wise men" in Spanish writing in the sixteenth and seventeenth centuries, see Monroe Z. Hafter, *Gracián and Perfection: Spanish Moralists of the Seventeenth Century* (Cambridge, Mass., 1966), 77-84.

[23] *QOCV*, p. 141: *I look upon my cheeks submerged, my sight poured out of two urns over the altars of the two Castiles.* Cf. *QOCV*, p. 595, Quevedo's use of an Alciati emblem, "El ciego lleva a cuestas al tullido."

And in a more patently emblematic style the anonymous author of a sonnet to an elm ravaged by winter pondered the relationship between the picture in words and his moral conclusion, stated separately in the subtitle as "la eternidad de las penas." [24] Gracián significantly follows an emblematic conceit from Alciati with "otra gran moralidad" in which Anastasio Pantaleón de Ribera pondered in conceitful simile the case of the rash almond-tree whose early flower is blighted by the frost, and the wiser mulberry tree. The sonnet ends with what might have stood as the epigraph to an emblem:

> Ese antigo moral tu ejemplo sea,
> que la injuria temiendo, que padeces,
> en tu mismo peligro se amenaza. [25]

But such incidental use of emblematic technique is not the main point of the present argument: what counted was the habit and training. One of the various emblems by Alciati which Gracián discussed was that of the helmet in which a swarm of bees had made its home, and which is now filled with delicious honey. [26] "The profound Alciati," commented Gracián, "took the opportunity from this to ponder the abundance of peace and her delights. He painted her thus, crowned with bees, in a sententious emblem." Alciati's epigraph pointed the moral in a final couplet:

> Arma procul jaceant; fas sit tunc sumere bellum,
> quando aliter pacis non potes arte frui.

What had impressed Gracián was the paradox, and the emblematist's ability to discover an unexpected relatedness between the symbol of war and that of sweetness. He took another example from Góngora, in which the poet had said of a lady that when she came out, the birds greeted her because they believed that day had dawned for the second time. [27] For Gracián both conceits exem-

---

[24] *Poesías varias de grandes ingenios españoles* (1654), ed. J. M. B. (Zaragoza, 1946), p. 163.

[25] *GOC*, pp. 295-296: *May that old mulberry tree be your example, which fearing that injury which you [now] suffer, feels the threat from your own danger.* The editor signifies in a note that Pantaleón's poem was derived from another of Alciati's emblems.

[26] *GOC*, p. 328.

[27] *GOC*, pp. 327-328: "Tomó ocasión de aquí el profundo Alciato para ponderar la abundancia de la paz y sus delicias; pintóla así, coronada de abejas, en un sentencioso emblema."

plified the same qualities. But they were also the product of the same discipline and intellectual habit.

Whilst the search for the unexpected relatedness was common to emblematist and poet in this period — a fact that of itself undermines the case for making the emblem the unique origin of the conceit — the emblem whetted the reader's appetite for the hidden meaning in the enigmatic and obscure. It also sharpened his ability to draw moral, or philosophic, conclusions from a series of visual images, and exercised the mind of both poet and reader in the art of making the leap, the longer the better, from object to metaphor, from situation to analogy. Lastly the emblem confirmed the view that logic and order were outstanding qualities in a work of art, since the emblematist often sought to give his reader a topic whose minutest detail contributed to the symbolical significance of the whole.

The cult of the device may even have exceeded the emblem's importance in the vogue of *conceptismo*. Palace plays and masques, public processions, both religious and secular, the occasional individual display like the Count of Villamediana's hat bearing the device of some gold coins with the motto: "Son mis amores" — all these manifestations contributed indirectly to the whetting of the *conceptista* appetite. [28] The device, rather than bastardizing the common currency of pun or other word play, enhanced the latter's value, especially as it was construed by at least one critic as a "silent poetry." [29] For Faria y Sousa the device, along with emblems, enigmas and hieroglyphs, pregnant gestures and actions, all deserved our admiration, since "in silence they speak elegantly, and there is displayed in them the splendour of our thoughts." [30] The whole discussion, which is of symbolic and subtle expression, moves significantly from symbol to emblem or device, and thence to the *agudeza:* it is with an example of the spoken conceit that he

[28] See Shergold, esp. pp. 236-297, and Praz, I, 159. Gracián, in *Agudeza*, GOC, p. 397, recounts without attribution the story of Villamediana's "equivocación atrevida y peligrosa" in thus declaring that the Count's mistress was a royal one, the Queen. Faria y Sousa (*Noches claras*, p. 349) referred to "los varios libros de acutissimas empressas que goza el mundo." [Villamediana declared his love both to be money and to be royal, the word *reales*, implied, having both these meanings.]

[29] Père le Moine's *De l'Art des devises* (1666), in Praz, I, 52: "une Poësie, qui ne chante point, qui n'est composée que d'une Figure muette, et d'un mot qui parle pour elle à la veue."

[30] Faria y Sousa, *Noches claras*, p. 349: "cosas que mudas hablan elegantemente, y campean en ellas las galas de los pensamientos."

concludes; for Faria, as later for Gracián, all these techniques reveal the same process at work. Furthermore the social context of emblem, device, motto, or even witty remark, must not be forgotten or misunderstood. Mazzeo's critique of Praz's emblematic theory of the origin of the conceit calls for one further comment. He takes Praz to task for assuming that both conceit and emblem "are of the nature of the charade or riddle — the by-products of an amusing, light-hearted (perhaps perverse?) verbal and pictorial game." For Mazzeo such light-heartedness is quite inconsistent with the sublime poetry of the English metaphysicals. [31] Yet a study of the palace context of Mendoza's poems will suggest the importance of games in the composition of poetry, and as the quotations from Faria y Sousa and Père le Moine indicate, what we may now regard as frivolous was often in the seventeenth century treated with solemnity.

As I noted earlier, Praz closely associated the emblem with the epigram that accompanied it: for him both, in different ways, were a form of conceit. Certainly the epigram in seventeenth-century Spain enjoyed great sucess, a fact possibly explained in part by the admiration for Martial on the grounds of his Spanish origin. For Gracián Martial, "nuestro Bilbilitano," was "the first-born of the conceit (agudeza)," [32] and his comments on Martial's epigrams show an appreciation of the conceptista qualities in the Latin poet. In one case Martial had demonstrated brilliantly his ability to make play with varying uses of the same verb; in another he had observed that the wild animals learned their ferocity from man, a conceit whose excellence for Gracián lay in the paradox that man was fiercer than the tiger, the symbol of ferocity. [33] The desire to emulate Martial in Spanish is suggested by the various attempts to render his epigrams into Spanish: Quevedo, López de Zárate, Bartolomé Leonardo de Argensola and Fernando de la Torre Farfán all tried their hand, whilst Juan de Alarcón regaled theatre audiences with his paraphrases of the epigrammatist. Martial's standing is indicated too by Agustín Collado del Hierro, who in his prologue to Salcedo

---

[31] "A Critique," p. 91. But see also Praz (The Flaming Heart, p. 207 et seq.), who shows the willingness of Crashaw and his contemporaries, including Ledesma, to indulge in the most incredibly tasteless word-play.

[32] GOC, p. 433 ("our native of Bilbilis [= Calatayud]"), and p. 258: "el primogénito de la agudeza."

[33] GOC, p. 396 and p. 325. For Gracián the earlier word-play is in the same category as the equívocos of Alonso de Ledesma, the second concepto contains the "picante de la agudeza viva y verdadera."

Coronel's *Rimas* (1627) quoted Martial, praised his wit (*agudeza*), and mentioned how the contemporary reader esteemed him, along with Tibullus and Persius among others, for his "erudite brevity." [34]

But the "erudite brevity" of the epigram in general was greatly appreciated, as may be judged by the popularity, in Spain as elsewhere, of the Welsh epigrammatist John Owen, and by the numerous attempts by various Spanish authors to write epigrams. [35] Mario Praz's indication of the popularity of the *Greek Anthology* in Europe at this time is borne out in Spain by the knowledge of it shown by Quevedo's editor and commentator González de Salas. [36] The sonnet in particular was regarded widely as an epigrammatic form: the authority for this notion went back at least as far as Fernando de Herrera's *Anotaciones* (1580), and so frequently did the poets conform to theoretical injunction that Gracián simply stated that "the sonnet corresponds to the Latin epigram." [37] We indeed find innumerable references to sonnets as "epigramas," and the way in which the epigrammatic model affected composition is suggested in two statements by Lope de Vega. The first is a passage from *El Laurel de Apolo* in praise of certain sonnets:

> ¡O cuán ricos sonetos
> De erudicion y estilo! ¡Con qué llave
> Cerraban sus concetos!
> ¡Qué conclusión, qué admiración, qué grave!
> Porque no es epigrama
> El que por varias sendas se derrama,
> O que la conclusion tiene tan fria,
> Que burla al que la espera, y desconfia. [38]

---

[34] García Salcedo Coronel, *Rimas* (Madrid, 1627), prologue: "breuedad erudita." See also Gabriel del Corral, *La Cintia de Aranjuez* (Madrid, 1629), prologue; and Salas Barbadillo's praise for some "coplas todas Marcialistas" in *El cortesano descortés* (Madrid, 1621), *Tema quinto*, f. 103.

[35] On Owen, see *DNB* and *Y Bywgraffiadur Cymreig*. Spanish translations of his work appeared in 1674 and 1682 (see Anthony A. Giulian, *Martial and the Epigram in Spain in the Sixteenth and Seventeenth Centuries*, Philadelphia, 1930, pp. 102-107).

[36] See *Studies*, I, 18, and *The Flaming Heart*, p. 208. Also *QOCV*, p. 562, and p. 561, where G. de S. says of a sonnet: "Es imitación de epigrammas griegos y latinos."

[37] See *Obras de Garci Lasso de la Vega con anotaciones de Fernando de Herrera* (Sevilla, 1580), p. 175, commentary on Sonnet XXIII, emphasizing the importance of the strong ending; *GOC*, p. 498: "El soneto corresponde al epigrama latino." That Lope regarded the sonnet as a conceptist form is clear from his words "haviendo este género de ser de conceptos" (see J. F. Montesinos, *Estudios sobre Lope*, Madrid, 1951, p. 128). Collado del Hierro praising Salcedo Coronel's sonnets in the latter's *Rimas* (1627), prologue, says: "siruen en la lengua Española en lugar de los Epigramas y Odas Griegas y Latinas." On the general point, see Praz, *The Flaming Heart*, p. 208.

[38] *Laurel*, in *BAE*, XXXVIII, p. 226: *Oh! What sonnets rich in learning and style! With what a key did they close their conceits! What an ending, what cause for wonder,*

Secondly, the appropriateness of the *sententia* to the strong ending is made fun of by Lope in a commentary on the making of a love sonnet: arriving at the second sextet he says that he is now "drawing out the *sententia* by the nape of the neck." [39]

The association of the epigram with the conceit is again a consequence of the stylistic preferences of the period, and part of a wider fondness for pithy and sententious concision. Here too we meet a past attempt to give the conceit a single explanation, namely that it had its origin in the change in erudite taste brought about by the gradual reaction against Ciceronian style with its rolling cadences; and the preference for the Senecan style with its abruptness, avoidance of balanced periods, frequent use of parentheses, fondness for *sententiae,* and indulgence in *acumina* (subtle points or conceits). [40] But as with the emblem the vital point is not the question of origin, but the fact that the new erudite taste helped determine that certain forms of expression would be recognized and cultivated as conceits. The cult of the Senecan style was given impetus by Justus Lipsius who propagated it by exhortation and example. Furthermore he helped establish a new canon of classical excellence, in which a prominent place was given to authors who shared certain basic features with Seneca: in particular for Tacitus and other Latin writers of the Silver Age. [41]

Spain reacted to this shift in taste, and some measure of Lipsius's extraordinary spell is conveyed by the Peruvian Diego de León Pinelo (who in reality was critical of Lipsius), describing his reactions to a passage of Lipsian prose: "My sleepiness suddenly shaken off, the style binds me in its spell, I let myself be enraptured by the eloquence as by a siren, and [I am] seduced by the most pleasing elegance of the words." [42] The many panegyrics evoked by Lipsius's

---

what solemnity! Because that which spreads itself over many a path is no epigram, nor that which has an ending so cold that it cheats and awakens the mistrust of the one who is waiting for it.

[39] *Obras escogidas,* II, p. 313: "Ya saco la sentencia del cogote."

[40] See Maurice W. Croll, "Attic Prose in the Seventeenth Century," *Studies in Philology,* XVIII (1921), 79-128 and his "Juste Lipse et le mouvement anticicéronien à la fin du XVIe et au début du XVIIe siècle," *Revue du Seizième Siècle,* II (1914), 200-242, cf. "The Baroque Style in Prose," in *Studies in English Philology: A Miscellany in Honor of Frederick Klaeber,* ed. K. Malone and M. B. Rund (Minneapolis, 1929), pp. 427-456; also George Williamson, *The Senecan Amble: a Study in Prose Form from Bacon to Collier* (London, 1951).

[41] See Croll, "Juste Lipse," and Williamson, *passim.*

[42] See quotation in Antonello Gerbi, "Diego de León Pinelo contra Justo Lipsio," *Fénix* (Lima), II (1945), 188-231 and 601-612: "... me encanta el estilo, me dejo raptar

name prove that this was no out-of-the-ordinary reaction, and the published correspondence between Lipsius and his Spanish admirers not only reflects the depth of their admiration for the Belgian humanist, but reveals in some cases the desire to emulate Lipsius's Latin style. [43] The most interesting case is Quevedo's, since one may observe in his letters to Lipsius not only the elegant brevity of the poet's Latin, but also the closeness between it and the conceits of his own Spanish verse. In a letter of 1604 he comments thus on the contrast between the ravages of war in the Low Countries, and those of peace in Spain: "Vos belli praeda estis. Nos otij, et ignorantiae. Ibi miles noster, opesque consumuntur. Hic nos consumimur." [44] Gracián could well have considered this as a conceptist parallel, stiffened by concision and syntactic counterpointing, and given added power by the apparent superiority of war over peace. The Lipsian discipline certainly exercised the *conceptista* writer, and Lipsius's missionary zeal strengthened the conceit by lending it the authority of a new and different classical canon.

And that new canon included, apart from Seneca and Tacitus, the names of Pliny the Younger, Velleius Paterculus and Sallust, whose claims Lipsius stressed, since they (and indeed the Silver Age in general) possessed in greater measure the qualities of style now being courted. The new taste finds clear reflexions in Spain: Gracián loved Tacitus for his devotion to the *agudeza*, whilst Velleius Paterculus was the "*non plus ultra* of the conceit, of elegance, and of eloquence." [45] We have already seen the respect accorded Martial: the other poets of the Silver Age likewise received their meed of praise. Góngora, whose *Polifemo* had been inspired by Ovid, drew a parallel between the obscurity of his *Soledades* and the "obscurity and intricate style" of the *Metamorphoses,* whose author for John

---

por la elocuencia como por una sirena, y [estoy] seducido por la amenísima elegancia de las palabras."

[43] See Alejandro Ramírez, *Epistolario de Justo Lipsio y los españoles (1577-1606),* Madrid, 1966, texts and introduction. Also Quevedo, *Obras completas,* ed. L. Astrana Marín, II (*Obras en verso*), Madrid, 1932, pp. 1171-1180.

[44] Ramírez, p. 400.

[45] On Tacitus, see *GOC,* p. 354, and p. 500: "Lo que admira en Tácito es la copia con tanta sutileza." Velleius's works are "el *non plus ultra* de la agudeza, del aliño y de la elocuencia" (p. 502). Quevedo is anxious to show Lipsius his knowledge of the latter's *C. Velleius Paterculus cum animadversionibus* (see Ramírez, pp. 400-401). And presumably a similar desire moved Lope in his ref. in *La Filomena* (Madrid, 1621, f. 185ᵛ).

Donne had been possessed of a "sweet witty soul"; [46] and Suárez de Figueroa writing of the "new poetry" not long afterwards, commented: "In recent years some have followed a new form of composition (in the style of Statius's *Silvae*), founded on obscuring the ideas through interposing words and using ablative absolutes and the suppression of articles, yet displaying care in the elegance of phrase and locution." [47] Furthermore, the comments of González de Salas, editor of *El Parnaso español* (1648), on the sources of Quevedo's poems suggest frequent inspiration from Juvenal, Persius, and of course Martial; [48] and Pellicer y Tovar in some remarks on Paravicino claims that the greatest of *conceptista* preachers had been "the first to introduce to the darkness of Spanish eloquence the lights of both Greece and Rome," a mystifying statement which, however, in the context of the whole passage alludes to the influence on Paravicino of those Greek and Roman writers who "imitated those of Asia," that is to say the practisers of Asianic prose who in a later era helped form Lipsian style. [49] All these references suggest how Spanish poets might be tempted to use examples and techniques from the post-classical age that were in harmony with the new practice they were establishing.

"That poem which had a star, and a divine one:" Gracián thus alluded in conceptist fashion to Antonio de Mendoza's popular poem about the *stella maris*, the *Vida de Nuestra Señora*; itself a very *conceptista* work. [50] But it belonged to a tradition in which a recognizable *conceptismo* had existed from very early times. Indeed one may argue that in the Christian tradition Christ's death was itself a *concepto*, there being no more profound paradox than that the Son of God should die to redeem the pledges of those in sinful

---

[46] Góngora, *Obras*, p. 896, and quot. in J. Donne, *The Divine Poems*, preface by Helen Gardner, p. xxiii, Note. Ovid stood just at the opening of the Silver Age.

[47] Cristóbal de Suárez de Figueroa, *Plaza universal de todas ciencias y artes...* (Madrid, 1615), f. 358: "Algunos siguen de poco a esta parte, vn nueuo genero de composicion (almodo de Estacio en las siluas) fundado en escurecer los concetos con / verso interposiciones de palabras, y ablatiuos absolutos, sin articulos, aunque cuydadosa en la elegancia de frases y elocuciones," cf. Faria y Sousa's comparison of Góngora with Statius: both great poets, but not to be imitated (*Fuente de Aganipe o Rimas varias*, Madrid, 1646, signature, b8v).

[48] *QOCV*, *passim*, footnote refs. to sources.

[49] In Anastasio Pantaleón de Ribera, *Obras*, ed. J. Pellicer y Tovar (Madrid, 1634), prologue by editor: Paravicino was "el primero que introduxo a las tinieblas de la Eloquencia Española, las luzes Griegas, i Latinas."

[50] In *Agudeza* (1642), *GOC*, p. 1226: "aquel poema que tuvo estrella, y divina." See also ch. VI here.

debt to the Father; the Church fathers too had noted the conceit-ful paradox of the *felix culpa*. Not surprisingly Gracián drew some examples of the conceit from patristic writings, alluding for instance to St. Augustine's "correspondencia" between the Virgin's marriage first to a carpenter and then to the architect of Heaven. [51] But within the literary tradition of a more recent period, the analogical and metaphoric vitality is what is important for the eventual emergence of poetic *conceptismo* — the habit of typological interpretation made it natural to understand for instance the crossing of the Red Sea as man's redemption from Sin; [52] a belief in symbolic acts or gestures could make a nun regard the carrying of wood into the kitchen as the carrying of the Cross; [53] the *exempla* of the preacher made it second nature to demonstrate the profundities of theology by reference to everyday happenings and objects. [54] One of the paths leading to *conceptismo* emerges from such a background.

Michel Darbord in discussing an earlier Spanish devotional poetry has shown how for instance El Cartujano, Juan de Padilla, in his *Retablo de la Vida de Cristo,* pictured the Cross in primitively conceptist terms, in the sense that the poet has taken a metaphor (that of the flag as heraldic device) and traced the similarity between it and Christ's Passion:

> Los altos pendones del rey de la gloria
> vemos en tinta muy negra tendidos
> de cruzes de sangre sotil esculpidos. [55]

---

[51] In *Agudeza, GOC,* p. 246: St. Augustine had made Our Lady "centro de su agudeza."

[52] For typology's influence on poetry, see Rosemond Tuve, *A Reading of George Herbert* (London, 1952), *passim*. And cf. *Vida de Nuestra Señora*: "¿Quien duda, quien, gran María, / que libre, sino el Bermejo, / pasaste aquel de la culpa / mar, tan justa-mente negro?" (*MOP,* I, 52). For general discussion, see Émile Mâle, *The Gothic Image: Religious Art in France of the Thirteenth Century,* trans. Dora Thussey (London, The Fontana Library, 1961), pp. 131-175, and Jean Daniélou, *From Shadows to Reality: Studies in the Biblical Typology of the Fathers,* trans. Dom Wulstan Hibberd (London, 1960).

[53] For this and like symbolic actions, see Johan Huizinga, *The Waning of the Middle Ages* (London, 1952), p. 173 *et seq.*

[54] See G. R. Owst, *Literature and Pulpit in Medieval England* (Cambridge, 1933), Ch. IV, esp. pp. 188-209; and Keith Whinnom, "El origen de las comparaciones religiosas del Siglo de Oro: Mendoza, Montesino y Román," *RFE,* XLVI (1963), 263-285.

[55] Michel Darbord, *La Poésie religieuse espagnole des Rois Catholiques à Philippe II* (Paris, 1965), p. 126: *We see the tall banners of the King of Glory laid (?) in a black ink, and marked out with crosses of fine blood.*

The same poet, in using another of the traditional symbols of Christ's passion, the mystical winepress, is more frankly conceptist:

> Este es aquel que descalço y en cueros
> piso en el lagar de la cruz fabricado
> con lança diviso su santo costado. [56]

The Old Testament image of the one who had "trodden the winepress alone" (*Isaiah*, 63,3) originated the conceit of Christ the winepresser treading down the grapes of Adam's sin. Similarly Montesino in his *Coplas de la Cruz* refers to the Cross as a heavenly banner, a flowering tree, a brooch set with Christ's "divine limbs." Such images, and other more plebeian ones, were in part the legacy of medieval moralistic writing, in part the creation of modern poets. Recently E. M. Wilson has drawn attention to the continuation of the extravagant metaphor, often homely and everyday, in the religious prose-writing of the sixteenth century in Spain: Domingo de Valtanas comparing faith to the link-boy lighting us only as far as the gates of Heaven, Malón de Chaide notoriously comparing Christ to an ass bearing our sins in His Passion but rising like a sturdy elephant at the Resurrection. [57] Strictly within the poetic field, the *a lo divino* tradition (in which profane poems were adapted to provide holy meanings) provides too in the late sixteenth century a means of strengthening the practice of seeking out and developing *correspondencias*, sometimes of a striking kind; such as when a pastoral poem by Garcilaso about the lovesick shepherd, having passed through a quite effective intermediate form by Sebastián de Córdoba, emerges finally as one of St. John of the Cross's most beautiful poems to the Passion:

> Y a cabo de un gran rato se ha encumbrado
> en un árbol, do abrió sus brazos bellos,
> y muerto se há quedado asido de ellos,
> el pecho del amor muy lastimado. [58]

---

[56] Darbord, p. 129: *This is the one who unshod and naked, his holy side pierced by a lance, trod in the winepress made out of the cross.*

[57] Darbord, p. 209. See Whinnom, "El origen," and E. M. Wilson, "Spanish and English Religious Poetry of the Seventeenth Century," *Journal of Ecclesiastical History*, IX (1958), 38-53.

[58] See Dámaso Alonso, *La poesía de San Juan de la Cruz: Desde esta ladera* (Madrid, 1942), pp. 47-61, quot. on p. 58: *And after a long while he climbed on to a tree where he opened his lovely arms, and held fast by them he died, his bosom sorely wounded by love.*

However, whilst this habit of metaphoric *correspondencias* goes far towards explaining one kind of *conceptismo* in the religious poetry of the sixteenth and early seventeenth centuries, it does not account for the transference of such a practice to secular verse. Part of the significance of Alonso de Ledesma is that we may observe that transference in the work of a single poet. His *Conceptos espirituales* (1600) by its very title and content makes explicit that the earlier practices we have described were a recognizable *conceptismo*. In a prologue to this popular devotional work, an Augustinian prior demonstrated its connexion with the preaching tradition — preachers should read the book because it contains "verbal ornaments of fine conceits" that they have a need of. [59] The *conceptos* are mainly limited to what the prologue calls "metaphors and perpetual allegories," the kind of metaphoric *correspondencias* we have been discussing; but which are reminiscent too of Ledesma's work as emblematist, because the poems require the reader to imagine the picture, trace its significant detail, and finally reflect on its moral or religious significance. So we may instance Christ's Cross as the key that opened the lock in heaven's door, or a pen which God dipped in His own blood. [60] Such extravagant metaphors (more familiar perhaps in an English guise, as in the poems of George Herbert, or more particularly those of Richard Crashaw) owed their popularity in Europe to the vogue of a Jesuit poetry that specialized in this kind of conceit, a fact that may be relevant to Ledesma's use of them. His acceptability and usefulness to the contemporary preacher underline another relevant fact: that the second half of the sixteenth century in Spain had witnessed a growing taste for conceit and extravagant metaphor in sermons, which in the course of the early seventeenth century became the subject of censure. The fact that criticism was often directed by the Jesuits against the excesses of a style of preaching prevalent among themselves again suggests a link with the extravagant

---

[59] Alfonso de Ledesma, *Conceptos espirituales* (ed. Madrid, 1602), prologue by Juan de Arenas: "Y pues que los que seruimos a Dios en el ministerio de la predicacion, nos hemos de valer de redobles en palabras de conceptos delgados... gastemos tiempo en este libro, pues nos ofrece tales conceptos." For *redobles*, see E. Pujol, "Les Ressources instrumentales et leur rôle dans la musique pour vihuela et pour guitare au XVIᵉ siècle et au XVIIᵉ," in *La Musique instrumentale de la Renaissance: Études réunies et présentées par Jean Jacquot* (Paris, 1955), p. 207: "passages plus ou moins rapides à une seule voix."

[60] *Conceptos espirituales,* p. 87, and p. 90.

conceptismo of Jesuit poetry. [61] Ledesma is highly significant therefore for bringing together, possibly in a conscious way, the traditional and the new. But it is the next step which perhaps gives him greater significance, for in another of his volumes, the *Romancero y monstro imaginado* (1616), he applied the technique of religious *conceptismo* to a secular subject. Thus Philip III's retirement to the Escorial after an attack of gout is pictured after the metaphor of a galley in a storm, whilst the Queen's loneliness in her husband's absence is conveyed "in the metaphor of the Sun and Moon." [62] The continuity between Ledesma's experiments and those of Góngora is suggested by Salcedo Coronel's comment on a line from the *Soledades* "El arco del camino pues torcido": "Don Luis describes the road *in the metaphor* of a bow." [63] For Edward M. Wilson the technique of continued metaphor is the essence of the conceit. [64] Certainly Góngora used it, as did Mendoza occasionally, particularly in his *Life of the Virgin*. Nevertheless we have seen that it is only one of the various forms of *concepto*.

One other important source of *conceptismo* requires discussion. J. A. Mazzeo in reviewing various theories for the origin of the conceit was critical of the view of Helmut Hatzfeld that metaphysical poetry was a decadent and exaggerated version of the earlier Petrarchan and troubadour traditions. Mazzeo objected that the metaphysical or conceptist movement was too different a creature to allow of such a forbear. [65] The evidence from Spain nevertheless suggests a continuous stream of *conceptismo* in the development from the troubadour *Cancionero* poetry of the fifteenth century, via the palace poetry of the sixteenth, into the court poetry of the seventeenth. Its source lay originally in the paradox of troubadour suffering bringing both death and satisfaction, and had found expression in the *dolce stil nuovo* and in Petrarch:

---

[61] See E. Correa Calderón, "Gracián y la oratoria barroca," in *Strenae. Estudios de filología e historia dedicados al Profesor Manuel García Blanco* (Salamanca, 1962), pp. 131-138, and Praz, *The Flaming Heart*, p. 217 *et seq.*

[62] Alonso de Ledesma, *Romancero y monstro imaginado* (Lérida, 1616), f. 1, and ff. 9-10v.

[63] Luis de Góngora, *Soledades de D. Luis de Gongora Comentadas por D. Garcia de Salzedo Coronel* (Madrid, 1636), f. 74v.

[64] Wilson, op. cit., p. 43.

[65] Mazzeo, "A Critique," p. 89, referring to Helmut Hatzfeld, "A Clarification of the Baroque Problem in the Romance Literatures," *Comparative Literature,* I (1949), 115-116.

O viva morte, o dilettoso male,
come puoi tanto in me, s'io no'l consento? [66]

The Castilian poets of the fifteenth century continued to deal in such intellectual subtleties, based largely on syntactical play, paradox and antithesis. [67] Gracián in the *Agudeza* showed great admiration for the subtle paradoxes that the *Cancionero* poets used in order to justify their extravagant statements. He quoted one by Lope de Sosa:

La vida, aunque de pasión
no querría yo perdella,
por no perder la ocasión
que tengo de estar sin ella. [68]

But an example from Pedro de Cartagena seems nearer to the kind of *conceptismo* practised by Mendoza or Villamediana, because it goes beyond mere verbal play towards a psychological self-analysis, in which the conceit has been used as a tool rather than merely as an ornamental device:

No se qual me sea mejor
la memoria o que se pierda,
que oluidarme es gran dolor
y acordarme desacuerda. [69]

Rafael Lapesa drew attention to the continuation of this style of writing in the octosyllabic palace poetry of the sixteenth century: "From the middle of the fifteenth century onwards, several generations of poets took to having conceits in their love *coplas*. Thus there was reached a tense condensation, an exact adjustment as between the emotion, tightened by the *agudeza,* and its expression in verses that were precise, and had a sharp edge." [70] This poetry

---

[66] Petrarch, *Canzoniere,* CXXXII. L. P. Thomas (op. cit., pp. 66-68), far from agreeing with Mazzeo, emphasized the Troubadour influences on Marino, and made the essential point that in Spain the *Cancionero* tradition was suffocated by Renaissance influences, but preserved in religious poetry and that of the people.

[67] See Rafael Lapesa, *Trayectoria poética de Garcilaso* (Madrid, 1948), pp. 5-34.

[68] *GOC,* p. 343: *I should not want to lose my life (even though it makes me suffer) so as not to lose the chance I have of being without life.*

[69] *Cancionero castellano del siglo XV,* ed. R. Foulché-Delbosc, II (Madrid, 1915), 523: *I do not know which best suits me, having a memory or losing it, for to forget causes me great pain, and to remember upsets me.*

[70] Rafael Lapesa, "Poesía de cancionero y poesía italianizante," in *Strenae,* p. 264: "Varias generaciones de poetas se dedican, desde mediados del siglo XV, a afilar conceptos en sus coplas de amores. Así se llegó a una condensación nerviosa, a un ajuste exacto entre el sentimiento, atesado por la agudeza, y la expresión en versos cortantes y precisos."

is brought closer to that of later court poets like Antonio de Mendoza by a number of features: it was courtly, clever but not learned, and well-adapted to the needs of improvisation and the subtleties of gallantry; furthermore its *conceptismo* was not metaphoric, but based on the exploitation of rhetorical and syntactical techniques.

The continuing relevance of this *Cancionero conceptismo* is shown in its use in the early seventeenth century. In discussing Antonio de Mendoza's octosyllabic poems I shall refer to their occasional deliberate archaism, a sign of the desire to establish a clear line of poetic descent. I shall also draw attention to Lope de Vega's praise for the *conceptos* (his word) of the poets of the *Cancionero*. [71] But the most significant indication that the *conceptista* tradition was being continued is the use of older poetic material, either because the poet recognized and appreciated a respected source, or because the material itself had been handed down as part of an oral *conceptista* tradition. Perhaps the most remarkable example of this technique may be found in the line "Yo sin vos, sin mí, sin Dios." A fifteenth-century *mote* (glossed in turn by Cartagena and Jorge Manrique in the same period, and used in the succeeding century by other poets), it became eventually the basis of a beautiful conceptist exercise in Lope de Vega's *El castigo sin venganza*. [72] And as an instance of more recent *Cancionero* type material, a *villancico* by Juan Boscán (1493?-1542), itself based on a fifteenth-century conceit, inspired some lines in Calderón's *Troya abrasada*. Part of the Boscán version reads:

> Si no os hubiera mirado
> no penara,
> pero tampoco os mirara.
> Veros harto mal ha sido,
> mas no veros peor fuera;
> no quedara tan perdido
> pero mucho más perdiera. [73]

---

[71] See p. 129. Ledesma (*Juegos de Noche Buena*, Madrid, 1611, prologue) commented on the greater suitability of the octosyllabic lines to the conceit: "en este genero de verso luze mas qualquier concepto."

[72] Lapesa, pp. 274-279: "Without you, without me and without God." The popularity of the *mote* is shown in Edward M. Wilson and Jack Sage, *Poesías líricas*, pp. 118-120.

[73] Sage and Wilson, p. 121: *If I had not looked at you, I should not be suffering, but neither would I have looked at you. To see you has been evil enough, but not to see you would be worse; I should not find myself so lost a soul, but I should lose much more.*

The continuity in sentiment and conceptist expression is plain from a *letra* to which Antonio de Mendoza wrote some *coplas:*

>Aborrecedme, y jamás
>mostréis los ojos serenos,
>que no es el deberos menos
>la razón de veros más. [74]

We do not know whether this *letra* was also the work of Mendoza. But it might as easily have come from a sixteenth-century poet, or derived from an even earlier form! All the same it must be emphasized that more frequently what Mendoza and his contemporaries made of the idiom was a new language; taut, expressive, highly sophisticated, in which the alembicated expression of an earlier generation has gone through a new distillation:

>Lisi, pues ya no he de verte,
>muera yo de mi tristeza,
>que morir de tu belleza
>no lo merece mi muerte:
>si se lograre en quererte,
>yo la quiero tan perdida,
>que muriendo de mi vida
>aun pierda el morir de ti. [75]

Gracián emphasized that the basic process in the *concepto* was the perception by the mind of a correspondence between correlates, [76] but the fields in which that process operated might vary considerably. The present survey has suggested certain factors that would help to modify the inward eye so as to apprehend and appreciate some kinds of relatedness more than others. The complex nature of the situation is suggested by the case of metaphor as a form of *concepto*. When Góngora's critics complained of him as a poet who juggled with tropes and figures, the reason might well

---

[74] *MOP*, II, 65: *Despise me and never show me serenity in your gaze, for to be less in your debt is not the reason for seeing you more.*

[75] *MOP*, II, 93-94: *Lisi, since I am not to see you any more, may I die of my sadness, for my death does not deserve to die of your beauty. If death were to be encompassed by love of you, I want a death so doomed and lost, that, dying of my own life, I should still lose the chance of dying of you.*

[76] *GOC*, p. 265: "Siempre el hallar correspondencia entre los correlatos es fundamento de toda sutileza." See on this point Mazzeo, "A Seventeenth-Century Theory," pp. 247-248.

be that as a learned poet he was reflecting the recent shift of interest from Aristotle's *Poetics* to his *Rhetoric* (a text that showed more preoccupation with metaphor); [77] but he might also have been applying in a different context the extravagant images of the Jesuit Latin poets; he might, on the other hand, have been developing a stage further the metaphoric exuberance of a Ledesma, or of some of the sixteenth-century moralists.

But whether the poetic conceit was of the metaphoric kind, or derived from the pithiness of the epigram, or the rhetorical pointing of Lipsius, one other factor perhaps more than any other determined that pre-existing forms of latent or un-self-conscious *conceptismo* now became part of a new vogue: the insistence on the power of the *ingenium,* man's inventive faculty, that which permitted the *inventio novi.* [78] Gracián returns time and again to this point: in the conceit there is some special circumstance, recognized by the *ingenium,* that raises a particular relationship (be it metaphor, paradox, antithesis or word play) above the level of the ordinary. It must contain "the spice of live and real wit." [79]

It is important, in the light of Gracián's theory and of the poet's practice, to emphasize that the conceit was not necessarily extravagant like Góngora's catachreses. There was place in it also for the multiple organic conceit, as in the *poema en metáfora,* in which the *conceptos* had been welded into a carefully constructed whole; place also for a delicate conceit expressing "a certain harmony and agreeable correspondence that the terms express among themselves, or with the subject," and which Gracián instanced with some lines from Mendoza's *Life of the Virgin:*

> Extraña, venera, admira,
> tan soberanos portentos,
> que Juan es la *voz de un mudo*
> y ella es la *vista de un ciego.* [80]

---

[77] See e.g. Francisco Cascales, *Cartas filológicas,* Clás. Cast., I (Madrid, 1930), 180-181: "palabras trastornadas con catacreses y metáforas licenciosas." For the influence of Aristotle's *Rhetoric,* see e.g. Mazzeo in "A Seventeenth-Century Theory," pp. 245-246.

[78] See Mazzeo, "A Seventeenth-Century Theory," and "Poetic of Correspondence," esp. pp. 228-232. Also Curtius, op. cit., p. 297.

[79] *GOC,* p. 297: "Siempre ha de haber alguna circunstancia especial... para levantar la comparación conceptuosa, etc."; and p. 325: "el picante de la agudeza viva y verdadera."

[80] *GOC,* p. 246: "una cierta armonía y agradable correspondencia que dicen entre sí los términos, o con el sujeto"; and p. 248: *Wonder at, venerate, and admire such sovereign portents, for John is the voice of a dumb man, and she the sight of a blind one.*

And finally one further distinction, noted by Gracián and relevant to Mendoza: in addition to the *agudezas de concepto,* characterized by subtleties of thought, with which we have been principally concerned there were also *agudezas verbales,* dependent on sheer word play. [81] Among the latter were two important categories, the *agudezas por paronomasia* with play on words of almost identical form (for instance Mendoza's "le quitas fieras, y le dejas flores"); [82] and the *ingenioso equívoco,* defined by Gracián as "like a word with a double-edge and a meaning in two different lights." [83] This, the *double entendre,* was for Gracián the popular conceit, and he saw it as a device more appropriate to the burlesque or satirical form than to serious poetry. [84] But it also had a place in the latter, as we may judge from Gracián's examples, and from Mendoza's *Life of the Virgin.* Sr. Muñoz Cortés in discussing the place of metaphor in the poetry of that period drew an interesting distinction between two kinds: one was "idealizing, Gongorine," the characteristic hyperbolic, even catachretic, metaphor of the *Soledades;* the other, with which the *equívoco* was associated, sought to deflate the object by means of the trope. [85] We may quote from Quevedo — since according to Gracián Don Francisco was the first to make up compositions on the basis of continuous punning — an instance in which the *equívoco* combines effectively with metaphor:

> Mancebitos de la carda,
> los que vivís de la hoja,
> como gusanos de seda
> tejiendo la cárcel propria. [86]

The poem is a *jácara,* a vision of low life in which the deflationary use of trope serves to heighten the impression that the idealization of the pastoral world or that of courtly love is being mocked. It is

---

[81] *GOC,* esp. *Discurso XXXI, et seq.*

[82] *GOC,* p. 254, and *MOP,* II, 193: *From her you take away wild beasts, and leave her flowers.*

[83] *GOC,* p. 394: "como una palabra de dos cortes y un significar a dos luces."

[84] *GOC,* p. 391: "la popular de las agudezas."

[85] Manuel Muñoz Cortés, "Aspectos estilísticos de Vélez de Guevara en su *Diablo Cojuelo," RFE,* XXVII (1943), 48-76.

[86] *GOC,* p. 399, and *QOCV,* p. 1240: *You hoodlums that live off the blade, like silkworms weaving your own prison.* The initiating *equívoco* is *hoja,* both "swordblade" and "blade of grass," etc.

a technique used also by Antonio de Mendoza, though as we shall see not only in a burlesque vein.

In conclusion, Gracián, like other literary theorists of his time, often recognized the conceit in a "witty" form of some rhetorical figure. [87] For J. A. Mazzeo such a view was an aspect of a wider failure to distinguish the conceit as something different from the schemes of rhetoric:

> The idea that 'plain' expression is studied by the science of grammar while rhetoric rules the domain of all ornate or non-literal expression was still dominant. The hegemony of this idea in all thinking about literary criticism made it inevitable that, when discussing all 'ornate' expression including poetry, the theorists should fall back on the abstract schemes and definitions of traditional rhetoric. [88]

This may well have been the case. But it overlooks one important practical aspect; the poets shared this notion of the rule of rhetoric with the theorist, and to that extent therefore were likely to discover some at least of their conceits in the rhetorical devices which formed the basis of their poetic practice.

The present survey casts some light on Mendoza's practice of poetry. It is not being suggested that he was in a position to respond to all the various formative pressures noted: indeed as an "ingenio lego," however polished, his capacity to draw directly on the more learned practices and devices of classical poetry, or of the modern Neo-Stoics was probably limited. Nevertheless his habits were partly a product of the culture that nurtured him, and often he could acquire from the practice of his more learned friends that which he did not know by precept. In two spheres his practice of conceptist art reveals direct knowledge: his long religious poem evidently owes something to the tradition of religious *conceptismo* outlined here; and his courtly love poems, particularly the glosses, *coplas,* and *redondillas* reflect an intimate knowledge of the tradition which, partly under the spur of a fashionable conceptist theory, was being metamorphosed into something that was at the same time old and new.

---

[87] *GOC*, e.g. p. 453: "...la agudeza tiene por materia y por fundamento muchas de las figuras retóricas."

[88] "Poetic of Correspondence," p. 223.

IV

POETRY, A COURTLY ART

Pourquoi toujours des bergers?;
on ne voit que cela partout.

(M. Jourdain in Molière's
Le Bourgeois Gentilhomme)

T H E emergence of a specifically courtly art in Spain at the beginning of the seventeenth century was an important development.
The poetry of the previous century had certainly been courtly too,
in the sense that many of its practitioners were noblemen, and
members of the court; its themes and sentiments also, inspired by
a mixture of courtly love, the influence of Petrarch, and Neopla-
tonism, were appropriate to an aristocratic society. But it had not
needed a specifically noble milieu in order to thrive, so that although
a palace poetry had certainly existed and was to become a determining factor in the new courtly art, it would not be subsequently
regarded as the central tradition, represented by Garcilaso, Boscán,
and Fernando de Herrera.

That this courtly art emerged late is probably explained by
Philip II's lack of interest in making his court a great centre for
poetic activity, an attitude very different from those of the two
succeeding Philips. However, the forces which would shape the
courtly poetic tradition were already at work from the middle of
the sixteenth century onwards. The most significant was probably the
chivalric code whose ideal of knightly service had achieved a memorable recrudescence in Castiglione's *Courtier* (1528), and found an
instinctive response in a Spanish court dominated now by the strict
etiquette and formalized manners of the Burgundian tradition. [1]
Castiglione's treatise too had helped create a conviction among the

---

[1] See Karl Brandi, *The Emperor Charles V: The Growth and Destiny of a Man and
of a World-Empire*, trans. C. V. Wedgwood, 2nd impression (London, 1949), esp. pp. 25-
32 and pp. 81-82. The evidence in this chapter covers approximately a hundred years.
What is being considered is persistence rather than change, and the phenomena discussed
reveal substantial continuity.

aristocracy that true nobility was not just of the blood, but of
the mind, and a modest cultivation of the arts could be counted a
virtue. The true courtier was recognizable above all by his genteel
devotion to the fair sex, and to a seemly, non-sensual love. Furthermore, such love, claimed Castiglione, distinguished the nobleman
from the lower orders, who of course had to make do with mere
lustful desires — this snob element in the cultivation of Castiglione's
Platonic love probably helped popularize it, and in so doing gave
it a more important role in poetry. [2] The *Courtier* had helped establish another tradition too, soon fortified by the further example of
Marguerite of Navarre's *Heptameron,* which shared with Castiglione
"la même conception de la vie polie, de la conversation, de 'l'amour
honneste.' " [3] Castiglione, drawing in part on the actual practice
of the Italian courts and giving currency to what he described as
the custom of the court of Urbino, had emphasized the communal
side to the true courtier's life: the ideal of nobility was something which people practised together, something also which they
discussed and judged in conclave. [4] The influence of these views
and their continuing relevance to actual practice are obvious from
the titles of many of the Spanish court poems of the seventeenth
century, but the most interesting picture of an Urbinian court in
a Spanish setting may be seen in Luis Milán's *El Cortesano* (1561),
modelled on Castiglione's treatise, but based on the customs and
manners of the Valencian court of the Duke of Calabria. [5] Milán
furthermore revealed elsewhere his dedication to Castiglione's ideal:
his *Libro de motes de damas y caualleros* contains in its prologue a
spirited exaltation of courtly values, and gives expression to the
view of the court community as one in which the *caballero* does
knightly obeisance to the ladies, and derives from them those qualities and delights which they are able to confer: "The gentleman
does not appear a gentleman, nor a knight a knight, except when,

---

[2] See John C. Nelson, *Renaissance Theory of Love: The Context of Giordano Bruno's
'Eroici furori'* (New York, 1958), p. 74.

[3] Abel Lefranc, *Grands Écrivains français de la Renaissance* (Paris, 1914), p. 239.

[4] References here to Spanish translation by Juan Boscán, *El Cortesano,* Austral, 2nd. edn.
(Buenos Aires, 1946). Perhaps the nearest Spanish equivalent, in method of discussion,
courtly atmosphere, and presentation of the courtly ideal is Gabriel Bocángel's discourse
on the *Amante cortesano* (1627) — see *Obras,* I, 146-174.

[5] In *Colección de libros españoles raros ó curiosos,* VII (Madrid, 1874). *The Libro
de motes* follows, in this edition, on pp. 473-502.

through serving the ladies with such services, work is changed to rest, gazing into contentment, and thought into happiness." [6]

Milán's *Cortesano* portrays an aristocratic setting that differs from that of the Italian model in two significant ways. Firstly, in the Valencian noblemen's lives, the chivalric motif is much plainer than in Castiglione, in which it remains an assumption rather than a practice. Here in contrast the mottoes and devices, as well as the numerous references to chivalric themes, provide evidence of the continuing relevance of chivalry to people's lives, evidence further echoed in the public spectacles of Spain from mid-century onwards, and in the emblematic and chivalric entertainments of the beginning of the seventeenth century. [7] In the second place, the practice of poetry plays a much more important part in Milán's treatise than in Castiglione's; and the poems, in giving expression to courtly gallantry, not only echo the sentiments of the *Cancionero* tradition, but are couched in forms — especially the *villancico* and the *glosa* — that will later characterize the writing of the poets of the court of Philip the Third and Fourth.

Milán's *Cortesano* reflects another aspect of the Spanish courtly milieu: courtiers spent part of their time discussing the case book of love. The questions of love which Marguerite of Navarre said were discussed at her brother's Parisian court, and whose nature is echoed in the *Heptameron* itself, [8] were probably a common feature of aristocratic life over a much longer period. Originally a medieval practice, the debates of love probably enjoyed greater favour owing to Castiglione's success, and that of others, in making profane love a respectable subject. [9] So courtiers, in trying to live according to the new code of gentility, might spend their hours together mulling over the niceties and dubieties which were the by-product of love's alchemy. The taste in Spain for such discussion is suggested by the existence of a Spanish translation of Ortensio Lando's famous collection of the doubts of love, *Quattro*

---

[6] Milán, p. 474: "No parece el señor tan señor, ni el caballero tan caballero, sino sirviendo las damas con tales servicios, que el trabajo se convierta en descanso, y el mirar en contentamiento, y el pensar en alegría."

[7] See N. D. Shergold, *A History of the Spanish Stage*, p. 237 and p. 241. The Burgundian love of chivalric spectacle and pageantry is also relevant: see e.g. Brandi, p. 82, and Shergold, pp. 239-240.

[8] See Lefranc, p. 215.

[9] Nelson, in his ch. "Love Treatises" (pp. 73-74 and *passim*), discusses the part played by the *dubbi*, the doubts of love, in the various handbooks of the sixteenth century.

libri de dubbi con le solutioni a ciascun dubbio accommodate (Venice, 1552). [10] Although the evidence for the actual practice of these doubts and questions lies mainly in literature, there is good reason for thinking that the fictional context has only preserved in a stylized form a common ritual of aristocratic life. For instance Alonso Núñez de Reinoso in his *Historia de los amores de Clareo y Florisea* (1552) has depicted at a ducal palace an ideal court among whose "honestos ejercicios" ("seemly practices") were the debates on the questions of love. [11] The author, who had long lived in Italy, may be describing a situation with which he was more familiar in an Italian court, but the setting was probably universal. After a day's hunting, the party returned to the palace, and then after dinner, at the duke's command, the debate began, the contenders being a lady and a gentleman. Melisena asked which was the more difficult, to feign love, or to hide one's feeling though actually being in love, to which Roselindos gave reply. Melisena then passed on to another question, Roselindos again responded, the process being repeated until Clareo, a visitor, was asked to put *his* question. Pierre Brantôme in recalling his experiences at the Spanish court in the mid-sixteenth century mentioned having participated in a similar, though briefer, debate. He commented on the fact that it was usual in Spain to have conversation with the ladies, and cites the case of one who came up to him with the question: "Which was the greatest fire of love, that of the widow, the married woman, or the young girl?" [12] This was indeed a very old question, and the archaic nature of much of such material is plain too from another question from a fifteenth-century handbook of love, which was still a courtly theme of conversation in the second half of the sixteenth century: the topic was

---

[10] See ref. in T. F. Crane, *Italian Social Customs of the Sixteenth Century and their Influence on the Literatures of Europe* (New Haven, 1920), p. 152. The trans. appeared in Antwerp in 1575. I am indebted to Crane (esp. pp. 565-659) for a no. of refs. below. On the medieval background of the questions of love, see Crane, p. 6 *et seq.*, Rudolph Schevill, "Some Forms of the Riddle Question and the Exercise of the Wits in Popular Fiction and Formal Literature," *University of California Publications in Modern Philology*, II (1910-1912), 183-237, Guiseppe Zonta, "Rileggendo Andrea Cappellano," *Studi Medievali*, III (1908-1911), 49-68, and his "Arbitrati reali o questioni giocose," ibid., 603-637. Also P. Rajna, "L'Episodio delle questioni d'amore nel *Ficolo* del Boccaccio," *Romania*, XXXI (1902), 28-81.

[11] The text in *Novelistas anteriores a Cervantes*, BAE, III, pp. 433-468, the debate on pp. 442-443.

[12] Pierre Brantôme, *Œuvres complètes*, IX (Paris, 1876), p. 531: "Qual era mayor fuego d'amor, el de la biuda, el de la casada, o de la hija moça?" Crane also mentions this question, drawing attention to its popularity and earlier history (p. 21 and p. 82).

whether love was more likely to make a wise man crazy, or a crazy man wise. [13]

When Clareo put *his* question, what ensued was a variant form of the debate. Clareo told a story, and then within its context posed a particular question of love. This time different members of the gathering made their answer, until finally one of the people present gave a reply that met with general approval. This pattern may be seen also to have been the basis of the long debate on love in the Fourth Book of Cervantes's *Galatea* (1585), or of the questions and answers on love in the Fourth Book of the *Diana*. [14] In discussions such as these there was opportunity not only for single contenders to duel with each other, but for the whole company to participate.

That the practice of such debate continued into the seventeenth century in Spain is probably indicated by the various games and entertainments (including discussion) in Tirso de Molina's *Cigarrales* (1621), and in some sophisticated *preguntas* (questions) in Calderón's *Secreto a voces*. [15] But in Gabriel Bocángel's *El amante cortesano* we come nearer reality. The author depicts what may have been the real setting of the house of Antonia de Mendoza, the Doña Antandra of the discourse. [16] The discussion on the nature of love is serious and philosophic after the manner of Castiglione's famous Fourth Book of the Courtier, but there is place also for the questions of love, the topic in this instance being the style appropriate to the correspondence between lovers, contrary points of view being presented by Gerarda and Nise. The debate proceeded awhile, until both ladies finally formulated an agreed opinion.

Returning to Book IV of the *Galatea,* we recall that the discussion sprang originally from people's comments on a poem by one of the shepherds. The situation is paralleled in Gabriel del Corral's *La Cintia de Aranjuez* (1629), where the advice, given in a ballad, to love in silence becomes the topic of argument of the assembled

---

[13] Nelson, p. 74.

[14] Cervantes, *Obras completas*, 692-705, and Jorge de Montemayor, *Los siete libros de la Diana,* ed. E. Moreno Báez (Madrid, 1955), pp. 180-185 and 220-227.

[15] Refs. in Crane, p. 586 *et seq.* See also account of Tirso's *El bandolero*, ibid., pp. 606-608. There is an interesting ref. in Cristóbal Suárez de Figueroa's *El pasajero* of 1617 (ed. F. Rodríguez Marín, Madrid, 1913), where in debating some questions of love, an interlocutor remarks: "... será razón conceder tiempo á otras preguntas, porque no se pase la siesta en sola una" (p. 162).

[16] *Obras*, I, esp. 168-169. For Antandra, see Note 45 below.

company. [17] The association in one way or another between poetry
and debate was not new. Both T. F. Crane and Rudolph Schevill indicated that the debates on love and other matters not only had a
place in the *Cancionero general* (1511) or the *Cancionero de Baena*
(1445), but had an earlier origin in the poetic contests of Troubadour
poetry. [18] Schevill argued also for a connexion between medieval
academic debate and the contests of the Troubadour minstrels, and
suggested that the tone of an academic atmosphere eventually became transformed in the sixteenth century into the tone of courtly
gallantry. The association in common practice between the questions
of love, and poetry is made plain in *El Crotalón* (1552), where in
one scene "questiones y preguntas de amores" alternate with the
composition of sonnets and *coplas* as the basis for the amusement
of a group of people. [19] What must be emphasized is that since the
questions of love were forms of debate, the premium was on wit,
pungency and pithiness, so that where the debate was in verse the
traditional Castilian metres were a natural choice, since they expressed a "subtle kind of poetry." [20]

A contemporary of Antonio de Mendoza, Anastasio Pantaleón de
Ribera, reveals in one poem the continuing role of the debates of
love in an aristocratic society. He addressed, in the name of a certain Doña Inés (presumably president of the assembly), a *romance*
to a "gathering of ladies" who met in what is picturesquely called
a "House of Conversation." Pantaleón reviews in turn the experience
in love, as well as the viewpoints, of the female company, and significantly, the purpose of the whole exercise is summed up thus in
one of the verses:

> Todo es amar, y pues oy
> a fuerza de coplas
> adivinar el estado
> de cada amante me toca. [21]

---

[17] Gabriel del Corral, *La Cintia de Aranjuez, prosas y versos* (Madrid, 1629), ff. 145-148.

[18] Crane, pp. 6-17, and Schevill, pp. 224-225. In the *Cancionero general* (ed. A. Rodríguez-Moñino, Madrid, 1958, ff. clv-clxv) there are a large number of *preguntas* and
respuestas, many on love.

[19] In Schevill, p. 228, Note.

[20] The phrase is used by one of the *Cancionero* poets, Fernán Pérez de Guzmán, quot.
in Andrée Collard, *Nueva poesía: conceptismo, culteranismo en la crítica española* (Madrid,
1967), p. 86. See also Lapesa, "Poesía de Cancionero," *passim*.

[21] "A vna Junta de Damas y S[eñor]es q[ue] se hazia en vna Cassa de Conuersazion,
diziendo dona Y[nes?] a todos," BNM MS 3884, *Poesías varias*, I, ff. 355v-357: *All is*

The situation is reminiscent of the *salons* of the French *précieuses,*
but what is important for an understanding of the court poetry of
Spain at this time is the fondness shown here for the group examination and analysis of the experience of love. The *dubbi* of conduct
and feeling made the courtier particularly responsive to the fine
distinctions in love's code, as well as to its expressions in language.
In France too in the early decades of the seventeenth century
the so-called *poésie galante* (similar in many ways to the work of the
Spanish court poets) reflected the fact that the aristocracy had sharpened its ear to the demands of minute emotional, and intellectual
analysis. Saint-Évremond recalling the society which he had abandoned for England in mid-century told how in the company of the
précieux masters:

> ...se font distinguer les fiertés des rigueurs;
> Les dédains des mépris, les tourments des langueurs;
> On y sait démêler la crainte et les allarmes;
> Discerner les attraits, les appas, et les charmes. [22]

Mendoza certainly expected of his audience a like sensitivity and
interest, and if much of his poetry remains inaccessible it is often
because our ear is not attuned to such tremulous variations of signal.

The second determining force in fashioning Spanish court poetry
was the vogue of the pastoral novel. Jorge de Montemayor's *Diana*
(1559?) ensured the success of a genre that would combine elements
from classical and Italian pastoral with the psychological subtleties
that Diego de San Pedro's *Arnalte y Lucinda* and *Cárcel de Amor*
had brought to the incipient novel form: the *Diana* also first infused
the pastoral genre with the spirit of Platonic love, [23] and may well
have given a new impetus to the tradition of courtly love and the
Petrarchan convention. Eventually too the pastoral novel helped in

---

love, and so today by dint of coplas it is my task to guess at the state (of mind?)
of each lover. The stanza suggests regular discussion of this kind in the *salon.*

22 See *Œuvres de Monsieur de Saint-Évremond, Publiées sur ses manuscrits...,* 4th
edn. (Amsterdam, 1726), I, p. 132 of second series. The female experts declare their
intention to return another day for discussion of "un autre point d'Amour." The author
never returned to France after his arrival in England in 1662. See also the ch. "La
Poésie galante" in Renée Winegarten, *French Lyric Poetry in the Age of Malherbe*
(Manchester, 1954).

23 See Mia Gerhardt, *La Pastorale: Essai d'analyse littéraire* (Assen, 1950), p. 187.

some measure at any rate to establish the pastoral ballad in Spain as a favourite form, but it is an irony of literary history that the pastoral ballad, despite a dependence on the same convention of a courtly, Platonic love, did not originate in the verse interludes of the pastoral novel, but arose independently out of the revitalized ballad tradition, the *romancero nuevo,* in which gradually towards the end of the sixteenth century the ballad on Moorish themes (the *romance morisco*) was ousted by its bucolic rival. [24]

When, after Philip II's death in 1598, the Spanish court began to dedicate itself with greater enthusiasm to the arts, the twin forces to which I have alluded could more effectively mould the courtly ideal. Ironically, the period which responded with delight to Cervantes's tilt at the chivalric and pastoral genres was also witness to a growing fondness in noble circles for entertainments based on the books of chivalry, and for acting out the pastoral life in the world of everyday. Don Quixote's encounter with some gentlefolk on safari playing at shepherds in eclogues by Garcilaso and Camoens is nearer actual practice than we might imagine, [25] whilst Lope de Vega's *Arcadia* (1598), which cast only a flimsy covering of anonymity over the background and personages of the House of Alba, makes clear in a way that other *romans à clé* like the *Galatea* and the *Diana* did not, that the milieu was really aristocratic, and that some of the episodes might possibly have been acted out in reality. [26] If the shepherd of pastoral had always been a gentleman, it was now the turn of the gentleman to assume the shepherd's guise.

The emergence of what may be called the Manzanarian idyll was a central feature of the new palace poetic tradition. The pastoral in Spain had long made certain landscapes its own, but the association with Tagus or Pisuerga or Guadalquivir had possessed little lasting significance. Things change with the return of the Spanish capital to Madrid after its brief sojourn in Valladolid (1601-6); the pastoral henceforth will become increasingly linked with the royal palace on the Manzanares at Madrid, and the spring palace not far away in Aranjuez at the confluence of the Tagus and Jarama.

---

[24] See R. Menéndez Pelayo, *Romancero hispánico: (hispano-portugués, americano y sefardí* [Madrid, 1953], II, 125 *et seq.* Also José F. Montesinos, "Algunos problemas del *Romancero nuevo,*" *RPh,* VI (1952-53), 231-247.

[25] *Don Quixote,* Part 2, Ch. LVIII.

[26] See e.g. Rennert and Castro, pp. 88-95, and José F. Montesinos, *Estudios sobre Lope de Vega* (México, 1951), p. 165 *et seq.*

Pedro Liñán de Riaza, an early master of the *romancero nuevo* who died in 1607, evokes what would subsequently become the dominant tradition when he cries:

> Serranos de Manzanares
> yo me muero por Inés
> cortesana en el aseo
> labradora en guardar fe. [27]

Góngora in 1609 might allude ironically to a landscape peopled by shepherdesses in farthingales:

> Cantar pensé en sus márgenes amenos
> cuantas Dianas Manzanares mira. [28]

The strength of this pastoral myth grew during the remaining years of Philip III's reign but was only to reach its climax after the accession of his son. Even before the beginning of their reign, the shepherd-king Fileno and his French wife Belisa were acknowledged as monarchs of a court in which figured a glittering host of "goddess peasant-girls." [29] Mendoza, entering upon this inheritance in the early sixteen-twenties, was swiftly to exploit it. The myth of the shepherd-king gave the literary milieu of the Manzanarian court its peculiar nobility and tenderness, for there was place in it only for the appropriate emotions and gestures.

We have seen how the *Courtier* and the pastoral genre helped mould an emergent courtly tradition in Spain. Subsequent developments there during the first half of the seventeenth century intensified further certain moral and social values which in turn influenced the course of poetry. *Galanteo* (gallantry) had been given a place in Castiglione's treatise, but the Spanish court in the early seventeenth century pursued it almost with vehemence. Diego Duque de Estrada, in his very lively *Comentarios del desengañado*, describes for

---

[27] Pedro Liñán de Riaza, *Rimas* (Zaragoza, 1876), p. 118: *You mountain-lads of the Manzanares, I die for Inés, in her neatness a lady of the court, but a peasant-girl in keeping faith.*

[28] Góngora, ed. Millé, p. 582: *I thought to celebrate on Manzanares's pleasant margins as many Dianas as that river spies.*

[29] The phrase "Deidad labradora" is Góngora's, from a ballad of 1620 (ed. Millé, p. 231). For Fileno and Belisa at their spring court, see another poem dated 1620 (ed. Millé, p. 224); these titles became common currency in Mendoza's poems in the two following decades.

instance the way in which he and his fellows spent their youth at
court at the very beginning of the century: "To spend and to triumph, to shine among knights, to play gallant among ladies, and to
let the vine branch bend where the gardener wishes." [30] In this list
extravagance and show were not really separate from gallantry: they
were essential aspects of it. Vittorio Siri, commenting on the young
Count Olivares's flamboyant courtship of Inés de Zúñiga, gave some
details of *galanteo* at the Spanish court. [31] The *caballeros,* he said,
so vied with each other in extravagance that they sometimes ruined
themselves, and such behaviour, far from being condemned, was applauded by the court and the royal family.

So intense was the pursuit of gallantry that it sometimes over-
rode obligations of court etiquette. Mme D'Aulnoy, in mid-century,
related how Spanish courtiers in love might, as a sign of their dis-
traction, keep their hats on in the Queen's presence. The official
explanation of this omission was that they were *embebecidos* (lost in
wonder), a term equally applicable to Zabaleta's lovers who gazed
enraptured at their beloved's picture. [32] But for Mme D'Aulnoy gallantry was already in a decline, and with a vague gesture she hints
that the Golden Age may have been in the reign of Charles V. [33]
One thing is certain — in Pierre Brantôme's time ladies in Spain
were already the subject of reverence: whenever one was spied, he
said, the cry would go up of *lugar a las damas,* and everyone would
bow and pay respect. [34] Little wonder then that by the early

---

[30] Diego Duque de Estrada, *Comentarios del desengañado ó sea Vida de D. Diego
Duque de Estrada escrita por él mismo,* in *Memorial histórico español: Colección de
documentos, opúsculos y antigüedades,* XII (Madrid, 1860), pp. 21-22: "gastar y triunfar,
lucir entre caballeros, galantear entre damas y plegarse el sarmiento donde quieren los
hortelanos." Don Diego was born in 1589, and came to court at the age of fourteen.

[31] Vittorio Siri, *Anécdotas del gobierno del Conde-Duque de Olivares,* trans. and ed.
Felipe Ximénez de Sandoval (Madrid, 1946), pp. 42-43. The trans. is of the French
version, *Anecdotes du Ministere du Comte Duc d'Olivarès, Tirées & traduites de l'Italien
du Mercurio Siry, par Monsieur de Valdory* (Bruxelles, 1722). The original account is in
Il Mercurio Ouero Historia de' correnti tempi (Casale, 1644). *Galanteo* was a neologism,
and censured (see Dámaso Alonso, *La lengua poética...,* p. 101). See also *FC,* p. 238
for a mocking ref. to *galantería.* Martin Hume (p. 55, Note) quotes the Venetian ambassador's account of lavish "gallanting" at the Spanish court at the time of the Count-
Duke's fall.

[32] Mme D'Aulnoy, *Relation d'un voyage d'Espagne où est exactement décrit l'Estat
de la Cour de ce Royaume, & de son gouuernement,* new edn. (Paris, 1668), p. 104,
and Juan de Zabaleta, *El Dia de Fiesta. Primera Parte. Que contiene el Dia de Fiesta por
la mañana...* (Coimbra, 1666), pp. 31-32.

[33] D'Aulnoy, pp. 106-107. For her vagueness and lack of precision, see Gabriel Maura
Gamazo and Agustín G. de Amezúa, *Fantasías y realidades del viaje a Madrid de la condesa d'Aulnoy* (Madrid, 1943).

[34] Brantôme, IX, 524-525.

seventeenth century Spain was regarded by visiting Frenchmen as the home of gallantry, and a model for the French court. [35] We may deduce therefore from all this that Mendoza was not exaggerating when, in *Querer por solo querer*, in the course of a dialogue on the conventions of courtship he refers to "la Religion de las damas": [36] they were indeed the centre of a cult.

How was court poetry affected by these developments? Firstly, love and courtship, basic material for most of Mendoza's poems, must have been a constant preoccupation and topic of conversation. Also, the gallant's devotion to verse seems almost to have been an obligatory characteristic, [37] and in cases where the fount of inspiration did not run freely the poets wrote verse on request in order to facilitate amorous conquest. [38] There existed also a more subtle relationship between *galanteo* and poetry: in a society dominated by the ideal of gallantry, yet haunted by its own proneness to violence, poetry was a medium which legitimized and controlled feeling, thus ensuring a more proper relation between the sexes. [39] The Manzanarian idyll, far from being a mere charade, was in reality a necessary myth.

Mendoza's poetry both expresses and exemplifies the communal life of such a court society. Although the courtly love-poem in its extolment of the *dama* and of the poet's passion for her expressed, in theory, a private relationship, this was not always so in practice.

---

[35] See Maurice Magendie, *La Politesse mondaine et les théories de l'honnêteté en France au xviie siècle, de 1600 à 1660* (Paris, 1925), pp. 99-100, and Gustave Reynier, *La Femme au xviie siècle* (Paris, 1933), p. 21. Magendie (pp. 423-424) claimed that the Spanish theatre, "qui avait spiritualisé l'amour," had been a dominant factor in winning over Mme de Sablé to the ideal of gallantry — she it was who took it back with her to France. If such was the case, the Spanish theatre may well have been an important social influence on gallant standards in Spain.

[36] *FC*, p. 353. Saint-Évremond echoed the phrase in asserting that the *précieuses* had made love "une espèce de religion" (I, 134). Their offence consisted in the substitution of intellectualization for feeling. In contrast, Mendoza's phrase is used in a defence of gallantry, though his sympathy was probably with the opposing view, that gallantry makes assiduity and show into the prime virtues (cf. *loa*, in *MOP*, III, 37-44, where he argues that the palace would only admit "galanterías modestas").

[37] See e.g. Zabaleta, *...por la mañana*, pp. 95-106, "El Poeta"; and his *El Dia de Fiesta por la tarde. Parte secunda del Dia de Fiesta...* (Madrid, 1660), ff. 61v-63, where mention is made of an academy subject over which a young poet is much exercised: it is "to a lady in the lace of whose shoe a flower was caught, as she ran through a garden." Of this kind of poetry Zabaleta asks: "What benefit do the poets derive from driving the ladies mad?"

[38] See e.g. Zabaleta, *...por la mañana*, p. 105. Cf. p. 46 here.

[39] See also Octave Nadal, *Le Sentiment de l'amour dans l'œuvre de Pierre Corneille*, 4th edn. (Paris, 1948), p. 41 and pp. 46-48.

Certainly a few of Mendoza's poems express a genuine love, but
in many cases (possibly the majority), they presumably afforded
entertainment for the company in the shape of songs, or recitations. [40]
A perusal of his poetry suggests three main types: in one the
relation is that between poet and patroness, be it the Countess of
Olivares, or the Duchess of Medina de Ríoseco; in another the
relationship may have been innocently flirtatious, as in the compositions for María de Guzmán as Amariles, or the Queen as Belisa;
in a third type the relationship, genuine or assumed, is with a less
distinguished but favoured *dama* among the assembled company.

The last type obviously lent itself to the greatest number of
variations. The ancient code of *senhal,* the oath of secrecy about
the identity of one's beloved, was part of the archaism of court
poetry at this time, but it was also part of the fun. [41] The *mote* for
one of Mendoza's glosses described the convention succinctly:

> Sin que se sepa por quién,
> morir quiero, y quiero bien. [42]

And when Narcisa is addressed in the subsequent verses, one may
presume that the assembled ladies sought hard to identify the object
of the poet's affections. A poem to Amariles fulfilled a different
function. If the recipient of the poet's attentions was really María de
Guzmán, the favourite's daughter, then it was not the purpose of
senhal to hide that identity. The opening stanza:

> El Alma tengo encargada
> y mi cuidado al silencio
> si le revelan los ojos
> me habran faltado del secreto. [43]

---

[40] e.g. Juan Vélez recited some *redondillas* by Mendoza at an academy in 1638 (*MOP,*
III, 134-136). The importance of song settings is discussed in chapter VIII.

[41] *Senhal* in the *Cancionero* poetry is mentioned in my forthcoming "*Pintura*: a Seventeenth-century Court Genre." As part of the "game of love" earlier at the English court
it is discussed in John Stevens, *Music & Poetry in the Early Tudor Court* (London, 1961),
p. 216.

[42] *MOP,* II, 161-162: *Without anyone knowing at whose hand, I wish to die, and
strongly wish to do so* [also = *I love well*]. John Stevens comments aptly: "...looked
at from the audience's point of view, the love-lyric was a confidence which they were
intended to overhear, a loud whisper" (p. 216).

[43] Hisp. Soc. Am. *MS HC*: 371/224, f. 82: *Silence has my soul and my care in
charge. If my eyes reveal it, they will have betrayed the secret.*

sought rather to give the girl a factitious sense of being singled out for affection, and envied for it by the audience. Indeed a *senhal* too well preserved was not as entertaining as one that gave helpful clues. A set of *décimas* uses a riddle technique, the opening stanza containing an allusion to the girl's name, María, and managing also to suggest playfully that she is both *bella* and *bellaca*. [44] However, the most popular variant on the *senhal* — and to call it secrecy in this period is a misnomer — was the genre of *pintura*, or *retrato de una dama*. [45] In the Spanish theatre of the early seventeenth century portraiture was a fairly common device, for an obvious reason, that it was an occasion for poetry. At court, however, it was both a source of poetry and a focus of social interest. Often associated with the pastoral charade, it may have been practised in idyllic surroundings, such as the palace gardens, or the grounds at Aranjuez: the opening of one *pintura* significantly mentions both idyllic pretence and the presence of an audience:

> Si quereis tener buen dia
> pastores los del Aldea
> venid a ver a Lysarda
> lograreis tan grande dicha.

And a poem by Gabriel Bocángel calls the young shepherds to come and "look at" the portrait:

> Al retrato de Antandra
> Venid zagales.

Sometimes a whole group of ladies would be portrayed, such as when Antonio de Mendoza submitted to the Countess-Duchess the *pintura* of these "goddesses" in turn. Indeed the resident vates were not the only ones to compose such portraits, for some of the noble ladies tried their hand; some like Doña Antonia (possibly

---

[44] *MOP*, III, 175-177. *Bella* (beautiful) and *bellaca* (wicked).

[45] See my *"Pintura"* for a fuller discussion of the points below. The quotation from Mendoza is in *MOP*, II, 56, and Antandra is discussed by R. Benítez Claros, *Vida y poesía de Bocángel* (Madrid, 1950), pp. 160-161. She may also be the *Cantadorcita* of Mendoza's II, 102-104, the lady "muy dada a las coplas" in I, 266-268 and "la Autora" of III, 142-144. The quotations from the article translate: *If you shepherds from the village wish to have a good day, come and see Lisarda, you will achieve such happiness*; and *Come shepherd-lads to see Antandra's portrait.*

Bocángel's Antandra, Antonia de Mendoza) or Doña Catalina Clara are known practisers of the genre. There were occasions when the *amada* requested the gallant to make a poetic portrait of her, the equivalent to the portrait which the lover often carried, and Don Antonio's talent may often have been bent to serve that need. Again, on occasion, the assembled company would have given the order beforehand for a *pintura* to be performed for their enjoyment.

Don Antonio, "El muchísimo Mendoza / pícaro de gran primor" (so he once described himself in expressing his relation with the ever solicitous ladies), [46] was sought after not only for tasks such as these, but because, along with other courtiers, he maintained the supply of poetry which the palace needed. His service to his patrons has been commented on in an earlier chapter. Rather different was his relation with palace poetasters, particularly women, with whom he exchanged verses. He upbraids a lady for giving currency to some verses he had sent her. [47] He adds "I glossed the verse for you," and says that he has sent piles to her place of retreat. By the time the poet has reached the middle of his poem, some more verses arrive from the lady, a suggestion possibly of the regularity of this poetic correspondence. Don Antonio on another occasion receives a request from a lady to burn some papers sent him — perhaps she thought that they might incriminate her — and he sends her a note to indicate that he is obeying her despite this further proof of her cruelty. And in a further reference to this, or another, holocaust, he calls on his lady to admit her apostasy in love's religion:

> será tu mano en su fuego
> un inquisidor de nieve. [48]

There can be little doubt that such papers, whether the love they expressed was genuine or not, were in the established courtly

---

[46] *MOP*, I, 245-247. The "rascal of great elegance," who had invited the ladies to a *merienda*, regaled them with individual poetic miniatures.

[47] *MOP*, II, 76-80: "Yo glosé por vos el verso;" this very difficult poem alludes also to the favour now enjoyed at the palace by Jerónimo de Villaizán. On the practice of palace flirtation, "discreteo cortesano," see Otis H. Green's *Courtly Love in Quevedo* (Boulder, Colorado, 1952), pp. 33-38.

[48] *MOP*, II, 134, and II, 142-143: *your hand in their fire will be an inquisitor of snow.*

convention, whose strength is bizarrely reflected in the fact that an invitation to dinner sent to the poet by some ladies was couched in ballad form, and attended with the customary *senhal*. [49]

Mention has been made of the doubts and questions of love. Mendoza's participation in this kind of entertainment is plain from two sets of *décimas* giving varying replies to the question whether it was better to love by fate or by choice. [50] Another poem is made up of a series of questions with comments, the ladies to whom the piece is addressed being invited to offer solutions to these *dubbi*. [51] On another occasion Mendoza's advice was sought over the appropriate answer to a "subtle and acute question," originally proposed by the Count de la Roca, as to which was better for the gallant, to be near his beloved, but hidden from her behind her back, or far away and facing her. Mendoza obviously found the topic a challenge to his wit (if not to his poetic instinct), for he wrote eighteen *décimas* in reply. A hint of the circumstances in which such poetry was composed is given when Mendoza, perhaps with an implied apology for the poor standard of the verses, interjects: "This is an improvised *copla*." [52] We may suspect that the poet wrote many similar *coplas* on the subject of the doubts and questions of love, probably improvised and rendered thus more perishable. With characteristic narcissism he alludes to this genre as a speciality of his, when he begins a *décima* to Amariles with the words: "I, the greatest asker of questions" [53] — it was after all a speciality much called for in palace life.

Other aspects of the "game of love" also gave the palace poet his opportunity. Some were old conventions, such as sending the replica of a heart as a symbol of affection: Don Antonio, for instance, expatiated in one poem on the hardness of the lady's real heart in comparison with the crystal one sent to the gallant; and the common poetic image of the relation between lover and beloved as that between the graceful bird and the bird of prey may reflect an older

---

[49] The poet's reply, addressed to "whoever you may be," comments disparagingly on the impropriety of a "forestful of nymphs" guzzling (*MOP*, I, 215-217).

[50] Hisp. Soc. Am. *MS HC*: 371/224, ff. 42-43v.

[51] Hisp. Soc. Am. *MS HC*: 371/224, ff. 99v-100v, "Pidiendo a las Damas de Palacio soluccion de algunas dudas." The authenticity of this poem is not certain.

[52] *MOP*, I, 221-227: "tan sutil, y aguda / cuestión" and "esta copla es de repente."

[53] *MOP*, II, 158: "Yo el mayor preguntador."

tradition of the use of the images of hunting in describing love. [54] In some instances it is not clear whether the poet was exploiting an established convention, or commenting on genuine, if curious, circumstances: such is the case when he embroidered on the occasion when, after the end of a love affair, a clock and a death's head remained in the gallant's hands. [55] On the other hand, the topic of the lady who preferred to look at a corpse to looking on her lover was more probably the poet's own creation. [56] In another piece Don Antonio is helping a comrade less well endowed to comment aptly on an unusual occurrence. On behalf of the Count-Duke's illegitimate son he addressed a ballad to a lady of the court, who on seeing the gentleman in question on Christmas Eve, had put out the lantern she was carrying to the Royal Chapel:

> ¿Por qué la matáis? ¿Qué ha hecho?
> ¡oh pasión de la belleza!
> que antiguo es en la hermosura
> el querer que todo muera. [57]

The gallant got perhaps better poetry than he deserved.

In a court given to polite conversation, the nature of the language used was an important consideration. Castiglione, realizing this, had devoted a chapter or two to the question: his attitude may be summed up in the proposition that all forms of affectation in language should be condemned, but that there was place for wit. [58] One cannot determine the linguistic norms of the Spanish court by what Castiglione may or may not have said, yet his influence may

---

[54] On these conventions, see John Stevens, pp. 209-210, and p. 15. The long-established association of women and birds may be seen in the *Cancionero general* (ed. R-Moñino, f. clxxxiii), where a *juego trobado* associates the ladies not only with trees, but also with birds, the *garza real, neblí*, etc. The tradition is still alive in the poetry of the seventeenth century, e.g. "Garza real que en puntas desiguales" (*MOP*, III, 229). On the antiquity of this association and its persistence, see also Tamara Talbot Rice, *A Concise History of Russian Art* (London, 1963), pp. 11-12, as well as E. de Jongh, "Erotica in Vogelperspectief. De dubbelzinnigheid van een reeks 17de eeuwse genrevoorstellingen," *Simiolus* (Amsterdam), III (1969), 22-74. Cf. *MOP*, II, 153: "Ya es la diestra montería / vuelo de amor, y tan alto / que están bajas las estrellas / a las garzas de Palacio."

[55] *MOP*, I, 279-282.

[56] *MOP*, I, 287-291.

[57] *MOP*, II, 263-264: *Why do you snuff out the light? What has it done? Oh passion from which beauty suffers! How ancient in loveliness is the wish that all may die.* The lady was the Countess of Sirvela.

[58] *El Cortesano*, esp. ch. VI. Bocángel also insists on lack of affectation in his "amante cortesano" (*Obras*, I, 160-161 and 168-169).

have been considerable in this respect as in others. The desire to avoid affectation, as will later be seen, could have been a factor in the court's preference for *conceptista* wit over *culterano* pretentiousness: [59] on the other hand, a preciosity bred of fastidiousness must sometimes have acted as a pressure towards over-elaboration of speech, or a search for more seemly expression. [60] We shall look at these points in turn.

The question of wit is plainer, and more important. The evidence clearly shows that in the latter half of the sixteenth century and the beginning of the seventeenth, the Spanish court had a reputation for wit. Brantôme claimed that the Spanish nation was "fort prompte d'esprit, et de belles parolles profférées à l'improviste," and that Spaniards would spare nothing to make a *bon mot*. [61] In particular Spanish women were singled out for their special gift of *donaire*: Brantôme had considerable occasion to draw upon it; [62] Camillo Borghese, who visited the court in 1594, noted that the women there were "quick-witted"; [63] whilst Pinheiro da Vega at the beginning of the new century praised them for their wit and quick sallies: "And rarely will they say anything to them to which they do not give a better reply." [64] That this reputation was to last for a long time is suggested by some words of Zabaleta referring to how ugly women overcome their prey: "They prick the men's pleasure with the witty goad of words." [65]

Wit however was obviously the prerogative of both sexes, and the dialogue between them was possibly the most characteristic aspect of Spanish court life. In *Querer por solo querer*, Mendoza, in

---

[59] See ch. VII. J. Entrambasaguas drew attention to the "popular character" of *conceptismo* as distinct from *culteranismo*: the latter presumably smacked too much of pedantry (see *Estudios sobre Lope de Vega*, I [Madrid, 1946], p. 80 and Note).

[60] For the mechanism of linguistic preciosity, see Roger Lathuillère, *La Préciosité: Étude historique et linguistique*, vol. I (*Position du problème — les origines*), Genève, 1966, p. 301.

[61] Pierre Brantôme, *Œuvres complètes*, VII (Paris, 1873), p. 5 and p. 195. For the Spaniard's own pride in his wit, see Collard, *Nueva poesía*, pp. 85-89.

[62] Brantôme, e.g. *Discours d'aucunes rodomontades et gentilles rencontres et parolles espaignolles*, in vol. VII, pp. 1-177, and *La Vie des dames galantes*, op. cit., VII-IX, *passim*.

[63] In J. García Mercadal, *España vista por los extranjeros* (Madrid, no date), II, 272-273: "prontas de ingenio."

[64] Tomé Pinheiro da Vega, *Fastiginia o Fastos geniales*, trans. Narciso Alonso Cortés (Valladolid, 1916), p. 18: "Y raramente les dirán una cosa á que no respondan otra mejor."

[65] Zabaleta, ... *por la mañana*, pp. 238-240: "Pícanles el gusto con la agudeza de las palabras."

trying to lay down the behaviour appropriate to a court lady and her male companion, allows us to catch something of the tones and gestures of palace society in that age:

> Que la gala, y la blandura,
> donayre, y gusto excelente,
> es profession màs decente
> de la bizarra hermosura.
> La burla, el chiste, el concepto,
> y la platica tambien,
> de quien es galan, y quien
> fino, atinado, y discreto. [66]

The cultivation of wit does not of itself create a *conceptista* art: indeed, I have commented earlier on the literary and cultural influences that helped its coming. But the milieu I have just described was evidently a very favourable one. The evidence suggests too the existence of a taste, not necessarily an exclusively courtly one, for the sort of colourful metaphorical *concepto* we find in Mendoza's poems. Brantôme, for example, referred to a courtier's witty description of an old duenna bringing up the rear of the handsome entourage of Philip II's third wife, Elizabeth of Valois: "This lady looks like the figure of death at the end of a gold or jewelled rosary." [67] And Borghese instances a woman bathing in the Manzanares who, on revealing to the Italian and his companions more of herself than she had intended, cried out: "Gentlemen, you have seen the pot with room for so much flesh in it." [68] It would appear therefore that the kind of remarks that found their way into the *Floresta española* (1574) of Melchor de Santa Cruz were not isolated examples, but the reflection of a society that had lived by its wit.

Another, rather different, aspect of metaphorical language at court is important in itself, as well as providing a bridge to the subject of preciosity, with which we shall deal in conclusion.

---

[66] *FC*, p. 352. The context wishes to emphasize how much more appropriate to women are gallant pursuits, than warlike ones: *For show and tender words, wit, and excellent taste are a more seemly profession for brave beauty. And the jest, the joke, the conceit, and conversation, likewise, for the one who is gallant, refined, and worldy-wise.*

[67] Brantôme, VII, 196: "Esta dama parece la muerte al cabo de un rosario de oro o de pedrerías."

[68] García Mercadal, II, 273: "Señores, habéis visto la olla, que tanta carne cabe en ella."

Pinheiro da Vega commented on lovers' jargon at the Spanish court, such as "my loved one has that heart by which I live." He goes on to say: "Of these are born those philosophic expressions of love, 'to depart without one's soul' and 'to go possessed of someone else's soul', and those impossibilities so well vouched for:

> Quitásteme en Leandro a mí la vida
> que, à no ser muerto yo, no fuera muerta.
> (Conde de Salinas)

meaning that for Leander to die, death would have to seek his soul in Hero, and for Hero to perish, death would have to take away her life in Leander." [69]

This quotation is significant for a number of reasons. It shows to what extent a recognizable *conceptismo* was part of the court lovers' language; it suggests a line of continuity between the poetic paradoxes of courtly love (as expressed in the *Cancionero* or Petrarchan tradition) and the everyday conduct of love in the early years of the century; and the commentator, by going on, in natural succession, to cite the Count of Salinas, imitates what must have been the original transformation of a habit of thought into the language of poetry.

The linguistic eccentricity to which Pinheiro drew attention is, in one sense, a manifestation of the *précieux* spirit: an emotion is dressed in over-elaborate finery, thus removing it from the sphere of the vulgar. When that process is applied to the description, or denotation, of objects, we have a more usual form of preciosity. In the first half of the seventeenth century in Spain, the *précieux* phenomenon mingled with that of *culteranismo*, [70] for an inflated erudition was really an aspect of the *précieux* mechanism. So, for instance, Quevedo in his *La culta latiniparla* (1626?) makes fun not only of certain ladies' false pedantry, but of the desire to disguise

---

[69] *Fastiginia*, prologue: "mi amado me tiene el corazón con que vivo," and: "De aquí nacen aquellas filosofías amorosas —*partir sin alma*— y *ir con alma ajena*, y aquellos imposibles tan averiguados: ...entendiendo que para morir Leandro, era necesario buscara la muerte su alma en Hero, y para perecer Hero, quitarle la vida en Leandro." Pinheiro's Salinas text is suspect. A better version runs: "quitasteme en Leandro a mi la Vida, / y a no auer muerto no fuera muerto, / que tan sin alma como esta Viuia" (see BNM MS 3657, f. 590). The Count's liking for these alembications is attested elsewhere, e.g. "Donde os he de buscar para hallarme / Si yo sali de mí para buscaros / y vos de vos huys por esconderos?" (BNM MS 3922, *Parnaso español 14*, f. 340).

[70] The relation is discussed in Lathuillère, I, 299 *et seq.*

the vulgarity of objects, or their supposed offensiveness. In proffering advice he advocates among other things the use of *cecina de leche* (jerked beef of milk) instead of *queso* (cheese), and "purple kalends" to refer to menstruation. [71] Quevedo's examples are presumably drawn from the imagination rather than actual speech, but the Spanish version of the Italian book of etiquette, *Galateo,* advocated a similar approach to language: *retrayendo,* for instance, was to be used in preference to *reculando,* presumably because of the latter's association with *culo* (arse). [72] And we would probably recognize as *précieux* the poet's tendency, mocked at by Zabaleta, to eschew the ordinary word for ladies' shoes or slippers, and substitute for them *coturnos* (buskins) — a tragedy indeed, jests the author. Zabaleta also mentioned a different form of artificiality, the use of flower language in referring to ladies: So-and-So Jasmin, and So-and-So Rose, etc. [73] The implication in this instance is not different from that in the popular court genre of "portraiture," where the *précieux* overtones are conveyed by the almost obligatory use of a language of substitution in poetic description, so that the lady's hair is necessarily turned to gold, her teeth to pearls. [74]

When Lope de Vega, in some valedictory verses heralding the publication of the Spanish *Galateo* in 1595, welcomed the arrival of "la curiosa Princesa Cortesia," he could hardly have foreseen what an exigent mistress she would become. [75] It is very difficult to gauge, however, the actual extent of the influence of preciosity at court. The acerbity of the attack on *culteranismo* reflects the power of the opposing view that language should eschew affectation. [76] It is significant also that despite social similarities and the subjection to

---

[71] *QOCP,* p. 788. For this type of figure in the theatre, see e.g. Calderón's *No hay burlas con el amor* (in *BAE,* IX, 309-328): Beatriz finds it distasteful to say the word *guantes* (gloves), because it is a "frase vulgar" (p. 312).

[72] Lucas Gracián Dantisco, *Galateo Español. De lo que se deue hazer, y guardar en la comun conuersacion para ser bien quisto y amado de las gentes...* (Barcelona, 1595), f. 84. The book originally appeared in Spanish in 1582, and was later republished in 1621.

[73] Zabaleta, ... *por la tarde,* ff. 62ᵛ-63; and f. 74ᵛ.

[74] See my article "*Pintura.*" Zabaleta (... *por la tarde,* pp. 99-100) comments that these attributes are "materiales tan precisos para esta obra, q[ue] los Poetas buenos, y malos vsan de ellos, de la manera que vsan de vnos colores mismos los buenos, y los malos pintores."

[75] *Galateo español,* f. 6ᵛ. Lope's own contribution to the vogue, in his play *La cortesia en España* and elsewhere, has been analysed by Pauline Marshall in her edition of Alonso Jerónimo de Salas Barbadillo, *El caballero perfecto* (Boulder, Colorado, 1949), pp. xxii-xxxiv.

[76] See e.g. Dámaso Alonso, *La lengua poética...*, *passim.*

similar forces, preciosity in Spain did not attain the importance it did in France. Yet the *précieux* must be taken into account as a potential force in the Spanish court milieu, expressing itself more perhaps as a retreat into idealized portrayal of life than into an artificiality of language. The latter, however, as we have seen, was not altogether absent, and in the course of reviewing Mendoza's poetry we shall have occasion to point to the influence of *précieux* tendencies.

Mendoza showed too a natural interest in the language of polite society, and the fact that as a dramatist he sometimes concerned himself with a social class still attempting to make its way to the top, made him sensitive to the ridiculous aspects of linguistic self-improvement. It was a quest that Salas Barbadillo satirized in an interlude, *Los mirones de la corte:* "You who want to speak properly are a thief who snatches his neighbour's phrases because they are elegant." [77] It was so easy for emulation to be misinterpreted as filching! Mendoza likewise poked fun at the tendency of certain people to use affected vocabulary — in *Cada loco con su tema* we hear of the gallant who uses modish words like *galantería,* or *desvalido* or *desaire,* and in the same play he comments on how one fashionable phrase has supplanted another: *de buen aire* has been replaced by *de buen garbo* as a description of a woman of fine appearance. [78] Such a sensitive reaction to people's speech has two important aspects: on the one hand, it made linguistic affectation the material (and the reason) for satire; on the other, it made the quest for linguistic purity and the avoidance of affectation a more important aim in the composition of poetry.

I have tried in the present chapter to focus attention on the milieu in which Mendoza worked. Like his fellow poets he believed that the poetry of the court was superior in standards, and by implication, different, to its equivalent outside. [79] This claim, however exaggerated, could command recognition to the extent that courtly poetry was an expression of a society governed by standards of etiquette and gallantry that were deemed superior to those of

---

[77] See E. Cotarelo, *Entremeses,* I, 255: "Vos, que deseáis hablar bien, sois ladrón de las frases de vuestro vecino, porque las que tiene son elegantes."

[78] See *FC,* pp. 237-238.

[79] See e.g. pp. 222-224 here.

the *vulgo liviano*. Poetry too, through the significant role it played in the business of gallantry and *bienséance,* carried its own presumption of superiority. In such a setting Mendoza might well feel flattered about the art he practised. And his conviction that he was the best poet in the world, [80] would be strengthened by his sense that he ministered to a real need in a society drawn towards an unattainable ideal. It was the poet after all who could offer the court an idealized projection of itself and its members; and when one looked through the magic glass of poetry no shadow of disillusion ever fell across the elm walks of Aranjuez.

[80] See Cotarelo, *Rojas Zorrilla,* pp. 59-60. Says Rojas in his academy *vejamen* listing a series of impossible requests: "Quieres que le haga creer al Sr. D. Antonio de Mendoza que no es el mayor poeta del orbe?"

V

MENDOZA'S POETRY

ROMANCES AND ALLIED FORMS

M E N D O Z A ' S favourite poetic form was the *romance* in quatrains
(cuartetas), a variation of the traditional octosyllabic, assonantic
ballad metre that had come into prominence with the *romancero*
nuevo, a modern ballad tradition that flowered in the final decade
of the sixteenth century, and which lent itself to musical setting, an
important fact in Mendoza's own case, as we shall see. [1] Mendoza
adhered to, and enlarged, that tradition by his predilection for the
pastoral ballad to which the *romancero nuevo* had given an impetus.

The pastoral ballad, as distinct from the old narrative *romance*,
was essentially a conventional piece. Thematically it allowed little
room for manoeuvre; its sentiments by tradition were those of
courtly love, its geography a flowing river and a level sward, and
its characteristic voice a lyrical utterance of medium intensity,
limited range and comparative brevity. Hence the poem's very
conventionality tended, paradoxically, to call for a treatment that
was novel, lending itself admirably to the *conceptista* technique,
which drew attention to the passing detail more than to the overall
effect. With an endowment both limited and apt, Mendoza made
his reputation largely in this narrow field. In this regard Mendoza
differed from Lope de Vega, who had probably helped to inspire
him. Lope seized on the ballad as something to exploit masterfully
with an insouciant virtuosity, whereas Mendoza used it as a con-
venient, even cosy, form within which he had no need to exert
himself.

Mendoza naturally adopted the Manzanarian idyll, and even
where the pastoral background is missing, his ballads preserve the
bucolic names, and the sentiments of courtly love. The poet, too,
often assumed a shepherd's name: as Lope de Vega had been

---

[1] See ch. VIII.

Belisardo, or Liñán Riselo, so Antonio de Mendoza was Antandro.
Fileno and Belisa who figure in a number of these poems were the
King and Queen in pastoral disguise, and even in the case of
other pastoral pseudonyms we sense that a continuous identity is
hidden. The backgrounds to these shepherds' loves are Madrid (the
palace gardens as well as the *Soto* along the Manzanares), and
the banks of the Tagus and Jarama at Aranjuez during the months
spent at the Spring palace, an annual ritual that offered the poet
recurring inspiration:

> Las que ayer partieron flores
> con abril por Manzanares,
> y en verde airosa batalla
> el campo les deja el valle.
> Hoy más esquivas desdeñan
> del Tajo *la* hermosa margen   [*en* in PMS]
> hasta los floridos meses
> por el nombre de galanes. [2]

In a setting so formal, and an art so formalized, it would be
pointless to look to true feeling as a tracer to Mendoza's more
authentic poetry. The fact is that some of Mendoza's best *romances*
give the impression of being utterly conventional in sentiment: the
poet has used courtly love merely in order to pin-point a moment,
or a mood. Mendoza also displayed a sly ambivalence towards his
material. He sensed that, just as the smiling mask forbids the real
smile, so the court poet as master of conventionality cannot reveal
true feeling because all feeling is made to appear as true. In a
billet doux he frankly admits to Narcisa that he has a:

> Discreción billeteada
> donde en necia pulidez
> vive cautivo el sentir
> muere encantado el querer. [3]

Having participated in the poet's sense that the game of love may
somehow preclude real love, the reader is led on to conclude that

---

[2] *MOP*, II, 151-152: *Those who yesterday shared flowers with April along the Manzanares — and to whom the valley offers battlefield for green and graceful skirmish —
today, more aloof, on Tagus's lovely banks, disdain even the flowering months because
of their being called gallant.*

[3] *MOP*, III, 84-91, quot. on p. 85: *A billet-doux* sort of *discretion in which, with
stupid polish, feeling lives captive, and love dies under a spell.*

in Mendoza's world of enchanted feeling, the disenchantment may at any moment happen: the protestation of loyalty may only succeed in suggesting the possibility of disloyalty, the desire to immortalize may only hasten the approach of time's wingèd chariot. This double standard, that both asserts and destroys, is an essential part of Mendoza's originality, and of the reader's reaction to him.

An ambivalence lurks too in Mendoza's sense of the social context of his poems. That much of the attitudinizing was feigned, or exaggerated, is obvious. What gives the poet originality is the suppleness of his approach. Though a man of noble stock, he was inferior in degree of nobility and in station to many of his audience, and his sense of that inferiority obtrudes in his poetry in unusual ways. Sometimes, Antonio de Mendoza (as had Clément Marot a century earlier in his posture of eternal loyalty and devotion to his royal mistress) went beyond the conventional self-abasement of the lover, and candidly introduced his sense of the real social gap between himself and the woman he loved, or affected to love:

> En tan alta parte adoro
> que es imposible el favor. [4]

At other moments, where the audience shared the poet's awareness of social inferiority, dutiful respect is changed into the language of passion. Thus, when he addresses his Queen, the self-abasement of the courtier becomes the adulation of the troubadour for his lady. Mendoza here is exploiting a literary convention that extended back, beyond Villasandino in the fifteenth century, to an earlier medieval antiquity. Probably part of that deliberate archaism to which I have already referred, this technique also served in Mendoza's case to slough off an uncomforting sense of belonging below the salt.

The pastoral ballad was primarily an opportunity for ringing the changes on the themes of love, disdain and despair, as well as for evoking the beauty of the shepherdesses and their landscape. Originality here lies in the novel comparison, the unexpected image, the well-balanced antitheses, or other forms of conceit. For instance, having pointed to the stream which eventually escapes

---

[4] *MOP*, I, 175: *In so high a place do I adore, that favour is out of the question.*

the mountain's cruel clutches, the poet asks the lady whether men cannot likewise escape the "hard bluffs of your savage disfavours" (*MOP*, II, 100). Or, in order to advance his suit, the poet tells how in nature doom overcomes those that show ingratitude: the proud rose growing among thorns would not let itself be plucked, but eventually it yielded to the scythe's blade (*MOP*, II, 260). At other times, the paradox at the heart of courtly love (that love, made the poet both to seek death as the solution to his despair, and to seek life as the only means of perpetuating the glorious agony of his passion) became a fruitful source of the conceit. That same tradition provided, in the form of hairsplitting quiddities, an extension into poetry of the courtly discussions on love to which I alluded earlier. The examples are many. Here is the opening of one poem:

> Después que muero por vos,
> quiero yo vivir conmigo,
> que si dejara de amaros,
> me aborreciera yo mismo.
> Si el quereros es ofensa,
> es error muy entendido,
> que no amaros ¿quién tan necio
> querrá acaballo consigo? [5]

On other occasions, the *conceptos* that the poet seeks have not sprung from the conventions of love, but from some aspect of the setting, or of the occasion. In some famous verses Mendoza suggested how the competitive spirit of springtime had spread from the earth to the sky:

> Compitiendo con las selvas,
> donde las flores madrugan,
> los pájaros en el viento
> forman abriles de pluma. [6]

---

[5] *MOP*, II, 38: *Ever since I have been dying because of you, I have wished to live by myself (and at peace), for if I ceased to love you, I should hate myself. If to love you is an offence, it is a very understandable error, for not to love you — who would be so stupid as to do away with himself?*

[6] *MOP*, I, 196: *Competing with the woods where the flowers awake early, the birds in the wind are building Aprils of feathers.* The poem is entitled "Trovado" in *PMS*, p. 189. See also p. 205 here.

In another poem he has caught Celinda in a moment of sadness
— and at once the realization that the one who causes love's
distress in others may herself be prone to that condition sets off
the following salvo of *conceptos:*

> Qué alegre de veros triste
> Celinda el amor quedó,
> que tristes lágrimas bellas
> alegrías son de amor.
> Venganzas son de infinitas
> todas las que lloráis hoy;
> y si en penas tiene el cielo
> tenga lágrimas el sol. [7]

Hyperbole was an important word in the language of conceit,
and the poet's own realization of this is clearly stated in one piece:

> Pinceles dulces de pluma,
> floridos, tiernos, y alegres,
> que en el abril de un romance
> las flores pintáis más verdes. [8]

These lines suggest other characteristic qualities too, richness of
setting, and a combination of tender feeling and gaiety. The *pincel* is
a significant image, for Mendoza was conscious of the pictorial
artistry by which he might capture moment, movement and
atmosphere. There is a paradox here: the quality of painting in
Mendoza's work has often been conveyed not by a heavy sensuous-
ness, but by the abstractive quality of his *conceptista* technique. In
coaxing out some unexpected relatedness the poet has reduced the
scene to its elements, so that we catch it, as it were, in the very act
of unbecoming:

> Furias esgrimiendo el sol,
> flores y plantas enoja,
> y es de los campos aliento
> el alba en tibieza hermosa.

---

[7] *MOP*, II, 320: *How happy was love, Celinda, to see you sad; for lovely sad tears
are the happiness of love. Those tears that today you shed are a revenge for an infinity
of them; and if love has heaven itself suffer, let the sun shed tears.*

[8] *MOP*, II, 148: *Sweet feathered paint-brushes (flowering, tender, and gay), which in
the April of a ballad paint the flowers greener.*

> Riesgos avisa el arroyo
> en corrientes presurosas,
> y esconde mayor peligro
> el agua en serenas ondas.
> Preciado el clavel de ardiente
> blasone vivezas rojas,
> que más tiernos ojos pide
> bien desmayada una rosa. [9]

It is the aim of the painter to record and preserve. Mendoza in using his abstractive technique has frequently immortalized the contingent, or the fleeting, by transforming it into a "higher" state, a process that immediately recalls the *desrealización* exemplified in much of the poetry of the period. A correspondence exists between Góngora's Galatea who drinks along the "arcaduz de su mano" ("aqueduct of her hand") and Mendoza's Juana who threatens her fairness with "mil nevadas" ("a thousand snowstorms") as she uses her hand to sprinkle water on her face (*MOP*, II, 383). But the correspondence conceals an underlying difference. In Góngora the *desrealización* accords with a desire to portray perfection in nature; in Mendoza under the presumption of natural perfection is subsumed mortal man's attempt to hold back the destructive power of time. The theme of "Oh temps! suspends ton vol" is not generally explicit in Mendoza, but in these ballads its pathos is often present where least sought after, the bitter residue of a poem's chemistry:

> Amariles, que bizarra
> dulcemente desdeñosa
> pisa del mundo las quejas,
> niega de amor las victorias.
> No concede a las estrellas
> el común imperio en todas,
> que están en su pecho helado
> flacamente poderosas.
> Sus gallardas perfecciones
> de leyes despreciadoras

---

[9] *MOP*, II, 246. The poem contrasts the greater danger from the beauty of a quiet woman with that of the more flashy sort: *The sun, with its foil tracing fury, angers plants and flowers, whilst dawn in beautiful warmth seems the breath of the countryside. The stream in its hastening currents gives warning of risk, but hides a greater danger in quiet waters. Let the carnation (proud of its ardour) show off its lively reds, but a swooning rose seeks out more tender eyes.*

de un pastorcillo la voz
de esta manera ocasionan.
No blasones de libre
niña del valle,
que hace amor cadenas
de libertades. [10]

Excessive fertility and a carefree attitude to composition have spoiled many of these pastoral ballads at their most promising. Despite this, abundant examples remain to prove Mendoza to have been a master of the form. It is difficult none the less to determine which ballads represent his greatest achievement, since we are inevitably conscious of the gap between our taste and that of Mendoza's audience. The popularity of "Después que muero por vos" (whose opening verses were earlier quoted) or of "Quien ama correspondido," made up of verses like:

Quien ser amado pretende
es indigno del favor,
que no obliga por amar
quien por obligar amó. [11]

proves how Mendoza was appreciated for that kind of intellectual play which was an essential part of the *concepto*. Furthermore, we are no longer in a position to meet the sense of occasion. To quote an instance: in a ballad contrasting two spells of unseasonable weather at Aranjuez and the palace of El Pardo, we may manage to respond to the poet's clever evocation of a reversal of the seasons and to his identification of Queen Belisa with the goddess who controls nature, only to find that, as the poet comments in turn on the important members of the assembly, each *conceptista* salvo (that probably awakened the audience's wholehearted response) now thuds dully in our ears (*MOP*, II, 52-55).

Understandably therefore I prefer those ballads whose appeal is direct, simple, and touching. But even at their simplest their keen

---

[10] *MOP*, I, 172-173: *Amariles, bravely, gently disdainful of the world's complaints, denies love's victories. She does not concede the stars their common sway over all women, for in her icy bosom they are weakly powerful. Her sprightly perfections, disregarding laws, occasion thus a little shepherd's voice: Do not boast of your freedom, child of the valley, for love makes chains out of freedoms.*

[11] *MOP*, II, 380: *The one who claims to be loved is unworthy of favour, for the man who loved in order to oblige does not oblige by his love.*

intellectual edge, and sharp sententiousness give them a very characteristic quality:

> Heridas en un rendido
> nunca fueron de valiente,
> y más flaqueza descubre
> quien mata, que no quien muere.
> A sangre mil veces fría
> es segunda vez aleve
> rigor, que busca más vida
> donde no cabe otra muerte. [12]

In the best poems, such keenness is tempered by a sensuous touch and a real feeling for nature. They display too in greatest measure the poet's extraordinary sense of rhythm:

> Oh qué bien descoge al viento
> la garza airosa las alas,
> y sobre las nubes negras
> tremolan las plumas blancas. [13]

To select one ballad for quotation in full is difficult, since it should display not only technical merit, but also characteristic qualities. The following *romance* is as deserving as any, for it brings together the essentially occasional nature of Mendoza's verse, its deliberate conventionality, its treatment of the ephemeral as the very heart of a poem, as well as its sudden display of virtuosity when he improvises with verve and assurance. And beneath the conventional exterior there throbs a universal sadness, as we share the shepherd's discovery that even a beautiful shepherdess, who causes men's unhappiness, herself suffers grief:

> Diez y siete primaveras
> tiene la niña de plata
> y dice el sol, que a sus ojos
> debe todas las mañanas.
> Melancólica y enferma

---

[12] MOP, II, 172: *The wounds inflicted on the one who has yielded were never made by a brave man, and the one who kills shows more weakness than the one who dies. A rigour a thousand times cold-blooded, which seeks out more life where death finds no more room, it is doubly treacherous.*

[13] MOP, II, 128-129: *How well the graceful heron spreads its wings to the wind, unfurling white feathers against black clouds.*

las iras del río pasa,
que con parecer divina
en esto se muestra humana.
¡Que entendida que se sufre!
¡qué sola que se acompaña!
que aunque el cuerpo es tan hermoso
tiene más hermosa el alma.
Sólo el dueño que la goza
mereció partes tan altas,
que no siempre la hermosura
ha de nacer desdichada.
Yo la vi nevar jazmines
y bebérselos el alba;
yo la vi llorar estrellas
por dos esferas de nácar.
¡Qué tristes están las flores
después que no ven su cara!
¡qué retiradas las aves!
¡qué perezosas las aguas!
Lauro que suspenso admira
en su belleza sus ansias,
por divertir a Jacinta
de esta manera le canta:

Estribillo

Serenad vuestro cielo,
zagala hermosa,
porque canten las aves,
las fuentes corran.
Llore celos el alba,
victorias, victorias amor,
tengan flores los prados
y rayos el sol.
Divina Jacinta,
alma de estos montes,
cielo de la tierra,
mayo de las flores.
No cubra la noche
vuestras dos auroras
porque canten las aves, etc. [14]

---

[14] *MOP*, II, 377-378: *The girl of silver has seventeen springs, and the sun says it owes each morning to her eyes. Melancholy and sick she suffers the river's anger, for though she seems divine, in this she shows herself human. How wise she is in her suffering! How much alone among those who accompany her! For though her body is beautiful, her soul is more so. Only the master who enjoys her favours deserved such lofty qualities, for it is not every day that beauty must be born sad. I saw in her a snow*

The poet's success in the religious ballad with a rural background suggests that he could well have written earthy pastoral *romances* in the manner of Liñán de Riaza, it suggests also his familiarity with a tradition extending back beyond the *romancero nuevo* to Encina, but whose immediate representatives were Góngora in his Christmas pieces, Lope in his *Pastores de Belén* (1612), or Alonso de Ledesma in the "peasant" pieces in his *Conceptos espirituales*. Mendoza seems nearest to Lope in his penetration into the popular spirit, as we see from the opening to a poem which evokes a village celebration of the Feast of Saint John the Evangelist:

> Alegre vienes, Pastor,
> ¿qué hay Pascual?, ¿qué hay Bartolejo?
> Todos estamos aquí,
> dejadme ver, que a eso vengo. [15]

But is was the *jácara* that lay closest to Mendoza's poetic instinct, for it combined a sense of the popular with a witty, metaphoric style different from that of the pastoral ballads. Despite hints of an even earlier origin the *jácara* can be linked with the vogue for thieves' slang and for Juan Hidalgo's *Romances de germanía de varios autores* (1609) which described the life of the underworld. [16] It required the genius of a Quevedo to establish the *jácara* (so named because its purpose was to describe the life of the *jaques* [hoodlums]) as a literary form: Quevedo's famous letter from Escarramán to la Méndez, a poetic address by a gangster to his moll, may well have been the precursor of numerous *jácaras* in the same vein. The "wicked youth of Escarramán whom poetry celebrates" — Góngora's words — fascinated other poets including Mendoza, who contributed his own

---

shower of jasmin which the dawn drank up; I saw her weep stars through two spheres of mother-of-pearl. How sad the flowers at not seeing her face! The birds are in retreat, the waters laze! Lauro, who in wonderment admires in her beauty the image of her anxieties, sings thus to Jacinta, in order to amuse her: Chorus: Uncloud your sky, lovely shepherdess, so that the birds may sing, the springs flow. Let dawn weep its jealousy, let love have victory, the meadows flowers, the sun its rays. Divine Jacinta, soul of these hills, heaven of this earth, Maytime of the flowers. May night not cover your double dawn, so that the birds may sing, etc.

[15] *MOP*, III, 289: *You look happy, shepherd! How goes it, Jack? How goes it, Jim? We are all here, let me take a look, for that is why I've come.* A number of similar poems are found in the unpublished Hisp. Soc. Am. *MS HC*: 371/224, as well as in BNM *MS 3700*: in the latter Mendoza's pieces alternate with similar ones by Lope and Luis Vélez.

[16] See J. M. Hill, *Poesías germanescas*, p. vii *et seq.*, Pidal, *Romancero*, II, p. 200 *et seq.*, and Cotarelo, *Colección de entremeses*, I, NBAE, XVII, p. CCLXXIV *et seq.*

Escarramán poem, an evocation of the life of the galley-slave barracks in Cadiz. [17] It has been claimed, perhaps wrongly, that the high-water mark of this genre was around 1613, and if Mendoza's poem was written at that time, it belongs among his earlier compositions. [18] In fact Mendoza's more characteristic exercise in the genre lies in a more interesting direction. Only one step lay between an evocation of the underworld and the depiction of picturesque scenes from popular life, and it is the latter rather than the former which attracted Mendoza. Sometimes introducing colourful characters such as Toribio or Inesilla that were used by other poets, he could establish with his audience a *rapport* based on the complicity of shared knowledge. Of these poems his most famous is "Con sus trapos Inesilla," which in a short, quite distinct, and most effective version appeared in the 1636 Zaragoza edition of the *Primavera y flor de los mejores romances*. [19] The fuller version tells of a Galician, wounded in a drunken brawl, who receives the consolations of a washer-girl called Inés. A quarrel is about to ensue between the Galician and a rival who has arrived on the scene, when a second girl appears and squabbles with Inés, who after calling her a whore, hits her in the face with her slipper. The poem ends in a dance, the other girl defending herself against the charge of whoredom:

> Ramerita me llama
> la picaruela,
> siendo destas ramas
> una alameda.
> La chinela me tira,
> y es gran perdición
> que me tire con una
> quien no tiene dos. [20]

---

[17] *QOCV*, pp. 1225-1228; Góngora, ed. Millé, p. 153: "la juventud traviesa / del cantado Escarramán;" and *MOP*, III, 92-95.

[18] See Pidal, op. cit., II, p. 201. Mendoza's piece was more probably written during the Andalusian journey of 1624: the King visited Cadiz, the time of year corresponding closely to that of Escarramán's letter.

[19] *Primavera* (1636), ed. Montesinos, p. 221-222, *MOP* text, I, 176-180 [=*FC* text]. The poem also appeared for instance in *PMS*, pp. 86-92 (where it is called a "xacara"), BNM *MS* 3795, f. 312, without attribution, and BNM *MS* 3700, f. 65ᵛ.

[20] *MOP*, I, 180: *The little rascal calls me a whore* (ramera), *she being of these branches* (ramas) *a whole gladeful. She throws her slipper at me, and it is a real sin that I should be pelted with one by a girl who doesn't have two to her name.*

Cervantes in *La gitanilla* described the *jácara* as a "danza cantada." Here, as elsewhere, we meet the importance of musical setting and accompaniment in Mendoza's poems. The genre's place in court entertainment, as well as the public occasions that the poet sometimes had in mind, is suggested by a *jácara* written for a theatrical evening in the *Retiro* on St. John's Eve 1638. He evokes the gaiety and noise, the splendour of the ladies, the abundance of music and song, the shouting and squabbling in the Prado outside. The opening verse, with its lilting rhythm, captures both the occasion, and the popularity of the *jácara* itself:

> Jacarilla, jacarilla,
> airoso y verde solaz
> de toda fiesta, el gran día
> de la noche de San Juan. [21]

Three other poems akin to "Con sus trapos Inesilla," though not explicitly referred to as *jácaras,* possibly represent, when taken together, Mendoza's highest poetic achievement, a view confirmed by their popularity. His *romancillo* (a six-syllabled ballad) "El alba Marica" evokes the scene when a young girl goes down to the Manzanares in the evening to bathe. The poem's opening stanzas could hardly be surpassed for wit and brilliance:

> El alba Marica,
> el alba es que sale
> allá va, señores,
> no se aparte nadie.
> A lavarse al soto,
> donde está en las tardes,
> el río en los huesos,
> y Madrid en carnes. [22]

The portrait of Marica (a variant on the genre called *pintura,* of which I shall have more to say) maintains the initial brilliance, but

---

[21] *MOP,* III, 68: *Jacarilla, Jacarilla, sprightly and verdant amusement of every* fiesta, *on this great day of the Eve of St. John.*

[22] *MOP,* II, 195-197: *It is the dawn, Marica, the dawn coming up (there she goes, sirs, let no-one turn away). On her way to the* Soto *to bathe, where in the evenings the river is stripped to dry bone, and Madrid is there in naked flesh* [The river's dryness in summer was proverbial]. The poem is found for instance in BNM *MS 3700,* f. 130v without attribution, BNM *MS 3795,* f. 213, *PMS* p. 288, and *Cancionero de 1628,* p. 287 (attributed to Góngora). *MOP* publishes the Alfay text of *Poesías varias* (1654). For the Quevedo attributions, see *QOCV,* p. cxx *et seq.*

technical virtuosity is at its very best in describing one of those
wonderful Madrid sunsets above the Manzanares, as Marica's body
turns the river to flame:

> Ya don Fulanito
> de Caniculares,
> nacido en la India,
> y barbado en Flandes.
> Daba en el ocaso
> con sus rocinantes,
> relinchos de nubes,
> coces de celajes
> ....
> Cuando Mariquilla
> quiere por templarse,
> que se encienda el río,
> que la luz se bañe. [23]

The animism and metaphoric exuberance here are reminiscent
of Lorca's *Romancero gitano*, whilst the deliberate exploitation of
bathos belongs to a tradition in which Góngora and Quevedo had
excelled.

Another poem "Al río bajan tres moras," on a similar and indeed
popular subject, is less successful as a whole, but contains some
excellent verses in praise of the three girls' beauty:

> Su cabello al sol escribe
> lecciones, y leyes de oro,
> y es breve papel el viento
> a los rasgos de sus ojos.
> A trenzar bajaron todas
> el campanario del moño,
> que de alto cayó, y de necio;
> así fuera de otros locos.
> Rubio, morenete, y blanco,
> es el *torno* boquirrojo,   [*terno* in *PMS*]
> que en todo calor, y temple
> es lindo clima lo hermoso. [24]

---

[23] *MOP*, II, 196: *Already Don So-and-So Dog-days (born in India and bearded in
Flanders) with his nags gave out in the west neighs of clouds and kicks of skyscapes...
When little Marica, in order to keep warm, wishes the river to burst into flame, and the
light to take a bath.*

[24] The lines in *MOP*, II, 135-137 run "Al río van tres gallegas / sin ningun turco en
el rostro," but the reading in *PMS*, p. 433 makes better sense of the word-play: *Their*

The third piece, which appeared in the 1641 Madrid edition of the *Primavera y flor,* and is represented in a longer, and more rambling, form in one of the manuscripts, is the "Villana de Leganés." In the shorter version it is a lovely poem, which may be quoted in its entirety:

> Villana de Leganes,
> segundo abril de la corte,
> que a Madrid lleuas tan verdes
> los años como las flores,
> que sencillamente hermosa
> los engaños desconoces
> de vn aplauso que florido
> tambien caduca a la noche:
> toda flor es peligrosa,
> o bien se pause o se corte,
> que entre ser flor y perderse
> no muda peligro el nombre.
> Todo es salteos la villa
> y seguro qualquier monte,
> que la malicia y la culpa
> siempre andan en trage de hombre.
> En viajes de amor no aprueuo
> seguir por la altura el norte,
> que es gran baxio, y lo vano
> todo en espuma se rompe.
> Mira no te hallen de cera
> essos *principios* de bronce   [*principes* MS 2802]
> y te lleuen desde el carro
> a Carrion de los Condes. [25]

---

hair writes lessons and laws of gold for the sun, and the wind is a short leaf of paper for the flourishes of their eyes [the text plays on *rasgo* (flourish, stroke) and *rasgado,* used of large, wide eyes]. *They all came down to plait their bell-tower of a bun, which fell down for being so high (and so stupid); would that it proved the same with other madmen. The red-lipped trinity is fair, dark, and white, for in every temperature and temper, beauty is a pretty sort of climate.*

[25] *MOP,* II, 341-342 [= Palacio MS 2802, f. 24v], and *Primavera,* pp. 238-239: *Peasant-girl of Leganés, a second April of the court, who carries her years to court as green as her flowers, who simple in her beauty* ["simplex munditiis"?] *knows nothing of the deceptions of an applause which, like a flower, also fades at nightfall. Every flower is in danger, whether it is cut or left, for between being flower and being damned, danger does not change its name. The capital is all highway robbery, and any mountain-top [in comparison] is safe, for malice and sin always wear men's clothes. On journeys of love I do not approve following a compass-north through deep waters* [the text plays on the *altura* (depth) of the sea and the high, noble classes] *for it is a great shallow, and vanity breaks foaming upon it. See that those bronze princes do not find you made of wax, and take you from their coach to Carrión de los Condes.* [In epic legend the Counts of Carrión abandoned their spouses, the daughters of the Cid.]

The *jácara,* as Menéndez Pidal has pointed out, lasted down into
the eighteenth century. [26] By that time its nature had changed,
for the *Diccionario de autoridades* defined it as a poem in ballad
metre which related "some particular or out-of-the-ordinary incident." [27] In the type that Mendoza called the "jácara honesta," this
development is prefigured. Such a piece was the one evoking the
Retiro on St. John's Eve, to which attention was earlier drawn. In
another poem a Prince of Thebes recounts his life (*MOP,* II, 71),
in a third an old servant appeals to his master not to neglect him
(*MOP,* III, 14). The only obvious link with the traditional *jácara*
is the preference for the *estilo donoso,* a fact which draws these
pieces and the *jácaras* proper near to the witty, metaphorical *romances* of Góngora and Quevedo: indeed it helps to explain why certain
poems in this group have been attributed to all three poets. Yet, one
distinction must be made here. In the burlesque *romances* of Góngora or Quevedo, as well as in poems like "El alba Marica," we
see the relevance of Sr. Muñoz Cortés's point that the trope (in the
shape of the catachresis or *ingenioso equívoco*) could be used to
deflate its object, and that the representation of the crudities of
low life made mock of the ideal world that had long been expressed
by the more conventional poetry. [28] On the other hand, the *jácara
honesta,* and its extension into the *pintura* with which we deal next,
suggests that the metaphoric style was no longer apt only for satire
and burlesque; its pyrotechnic brilliance had assured it a place
among the more serious forms of poetry.

The genre called *pintura,* or *pintar una dama,* was much older
than Mendoza. Indeed in one sense it is medieval. But its emergence
now as a recognizable genre may certainly be traced at least as far
back as an early Gongorine poem of 1590. [29] Two important points
in its development are significant for us. In the first place, the *pintura*

---

[26] *Romancero,* II, 202. Calderón in an interlude, *Las jácaras,* depicted a lady who had
a mania for the genre.

[27] *Diccionario de la lengua castellana,* ed. Real Ac. Esp. (Madrid, 1726-39): "algun
sucesso particular o extrano."

[28] See p. 85. That Mendoza was aware of breaking new ground is suggested by
the opening of a poem to the Virgin of Almudena: "en jacara, y modo nuevo" (*MOP,*
III, 250).

[29] See my "Pintura."

played a part in the activities of the literary academies, for Álvaro Cubillo de Aragón drew attention to the practice of calling on their members to "paint" certain types, an old woman, a bald man, and so on. Secondly, as was earlier shown, the *pintura* became a quite popular court genre, and was often made in response to a request from the audience for a *retrato* of someone or other. A number of Mendoza's poems came about as a form of improvisation, among them probably some of his poetic portraits. Certainly he regarded the *pintura* as a great opportunity for releasing a torrent of *conceptos,* largely of the metaphorical kind associated with the *estilo donoso:*

> Cuánta perfección escribe
> en púrpuras de cristales
> el cielo, tiembla en sus ojos
> a los rasgos de azabache.
> En sus desdeñosos labios
> florecido todo un áspid,
> nadie a su veneno debe
> la queja de morir tarde.
> ....
>
> Espadas blancas de amor,
> cristal envainado en carne,
> sus manos mejor que treguas
> son desafío en el guante. [30]

And the presence of an audience is suggested by the abundance of such extravagant hyperboles, conceits thrown up so that the assembly might gasp at their brilliance and daring. His desire to respond to the expectation of these sallies of *conceptos* is implied when he comments in another *pintura* on the impossibility of ever introducing any image suggestive of age in describing someone so young:

> mas cosa vieja en la niña
> ni aun en conceptos se atreve. [31]

---

[30] *MOP*, II, 357: *As much perfection as heaven writes in purples of crystal trembles in her eyes at each jet-coloured flourish [of her eyelashes]. In her disdainful lips lurks a flowering asp, and no-one owes to its poison the complaint that he is long in dying... White swords of love [armas blancas = swordarms], crystal sheathed in flesh, her hands rather than signs of truce are a challenge inside a glove.*

[31] *MOP*, I, 199: *But a thing ancient in a girl so young one does not dare to suggest even in* conceptos.

Here the master's technical virtuosity has reached its limit, and he is telling his audience so.

If, as was earlier suggested, Mendoza sometimes saw himself as a painter in words, the exercise of the art of *pintura* would have intensified that feeling. He did on one occasion intimate a light-hearted comparison between his art and that of Velázquez, [32] but this goes only part of the way towards understanding his position. The *pintura* in a ballad about some court shepherdess might conceivably be akin to what Velázquez was attempting, but there were certain subjects in which the art of poetry could even excel the art of the painter in the task of description. When Mendoza, in some *redondillas* to which we shall later refer, makes it known that his present subject was one that even "Titian's brush" would not have attempted, [33] he is suggesting that there exists in the poet's pen a potential for description beyond that of any painter. Mendoza's success in the genre of poetic portraiture suggests that there was some truth in this.

J. F. Montesinos, in his study of the popular collection *Primavera y flor de los mejores romances* (Madrid, 1621) and its successors, drew attention to the archaic nature of the forms there included alongside the ballads. [34] He was probably right in associating this fact with the archaism of the convention of courtly love that so many of these poems expressed: if the poets were free to imitate the postures of the fifteenth-century troubadour, might they not also employ the more traditional Castilian poetic forms? It is noticeable, as corroboration of this view, that in Mendoza's case, the *endecha* (a form of *romancillo* with six-syllable assonantic quatrains), whose growing popularity was already attested in Pedro de Flores's *Ramillete de Flores. Sexta parte de flor de romances* (Lisboa, 1593), has ceased to be a lament, and expresses a wider range of themes in which perhaps sadness, that of love, predominates. Indeed at times the poet uses the *endecha* merely to embroider fancifully a pastoral

---

[32] *MOP*, II, 56. He calls on the audience to accept the accuracy of the *pintura* he has made. If anyone disagrees, "De Velázquez a las sombras / apele, a cuyos retratos / deben en los testimonios / fijas lisonjas los falsos."

[33] *MOP*, II, 226: "real jardín lo emprendiera / la ticiana pluma en vano." For the coming together here of pen and paint-brush, cf. archaic meaning of English "pencil."

[34] See *Primavera*, p. LIX *et seq.*

scene, such as that in which Amariles is addressed on her birthday, and four palace peasant-girls trip on to the stage:

> Salen a la fiesta
> cuatro labradoras
> de las flores vida,
> de los campos gloria. [35]

Such interest in the more traditional forms, and their adaptation to contemporary taste, may be seen in Mendoza's normal practice. On one occasion, with an almost solemn archaism, he experimented with the traditional (and defunct) *arte mayor* line (*MOP*, III, 115). More characteristic is his fondness for the varying traditional rhymed forms of the octosyllabic line: *coplas, glosas, letras* (or *letrillas*), *redondillas* and *seguidillas*. Some of these were already found in the anthologies at the end of the sixteenth century, some (especially the *seguidilla*) belong to a more recent vogue. Two points here are probably significant. These were often poems intended to be sung in public, and as Montesinos has pointed out with regard to one of those forms, Lope de Vega only distinguished between the *letra* and the *letrilla* by the length of the composition; they were both the same thing, words to be sung, "letras para cantar." [36] The second point suggests aristocracy of taste: the two outstanding noble poets of the day, Esquilache and Villamediana, showed considerable fondness for the *redondilla* form, and indeed a liking for other traditional forms like the *glosa*. It may well be that since these forms were used by these poets to convey highly proper sentiments in an intellectualized style, their charm and varying technical effects could be exploited without incurring the charge of plebeianism. Furthermore, as was seen earlier, there was a courtly precedent for such affection for the traditional Castilian metres.

Mendoza, like others of his contemporaries, showed a predilection for *coplas* forming a poetic commentary on opening *letras* which stated the poem's theme. This gave Mendoza the greatest opportunity for the display of wit, and though the appeal of this kind of exercise (so popular among other court poets such as Villamediana

---

[35] *MOP*, I, 260-261: *There come to the* fiesta *four peasant-girls, life of the flowers, glory of the fields.*

[36] On music, see *Primavera*, esp. p. LXIX *et seq.*, and Montesinos, *Estudios sobre Lope*, p. 138; on *seguidilla*, see *Primavera*, p. LXXVII *et seq.*

and Esquilache) has probably diminished, there remain moments when his virtuosity commands our admiration. For instance, part of his commentary on this *letra:*

> Hagamos de amor donaire,
> y de sus veras pastor,
> que los cuidados de amor
> aunque son fuego, son aire.

consists of these ingenious, and effective, lines:

> Mudando amor de elemento,
> las plumas, que por costumbre
> ardían en fina lumbre,
> se apagan en falso viento:
> los ojos, que en rendimiento,
> mares formaban de penas,
> surcan golfos de sirenas
> ya no el agua, sino el aire. [37]

But in the *coplas* form, Mendoza's greatest achievement was in the witty style already noted in the *jácaras.* As there, it seems particularly suited to the *pintura,* an example being this stanza which comments on a *letra* declaring the lover's willingness to enjoy even the woman's cruelty:

> Niña colérica, y leve,
> de amor lisonja cruel,
> toda chispa de clavel,
> toda pólvora de nieve:
> en cuya hermosura bebe
> milagros la fe sedienta,
> dulzuras toda en pimienta,
> toda almíbares en sal,
> *niña hermosa y celestial,*
> *ni ofendiendo tratas mal.* [38]

---

[37] *MOP*, I, 247-248: *Let us make light of love, shepherd, even of its serious side, for the cares of love, though they be fire, are [only] air. ... With love changing its element, those feathers* [of the heron?] *which were wont to burn in pure [and well-mannered] fire, are extinguished in a treacherous wind: those eyes which in submission formed seas of sorrow now cleave bays full of sirens — bays not of water but of air"* [*aire* seems also to carry the implications of *aura popularis*].

[38] *MOP*, I, 234-236: *Quick-tempered and frivolous girl, love's cruel flattery, she is all, the carnation spark of her lips [and wit], all, a [gun-] powder of snow; at whose beauty love, thirsting, drinks miracles, all of her, sweetness laced with spice [and anger],*

As suggested earlier the *coplas* and *glosas* were in part a deliberate archaism. It is not surprising, therefore, that the archaic quality is found not only in the choice of form, but also in the use of the subject matter. There is, of course, nothing unusual in the fact that most of these poems, like Mendoza's *romances,* are about courtly love. But significantly he sometimes seeks to express his thoughts in language and manner very reminiscent of the earlier *Cancionero* poetry. Thus on the following *letra* (whose author might be Mendoza, or else someone unknown):

> Sufriros y amaros quiero,
> niña hermosa y celestial,
> sin otro bien que este mal.

Don Antonio, in his first *copla* glossing the original verse's stark use of parallelism and antithesis, seeks to convey even more characteristically the flatness, one might even say the dullness, of the *Cancionero:*

> En vuestro hermoso desdén
> ya sé que no obra jamás
> más bien que el amaros más,
> y que más que amaros bien.
> Si está seguro este bien,
> y no hay más vida que amaros
> en morir, y en adoraros
> sobre todo lo que muero
> sufriros y amaros quiero. [39]

The *redondilla* form represents only a small, and on the whole insignificant, part of Mendoza's output, yet reference has to be made to part of a poem in *redondillas* in which he attempted to capture the magnificence of a fountain at the home of the Duke of Medina de Ríoseco:

> Penacho de sol, que en suma
> siembra en desperdicio leve

---

syrup kept in salt [and wit]; lovely and heavenly girl, you do not treat anyone badly even when you give offence.

[39] MOP, III, 147-148: I wish both to love and to suffer you, lovely and heavenly girl, without any happiness but this misfortune... In your lovely disdain I well know that the only happiness ever to operate [?] is loving you more, and going beyond just loving you well. If this happiness is secure, and life is only for loving you, [then] in dying and in adoring you (above all the dying), I wish both to love and suffer you.

de átomos de plata y nieve
cada rayo y cada pluma.
Cuyas garzotas tempranas
se rizan de las más bellas
lágrimas que llora en ellas
la envidia de las mañanas.
Mintiendo a lo natural
parece que desde el suelo
sus estrellas cierne el cielo
en harina de cristal.
Cándidas fraguas y bellas
sin duda que el centro aloja
que en buen aire el viento arroja
nevadas tantas centellas.
Desde los pardos confines
del abismo al cielo sube
y en flamante airosa nube
polvos nieva de jazmines. [40]

In their richness of imagination and the repeated (and fruitless) attempts to get it right, these verses call to mind the tradition of the Welsh *dyfalu* poems at their best. They represent also, almost with pathos, how the poet's brush was intent on preserving a vision which, even as it formed, was dissolved into nothingness.

The *redondillas* contain another hint of Mendoza's archaism. It may be recalled that Lope de Vega in his prologue to *El Isidro* (1599) had asked whether anything could equal a *redondilla* by Garci Sánchez or Diego de Mendoza, [41] and in his introduction to the poetic contest on the occasion of San Isidro's beatification (1620), he not only praised the "divine thoughts" of the "Cancioneros antiguos," but quoted from them verses in the *redondilla* form. [42] The

---

[40] *MOP*, II, 224-230, quot. on pp. 226-227: *A plume of sunshine, which in sum [and summa] scatters, in light-hearted profligacy, over each ray and each feather atoms of silver and of snow. Whose early crests are crinkled by the fairest tears shed in them by the envy of the mornings. In natural fashion telling a lie [and turning the order of nature into a lie], it appears as though the sky were, from the ground sieving the stars in a flour of crystal. Without doubt the centre holds forges both white [-hot] and beautiful, for the wind [of the bellows] throws gracefully [and into good air] so many snow-white sparks. From the dark confines of the abyss it soars skywards, and in an airy [and graceful], resplendent [and new] cloud it scatters a snowstorm of powdered jasmin.*

[41] *Obras completas de Lope de Vega*, ed. J. de Entrambasaguas, I (*Obras no dramáticas, I*), [Madrid, 1965], p. 274.

[42] Lope de Vega, *Obras escogidas*, II, 1572-1576: "divinos pensamientos" (p. 1573).

example of the *Cancionero* poets, and in particular that of the humanist poet Diego Hurtado de Mendoza, may have had its effect on Antonio de Mendoza, a kinsman, so that he may have wanted to emulate Don Diego's most significant poetic achievement, the *redondilla*. The majority of Antonio de Mendoza's exercises in that form do not suggest such emulation, but two sets, in fact linked together, are reminiscent of Don Diego's. These sets, both *cartas en redondillas* like those of Don Diego, are directed to a Marchioness called María. [43] They cover the usual sentiments, but make less pretence of being conventional *amour courtois* poems. They suggest, rather, a genuine social context, in which the lover's affections have been challenged by another's. Nevertheless, the reader suspects at moments in one poem that it is, so to speak, a put-up job, and that the rival is really the beautiful Amariles's husband, who can also relish the poetic performance. Two things are certain, the highly aristocratic milieu, and the tone of pastiche:

> Tardó el respeto en mostraros
> que os amaba, y aunque yo
> me perdía, no perdió
> ningún instante el amaros. [44]

But if this was indeed in part an attempt to imitate the manner of Don Diego's *redondillas* in epistolary form, one feels that Antonio de Mendoza was aware also of their primitive *conceptismo,* but refrained deliberately in the interest of emulation from exploiting its full potential. That this could have been the case is suggested by the strong contrast with other *redondillas* on a love theme, in which the style is characterized by brilliant *conceptos* similar to those of his *romances:*

> En guerra hermosa y segura
> de una y otra perfección,

---

[43] See *MOP*, II, 154-156, and II, 67-70. That the poems are associated is suggested by their position in *PMS*, pp. 463-466, and 467-472 respectively, being called there *Romance redondillas*, and *Redondillas*. The Marchioness was probably the Marquesa de Heliche, María de Guzmán, Olivares's daughter, the Amariles of many of Mendoza's poems. The public nature of the occasion is suggested by the appeal to Belisa, the Queen (II, 70), as witness to his love. The other poem suggests Amariles's love for someone else ("Que vos lo queráis más bien / lo conozco en vuestro amor" [II, 156]), presumably the Marquis.

[44] *MOP*, II, 69: *My sense of respect was slow to show you that I loved you, and though I was on the way to perdition, my love for you did not lose a single instant.*

ya es niña tu discreción
batalla de tu hermosura. [45]

Finally, in contrast to the forms which originated in an older native tradition, mention must be made of the madrigal, an Italian form, primarily connected of course with musical setting, whose heyday had been at the end of the sixteenth and the beginning of the seventeenth century. Perhaps in Mendoza's case too the madrigal was intended for a musical setting, though it would have been a great pity for the beauty of the words to get lost in the complexities of the polyphony, since these brief poems are among the poet's most beautiful compositions. He appears to have considered the madrigal especially appropriate to record a fleeting impression, or to develop a simple conceit. In one we catch a glimpse of Celaura's hair, brilliant in the shining sun; in another, the young shepherdess flees in vain, for she is pursued not by favour or desire, but by the inexorable hope of her lover. Mendoza in his madrigals comes closest to the daring catachreses of Góngora, as we can judge from the evocation of the footprint of the hunting bird who is his loved one:

Plumas calco de nieve,
hermosa planta breve
de altiva cazadora,
que en flecha voladora
del aire mismo fué terror ligero. [46]

The best madrigal perhaps is that in which the wave on the seashore is addressed as the divine fisher-girl, casting her fronds of water like nets to sea and sky:

Tiende las redes, ola,
pescadora divina,
más sola en peregrina
que en la ribera sola.
Si el cebo son tus ojos siempre bellos
saquear podrás la tierra, el mar con ellos;

---

[45] *MOP*, III, 136-138: *In a beautiful and safe (?) war between one perfection and another, your discretion, my girl, is at battle with your beauty.*

[46] For madrigals, see *MOP*, III, 96-99, quot. on p. 96: *Feathers, a trace made by snow, a brief and lovely foot (print) of a haughty huntress who upon a flying arrow was the swift terror of the air itself.*

tiende las redes, tiende, que bien puedes,
al aire, al cielo, dilatar las redes. [47]

It is not merely churlish to comment that the potential which
Mendoza shows here is greater than his achievement elsewhere.
Rather is it that in the madrigal he hits on a form appropriate to
his greatest talents: its formal brevity is well fitted to the poet's
brief flashes of wit, as well as to his restricted capacity for organic
form. And freed from the tyranny of the pastoral ballad, or of the
courtly *glosa*, he is able to exercise his imagination in a direction
that may fairly be described as impressionistic. The pictorial quality
in Mendoza's art would in any case make the term impressionistic
an acceptable one, but it can be used in a more precise sense: as
in the *redondillas* to the fountain, or in the *pintura* poems, vivid
language is used not in order to define, and thereby limit, an object,
but to recreate it out of those sensual particles that initially gave
it life, thus conveying to us a vision that is vague, elemental, yet
magical.

DÉCIMAS

Mendoza was almost certainly recognized in his own times as a
master of the ballad form. Yet even at the very outset of his court
career he enjoyed a reputation also as a composer of the ten-line
octosyllabic stanza known as the *décima*: certainly in 1620 Lope
de Vega acclaimed him as unequalled in that genre, [48] praise indeed
at a time when both Vicente Espinel, whose *espinela* had attained
such renown, and the Count of Villamediana (who used the *décima*
so frequently in his satirical attack on the members of the court)
were still practising their art. I have earlier indicated the clear
association during the period between the *décima* and the epigram.
And in Mendoza the form was used in two ways suggesting epigram-

---

[47] *MOP*, III, 96: *Spread your nets, oh wave, divine fisher-girl, more lovely in your
singularness, than in your solitude on the sea-shore. If your ever lovely eyes are the bait,
you will be able with them to plunder both sea and land; spread your nets, spread them,
well may you spread them to air and sky.* The poem, in the tradition of the piscatorial
eclogue, may be compared with some Gongorine pieces (e.g. *Obras*, ed. R. F.-D., I, 18
[dated 1581] and II, 215 [dated 1614]). Trillo de Figueroa (in *BAE*, XLII, p. 45), like
Mendoza, associates the casting of nets and love: "La red y el llanto sobre el mar tendía."

[48] Lope de Vega, *Obras escogidas*, II, 1583.

matic intent: it could stand tersely alone, its aim generally satirical
or epigrammatic, very often both; or it could — and more usually
did — stand as one of a number of stanzas making up a composition,
usually brief, concise and witty, of the kind that seventeenth-century
poets had learned to admire in Martial. In this second form Mendoza is often at his best, as the stanza's (and the poem's) brief com-
pass does not allow his wit too free a rein. The following verse from
a poem about a skinny female may be taken as an instance:

> Erase una señorita
> de hechura de cañamón,
> que del diacatolicón
> siempre casi necesita;
> en su airecito de pita
> más que alma tiene almarada,
> hecha de amor jeringada,
> en cuyo bebido rayo
> mira al buen gusto al soslayo,
> quiso fuese, y no hubo nada. [49]

The tautness here of image and word-play is significant, for although
these *décimas* vary greatly in subject from the numerous love poems
to a priapic eulogy, or an elegy, the style in general bears resemblance either to the metaphoric *conceptos* of the verse just quoted,
or to the parallelistic conceits of an epigrammatic stanza such as
this one to the Count-Duke as creator of the new palace of the
Retiro:

> Este edificio en tu acierto
> altamente fabricado,
> de todo esplendor poblado,
> de toda ambición desierto,
> fiel testigo, y nunca muerto
> será, de que nada en vano
> obrará tu soberano
> designio, y ingenio excelente,

---

[49] *MOP*, I, 311-313: *There was a young lady, a tiny little thing, almost always in
need of a purgative; with the look of a slender aloe she does not have a soul inside her
but a bodkin, made of love and syringed, in whose sharp-pointed ray she looks askance at
good taste. She tried hard, and nothing happened* [the last two lines refer to a famous
sonnet by Cervantes]. The clyster was a common source of amusing comment.

>   si donde pones la mente
>   *pusieras* también la mano. [50]   [*pusieres* in *PMS*]

Where a coincidence of style exists despite a wide variety of theme, the original association of the stanza form with epigrammatic and satirical verse may have led to the preservation of some of the latter's stylistic characteristics even in a quite different *décima* poem: thus what may have begun as an exercise in the *concepto* has drifted into a habit of *conceptismo*. Of the two kinds of epigrammatic style noted, the witty one is the less predominant, and what was more generally sought after may be deduced from a poem in answer to a specific request from the Count-Duke for a *concepto* to celebrate the King's birthday. The series of *décimas* opens thus:

>   Del Rey a los años bellos
>   va el concepto y por los dos
>   si ellos descansan en Vos
>   siempre Vos viváis en ellos.
>   Y a la par *gloriosa* de ellos   [*glorioso?*]
>   midan sus abriles tiernos
>   vuestros tempranos inviernos
>   que es bien en tanto alborozo
>   que os hagan sus años mozo
>   pues Vos los hacéis eternos. [51]

The poet obviously thought he was expected to perceive and develop an unusual, or striking, relationship containing that *picante* quality or *realce*, which Gracián later emphasized. The development was to be made with due attention to rhetorical devices such as parallelism, word-play, paradox and so forth. The present conceit has its basis in the interdependence of the King and his *privado*, in which each derives glory from the other, a notion which is then developed in three parallel, and paradoxical, statements: the King's years which "rest in peace" on the *privado's* shoulders are contrasted to the wish that the *privado* may "long live" to give service; the

---

[50] *MOP*, II, 64-65: *This edifice nobly built upon your right judgment, peopled with every splendour, deserted by every ambition, shall be a faithful and undying witness that your sovereign purpose and excellent genius will never work in vain, if where you put your mind you should also put your hand.*

[51] *MOP*, III, 200-201: *The* concepto *is to the King's fair years, and to both of you. If they rest upon you, may you always live in them. And likewise glorious through them, let their tender Aprils be the measure of your early winters, for it is proper in so much gaiety that his years [and his birthday] should make you young, since you make them eternal.*

monarch's tender spring should blossom in the solicitude of his adviser's early winter of wisdom; and if in the present festivities, the *privado* seems rumbustiously youthful, it must be remembered too that he guarantees his master's claim upon eternity.

This kind of *décima*, in which the whole stanza flows from an original conceit, is characteristic of Mendoza's practice. In a number of compositions, however, the initial conceit is the foundation on which a longer poem is built up. Such is the one that tells how a lady sent her lover a heart of crystal, telling him to take good care of it. The poet takes as his original conceit the idea that the woman's heart is itself like this hard crystal, a point of departure that affords an opportunity to develop ingenious paradoxes and subtle confusions. The opening stanza, making the point that what his beloved has really done is to send him her own hard heart, shows the kind of play in which the poet indulges:

> No fiáis, señora, mal,
> ni es aventurado el modo,
> por otro, que es alma todo,
> un corazón de cristal:
> no es copia, es original
> corazón tan duro, y frío,
> pero más alma, y más brío
> me *dirá* en el mal, que os muestro,   [*dará?*]
> tan muerto, y helado el vuestro,
> que tan encendido el mío. [52]

Gracián could have taken some examples of *conceptos por correspondencia y proporción* from this poem, as well he might have taken from another *décima* poem by Mendoza a few examples of the *agudeza de improporción y disonancia*, in which the poet brings out the opposition between the terms of the relationship he posits.[53] The subject here is the lady who preferred to look at a corpse rather than at the man who loved her. The initial conceit is twisted, turned, and seen from all angles, so that we may admire the poet's extraordinary ingenuity. As a good instance, let us take this verse which

---

[52] *MOP*, I, 277-278: *Lady, you do not either unwisely or rashly entrust in exchange for a heart that is all soul, another one of crystal: a heart so cold and so hard is not a copy but an original, but more soul and spirit will it give to me in this misfortune which I reveal to you, your heart being as dead and ice-cold as mine is aflame.*

[53] See chs. IV and V of the *Agudeza, GOC*, 245-259.

proclaims the lady's dominion even over death, and then deduces
from this that she has churlishly withdrawn her *imperium* from
the poet's own dead state:

En los fértiles y amenos
campos del morir, ¿quién nace
seguro?, ¿quién libre yace
de tus gloriosos venenos?
en los dilatados senos
del morir, ¿qué alma escondida
de ti vive?, y más rendida
la mía en amarte y verte,
si huyes tu vista a mi muerte,
niegas tu imperio a mi vida. 54

One notes here how the underlying paradox has triggered off
further ones: death's dominion is fertile and pleasant because it
receives the lady's attentions, yet within it are born (?!) men whose
freedom and security are threatened by the death-dealing poison
of the lady's heavenly beauty. This is a subtle poetry which gains
its effectiveness through the continuous current of the original conceit. In one sense, this type belongs to the same genre as the *poemas
en metáfora,* or the emblem: they share a central, proliferating, yet
organic conceit. Their difference from Mendoza lies in the latter's
dependence not on imagistic connexions but on discursive ones: the
framework is logical, even syllogistic. And his weakness in these
décimas lies in an inability to substitute, for the organic control of a
poem dominated and held together by a metaphor, an intellectual
control which would give to each stanza its proper, clear place in
the development of the whole.

Mendoza's *décimas* often betray the same triviality and carelessness as his *romances,* though the longer poems usually reveal some
concern for formal excellence. The predominant weaknesses spring
from the technique used: an over-elaboration of the conceit within
the discrete structure of the different stanzas, and a consequent lack
of organic form. Often too the pieces end, not because the compo-

---

54 *MOP,* I, 288-289: *In the fertile and pleasant fields of death, who is born safe?
Who is free of your glorious poisons? In the vast recesses of death, what soul can live
hidden from you? Whilst in my own soul's case, in greater submission, as it loves and
looks upon you, you deny your* imperium *over my life, if you avert your gaze from my
death.*

sition has reached its rounded close, but because the poet has discovered a better couplet than usual with which to mark the poem's conclusion. In consequence the reader is normally more aware of brilliant moments than of any concerted success. For instance it would be difficult to find a more outstanding case of Mendoza's highly concentrated and intellectualized art than the last stanza of a poem addressed to a lady who threw a snowball at her lover. The paradoxical coincidence of winter and summer in the snow of her hands and the fire of her eyes is here brought to its climax, and the basic assumptions and language of courtly love assume a new richness in the striking analogy between fire and ice in the alchemy of love, and in that of the elements:

> Nacen invierno, y verano
> de un cielo, y la tierra debe
> esto mismo en sol, y en nieve
> a tus ojos, y a tu mano:
> y tu cielo a quien en vano
> solicita mi dolor,
> de tu yelo, y de tu ardor
> introducido ha dejado
> en tu desdén lo nevado,
> y lo encendido en mi amor. [55]

But however satisfactory the stanza, the poem, overall, fails to convince.

Mendoza's most satisfying achievements with the *décima* are, not unexpectedly, in the single-stanza epigram. In conclusion let us consider two of these. The first typifies what may be called Martialesque inspiration, in the sense that we recognize in the occasion the sort of subject that Martial's wit immortalized. Yet Mendoza's treatment is very different from what we find in Baltasar de Alcázar, the most loyal imitator of Martial in Spanish. Alcázar's approach, like Martial's, is slow and cajoling, almost a sly, country humour. Mendoza's epigram by contrast (like Quevedo's, his nearest equivalent), is concise, trimmed to the bone, its form balanced, the

---

[55] *MOP*, II, 26-27. For title, see *PMS*, p. 124, "A una dama que le arrojo una pella de nieve": *Both winter and summer are born out of the same sky [=heaven, the lady], and earth owes this in sunshine and in snow to your eyes and your hand; and your heaven [=sky], whom my pain vainly implores, has left of its ice and its ardour the snow in your disdain and the fire in my love*. Hopewell Hudson, op. cit., p. 23, quotes a Latin epigram on this theme: the authorship is uncertain, but apparently ancient.

underlying *concepto* worked out in all its implications. The subject of the epigram is a cold woman who in fact burns with love for herself:

> Antandra, no es culpa leve
> que tanto fuego veamos
> en vos, y sólo tengamos
> noticias de vuestra nieve:
> si a vuestros labios se atreve
> el fuego en llama escondida,
> oh boca hermosa encendida
> de tanto ardiente clavel,
> avisaré a don Gabriel,
> que se quema la florida. [56]

The second *décima* is very different. It reveals the poet in one of his rare moments of moralizing, and its language and theme suggest the possible inspiration of Lipsius's *De constantia* and the classical legend of the Golden Age. Gracián admired this epigram, as well he might, for through paradoxical juxtaposition, and an extraordinary sensitivity to rhythm, Mendoza has transformed the trite into the definitive statement:

> Soledad, no hay compañía
> Mayor, donde el alma yace
> Consigo, y en ella nace
> Una verdad cada día:
> En esta breve armonía,
> Miro cuán breve reposa
> En un peligro la rosa,
> En un desmayo el jazmín:
> Y que sólo el alma al fin
> Permanece siempre hermosa. [57]

---

[56] *MOP*, II, 59-60. Antandra may be Bocángel's Antonia de Mendoza: *Antandra, it is not a trivial offence that we should note so much fire in you, having only evidence of your snow [=cold disdain]. If fire in a hidden flame dares to show itself at your lips, oh lovely mouth aflame with so much burning carnation [of your lips], I shall tell Don Gabriel that the flower lady is burning [la florida* may also indicate the American colony, subject to notorious depredations since the founding of St. Augustine in 1565].

[57] *MOP*, II, 203, reproducing text of the *Delicias de Apolo* (1670), gives as title "A la soledad de Nuestra Señora de Balma," whilst *PMS* (p. 536) says "En Alabanza de la Soledad." The poem also appeared in *Querer por solo querer* (*FC*, p. 359): *Solitude, there is no greater company, [than] where the soul keeps her own, and truth is born in her each single day. In this brief harmony I see how briefly the rose reposes in danger, the jasmin in a swoon, and that in the end only the soul remains always beautiful.* For Gracián's praise, see *Agudeza, GOC*, p. 293.

And like some of the other stanzas quoted, this one attests Mendoza's technical achievement with the *décima*. He stood in the same line as Vicente Espinel (whose *espinela* form he usually employed), yet the contrast between the two poets brings out Mendoza's skill. Espinel, who used the *décima* in courtly love poems glossing some *mote* or other (a form which Mendoza used, incidentally, only once), wrote in a cosy, smooth manner, trimming the poetic statement to the shape of the stanza:

> Vuestra voluntad me culpa,
> Y en biuo fuego me abraso,
> Pues sin relatarme el caso
> Me condenays a la culpa. [58]

Mendoza, in contrast, opens out the *décima*, elbowing his way through it with gusto and originality, changing its rhythm through bold *enjambement*, and introducing parallelisms that give the stanza shape rather than let it sag; and his material, however conventional, is treated as a challenge to brilliance.

SONNETS

"I wish to recite a sonnet, but do not dare, for each of these young ladies will ask for one." [59] Such arrogance suggests the literary lion: presumably Mendoza's sonnets, like his *romances* and *décimas,* were greatly appreciated. Certainly, he wrote a fair number of them, some seventy in all. But though the sonnet offered greater scope and range than the pastoral ballad or the *décima*, the poet's exercises afford scant opportunity to know Antonio de Mendoza more intimately: a few rather mawkish protests of loyalty to the Count-Duke; a promising love-poem to his second wife, in which *conceptista* sallies triumph eventually over what had seemed real affection; and a number of sonnets that express the poet's special

---

[58] Vicente Espinel, *Diversas rimas*, ed. Dorothy Clotelle Clarke (New York, 1956), p. 181: *Your will finds fault with me, and I burn in living fire. For without giving me the case-history, you condemn me to blame.* See also her "A note on the *décima* or *espinela*," *HR*, VI (1939), 155-158, and "Sobre la espinela," *RFE*, XXIII (1936), 293-304.

[59] *MOP*, III, 227: "Decir quiero un soneto, y no me atrevo, / que pedirá un soneto cada una."

devotion to the Virgin. [60] Occasionally, a moral preoccupation does find utterance: the withered elm fashionably comments on time's passing; a well-known sonnet expresses disillusion with the world, and the poet's search for solace in solitude. [61] But nowhere does he deal with that most popular of themes among his literary friends and contemporaries, death. There are indeed a number of other negative factors. We find sparse reference to classical themes or to mythology, even though these elements were very popular in the contemporary sonnet. And despite the coincidence in some regards between Quevedo's sonnets and those of Mendoza, subjects such as Quevedo's "A Aminta, que se cubrió los ojos con la mano" are lacking. Quevedo's opening lines:

> Lo que me quita en fuego, me da en nieve
> la mano que tus ojos me recata. [62]

have their equivalent in abundance among the poems dealt with earlier here, but for some reason Mendoza eschewed these topics in the sonnet form. It could be that he associated the witty octosyllable with this type of *conceptista* play, and reserved for the Italian hendecasyllable a more central feature of the Petrarchan tradition, a more solemn portrayal of the lover's posture before his beloved.

The sonnets divide roughly into three groups, the patriotic, the devotional and those that treat of love. A further division, commonly made in that age, suggests itself; the heroic, and the lyrical. The patriotic and religious muse called for a high style appropriate to the epic, whereas the lyrical vein, as in love poetry, could be content with the middle style, which offered more freedom, courting elegance at one moment, and skirting the colloquial at the next. Whereas the choice of an appropriate height of style was not an obvious concern in the compositions we discussed earlier, it was often so in the sonnet: the death of Gustavus Adolphus, or an address to Our Lady of Montserrat, required a more solemn voice and a diction at times enriched by learned words with their tell-tale dactylic

---

[60] *MOP*, III, 224 (e.g.), 223, and 253-255.

[61] *MOP*, II, 199, and 192.

[62] *QOCV*, p. 342: *The hand which hides from me your eyes, gives me, in snow, what it takes from me in fire.*

rhythm, or by an unusual word-order. Gustavus Adolphus's conquests, for example, are thus evoked:

> Segundo Atila penetró sediento
> de imperio justo el septentrión y ardiente
> los términos turbó del occidente
> armada tempestad, rayo sangriento. [63]

Not unexpectedly this and other patriotic poems have the same ringing eloquence as Fernando de Herrera's at the time of Lepanto, or as equivalent compositions by Mendoza's own contemporaries, Soto de Rojas, Salas Barbadillo, even Lope de Vega and Quevedo. Mendoza's sonnets in this vein can claim originality on one count: they were often written close to the personages or events they describe. For instance he extracted, rather ineffectively, some political capital out of the moment when Prince Charles of England, on a visit to the Spanish court, knelt during the celebration of Mass; or he marked Philip IV's entry into a masked ball in another piece. [64]

Most interest attaches to the poet's love sonnets and to his occasional treatment of a moral theme. Courtly love had lingered on in the sonnet as in the pastoral ballad. At this late date what surprises is the elaborately traditional treatment of the code in a poet like Villamediana, or in some of Quevedo. [65] In Mendoza there are clearer signs of impending change. Admittedly most of the sonnets from the play *Querer por solo querer,* which dealt with a chivalresque subject, are in the authentic tradition in so far as sentiment and posture are concerned:

> Amar quiero sin premio, y nunca puedo,
> que amar es premio: padecer querría,
> y el dolor tanto agrada el alma mía,
> que deste gusto escrupuloso quedo. [66]

---

[63] *MOP,* III, 218: *A second Attila, burning and thirsting for just dominion, he broke through the north, and disturbed the boundaries of the west, an armed tempest and a bloody thunderbolt.* Mendoza here and in the two other sonnets on this subject mixes admiration with hatred (*MOP,* III, 218-219), an attitude shared with his contemporaries (see J. M. Jover, *1635: Historia de una polémica,* p. 425).

[64] *MOP,* III, 228, and 234.

[65] See Otis H. Green, *Courtly Love in Quevedo* (Boulder, Colorado, 1952) and his *Spain and the Western Tradition,* I (Madison, 1963), 252-257.

[66] *MOP,* II, 190: *I wish to love with no prize, but cannot, for to love is itself a prize; I should like to suffer, but pain so pleases my soul that I feel scruples over this pleasure.*

But as in this case many poems veer away from emotional interest towards epigrammatic point. And in some cases, even when — as in a poem on self-torture — the lover's feeling is at its very maximum, it is not conveyed to the reader, since the poet's attention has been wholly given to rhetorical structure, or to sententious comment. [67] The characteristically sensuous appeal of the Garcilasan sonnet has given way to something different. Where feeling is produced in the reader it is kindled on reflexion, rather than conveyed there by sensorial means.

What is the nature of the underlying change? As was intimated in an earlier chapter, it is connected with the tendency to see the sonnet as an epigram. The structure of the Garcilasan sonnet, with its architectonic balance, its sensuous counterpointing, its smoothness of flow, may still be observed in Villamediana, Esquilache, and occasionally even in Góngora or Mendoza. But in Don Antonio, as in some of his other contemporaries, the sonnet appears at times to be moving towards different ends. In particular, there is a shift towards more rational discourse, towards that which Eliot, in relation to English metaphysical wit, memorably described as "a tough reasonableness beneath the slight lyric grace." [68] The discursive method was by no means entirely absent in the earlier sonnets — one thinks even of Garcilaso in this context — but now in Lope de Vega (who might well have been Mendoza's mentor), and in some of Lope's other contemporaries, a more deliberate use of this approach is found. The sonnet conveys frequently a reasoned argument brought to its culmination in the second tercet, or the closing line. In other instances, the earlier part builds up a picture, or series of pictures, whose epigrammatic point is displayed in the sonnet's conclusion. In all this, the reader's task has changed somewhat. He is now called upon to make sense of the detail and its epigrammatic significance in much the same way as his eye has learnt to make sense of the emblems of Alciati, Covarrubias or Ledesma. Not unnaturally, the sonnet's substructure has also been modified. In place of sensuous counterpoint ("cestillos blancos de purpúreas rosas") we find a balance of conceits ("aquella eterna

---

[67] Cf. Gracián's remark on Mendoza, "sentencioso como siempre" (*GOC*, p. 1236).

[68] T. S. Eliot, essay on Marvell, in *Selected Essays*, 2nd edn., reprinted (London, 1945), p. 293.

luz, que en llama breve"), and the sonnet's whole movement forward is determined by the pattern of argument, rhetoric, or wit. Put in rather different terms, this is a poetic style that reflects the vogue for Seneca and Tacitus, rather than the earlier vogue of the Ciceronian style.

Another important change is that of tone. Wilson's words in the *Arte of Rhetorique* (1560) concerning the low style, that it "goe plainly to worke, and speake altogether in common wordes" [69] may be applied more aptly to Lope de Vega's sonnets than to those of Mendoza, but in both poets there is an approximation to a conversational tone. In Mendoza's case this is seen more in the rhythm of the lines, the lack of end-stopping and the use of *enjambement* than in the choice of vocabulary, though at certain moments we find this as well:

> Quisiera yo quejarme, mas no creo
> que donde no se admiten tiernas quejas
> tengan enmienda justa mis agravios. [70]

Mendoza, however, should not be seen as the daring innovator. Though he is fond, for instance, of *enjambement,* he does not have recourse to it brazenly, as did Francisco de Rioja; nor does he break up his lines into brusque word-lists as frequently did Lope de Vega:

> Desmayarse, atreverse, estar furioso,
> Áspero, tierno, liberal, esquivo,
> Alentado, mortal, difunto, vivo,
> Leal, traidor, cobarde y animoso. [71]

Mendoza's liberties in contrast were taken with a certain solemnity and decorum. Another aspect of tone which both binds and separates Lope and his friend merits attention. Luis Rosales, in some memorable pages, attempted to define the essence of Garcilaso de la Vega's poetry, and its influence. He found it in Garcilaso's intimacy, his characteristic "transparencia al espíritu." Mendoza shared with his

---

[69] Quot. in Tuve, *Elizabethan and Metaphysical Imagery,* p. 232.

[70] *MOP,* III, 217: *I should like to complain, but I do not think that my offences would find just restitution where tender complaints are not admitted.*

[71] Lope de Vega, *Obras escogidas,* II, p. 73: *To swoon, to dare, to be angry, harsh, tender, generous, aloof, spirited, mortal, dead, live, loyal, treacherous, cowardly, and courageous.*

contemporaries their admiration for the Toledan poet, as he may indeed have reacted to the same intimate voice in the sonnets of Luis de Camoens, another prestige figure at this time. [72] That intimacy is heard again in Lope de Vega and some of his fellow artists: at moments we hear it too in Mendoza's sonnets, though often it is inhibited by solemnity of diction and rhetoric: despite the casualness of the rhythm, Mendoza's voice is more often of the pulpit than of the confessional.

But for all this, Don Antonio's most original contribution to the sonnet occurs where love's confession finds expression through a form dominated by keen intellectual control, and the desire to seek out antitheses and contrasts. The form itself prods the poet into looking sensitively and long at levels, or kinds, of experience that the older sonnet had ignored. And the poem's slow uncoiling through its various rhetorical stages reveals the complex and ambivalent experience which is love:

> Ojos del bien de amor, ricos y avaros
> si os miro no os turbéis, que si pudiera
> dejaros de mirar, no os ofendiera,
> que no me cuesta poco el enojaros.
> Mas si el alma se ocupa en contemplaros
> y de vuestra beldad la ley severa
> manda que mire, y que mirando muera,
> si miro y muero no debéis quejaros. [73]

So intimate here is the scene, so close to his beloved does the poet stand, that the reader is embarrassed to find himself an unintentional observer. In another sonnet the tone of voice, hushed and reverent, is at variance with the violence whose effects we see before our eyes:

> Tú que ignoras la oculta abierta herida
> que aun sangre tanta en estos rasgos vierte,

---

[72] See Luis Felipe Vivanco and Luis Rosales, *Antología de la poesía heroica del Imperio*, II, XVI *et seq.*, and Rosales, "La poesía cortesana," in *Studia philologica: homenaje ofrecido a Dámaso Alonso por sus amigos y discípulos...*, III (Madrid, 1963), esp. 290-302. Rosales (p. 302, Note) suggests how significant it is that Cervantes (see *Don Quixote*, Part 2, ch. LVIII) portrays a group intent on acting out eclogues by Garcilaso and Camoens. For Mendoza and Garcilaso, see p. 181.

[73] *MOP*, III, 217: *You, eyes, of love's treasure, rich and miserly, do not get troubled if I look at you, for if I could cease to look, I would not offend you, since to cause you annoyance means a lot to me. But if my soul is given over to contemplating you, and the severe law of your beauty commands me to look, and that by looking I die, if I look and die you must not complain.*

mira, que aun muda teme el ofenderte,
oye, que aun yace al daño agradecida.
Si curiosa, no digo enternecida,
quieres saber la mano hermosa y fuerte
a quien ira y dolor causa esta muerte,
esa es dueña y destrozo de mi vida. [74]

The spirituality of a few of these sonnets suggests their descent
from Salinas and Villamediana:

Si propia inclinación me lleva y guía
a tus divinos ojos celestiales

or: Cuerpo de tanto espíritu vestido. [75]

But the mature Mendoza, as in the two earlier quotations, is much
nearer Bocángel in interest and expression. What perhaps unites the
two poets more than anything else is their microscopic attention to
the relation between lover and beloved, as may be judged from the
opening of Bocángel's sonnet to the beginnings of love:

Venciste Filis; ya en el pecho mio,
oy la primer terneza se introduze,
y qual yelo en que el Sol infante luze,
llòro, mas con valor reuelde y frio.
Mengua mi obstinacion, no mi aluedrio,
que este afecto a que el hado me reduze,
no como ley, qual gusto se produze,
y si le doy lugar, no señorio. [76]

In comparison Mendoza suffers because often he sacrifices everything to the conceit, or pursues that conceit too inexorably, forgetting
the experience that it was intended to illuminate.

---

[74] *MOP*, III, 216: *You who know nothing of the hidden, open wound which still
pours out so much blood in these rents [and the pen flourishes of the verses?], just look,
for even when silent it [=the wound] fears to offend you, just listen, for it even feels
grateful for the harm inflicted. If out of curiosity (I do not say moved to pity), you
wish to know the strong and lovely hand to whom this death of mine causes anger and
sorrow, it is the mistress and destroyer of my life.*

[75] *MOP*, III, 242: *If an inward inclination takes and guides me towards your divine
and heavenly eyes;* and III, 239: *Body clothed in so much spirit.*

[76] *Obras*, I, 259-260: *You have conquered, Phyllis; already today the first tenderness
penetrates my breast, and like ice on which the infant sun shines, I weep, though with
a valour both rebellious and cold. It is my obstinacy and not my will that wanes, for
this affection to which fate subjects me, is felt not like a law, but like a pleasure, and if
I give way to it, I do not recognize its dominion.*

Mendoza's achievement in the sonnet form — and it is considerable — lies primarily in his skilful exploitation of the conceit. Let us examine first some characteristic points of departure, and then some of the devices used. In this examination Gracián, who quoted a number of Mendoza's sonnets, will help to bring us closer to the vantage point of the contemporary reader.

Since the conceit had its root in correspondence and relationship, its simplest form was a comparison — but one which possessed enough *realce* to raise it above the level of a mere rhetorical device. Thus in what may seem a rather obscure apostrophe to a heron, there is implied what Gracián termed a *semejanza conceptuosa* (conceitful simile) between a beautiful woman and that bird. The heron is told to stay with the poet, for in his love and respect she will be safe from the falcon's claws. [77] Mendoza elsewhere bids farewell to the litter that had carried him to Barcelona, and compares his embarrassingly uncomfortable journey through limbo with the condition of a claimant — whether to an appointment or to a woman's favour, it little matters (*MOP*, III, 226). Such comparisons, which spring from casual observation, either genuine or assumed, play a much more important role however in Lope de Vega's sonnets than they do here.

A different conceit sought to bring out the dissimilarity in the terms of comparison. In a sonnet earlier referred to, "A un amor secreto," the poet described a storm, but with the purpose of bringing out the contrast between an aggrieved Nature, and the lover's unprotesting constancy. [78] A poem to the leafless elm affords another example of this conceit. The tree's present state is contrasted with what it had been at the height of summer, a "flowering hyperbole." Gracián himself turned to the theme of the tree in autumn for examples of this *concepto por desemejanza* (conceit of dissimilarity) — it was a popular poetic theme, and an emblematic one. [79] Mendoza's own exercise in this vein might indeed have

---

[77] *MOP*, III, 229, and chapter X of the *Agudeza*.

[78] *MOP*, II, 191, text of *Querer por solo querer* (*FC*, p. 406). It has the title "A un amor secreto" in *PMS* (p. 265). Gracián, who quotes it (*GOC*, p. 294) as an example of a *concepto por desejemanza*, does not, surprisingly, draw on Lope de Vega, master of this conceit (e.g. *Poesías Líricas*, Clás. Cast., I, p. 236, "El ánimo solícito y turbado").

[79] *MOP*, II, 199: "hipérbole florido." See *GOC*, p. 292 and pp. 295-296, for Luis Carrillo de Sotomayor's "Enojo un tiempo fué tu cuello alzado" and Anastasio Pantaleón's "Tú que en la pompa ya de flores vana." For the leafless tree as emblem, see e.g. Praz, I, 87 and 104.

stood as the epigraph to an emblem, the moral *sententia* with which
it ends bringing it even nearer the emblematic tradition, when the
poet comments on the air's responsibility for the tree in its glory
as in its decline:

> De quien más me trató, quejarme puedo;
> mas ay, quién mejor que él matarme pudo:
> aire fué mi vivir, aire me quedo. [80]

The point is not that Mendoza drew on emblematic material, though
that may have been the case. Rather the coincidence here of the
emblematic and *conceptista* traditions illuminates what motivated
both emblem and conceit, since in this period man's visual experience was instinctively turned to moral and symbolic ends, the poet
or the emblematist finding meaningful conceits in comparing
actions or situations he had observed, with his own condition. This
pictorial approach links part of the English metaphysical tradition
with some of the Spanish *conceptista* poets: as George Herbert
pondered the similarity between the church floor and the human
heart, or Antonio de Mendoza the resemblance between a leafless
elm and certain truths about human life, the reader's attention is
directed to the poetic sleight of hand that goes on drawing further
dazzling conceits out of the grudging detail of the picture.

Only a short step separates the *conceptista* comparison from the
paradox, "a proposition as elevated as it is extravagant." The words
are Gracián's who took one of Mendoza's sonnets as an example. The
poem selected starts as a tirade against war, but at the opening of
the sextet, the reader to his astonishment discovers that the evocation
of this "barbarous law" has been merely the introduction to a
violent paradox, that war, despite all, is preferable to love:

> No quiero amor: más quiero dar despojos
> a la dura violencia de una espada,
> que a la blanda soberbia de unos ojos. [81]

---

[80] *MOP*, II, 199: *I can complain of the one who had most to do with me. But alas,
who better than he could kill me? My life was air, and air I remain.*

[81] *GOC*, p. 337 ("una propuesta tan ardua como extravagante"), which quotes this
sonnet as an example (*MOP*, II, 192-193): *I do not want love. I prefer to give my
attentions to the cruel violence of a sword rather than to the bland arrogance of a pair
of eyes* [*Despojos* (booty) was also used in the language of gallantry, cf. *BAE*, XLV,
p. 458: "yo admitiera despojos / De hombre de á pié?"].

A near relation of the paradox was a device termed by Gracián the "ingenious transposition." Here, within a certain set of circumstances, we come to what appears the wrong conclusion. So in a sonnet to Anarda on the death of her child, the dirge ends in a flirtatious compliment: since Anarda herself is heavenly, the child in dying has only exchanged one heaven for another. [82] What may seem to us a fundamental lack of proportion was frequently for the seventeenth-century reader the essence of a successful conceit.

Mendoza liked a form of *concepto* defined by Gracián as a "conceitful argument," tersely summed up in the sonnet's conclusion. [83] In one poem, having claimed that the fire from Lisi's eyes is greater than sun or volcano, greater too than could be extinguished by Arctic ice or even Lisi's icier hand, the poet concludes with this observation:

> Desengaño es sin queja a la esperanza
> que de Lisi el sujeto altivo hermoso
> no se pueda encender sino en sí mismo. [84]

This type of conceit is found also in Quevedo's sonnets, but characteristically the latter's *conceptos* are usually more outrageous in their brilliance. This technique of *epiphonema* or striking reflexion was taught in the schools as one of the resources of the epigrammatist, [85] and its place in the sonnet suggests the easy association of that form with the epigram.

But if there was room for the extravagant statement, the epigrammatist should not forget the homely and all-embracing truth. In the *sententia*, whose place was usually at the end of the sonnet, the poet's judgment seeks to go beyond the immediate context, and discover the wider truth: in this type of *agudeza*, said Gracián, "there come together ... liveliness of wit and sureness of judgment." [86] In one example Mendoza sums up the basis of the love code:

> ni hay más premio en amar que ser amante;

---

[82] "De las ingeniosas transposiciones," title of ch. XVII of the *Agudeza* (*GOC*, p. 311), and *MOP*, III, 240-241.

[83] Gracián, who entitled chapter XXXVI of the *Agudeza* "De los argumentos conceptuosos," mentioned its common use in concluding a sonnet (*GOC*, p. 410).

[84] *MOP*, III, 236: *It is for hope a disillusion (though an uncomplaining one) that the haughty, beautiful subject who is Lisi should only be able to catch fire in herself.*

[85] See Hopewell Hudson, pp. 4-6.

[86] *GOC*, p. 377: "concurren en ella [= operación] la viveza del ingenio y el acierto del juicio."

in another he reflects sententiously on the place of suffering in love:

> ¡Oh continua enseñada pesadumbre,
> sufrir sin novedad un triste amante,
> tanto debe un dolor a la costumbre! [87]

What of the more common devices in the sonnet's substructure? The poet could draw here not only on his reserve of wit and point, but on rhetorical usages admired in the compositions of the Silver Age as well as in the Fathers of the Church, and long taught as part of one's instruction in the art of writing. Of these devices the most important was antithesis, not only in the passing phrase ("esa es dueña y destrozo de mi vida" [*MOP*, III, 216]), but in concentrated groups, such as in the opening lines of a poem on the death of Prince Charles:

> Aquella eterna luz, que en llama breve
> sin años, siglos fué de resplandores. [88]

At other times antithesis is built into the structure of the entire sonnet. Such is the case when Mendoza brings out the contrast in all the things that surround his love: body, spirit; victor, vanquished; fire, cold; tenderness, harshness (*MOP*, III, 239).

If the antithesis commended itself because of its potential for extravagance, there was room also for parallelism, a gentler form of conceit. It claimed the reader's attention by its formal balance and appropriateness, and in the best examples the subtlety of meaning would not be fully expressed until the parallelism was complete. Sometimes, it could engage a whole sextet, or even an entire sonnet, and in such instances syntactical parallelism (e.g. three protases that correspond to three apodoses) takes the place of that based on substantives, or adjectives. It is the latter kind, however, that is most usual, and most pleasing. Here, for example, Mendoza, in addressing Spain, attempts to epitomize Philip IV's achievements in rescuing her from misery:

> te libra fuerte, sabio te acompaña
> valor divino, genio soberano. [89]

---

[87] *MOP*, III, 246: *nor is there more prize in love than being a lover;* and *MOP*, II, 192: *Oh continuous and well-trained sadness, for a sad lover to suffer in the ordinary way of business, so much does sorrow owe to habit.*

[88] *MOP*, III, 234. See also Note 94.

[89] *MOP*, III, 224-225: *there frees you by his strength, there accompanies you in his wisdom, a divine courage and a sovereign genius.*

This particular form of parallelism is very characteristic of Góngora's sonnets, even in his earliest period, and was to a large extent a logical outcome of the natural hemistichal balance of the hendeca-syllable, and the exploitation of time-honoured rhetorical adornment. What characterizes Mendoza's (or Góngora's) use of these features is not therefore the novelty, but the self-conscious deliberation with which they are applied.

Consonance or word-echo — for Gracián the epitome of the *agudeza* — [90] plays some part in Mendoza's sonnets. To list a few:

1. de mis sentidos: ay si desatados   (*MOP*, III, 255-256)

2. ver con saña el albor y el sol con ceño   (*MOP*, III, 235)

3. manda que mire, y que mirando muera,
si miro y muero no debéis quejaros   (*MOP*, III, 217)

Both the theme and the verbal play in the last example conforms to the practice of the Castilian *Cancionero* poets of the fifteenth century, and Mendoza's use of them brings to mind the point earlier made that some seventeenth-century poets deliberately emulated what they recognized as time-honoured *conceptos*. But Lope too, as Sr. Montesinos commented, made clear the view that however admirable was the traditional verse of the peninsula, the newer Italianate poetry was ultimately superior, and more artistic. [91] It may well be that, in the example quoted, archaism blended with a similar sense of superiority: if Mendoza was acknowledging the troubadour poet, he was at the same time putting him in his place, a niche in a predominantly Italianate design.

Lastly, reference must be made to another type of word-play, the *ingenioso equívoco* or pun. Except for long established puns like *hierro* — *yerro*, or *estrella* in the sense of star and fate, Mendoza's sonnets are not rich in this form of conceit. One again recalls Gracián's assertion that the *ingenioso equívoco* belonged to the

---

[90] This is Gracián's "agudeza por paronomasia, retruécano y jugar del vocablo," title of ch. xxxii of the *Agudeza*.

[91] Montesinos, *Estudios sobre Lope*, pp. 121-122.

world of burlesque rather than to serious poetry. [92] If the use of the witty style in the *pintura* suggested that Gracián's affirmation was too dogmatic, the evidence of Mendoza's sonnets certainly suggests that there was in it a basic truth.

In conclusion two of Mendoza's sonnets, both splendid, both different from each other, are given in full. The first, a poem to solitude, is probably his best-known, for it has found a place in the anthologies. Gracián cited it as an example of the virtue of variety in art: certainly the alternation of antitheses, parallelisms, paradoxes, and other subtleties awaken admiration, as does the way in which they are tied into an organic whole. But the impact of the poem is largely moral. However reminiscent the theme and language may be of the classical *tranquilla quies,* the traditional view of the corruptive influence of the "purpura regum" explains only part of the attitude adopted, and we sense that the poet was also giving expression to a personal disillusion with life at the court of Philip IV:

> Amable soledad, muda alegría,
> que ni escarmientos ves, ni ofensas lloras,
> segunda habitación de las auroras,
> de la verdad primera compañía.
> Tarde buscada paz del alma mía,
> que la vana inquietud del mundo ignoras,
> donde no la ambición hurta las horas,
> y entero nace para un hombre el día.
> ¡Dichosa tú, que nunca das venganza,
> ni de Palacio ves con propio daño
> la ofendida verdad de la mudanza,
> la sabrosa mentira del engaño,
> la dulce enfermedad de la esperanza,
> la pesada salud del desengaño! [93]

---

[92] See p. 85.

[93] *MOP*, II, 192, text of *Querer por solo querer* (*FC*, p. 413). Also *PMS*, p. 263: *Lovable solitude, quiet happiness, that does not need to profit by others' mistakes, nor weep at the offences it suffers, second dwelling-place of the dawn, truth's chosen company. Tardily sought peace of my soul, that knows nothing of the vain anxieties of the world, where ambition does not thieve the hours, and day is born whole for every man. Happy are you, who never take revenge, nor see at the Palace (to your detriment) the offended truth of someone's change of mind, the tasty lie of deception, the sweet sickness of hope, the tiresome [and so boring] health of disillusion.* Cf. Polo de Medina's *Ocios de la Soledad* (1633): "todas las horas vivirás iguales, / y en soledad, que es toda compañía, / desde que nace vivirás el día" (*Obras escogidas*, ed. Cossío, p. 275). For Gracián's comments, see *GOC*, pp. 240-241.

This poem, which may have first been heard at the performance of *Querer por solo querer*, is not technically adventurous, for it follows the natural contours of the sonnet form. The second example belongs to a later period, and was written to commemorate the death of Philip IV's brother, Prince Charles, in 1632. The approach to the sonnet and to the use of *conceptos* is much bolder. If the structure of the earlier piece is static, then this one is dynamic: as in some of his *décimas*, the poet seeks elbow-room within the poetic form. The technique remains that of antithesis, parallelism, paradox and the rest, but they are here used more outrageously. The language too is crisper, its rhythms more abrupt, the expression more abstract. Built on a series of antitheses that result from the initial paradoxes of death in youth, and eternity in time, the sonnet's conflict of opposites is sustained right up to the last tercet, in which the poet speaks of triumph in obedience, and of honour achieved in setting aside the realization of one's princely hopes:

> Aquella eterna luz, que en llama breve
> sin años, siglos fué de resplandores,
> entre sombras, espantos, entre errores
> sus lucimientos a lograr se atreve.
> En abriles bellísimo de nieve
> aun más Fénix de glorias que de flores
> a tantas suyas (más cuanto mayores)
> la misma eternidad tiempo les debe.
> Y en su semblante respiró lo humano,
> que en sus virtudes, todas evidencias,
> no supieron mentir las confianzas.
> En cuanto corazón triunfó su mano
> y a los pies de Felipe, en obediencias
> pobló de honor, de fe, sus esperanzas. [94]

---

[94] *MOP*, III, 234: *That eternal light, which in a brief flame was, without years, centuries of splendours, among shadows, horrors, errors, dares to show its shining successes. In Aprils most beautifully clad in snow* [= contrast between youth and experience], *even more a Phoenix in glories than in flowers, to so many of his glories (but how much greater ones!) does eternity herself owe a debt of time. And in his face there breathed that human understanding which the possession of confidences did not succeed in hiding in his virtues, there for all to see* [?]. *His hand triumphed in so far as it was heart, and at Philip's feet, in obedience, he clothed his hopes [of succession?] in honour and in faith.* On Prince Charles, see Marañón, *passim.* Mendoza's excessive praise for a dull-witted prince may seem surprising, but BM *Eg. MS*, ff. 172-202v, *Las Señas del S. Infante que esté en el Zielo*, shows that out of sincerity or political subtlety the poet sought to glamorize the dead Prince, as well as to show up the cordiality of the Count-Duke's relations with him.

This composition may be regarded as one of the best, and most advanced, examples of the seventeenth-century Spanish poet's concept of the sonnet as epigram. If part of its inspiration came from Martial and the *Greek Anthology*, and part from the concision of Silver Age Literature, its achievement nevertheless lies in its having taken the natural qualities of the epigrammatic form to a limit never foreseen by the classical masters.

VI

VIDA DE NUESTRA SEÑORA

W H E N Mendoza's *Vida* appeared posthumously at Seville in 1666, it did so owing to the good offices of the author's nephew, Antonio de Salcedo Hurtado de Mendoza, Marquis of Legarda. The poem was unfinished, and its editor has preserved the poet's note of an intention to make certain further additions. Certain stanzas which had been left unplaced at the end of the manuscript were furthermore incorporated into the text "where they have seemed most opportune." The editor, probably rightly, concluded that the *Vida* had never been given its "final polishing." [1]

These circumstances have led to the belief that the *Vida* was Mendoza's last work: Miguel Manescal for instance, editor of *El Fénix castellano,* described it as the "last gentle divine breath of that courtly swan," a view that receives apparent confirmation from some stanzas at the beginning of the poem:

> Yo que en desperdicios viles
> tanto traté, como ajenos,
> a mis años, que de tantos
> ni un solo instante me debo.
> Cobre ya de mí este solo,
> último advertido aliento. [2]

These lines at the very least evoke a man burdened with years and convinced of his closeness to death. Yet the evidence suggests that the poem, or at least the bulk of it, had existed long before the poet's death in 1644. Certainly Lope de Vega had seen the *Vida* in some shape or form by August 1628, when he commented on a copy which

---

[1] *MOP* (I, 44-141) reproduces the text of the 1666 edition, to which reference is made here. Where other texts suggest better readings, the variant has been noted alongside the quot. For the 1666 editor's comments, see I, 139-140.

[2] *MOP*, I, 48: *May I — who in vile squandering dealt with my years as someone else's property to such degree that with so many of them to my credit, I do not owe a single instant to myself — at last make on myself the charge of this last, sole, conscious(?) breath?* Manescal in his letter to the reader (see *MOP*, I, 146) refers to the "último suave divino aliento de aquel cortesano cisne."

he had requested the author to send him. Lope did not stint his praise: his only complaint was that, being unfinished, the poem as it were gets called away at the wrong moment:

> By that same Lady that obliged you to write it, pray steal (even though it be from His Majesty, whom God defend) a few hours to finish it: for human Majesty will surely put up with such neglect in order to do this service to a divine One. [3]

The context makes quite clear that the poem (though not referred to by title) was the *Vida,* and if the words "a few hours" are not a flatteringly optimistic assessment, the work, though unfinished, was not far from a completed state. Corroboration of the *Vida's* existence around this period is provided by Pérez de Montalbán, who referred to it in his *Para todos* (1632). [4] The only way to reconcile Mendoza's allusion to the weight of years with the evidence for a much earlier date of composition is either to assume that the poet wrote at some time in the late twenties, when death had seemed near to him; or more probably, that towards the end of his life he was still working on the poem, to which he added the stanzas quoted earlier. [5]

The poem (which even in its uncompleted form contained over 780 stanzas in ballad metre) was certainly Mendoza's most popular work, known to a considerable audience long before it appeared in print. Apart from the copies seen by Lope and Montalbán, that used by Gracián in the forties in compiling the first version of his *Agudeza* (1642), and the eight manuscripts noted by Benítez Claros, there are a further four copies in the Hispanic Society Collection in New York, another in a Parisian manuscript, and two (one complete, and one a fragment) in the Bodleian Library. The abundance of copies is further suggested by the fact that the copyist of the Hispanic Society *MS* B2414 corrected his text by reference to "various manuscripts," and that some of the texts, when compared with the 1666 Seville edition, suggest a rich and different manuscript tradition. [6]

---

[3] See Lope de Vega, *Epistolario,* IV, 101-102.

[4] See Juan Pérez de Montalbán, *Para todos. Exemplos morales humanos y divinos* (ed. Huesca, 1633), f. 55 of first series.

[5] Gracián may have preserved a tradition when he states in the *Agudeza* that Mendoza "comenzó, y parece que desconfió de poderlo acabar" (*GOC*, p. 449). But Gracián averred that the poet finally returned to his task, and completed it.

[6] For bibliography, see *MOP,* I, xviii *et seq.*, pp. 324-327 here, and *Hisp. Am. Cat.,* II, 246-247; later ref. to *MS HC* 411,27, a volume of *varios,* in *Hisp. Am. Cat.,* I, 160-166.

The printed version of 1666 led to wider acclaim. Though ten thousand copies were printed, these proved unequal to the demand, and in 1672 a further edition appeared in Naples. The work also reached a possibly different kind of public in the lyrical collection *Delicias de Apolo* (1670). Meanwhile the *Vida* had appeared in Mexico in 1668, the editor claiming that the poem had "achieved the applause of Europe, and was now being sought by the desires of America"! Subsequent European editions appeared in Madrid (1682) and Pamplona (1688). The poem was incorporated in the *Fénix castellano,* appeared in Valencia (1710), Milan (1723), and was finally reprinted in the text of the *Obras líricas y cómicas* (1728). A significant pointer to the poem's devotional, as distinct from its literary, value is the fact that those responsible for the editions of Naples, Madrid (1682), Pamplona and Valencia did not shrink from adding new material to the text for the greater edification of the readers. A further indication of its use in the practice of piety is its inclusion in Hispanic Society of America *MS HC* 411,27, a very large seventeenth-century collection of devotional and contemplative poetry.

The *Vida* was the product of two forces, one personal, the other social. Various poems indicate Mendoza's particular devotion to the Virgin, especially perhaps to Our Lady of Montserrat whom he regarded as having preserved him from error in his sexual life:

> borró la heroica fuerza de tus manos
> del yerro, y del incendio aun las señales. [7]

This was perhaps the obligation to which Lope de Vega referred in his letter of 1628 to the poet. But the poem was also part of the great tradition of Marian devotion that blossomed as a consequence of the Counter-Reformation. The interest was further stimulated by the controversy in the early seventeenth century over the Immaculate Conception. During the years 1615-1619 feasts in honour of the *Inmaculada* had been held in Seville, Granada and Baeza; Lope de Vega's *La limpieza no manchada* was commissioned by Salamanca University in 1618; and Mendoza himself referred to the spirited defence of the Virgin's "sagrada limpieza" made by Bishop

---

[7] *MOP*, III, 253: *the heroic power of your hands wiped out the marks of the branding-iron (of sin) and even of the fire.* See also *MOP*, II, 182-183, 187-188, and III, 243.

Jerónimo Bautista Lanuza. [8] Other poems in this period were written in Spain in Mary's honour: Baltasar Elisio's *Limpia concepción de la Virgen Señora Nuestra* (1618), Alonso de Bonilla's *Nombres y atributos de la ... Virgen* (1624), and Sebastián de Nieva Calvo's *La mejor mujer, madre y virgen* (1625). Most famous of all was José de Valdivielso's *Excelencias y muerte del glorioso patriarca y esposo de Nuestra Señora, San Joseph*, first published in 1604, and which by 1659 had gone through twenty-seven editions. But in addition to these long poems there were innumerable short lyric pieces like those by Lope de Vega in his *Pastores de Belén* (1612), Valdivielso, Ledesma, and Antonio de Mendoza himself.

One major factor sets Mendoza's *Vida* apart from the longer poems mentioned. The latter belong to the tradition of religious epic in Spain, and the treatment, style, even the use of the *octava rima* stanza, conform to the accepted pattern. A typical instance is the opening of Nieva Calvo's poem:

> La mejor muger canto, que dar pudo
> por Madre al mayorazgo, el Dios ama[n]te,
> la Torre de marfil, el fuerte Escudo,
> el Norte fixo, y Luna sin menguante. [9]

Mendoza's poem, despite its length, was essentially a lyrical work.

In his account of the Virgin's life from her Immaculate Conception to the *Transitus*, Mendoza incorporated an unusual mixture of elements. He showed a sound knowledge of Scripture, but also introduced traditional accounts like that of St. Joseph's jealousy; he was anxious to make incidental comment on the theological disputes concerning the Immaculate Conception, and to refer to Saint Ildefonsus's views on the *Transitus Mariae;* and he also introduced, in a strangely effective way, a parallel between Christ's childhood exile in Egypt, and Pompey's flight there after his defeat by Julius Caesar at the battle of Pharsalus, the latter account probably based on Book VIII of Lucan's *Pharsalia*. But the main part of the poem

---

[8] For Marian devotion see K. Vossler, *La poesía de la soledad en España* (Buenos Aires, 1946), p. 28. For Lanuza, see *MOP*, I, 53-54: he was author of *Homilias sobre los Evangelios* (Barbastro, 1621). See also P. Ángel Uribe, "La Inmaculada en la literatura franciscano-española," *Archivo Ibero-Americano*, 2ª época, XV (1955), 201-495, and T. D. Kendrick, *St. James in Spain* (London, 1960), esp. ch. VI, "The Marian War."

[9] Sebastián de Nieva Calvo, *La mejor muger, madre, y virgen* (Madrid, 1625), f. 1: *I sing the best woman that the loving God could give as mother to His eldest son, the ivory tower, the strong shield, the fixed north, and waneless moon.*

was built around the traditional stages in the Virgin's life, each one being elaborated lyrically, and with a devotional purpose in mind.

From the mid-sixteenth century onwards spiritual exercises and meditative devotions were given a new impetus by the Counter-Reformation. [10] St. Francis of Sales defined meditation as "an attentive thought iterated, or voluntarily intertained in the mynd, to excitate the will to holy affections and resolutions." Such a discipline was directed to the life of both Christ and the Virgin, in the first place through "imaginarie representation" to re-create some central aspect of the religious mystery, to reflect upon its truth, and ultimately to translate that truth into action. Louis L. Martz, in seeking to show how this discipline was reflected in English poetry of the late sixteenth and early seventeenth century, argued that the characteristic movement of the meditative poem was "a manner which deliberately evolves a subtle fusion of passion and thought, of concrete imagery and theological abstraction, presented in a sequence of articulated, climactic structure." [11] The possibility of a similar relation and influence must be borne in mind in examining Mendoza's *Vida*. At the same time it must be remembered that in the Spanish tradition meditative techniques had influenced poetry at a much earlier date, as may be judged from Ambrosio de Montesino's poetry, in which we find sections entitled "Contemplación" or "Contemplativa interrogación," and where the text is interspersed with prayer. More indicative of the influence of the kind of techniques to which Martz drew attention was the deliberate attempt, paralleled in the medieval exegetic tradition, of making the reader visualize some aspect of Christ's suffering, presumably as a preliminary to meditation. Montesino, for instance, having made his reader visualize the scourging of Christ, goes on to compose this prelude, and incentive, to meditation:

> La fuerza mas poderosa
> Que ata y encarcela,
> No es, mi Dios, soga nudosa,

---

[10] See general account in Louis L. Martz, *The Poetry of Meditation: A Study in English Religious Literature of the Seventeenth Century*, 2nd edn. (New Haven, 1962), p. 4 *et seq.*, and Pierre Pourrat, *Christian Spirituality*, trans. W. H. Mitchell and S. P. Jacques, 3 vols. (London, 1922-1927).

[11] Quots. and refs., in Martz, p. 15, p. 30 and p. 34. Martz's summary, made in relation to poems by Robert Southwell, is on p. 83.

Mas caridad espantosa,
Que nuestros males asuela. [12]

Mendoza's work, here as elsewhere, must be judged in the light of both what was old and new.

The Jesuit Order had deliberately stimulated the adoration of Mary as a means of deepening the religious experience of the people. [13] The traditional Sodalities of the Virgin, whose members bore a particular loyalty to her, assumed a new importance. The Sodalites' devotions were helped by treatises such as Gaspar Loarte's *Meditationes de Rosario Beatae Virginis* (Venice, 1573), or the older *Rosario della gloriosa vergine Maria* (Venice, 1522) by Alberto Castello. In Spain a text such as *El Rosario de Nuestra Señora la virgen María, y la manera de rezar los quince Misterios del Rosario* (Barcelona, 1591) sought like Robert Southwell's *Moeoniae* (1595) to place poetry at the disposal of religion, being in this case specifically aimed at "any sodalite *(confrade)* of our Lady of the Rosary, or any person that has devotion in the said holy Rosary." [14] The poems, some very simple *coplas*, were linked to the traditional meditations of the Rosary on the five joyful, the five dolorous, and the five glorious Mysteries of the Virgin. The verses were to be recited along with an appropriate prayer (also given in the book) for each Mystery, followed by one Paternoster, and ten Avemarias. The whole devotion was, if possible, to be said every day. [15] Martz has argued that much religious poetry of the period — as for instance Southwell's *Sequence on the Virgin Mary and Christ* or Donne's *Corona* — originated in Marian devotion, and had been influenced by it. Martz remarked

[12] See *Romancero y cancionero sagrados*, ed. Justo de Sancha, in *BAE*, XXXV, p. 415 and p. 417, quot. on p. 416: *The force most powerful to bind and imprison Thee is not, my God, a knotted rope, but a frightening love which burns up our sins.*

[13] See Martz, p. 96 *et seq.* On the history of the Rosary and the methods of devotion, see Herbert Thurston, "Our popular Devotions. II — The Rosary," *The Month*, XCVI (1900), 403-418, 513-527, 620-637, and XCVII (1901), 67-79, 172-188, 286-304, 383-404. The fifteen Mysteries [see Thurston, XCVI (1900), 620-632] were Annunciation, Visitation, Nativity, Presentation, Finding of Christ in the Temple; Gethsemane, Scourging, Crown of Thorns, Carrying of the Cross, Crucifixion; Resurrection, Ascension, Coming of the Holy Ghost, Assumption, Coronation.

[14] *El Rosario*, in *Cancionero de Nuestra Señora en el qual ay muy buenos romances, canciones y villancicos* (1591), ed. Valencia, 1952, prologue by Antonio Pérez Gómez, p. 99 *et seq.*: "qualquier confrade de nuestra Señora del Rosario, o qualquier persona que tuuiere devocion en el dicho sancto rosario." That this Sodality may have been connected with Our Lady of Montserrat is suggested by a poem in the accompanying *Cancionero*, "Laberinto a Nuestra Señora de Monserrate": in such a case Mendoza's devotion to this Virgin may indicate a connexion with this particular confraternity.

[15] *El Rosario*, p. 101.

of the Southwell poems that they possessed no organic development
but were rather "three or four witty, pious meditations on a given
mystery;" he remarked too on the similarity between such stanzaic
division and the meditative technique recommended by Loarte,
which divided each Mystery into three individual points which the
Christian might ponder. [16] We shall later examine to what extent
Mendoza conforms to such practice.

But even though the *coplas* of the *Rosario* and the *Vida* are both
the fruits of Marian devotion, Mendoza's poem is in contrast witty
and sophisticated, much more closely related to Crashaw's *Epigrammata sacra* (1634). Mario Praz, probably rightly, derived the latter
from a tradition of Jesuit sacred poetry. He argued also that Alonso
de Ledesma's riddling verses *Epigramas y hieroglíficos a la vida de
Cristo* (1625) were more naïve examples of the same art. [17] Accepting
the possible ultimate relevance of Jesuit poetry, the source of inspiration in Mendoza's case was more probably Ledesma than any
contemporary Latin tradition: the Ledesma of the much earlier
Conceptos espirituales as well as that of the *Epigramas*. Ledesma's
religious conceit is typified by his comment on Mary Magdalene's
hair, in which the liturgical image of the *Vexilla regis* of Christ's
Passion is daringly associated with Mary's display of love for her
Master:

> Hizo vandera el amor
> Maria de tus cabellos,
> y agora viene a ponellos
> a los pies del vencedor.
> Iusto es que postre por tierra
> las vanderas que arboladas,
> tendidas y desplegadas
> hizieron contra Dios guerra. [18]

Ledesma's brazenness is shown too in a conceit about St. Stephen,
who, showing good taste in dying for God, was the man who found

---

[16] See *The Poems of Robert Southwell, S. J.,* ed. James H. McDonald and Nancy
Pollard Brown (Oxford, 1967), and John Donne, *The Divine Poems,* ed. Helen Gardner
(Oxford, 1952), pp. 1-5. See Martz, p. 102.

[17] See *The Flaming Heart,* p. 214. On the difficulty of 'explaining' *concettista* poetry
merely by reference to tradition, see Empson's remark (in Martz, p. 92) that making
explicit, characteristics already found e.g. in the liturgy, was in itself possibly even
"worth calling a new style."

[18] *Conceptos espirituales,* pp. 327-328: *Love made a banner, Mary, of your hair, and
now comes to place it at the victor's feet. It is right that love should prostrate on the
ground those banners which, hoisted and unfurled, made war against God.*

the honey inside the lion of death that Samson, Christ, had slain. [19] The practical devotional value of such witticisms is suggested in some words by a brother of the Order of St. Bernard, who in a prologue to Ledesma's *Juegos de Noche Buena* (1611) praised "such subtle conceits, such finespun thoughts, such profitable discourses," by which presumably the reader was prompted to think afresh of the groundwork of his religion. [20]

Mendoza's *Vida*, like Southwell's *Sequence*, probably represents the coming together of two distinct, but not unrelated currents, that of popular Marian devotion and that of a more learned literary tradition. [21] But unlike the *Sequence* or the *coplas* of the *Rosario*, the *Vida* does not fit a particular pattern of devotion, though it incorporates the fifteen Mysteries. Of these only the Crowning of the Virgin (which the poet would presumably have reached in the completed poem) is absent, the rest being dealt with in turn, usually accompanied by an explicit marginal reference. The *Vida* too, with only sparse treatment of Christ's ministry, moves from the fifth joyful Mystery (The Finding of Christ in the Temple) to the first of the dolorous Mysteries (Gethsemane), as though the poet's plan were affected by a traditional schema of the Virgin's life.

However, if we look for the kind of point by point meditations that Martz described, we may conclude that Mendoza's elaboration of an individual Mystery is sometimes too extensive to have served as a meditative exercise. Nevertheless, he did preserve the aim mentioned by Loarte of making, under each heading, a number of points, rather than producing an organic composition. [22] And in the treatment of a few of the Mysteries the pattern corresponds more closely to that suggested by Martz. Christ's Resurrection, for instance (fifth of the Dolorous Mysteries), has only five *cuartetas*, in which two main points are made. The first runs thus:

---

[19] *Conceptos*, pp. 283-284. The conceit of the lion and the honey may owe something to Alciati's emblem (see p. 70 here).

[20] Alfonso de Ledesma, *Juegos de Noche Buena moralizados a la vida de Christo* (Madrid, 1611), prelim. ¶4, letter from Fray Lorenço de Zamora: "conceptos tan agudos, pensamientos tan delgados, discursos tan prouechosos."

[21] See Martz, p. 103: "the continental art of the sacred epigram (as found in Crashaw's *Epigrammata Sacra*) is combined with meditation on the life of Christ after the manner suggested by Southwell's fellow-Jesuit for meditation by the rosary."

[22] In Martz, p. 102.

11

> Resucita de sí mismo,
> no cual Fénix heredero
> de sus cenizas, que sólo
> de su amor se formó el fuego.
> Que unidamente a sí propio
> se volvió, tomando entero
> su ser, en el ya cobrado
> triunfante, glorioso cuerpo. [23]

Such distillation of theological concepts into poetic thought is singularly apt for meditation. The mind, having responded to the visual image of the Phoenix rising from its ashes, is invited to participate in a breathless perception of God's deeper mystery in the return of the Son of God to the Father.

Mendoza's possible debt to traditional exegesis of Scripture must be discussed, in the hope of discovering the extent to which his poetic practice responded to a *conceptismo* present in much older material. The *Vita Christi* of Ludolph of Saxony, who died in 1377, forms a useful comparison. "A mosaic structure which draws on a host of earlier writers, incorporating whole passages from other works," this voluminous text provided direct inspiration for Juan de Padilla's *Retablo de la Vida de Cristo,* and was a possible influence on Íñigo de Mendoza's *Vita Christi,* both works in the direct line of ascent from Antonio de Mendoza's poem. [24] Ludolph's work had also in part a contemplative purpose, another link with the poetry of Padilla, Íñigo de Mendoza, and Diego de San Pedro's *Pasión trobada.*

An examination of key-scenes found in both Ludolph and Mendoza suggests more differences than similarities. The various interpretative techniques, moral, allegorical, and anagogic, certainly created a host of potential conceits, but Antonio de Mendoza drew

---

[23] *MOP,* I, 126: *He is resurrected of Himself, not like a Phoenix the heir to his own ashes, for the fire was made only of His love. He returned in oneness to Himself, taking possession of His entire being in His now recovered, triumphant and glorious body.*

[24] See K. Whinnom, "The Supposed Sources of Inspiration of Spanish Fifteenth-Century Narrative Religious Verse," *Symposium,* XVII (1963), 269. For an account of the religious revival of the fifteenth century, see Albert Hyma, *The Christian Renaissance: A History of the "Devotio Moderna,"* 2nd edn. (Hamden, Connecticut, 1965). For the exegetic tradition's survival into the sixteenth century, see e.g. E. Ph. Goldschmidt, *Medieval Texts and Their First Appearance in Print* (London, 1943), on the dissemination of the Pseudo-Bonaventure *Meditationes,* reprinted some fifty times after 1500 (pp. 47-48); and Sister Mary Immaculate Bodenstedt, *The Vita Christi of Ludolphus the Carthusian* (Washington, 1944), esp. pp. 18-23. "Since 1472 more than sixty editions" were printed in various cities of Germany, France, Italy and Belgium (p. 19). The Spanish translation appeared in Alcalá in 1502-3.

much more frequently from his own imagination, or possibly at times from suggestions in Alonso de Ledesma, than from exegetic tradition. However, he certainly seemed conscious of the latter, and drew upon it occasionally. We may judge for instance by the treatment of Christ in the hands of his captors. Ludolph wrote: "quanto magis poenale fuit Christo, qui est dominus coeli et terrae, et quem coeli, et terra capere non poterant, violentorum quantum ex parte ipsorum erat, manibus capi et teneri." [25] This paradox inspired a *concepto* at two points in the *Vida*, firstly in the corresponding section of the poem:

¡Qué asombro! ¡Que Dios se mire
de los hombres prisionero! [26]

The paradox is then echoed in the Passion story, more emphasis being given this time to Christ's dominion over Heaven and Earth. [27]

Ludolph affirmed in his treatment of the Circumcision that this was the first of the six occasions when Christ spilled His blood for us: it was the "redemptionis initium," and furthermore "Non solum in virili, sed etiam in infantili aetate sanguinem suum pro nobis voluit fundere." [28] The anticipation of Christ's Passion is implicit in Southwell's and Crashaw's treatment of the theme: the former says that "with angring salve it smarts to heal our wound"; the latter in a Latin epigram (and even more in the English version) emphasizes the sacramental implications by inviting us to drink of Christ's blood. [29] Antonio de Mendoza in comparison is more theologically precise:

[25] *Vita Jesu Christi e quattuor evangeliis et scriptoribus orthodoxis concinnata per Ludolphum de Saxonia ex ordine Carthusianorum* (Parisiis et Romae, 1865), p. 614.

[26] MOP, I, 111-112: *What source of wonderment! That God should find himself a prisoner in men's hands.*

[27] MOP, I, 116, and p. 167 here.

[28] *Vita Christi*, pp. 43-47, quots. on p. 47. K. Whinnom discusses instructively (loc. cit., p. 281 *et seq.*) the parallel between Ludolph's comments on the Circumcision and those in Íñigo de Mendoza. What is significantly absent from Don Antonio's treatment of the episode is the emphasis in Ludolph and Íñigo de Mendoza on spiritual circumcision: one contrasts the excoriating attack on the vices of the court in Fray Íñigo with the later poet's preference for anodyne reflexions (see text of *Vita Christi* in Julio Rodríguez-Puértolas, *Fray Íñigo de Mendoza y sus "Coplas de Vita Christi"* [Madrid, 1968], pp. 399-407).

[29] See *The Poems of Robert Southwell, S. J.*, p. 7, and *The Poems English Latin and Greek of Richard Crashaw*, ed. L. C. Martin, 2nd edn. reprinted (Oxford, 1966), p. 38 and p. 98 ("To thee these first fruits of my growing death"). The latter's *An Himne for the Circumcision day of our Lord* (pp. 141-142) is content just to hint at the eventual redemption of our sin, here adumbrated.

> Tan temprana su doctrina
> como su sangre en excesos
> de amor, y obediencia pasa
> de todo, sino es de él mesmo. [30]

Christ's love thus adumbrated will later reveal itself fully; Christ too in submitting to Circumcision showed His willingness to obey the Law, a notion found in older tradition, and reflected in Ludolph's text. The anticipation of the Cross is stated more clearly in another stanza, which also brings out mankind's forgetfulness of sin:

> ¡Oh cuánto nuestros olvidos
> acusa! Que hacer le vemos
> en deuda, que no fué suya,
> tan temprano los remedios. [31]

In the episode of taking Christ's body to the tomb, traditional accounts emphasized that Christ showed, in death as in life, that He was rejected of man: "namque domum in vita non habuit, post mortem quoque in alieno sepulchro reconditur." [32] Mendoza takes and develops this parallel so fraught with paradox:

> Tierra a nadie negó el mundo,
> que todo es patria de un muerto,
> y hasta su entierro le cuesta
> a un difunto Dios un ruego. [33]

The originating notion has been sharpened by a clearer reference to the purchase of real estate, and by the epigrammatic reference to a dead man finding a homeland in any part of the globe. Finally the utter paradox of the Saviour who, even in His final act of redeeming our pledges, dies the death of a pauper is deepened by the allusion to Christ as no more (and no less!) than a "dead God."

As is the case with his Marian imagery, Mendoza occasionally has recourse to traditional images in the treatment of Christ's life.

---

[30] *MOP*, I, 84: *As early does His doctrine as His blood surpass, in excess of love and obedience, everything except Himself.* The obedience (see p. 85) was to the law of Solomon.

[31] *MOP*, I, 85: *Oh! How He accuses our forgetfulness! Since so soon, for a debt that was not His, He makes the remedy.*

[32] *Vita Christi*, p. 682.

[33] *MOP*, I, 125: *The world never denied anyone land, for all is homeland to a dead man, whilst even his burial costs a dead God one request.*

Nowhere is this clearer than in the sequence on the Resurrection. The reference here to Christ as the sun (frequent in Southwell or Crashaw on account of the word-play on *sun* and *son*) is originally scriptural, the Matthew Gospel (XIII, 43) referring thus to the just in heaven: "Tunc fulgebunt justi sicut sol in regno Patris." Ludolph's text emphasizes how Christ's resurrected body will shine even more brightly, for He is the *justitiae sol* (Malachi, IV, 2). And in the same section, in both Ludolph and Mendoza, the resurrecting Christ is associated with a Phoenix. [34]

Finally I note a *concepto* that only yields its significance in the light of exegetic tradition. In describing Mary Magdalene's anointing of Christ's feet, Mendoza alluded to a mean bystander's objection to this act:

> Un mísero en desperdicios,
> que en suavidades molesto,
> más que la fragancia, inunda
> su querella el aposento,
> con los pies de Dios se enoja. [35]

The last line remains enigmatic till we realize that this part of Scripture was interpreted *mystice* in the following way. Christ's feet were "pauperes" since they were the "inferior pars corporis mystici," and mankind, rich in sin, must shower upon them the abundance of its compassion and love. However, when we have, as often, failed in this task, "Contra pedes Domini stetimus, cum in peccatis positi, ejus itineribus renitebamur." [36] In Mendoza's text, therefore, the avarice of the complainant is associated with mankind's sinful anger directed against God, as symbolized by Christ's feet.

Ludolph's meditative technique is in clear contrast to Mendoza's *Vida*. In keeping with its Carthusian author's practical intentions, the volume sought frequently after occasions for reflexion, contemplation and prayer. Indeed the text is interspersed too, like the Barcelona *Rosario*, with prayers, as well as with incidental exhortations. The author tried in particular to make Christ's suffering

---

[34] See *Vida* text on p. 162 here, and Ludolph's *Vita*, p. 696.

[35] *MOP*, I, 105: *A man niggling over squandering, bothersome over luxuries, his complaint more than the fragrance floods the room... He gets annoyed with the feet of God.*

[36] *Vita Christi*, pp. 261-263, quots. on p. 261 and 262-263.

unbearably real, so that the Christian might be driven to meditate on His Passion. This morbid realism was reflected also in Spain in the poems of Íñigo de Mendoza and Juan de Padilla, as well as in Diego de San Pedro's *Pasión trobada*. [37] Mendoza's *Romance,* on the other hand, is in better taste, and almost tangential in method: the flagellation is a "fierce rain," and the tortures only wear themselves away on Christ. [38] Such refusal to assault the senses as a preliminary to meditation underlines Mendoza's divergence from tradition. If he emphasized the pictorial (as indeed had Juan de Padilla in the *Retablo de la Vida de Cristo*), Mendoza's understanding of poetic painting was very different: it was an evasive technique rather than an equivalent of the pathos-laden representations of his contemporary Gregorio Hernández. [39] Mendoza's poem in this regard shows little sign of that contemplative discipline noted by Martz in the poetry of Southwell and Donne, and earlier referred to in a quotation from Montesino.

However, the exegetic tradition, as distinct from the contemplative method, has left its mark even where the poet was in all probability not following it consciously: one may instance a part of the *Ecce homo* section, which dwells thus on the choice of Barabbas rather than Christ:

> En vez del Justo prefieren
> al más culpado, aprendiendo
> de poderosa costumbre
> su ruin elección el pueblo. [40]

This is dead poetry, but as commentary it follows the kind of moral or spiritual lessons that Ludolph drew, or repeated. By this means

---

[37] See "The Supposed Sources," p. 275 *et seq.* One may quote as an instance Diego de San Pedro's: "Que al tiempo que se açoto / la su carne delicada / como toda se [le] abrio / con la sangre que salio / tenia la [ropa] pegada" (quot. ibid., p. 276).

[38] *MOP*, I, 113.

[39] Juan de Padilla intended to paint four *Tablas* for his reredos (see e.g. the text in *Cancionero castellano del siglo XV*, ed. R. Foulché-Delbosc, *NBAE*, XIX, p. 427). His picture of Christ's death is frighteningly real: "El pecho sonaba con ronco latido, / los ojos abiertos, la vista turbada, / llena de sangre la boca sagrada" (p. 442). Mendoza's attitude is brought out also by the contrast with Lope de Vega's *romance, A la muerte de Cristo,* where, more in keeping with Ludolph or the Pseudo-Bonaventure, emphasis is placed on the Virgin's participation in Christ's suffering (see Lope in *Romancero y Cancionero sagrados,* p. 96; *Vita Christi,* pp. 663-665, and Pseudo-Bonaventure, *Meditations on the Life of Christ,* ed. Isa Ragusa and Rosalie B. Green, Princeton, N.J., 1961, pp. 333-335).

[40] *MOP*, I, 115: *In place of the Just One they prefer the most guilty, the people learning, by the power of custom, their own vile choice.*

as well as by the *conceptos* of image, parallelism, paradox (both traditional and original), the poet helped satisfy a public that did not come in search of a biographical account, but of a "celestial ambrosia" to be slowly sipped by the reader of devout turn of mind. In all likelihood too, here were to be found the *conceptos* which the poet himself claimed were drawn upon by Hortensio Paravicino, much as an earlier generation of preachers had taken their *conceptus praedicabiles* from Ledesma. [41]

At this distance in time proper appraisal of the *Vida* is difficult. A reader who can enjoy Crashaw's famous line on the turning of the water into wine at the wedding in Cana: "Nympha pudica Deum vidit et erubuit," [42] is more likely to respond to the *Vida* than one who cannot. Mendoza's subtlety and power of invention are beyond dispute, and once we have realized that the poet is not attempting a sustained narrative, but a series of lyrical episodes linked to a devotional purpose, we may more easily appreciate the extraordinary series of *conceptos,* some compounded into complicated metaphoric structures that amaze as well as baffle.

However, it must be admitted that the poet's lines often have a hard edge, not found in the best of his ballads and *décimas,* as though the stanzas had been chiselled, rather than moulded, into place. Furthermore some of the conceits court the obvious, others have suffered from an over-anxiety to maintain solemnity of diction by the introduction of *cultismos* and an artificial word-order. The fairest claim that may be made on the *Vida's* behalf is that it contains some beautiful stanzas. We may instance this evocation of Christ bearing His Cross:

> Si cielo y tierra en un soplo
> suyo se está manteniendo
> y firmes penden los astros
> del arbitrio de su dedo:
>   ¿Qué admiración les haría
> ver oprimir un madero
> sus hombros, a quien le fueran
> muchos mundos flaco peso? [43]

---

[41] Manescal's words in prologue to *FC* (*MOP*, I, 146). For Paravicino and Mendoza, see p. 34 here.

[42] See Richard Crashaw, p. 38.

[43] *MOP*, I, 116: *If heaven and earth are held up by a puff of His breath and the stars hang firmly by the arbitrament of His finger, how astonished they would be to see*

and his conceits are sometimes both original and frightening, as in this depiction of Christ the true vine suffering on the Cross:

> Clavado de pies, y manos
> no da más frutos, y hechos   [*nos das más frutos y*
> de rubíes un racimo   *hecho*. Hisp. Am. MS.]
> pagó el nombre de sarmiento. [44]

At such moments Mendoza's poetic power approaches Southwell's, though even at his best he lacks the Jesuit martyr's heart-felt devotion, and poignant naïveté.

Three features of the *Vida* merit particular mention. Firstly, the occasional pictorial texture, traceable in part to the poet's express aim of "painting" the various scenes from the Virgin's life; [45] and possibly to the notion that meditation should begin with the creation of a visual image. But if Mendoza's intention of painting such scenes was not very different in principle from Marino's attempts in the *Galleria* to recreate poetically some famous paintings of the Virgin, the Spanish poet was not consistently pictorial. Only at certain moments did he attempt portraiture; the Crown of Thorns for instance, or the *Transitus Mariae,* where he briefly evoked Christ receiving His Mother into heaven:

> Su celestial mano sola
> recibe el alma, en descuento
> de tantas veces glorioso
> depósito de su cuerpo.
> Sagrada nube circunda
> el suyo intacto, cubriendo
> con muchos sus resplandores
> más lucidos, que cubiertos. [46]

---

a piece of wood press down His shoulders, He to whom many worlds would be but a flimsy burden. (Cf. Southwell's Sinnes heavie loade, p. 17: "This Globe of earth doth thy one finger prop").

[44] *MOP*, I, 118: *Nailed hand and foot* [like on an espalier?], *He gives us more fruits, and Himself made a bunch of rubies, He paid for His own name of vine-shoot (and Sarmiento).* On the mystic winepress, see Darbord, p. 129, and p. 78 here.

[45] See the poet's note about unfinished sequences: "Hase de pintar..." (*MOP*, I, 140).

[46] *MOP*, I, 137: *His heavenly hand alone receives her soul, recompense for the receptacle so many times glorious of her body. A sacred cloud surrounds her undefiled body, veiling with its own many splendours, that which was hers — whose splendour was brighter (and more successful!) than it was veiled.*

Mendoza may also have understood "painting" in a different sense, that of conveying through the conceits a moral and religious portrait of his subject, similar to that which God the painter had done in first creating Mary. [47]

Pictorialism in its usual sense is here found in landscape rather than in portraiture, particularly where the pictorial could be combined with the grotesque, a combination not unknown elsewhere in this period, as in the poetry of Saint-Amant, or John Davies of Hereford. [48] Mendoza reserved such treatment for the traditional allegorical cold which held the world in its grip at the time of Christ's Nativity — and here he seems more grotesque than his Spanish contemporaries in their treatment of this theme — as well as for certain aspects of the Crucifixion. The grotesque element, however, in Mendoza is much less extreme than in John Davies, for instance; but it is present, as may be judged by part of the description of the snow at the Nativity:

> Mal discernidos los campos,
> y los ríos, los corderos
> beben hierba, y agua pacen
> de sed engañada hambrientos: [49]

and when the Temple veil was rent:

> Bramó el mar, abrió la tierra
> sus duros, temblados senos,
> y en ya cadáveres vivos
> la vida cobró sus muertos. [50]

The second feature of the *Vida* to warrant comment is the use of traditional religious images as the basis of its conceits. The Cross,

---

[47] Cf. *MOP*, I, 51: "En cuya valiente imagen, / de Dios pincel sin defectos, / son todas las gracias sombras, / son todas las culpas lejos." See also e.g. p. 61, st. 117. For symbol and moral quality in portraiture, see John Pope-Hennesy, *The Portrait in the Renaissance: The A. W. Mellon Lectures in the Fine Arts. 1963* (New York, N.Y., 1966), *passim*.

[48] See Odette de Mourgues, *Metaphysical, Précieux and Baroque Poetry* (Oxford, 1953), "The Macabre and the Morbid," pp. 88-93. See also p. 101, where she refers to such poetry's similarity with the painting of Hieronymus Bosch, a vogue figure in Spain at this time whose "insigne mano" (*MOP*, III, 15) is mentioned by Mendoza.

[49] *MOP*, I, 79: *With fields and rivers hardly distinguishable, the lambs drink grass and graze water, hungry with a deceived thirst.*

[50] *MOP*, I, 121: *The sea roared, earth opened her hard, trembling bosom, and life recovered its dead in now living corpses.*

for instance, is both tree and ship, *conceptos* already used in the liturgy. [51] Some of his images belonged to the language of Marian devotion, and were popular in the emblematic literature of the period. Of the fifteen titles of Mary, at least twelve find a place in the *Vida*. An interesting comparison may be made between the conceits composed by Mendoza and Southwell on the basis of the title *Stella maris* and Christ's title of *Sol justitiae:*

> Luciente, fecunda estrella
> del mar, donde en vez de puerto,
> navegante sol humano
> buscó tierra, y *halló cielo.*   [*tomó cielo.* Hisp. Am. MS.]

> Joy in the rising of our Orient starre,
> That shal bring forth the Sun that lent her light
> ....
> Load-starre of all ingolfd in wordly waves. [52]

Both poets have brought together the Sun and the Star, both understandably have connected them with seafaring, and have made them the starting-point of a paradox: in the one that Christ the sailor, in seeking earth, found a heaven in Mary's womb; in the other (echoing the liturgy, and punning on *Sun* and *Sonne*), bringing out the strange truth about Mary in the *Offertorium:* "genuisti qui te fecit."

Mendoza also embroidered on other less famous titles, sometimes with originality. *Turris David* is subtly incorporated into a chivalrous setting, not unknown in medieval Marian poetry. The Saviour at His birth is cruelly besieged by the cold fury of Nature, and when the poet presumes that Nature's opponent must be some cruel giant, he learns that it is:

> un niño hermoso,
> que está solo defendiendo

---

[51] *MOP*, I, 120. Cf. the liturgy: "Dulce lignum. Sola digna tu fuiste ferre saecli pretium, atque portum praeparare nauta mundo naufrago."

[52] *MOP*, I, 47: *Bright, fertile star of the sea, where in lieu of port, a sailing human sun sought land, and found a heaven.* Southwell, p. 3. On the Virgin's titles, see e.g. Antoine Vérard, *Heures à l'usage de Rouen* (1503), and Rosemary Freeman, *English Emblem Books* (London, 1948), p. 182. The association in both Southwell and Mendoza (as well as others) of the Star and the Sun may owe something to the memory of another of the Virgin's titles "Electa ut sol."

> la torre de una doncella,
> la muralla de un cabello. 53

Mendoza may have taken the hint from one of Ledesma's *Conceptos espirituales,* in which Christ is invoked as a poor knight in love with a lady who has thrown him over for "an ugly and clumsy monster," now in tyrannical possession of "this most beautiful tower." 54 But Ledesma's poem lacked imagistic clarity, since the lady, really the human soul, was also in some ways the Virgin. If Mendoza got his idea from Ledesma he has strengthened the logic; and the Virgin's tower defended against the might of human sinfulness by only a beautiful child is a moving image in which we sense the latent paradox of Christ's ultimate power. Southwell, drawing on similar traditional material, asserted the same paradox with even greater effectiveness:

> His Campe is pitched in a stall,
> His bulwarke but a broken wall:
> The Crib his trench, hay stalks his stakes,
> Of Sheepheards he his Muster makes. 55

Two other titles given to Mary were *pulchra ut luna* and *speculum sine macula.* The *equívoco* of *luna* as both "moon" and "glass" proved too strong an attraction for the poet to withstand. After describing Christ as a pearl conceived of the virgin flower's dew, Mendoza, in order to emphasize Mary's greater purity, continues:

> Las mismas fecundidades
> más purezas añadiendo,
> nunca manchada la luna
> más cristal quedó el espejo. 56

---

53 *MOP,* I, 81: *a beautiful child who is all alone defending a maiden's tower, the wall of one hair.* On Christ's medieval court, see Whinnom, "El origen," pp. 267-268, and Íñigo de Mendoza's *Vita Christi,* ed. Rodríguez-Puértolas, p. 477: "Asy nuestro redemptor, / como mañoso guerrero" becomes later "vencedor / en el campo del madero."

54 *Conceptos,* in *Cancionero sagrado,* p. 82. The "monstruo feo y torpe" may have suggested Mendoza's "feroz gigante / turbador, osado, feo."

55 Southwell, p. 14.

56 *MOP,* I, 80: *That very fecundity adding more purity, the unblemished moon-mirror's glass now became more crystal.* The image of Christ as the pearl inside Mary's shell may owe something to Ledesma, who uses the figure in his *Segunda parte de los conceptos Espirituales, y Morales* (Barcelona, 1607), p. 132 and in his *Epigramas y Hieroglificos a la vida de Cristo* (Madrid, 1625), f. 3ᵛ.

We descend here from the strained but beautiful *conceptos* of
knightly service to the kind of riddle found in Ledesma's *Enigmas
hechas para honesta recreación:* the poet has sacrificed so much to
intellectual subtlety that the poetry has got lost.

A final feature brings us closer to understanding what made
Mendoza's poem so popular. The clue lies with Gracián's discussion
of the "agudeza por alusión," which he defined as positing a
connexion "not by expressing it, but pointing to it mysteriously."
Gracián took as his first example the opening of Mendoza's *Vida,*
which dwelt on Mary's traditional titles and furthermore contained
"many other mysterious allusions." [57] This technique the critic
defined as "subtlety in cipher": it is the kind of intellectual, and
presumably spiritual, pleasure to be derived from Ledesma's
enigmas, or Alciati's emblems. Gracián quoted the following stanza
(not found incidentally in the 1666 edition):

> Prevención solicitada
> contra el ardiente veneno
> de aquel Serafín bizarro,
> antes luz y ahora fuego.

Mendoza thus alluded to the Virgin as a Second Eve treading upon
the serpent's head, thereby destroying the poison given to man
by the deadly Seraph, Lucifer. The allusions were not beyond the
reach of even the average reader, but they were woven together in
a pleasing way that tested, without taxing, the ability to interpret
subtlety and enigma. It may well have been that where we today
find the poet most baffling or tiresome, the seventeenth-century
reader found him sublime, approaching the role of diviner of holy
mysteries which Tesauro had assigned to the *concettista.*

But the ultimate secret of the *Vida's* popularity must lie in its
combination of aesthetic pleasure and spiritual edification. The first
element now makes only a limited impact, since today's reader,
unlike Mendoza's contemporaries, fails to respond fully to the
cultural medium in which the *Vida* was produced. For the seventeenth-century public, indeed, what we denote as aesthetic was only

---

[57] *GOC*, p. 449: "no exprimiéndola [relación], sino apuntándola misteriosamente,"
"otras muchas misteriosas alusiones," and "Sutileza en cifra." The quot. from the *Vida*
translates: *A remedy sought against the burning poison of that brave Seraph, once light
and now fire.*

part of the larger response, and indistinguishable from it. The situation may be characterized by some examples. The reader was familiar, for instance, with the liturgical image of the Ship of the Cross, an association whose pathos in the *Vida* was intensified by the use of a long and bold perpetual allegory. In Mendoza's description of the Crucifixion the elements are boats whose mooring lines have snapped in the tempest, the sun has been drowned, the moon has lost her tiller. The stars are part of the ship's entangled rigging. Finally the universe is shipwrecked, the rending of the Temple veil representing the tearing of the ship's canvas. Even now the metaphor's magnificent trajectory is not yet complete: the Cross, representing the ship's mast, is topped by Saint Elmo's fire, a sign of Christ's triumph over a shipwrecked world. Thus the hyperbole characteristic of Mendoza's poetic technique, as indeed of the poetry of the period in Spain and elsewhere, [58] was used to give a new veneer to an image that had perhaps, through over-familiarity, lost something of its lustre.

One can exemplify the same process at work elsewhere in the *Vida* — for instance in the long passage of Invocation, where the poet develops at length the marine images suggested by Mary's titles as Star of the Sea and "Loadstarre"; or again the episode of the Crown of Thorns, which forcefully brings together Christ's bloody sweat in the Garden, the immemorial connexion of the Red Sea with man's sinfulness (from which redemption would soon come), and the rich wine harvest of the Crucifixion:

> Rocíos purpúreos bañan
> su cabeza, guarneciendo
> de sangre aljófares puros
> su nevado, hermoso cuello.
> Si no son racimos rojos
> sus pardos lucientes crespos,
> son rizas, sangrientas ondas
> de mares ya más bermejos. [59]

---

[58] *MOP*, I, 120-122. For the vogue of hyperbole, see Frank J. Warnke, *European Metaphysical Poetry* (New Haven, 1961), pp. 2-3, along with the evidence of his selected poems.

[59] *MOP*, I, 49-50, and 114: *A purple dew bathes his head, pure pearls of blood adorn his lovely, snow-white neck. If those dark, shining locks are not red clusters, they are curling, bloody waves of seas now more scarlet.*

A final example concerns specifically the theme: "ego sum vitis." The image again is traditional, hallowed by Gospel and liturgy. The mystic winepress too, as was seen in an earlier chapter, was a long-established symbol of the Crucifixion, its associations echoed and renewed in the liturgical "arbor una nobilis" and its fruit, as well as in the reference to "vineam meam." Some measure of the common heritage, as well as of the varied treatment to which traditional material could be subjected, may be seen in the way that Mendoza and other devotional poets of the Counter-Reformation used the theme. Crashaw, with rather maudlin sentiment, caused the Vine to love the "crucis arbor" as it had loved the elm, an exercise perhaps in attaining a devotional object along the path of Latin lore. [60] William Alabaster, in a more homely vein, makes the vine which climbs the Cross offer welcome shade to the sinner scorched by the fire of his sin, or sees the grapes of the vine "swell with grace and heavenly lustre." Robert Southwell makes the "grape of blisse" distil "sweete wine at will." [61] Mendoza makes the cluster of grapes into a handful of valuable rubies, with which the vine itself, Christ, is as it were paid for. [62] Ledesma changes vine into pear-tree because he wishes to make play with a children's singing game consisting of a verse beginning "Este peral tiene peras." Ledesma opens his gloss thus:

> Es el árbol de la cruz
> Un frutal sabroso y sano,
> Cuya fruta es Dios y hombre
> Divino engerto y humano. [63]

If behind these coincidences (as well as divergences) of metaphor and interpretation there lay a common tradition, all five poets expressed it too by an equal zeal to discover ways of awakening (frequently by invoking everyday experience), the reader's considered response — an aim and method very similar to those of the medieval

---

[60] For winepress, see p. 78 here. Crashaw, p. 41.

[61] *The Sonnets of William Alabaster*, ed. G. M. Story and Helen Gardner (Oxford, 1959), p. 18 and p. 17. Southwell, p. 18.

[62] *MOP*, I, 118.

[63] Text of *Juegos de Noche Buena* (1605) in *Romancero y cancionero sagrados*, BAE, XXXV, pp. 151-181, quot. on p. 173: *This pear-tree has on it pears... The tree of the Cross is a tasty and healthy fruit-tree, whose fruit is both God and man, a graft both human and divine.* The line "Este peral..." is used as chorus throughout.

preacher, or of authors like the Pseudo-Bonaventure. But in addition the poets shared a sense of novelty and contemporaneity. G. M. Story's assertion that the peculiar quality of the verse of William Alabaster, a precursor of the metaphysical poets, comes from the fusion of "an old and widespread devotional tradition" with a "new poetic temper" could equally be applied to the other poets. [64] The lessons of Scripture or the traditional Christian symbols were now couched in a more fashionable language of paradox, or other form of conceit. [65] One may cite Mendoza's treatment of the binding of Christ's hands when He was taken prisoner. Taking a cue from a moral interpretation in traditional exegesis, that we are in like manner bound to Christ by His love ("ipsa enim charitas est vinculum, in quo anima Deo alligatur"), the poet develops the paradox of a love that binds us, the binders, to the one that we have bound. Though Christ is man's prisoner, He has in reality imprisoned us in His love:

> Ligan sus gloriosas manos,
> mas no a beneficios nuestros
> se las atan, que es su amor
> la prisión, pero no el preso. [66]

Taking what the exegetic tradition had already adumbrated as the basis of a paradox, Mendoza erected on it a conceitful structure that might appeal to the connoisseur of Alciati, or the admirer of Martial.

Let us return in conclusion to Martz's thesis about the relation between English devotional poetry and those stages in the *Scala Meditatoria* that the Ignatian tradition had helped to popularize. Some critics have argued that Spanish religious poetry was likewise affected by this meditative discipline or habit. Edward Sarmiento cited Fray Luis de León's poem to the Ascension as an instance of the process; Arthur Terry has suggested "the Ignatian concept of

---

[64] *The Sonnets*, General Introduction by Story, p. XXIII.

[65] For the change in preaching taste by the end of the sixteenth century, see Otis H. Green, "Se acicalaron los auditorios: An Aspect of the Spanish Literary Baroque," *HR*, XXVII (1959), 413-422. The Count of Salinas, objecting to the more alembicated manner, protested at Paravicino's preaching, and its "lenguaje crespo y entrincado... cõn cuidado escureçido" (BNM *MS* 3657, f. 609).

[66] Latin quot. in Ludolph, p. 615, *MOP*, I, 111: *They bind His hands; but not for our benefit, since it is His love that forms the prison, not He as prisoner.*

Colloquy" has affected, and developed, the "conversational urgency" of other devotional poems, such as Lope de Vega's "Qué tengo yo que mi amistad procuras?"; Edward Wilson, in interpreting a difficult Calderonian poem, *Psalle et Sile*, has sought to relate to it the pattern of three-fold meditation, which in turn engaged memory, understanding and will. [67] The argument in all these cases is plausible, although it is notoriously easy to impose upon a phenomenon an order that may be totally unrelated to it.

What does the *Vida* suggest? The evidence of Loarte's *Meditationes de Rosario Beatae Virginis,* to which reference was earlier made, should help produce a more balanced picture. There, in the manner described by Martz, each Mystery is meditated under three points, with appropriate amplification subsequently of each heading. "Imaginarie representation" is often used. For instance, Loarte gives this advice for meditating on the Ascension: "Doo nowe contemplate, with howe great sweetnes and affabilitie he talked to euerye one; with howe great charitie he blessed and comforted euerye one ... etc." The reader is then invited to re-create for himself the audience's reactions to Christ's disappearance from among men: "al that holye assembly felt, seing him mount vp thus triumphantly: how their heartes did rent in twaine through loue, and howe they melted againe with tears." [68] A study of Loarte's handbook throws into relief, however, one quite different but important point, that meditation embraced a number of features besides the *Scala Meditatoria,* in particular the consideration of abstract points of theology and morals. Let us consider, as one instance among many, the treatment of Gethsemane. Here in discussing Christ's exhortation to His disciples to pray, Loarte bids the reader consider the nature of prayer. Later in the same section Loarte comments on the "charitie and fatherlye care" which Christ showed His disciples. [69] Such aspects as these emphasize how the *Meditationes,* whatever they may have owed to the Ignatian discipline, belonged firmly to an

---

[67] See Luis de León, *The Original Poems,* ed. Edward Sarmiento (Manchester, 1953), p. 87; Arthur Terry, *An Anthology of Spanish Poetry, 1500-1700,* II (Oxford, 1968), pp. xix-xxi; E. M. Wilson, "A Key to Calderón's *Psalle et sile,*" in *Hispanic Studies in Honour of I. González Llubera,* ed. Frank Pierce and C. A. Jones (Oxford, 1959), pp. 438-440.

[68] I quote J. Fenne's version, *Instruction and Advertisements, How to Meditate the Misteries of the Rosarie of the most holy Virgin Mary. Written in Italian by the Reuerend Father Gaspar Loarte D. of Diuinitie of the Societie of Jesus. And newly translated into English* (Rouen?, 1600?), f. 84 and f. 85.

[69] Loarte, ff. 37-43, quot. on f. 40v.

older tradition of meditation and exegesis, exemplified for instance in Ludolph's *Vita Christi* and the Pseudo-Bonaventure. Furthermore, even the detail of the "imaginarie representations" in Loarte is sometimes reminiscent not of any intense meditative discipline, but of the desultory, and homely reflexions of the anonymous author of the *Meditationes Vitae Christi*.

Mendoza's *Vida*, like Loarte's handbook, is a reminder of the variety in the patterns of meditation. Mendoza did not share Loarte's fondness for "imaginarie representation" as a basic step in meditation; indeed, his avowed aim of "painting" is at variance with his usual lack of interest in the technique of composition of place. Again he made little use of the system of the three points (despite the obvious strength of Loarte's argument that this led to "lesse confusio[n]"). [70] These differences apart, the *Vida* belongs to Loarte and to older tradition by dint of other things; first, by the accumulation of myriad details, an equivalent of the smaller points in the amplifications of Loarte's text or the trivia of the Pseudo-Bonaventure, and likewise intended as spurs to reflexion; further, by those theological, moral, or merely desultory, reflexions that engaged the reader's passing attention, even if they did not command his response by a direct appeal to his imagination and senses. In addition the *Vida*'s subtleties in cipher which Gracián admired were a more sophisticated equivalent of a taste satisfied both by traditional exegesis and the meditative tradition.

The *Vida* therefore shows the need for caution in positing a relation between particular poems and meditative literature, unless that relation be defined in the wider and vaguer sense which Martz finally adopted in the preface to the second edition of his book. There he declares in favour of the "meditative poem" rather than the "meditative style," allowing too that such a poem is a "genre that may be composed in different styles." [71] Such a description accords better too with the definition and function of meditation as given by Loarte himself, that it "serue vs as a mirror, wherein, by eftons looking & taking view, we may with the eies of our soule see that, which with the eyes of our bodie we neither could nor can

---

[70] Loarte, f. 6ᵛ.
[71] Martz, p. xv.

see; and according to it direct and frame our life ..." [72] But one might hesitate to describe the *Vida* as a specifically meditative poem even within such an ample definition. A devotional poem, certainly, its intention to induce in the reader a serious and reflective concern for the truths of religion. Yet in temper the *Vida* is distant from the spirit of contemplation and prayer of the medieval Spanish poems we have discussed; distant, too, from these same features in Loarte, Ludolph, or the Barcelona *Rosario*. Here we may perhaps be in contact with some aspect of the author himself: a religious man, with a particular devotion to the Virgin, who nevertheless displayed an aloofness that may well correspond to the cool chemistry of the analyses of courtly sentiments in his secular poetry.

---

[72] Loarte, ff. 1v-2.

VII

A POET AND THE LITERARY TRADITION

ANTONIO de Mendoza did not generally seek to air his views on poetry. Two statements, however, cast considerable light on his attitude. In the first, part of his prose account of the great *Fiesta de Aranjuez* of 1622, he expressed the belief that the arts at court should be different, and superior, to what was offered to the ordinary public. "La decencia de Palacio," he averred, deserved an abler pen than his, even to give a just account of the entertainment, and in recognizing Villamediana's achievement in the *Gloria de Niquea* (performed at Aranjuez), Mendoza stressed how, normally, poetry was there given no more than a "brief licence," and that poets brought up outside "the severity of its school" were not adept at the art. [1]

The second statement was Mendoza's *aprobación*, written in 1639, for the Prince of Esquilache's *Obras divinas, y humanas en verso*. Mistaken attempts had been made, said Mendoza, to lead the Spanish language along new and dangerous paths — a tilt obviously at Góngora and his followers — but the real and royal road was that taken by Esquilache, to whose pen "en galas, purezas, co[n]ceptos, y primores, le deuen nuestros oidos, no menos el descanso, que la admiracion; sabiendo juntar lo que es tan dificil de vnir, como la dulçura, la propriedad, y la grandeza." [2] So deserving was this poet of our admiration that Mendoza concurred with a certain "great man," who affirmed that though many of Spain's men of genius deserved our envy, he himself would choose to write like the Prince of Esquilache.

---

[1] *MOP*, I, 1-26, esp. p. 7 and p. 9: "...la corta licencia, que se les concede en él [= Palacio] a los versos, y el atino con que se han de escribir, en que se ven poco prácticos los que se han criado lejos de la severidad de su escuela."

[2] Francisco de Borja, Príncipe de Esquilache, *Obras diuinas, y humanas en verso* (Madrid, 1648). The *aprobación* by Antonio de Mendoza is dated Madrid, 6 June 1639: *in splendour, purity, conceits and elegance our ears owe him no less solace than wonderment; knowing how to join together things as difficult to unite as sweetness, decorum and elevation.*

The passage yields its implications grudgingly, since the language
of criticism at this time was ill-adapted to describing lyric poetry. [3]
Furthermore, the terms of description were used by Gongorists as
well as by Góngora's detractors to express approval, an indication
of the words' ambiguity. However, the key seems to lie in the rare
combination of "sweetness, decorum, and elevation," a phrase whose
significance for Mendoza may be brought out by a brief examination
of Esquilache's poetry. The Prince's poems, in relation to prevalent
practice, were old-fashioned, well turned, and above all marked by
purity and unaffectedness of language, as well as by a pleasing
banality. Though Esquilache had apparently shown approval of
Góngora's experiments, his own practice avoided all extravagance
of diction or device; the sentiments of courtly love which his
poems often expressed were conducive to seemliness of emotion and
expression, so that here as well as in the occasional moral or religious
poem, an elevated style was apparent; and everywhere his verse
distilled a restful gentleness and limpidity:

> Ya del Octubre la inquietud primera,
> Anuncia del imbierno la venida,
> Y su lluuia pacifica, y dormida,
> Finge segunda, y breue primauera. [4]

How do we explain Mendoza's admiration for a poetry patently
unlike much of his own? The answer may be two-fold. Firstly,
however much Mendoza was influenced by Góngora — as may be
judged by the *culto* diction of parts of the *Romance* to the Virgin,
or the occasional sonnet — he was firmly persuaded that the Cor-
doban poet's experiments had been harmful: Mendoza here ranged
himself alongside Lope de Vega and Quevedo. He expressed his
view of the *gongoristas* unequivocally in *Cada loco con su tema*.
Góngora himself was "a most divine genius," but he was imitated
by "a hundred idiots." [5] The result was that art had become

---

[3] See W. C. Atkinson, "On Aristotle and the Concept of Lyric Poetry in Early Spanish
Criticism," *Estudios dedicados a Menéndez Pidal*, VI (Madrid, 1956), pp. 189-213. Andrée
Collard in her *Nueva poesia: conceptismo, culteranismo en la crítica española* (Madrid,
1967) has attempted to put some order into the terminological ambiguities.

[4] Esquilache, p. 8: *October's first disquiet announces winter's coming, and its peaceful,
somnolent rain simulates a second, and brief, spring.*

[5] *BAE*, XLV, 469: "Pulidamente se escribe / Entre gente ilustre, y vive / Culto el
metro y crespo el arte; / Hase escondido el Parnaso, / Y corre ya tan obscuro, / Que,

"convoluted" *(crespo)* — the Count of Salinas had used the same term in his complaint about Paravicino's sermons [6] — and poetry so obscure that Garcilaso, because of his very clarity, was no longer understood. Esquilache may therefore in contrast have represented the true tradition, characterized by linguistic purity. The love of *purezas* is expressed by Mendoza too in a *décima* to the Fountain of Batres on the estate of the Count of Arcos, and supposed to have been created by the poet Garcilaso de la Vega. He attributes the clarity and purity of the waters to the characteristic genius of the founder, who is thus addressed:

> tu ingenio le dió el ser clara,
> tu vena le halló el ser pura. [7]

The appeal to Garcilaso is in addition an appeal to tradition, a point of relevance also to Mendoza's view of Esquilache, who probably represented the true poetic descent; extending along one line via Fernando de Herrera to Garcilaso; and along another via Cristóbal de Castillejo and Diego Hurtado de Mendoza to the *Cancionero* poets.

Secondly, Esquilache, in both a literal and a metaphorical sense, was the prince of palace poets. His propriety and sense of elevation suited the palace muse; his exercise of courtly love, his practice of the Manzanarian idyll, his dalliance with the traditional *glosa* and *redondilla*, all emphasized a poetry of aristocratic descent; even the Prince's wit, though modest and unpretentious, was a natural part of the court heritage:

> De Mançanares al Soto
> Salio Lucinda vna tarde;
> Porque Mayo no se ausente,
> Y porque el dia no falte. [8]

---

por claro, terso y puro, / No se entiende á Garcilaso; / A un ingenio el mas divino / Imitan cien majaderos."

[6] See note 65 of ch. VI. Lope in contrast uses the word *crespo* in an approving sense — see Collard, p. 101.

[7] *MOP*, III, 180-181: *Your genius gave it the gift of clarity, your vein [of poetry] found it purity.* The *décima* is found with variants in Hisp. Soc. Am. MS B2464, f. 323 (see *Hisp. Am. Cat.*, I, 439), where it accompanies poems by other authors on the same subject.

[8] Esquilache, p. 442: *Lucinda left for the Soto of the Manzanares one evening, so that May should not be absent, nor day be missing.* Mendoza's fondness for the Prince's

For all the obvious differences in style Mendoza's practice developed, rather than denied, the essential characteristics of Esquilache's poetry. Furthermore, Mendoza's critical approval of Esquilache was shared by his friend Lope de Vega, who praised the Prince for having followed an "easy path, both plain and sanctioned" to poetry's high summit, and for having served as "so true an asylum for our language." [9]

Mendoza's view of the Gongorists provides a starting-point for a consideration of his position in the literary tradition. He was not consistent in his attitude to obscurity in poetry, [10] nor did he complain about the extravagance of the Gongorists' metaphors: what he criticized emphatically was their wrong-headed approach to language. Such an attitude was shared by two significant poets, younger than Mendoza, who admired the latter's work, and underwent his influence. For Polo de Medina, author of the *Academias del jardín* (1630), the Gongorists' obscurity was of verbal origin. [11] Gabriel Bocángel in the introduction to his *Rimas y prosas* (1627) likewise condemned "the cudgel blow of the puffed-up verse and ... the strange locution;" he wished to retain the word *culto* in his vocabulary, but defined it as the compounding of great elegance with great clarity. [12] Basically, however, the poetic practice of Polo, Bocángel and Mendoza had much in common with that of Góngora, apart from their reservations concerning the use of a learned or obscure vocabulary.

These three poets, all writing largely under the influence of the court, shared a common conviction, briefly the need to *feel* different from Góngora, if not to *be* different from him; and an insistence on

---

verse (as well as his ability to assimilate it to his own) is suggested by *MOP*, II, 344-345, where a *romance* was composed to an original *copla* and *estribillo* by Esquilache.

[9] In Rennert and Castro, p. 291 and Note: "Por fácil senda, permitida y llana ... a la alta cumbre vino," and "tan verdadero asilo de nuestra lengua."

[10] One may contrast his emphasis on clarity with the failure to condemn the Gongorists' obscurity in the Esquilache *aprobación*, and with the allusion he makes (*MOP*, II, 350) to his own "tenebrosa ... pluma."

[11] Polo de Medina, *Obras escogidas*, p. 75, and Collard, pp. 106-107. For Polo's view of Mendoza, see Note 24.

[12] *Obras*, I, 12-13: "el porrazo del verso hinchado, y de la estraña locucion," and "el compadecer la grande elegancia con la suma claridad." That a palace audience required a special linguistic treatment is suggested by Bocángel's insistence on the elevation normally appropriate to the epic style: so (I, 149) he calls for a combination of the *heroico* and the *claro*, and claims of his masque *El Nuevo Olimpo* (1649) that the diction is tempered between *Lirico* and *Heroyco* (II, 145). Bocángel in a poem of 1637 saluted "Mendoça prodigioso" and his fame (I, 409).

linguistic purity and clarity as the mark of the true poet. And
whether expressed in Mendoza's terms about the combination of
"sweetness, decorum, and elevation," in Bocángel's emphasis on both
elegance and clarity, or in Lope de Vega's description of Mendoza's
verse as "sweetly solemn," they all felt that purity should be
conjoined to an appropriate seemliness or gravity, a combination
also noted by Sebastián Francisco de Medrano, who praised Mendoza for being "without impropriety, sweet and majestic," and thus
appropriate to Palace decorum. [13] Lope de Vega in the context
already quoted goes on to sum up what for him, and probably for
many others in the period, was the essence of Mendoza. He was a

> Raro maestro del hablar süave,
> Gallardo en prosa y verso,
> Conceptuoso, fácil, puro y terso. [14]

In a text not outstanding for serious critical judgments, Lope's words
seem both sincere and apt: Don Antonio, whose gentle cadences
are indeed the hall-mark of most of his verses, possessed a genius
that matched cleverness with ease, rarely losing the clue of clarity
in exploring the labyrinth of wit. And the purity of his verse was in
the same stream as Esquilache, flowing ultimately from the fount
of Garcilaso. The consensus in such views as these concerning a
primarily courtly art may have been accidental, and in isolation,
should not be accorded much significance. But taken in conjunction
with the evidence presented below, it may help to show Mendoza's
place in relation to the tastes prevalent in his day.

   Joseph del Corral, a court official, began in 1625 to put together
a common-place book which presumably expressed his predilections
in poetry. [15] He disregarded the learned, Italianate works of his

[13] *Favores de las Musas* (Milan, 1631), f. 5ᵛ: "sin impropriedad, dulce y magestuoso."
The following contemporary encomiums of Mendoza may also be noted: Fernando Luis
de Vera y Mendoza, *Panegírico por la poesía* (1627), in *Revista de Bibliografía Nacional*,
II (1941), 335 (= f. 55); Luigi Carducho, *Diálogos de la pintura entre maestro y discípulo* (Madrid, 1629), f. 61; Joseph Pellicer y Tovar, *El fénix y su historia natural*
(Madrid, 1630), f. 63; Montalbán, *Para todos* (Huesca, 1633), f. 55 and f. 16 (of second
series); Salas Barbadillo, *Coronas del Parnaso y platos de las Musas* (Madrid, 1635),
f. 34, and f. 127ᵛ.
   [14] The "bizarro ingenio, dulcemente grave" was, claimed Lope, "a rare master of
gentle speech, sprightly in prose and verse, conceitful, fluent, pure and crystalline." (See
Laurel de Apolo, in *Obras no dramáticas*, BAE, XXXVIII, p. 198).
   [15] See E. M. Wilson, "The *Cancionero* of Don Joseph del Corral," HR, XXXV (1967),
141-160. I assume that the make-up of the *Cancionero* was homogeneous throughout — the
manuscript in its present form is mutilated, with about a half of the original material gone.

period, and showed a marked preference for poems of courtly love, and the Manzanarian idyll. His favourites included Lope de Vega, Esquilache, the Count of Salinas, Antonio de Mendoza (four of whose best-known poems appear), Luis Vélez de Guevara, and poems from the *Primavera y flor*. Góngora, on the other hand, is represented by only two poems, one a burlesque sonnet, the other a late and courtly *romance*. The pertinence for the *Cancionero* of the *Primavera y flor* throws into relief how the latter also reflected a certain kind of taste in the years (extending from 1621 to 1641) during which its various, and varying, editions appeared. More an anthology than a haphazard collection, it may well reflect too the predilection of noble patrons anxious to hear its poems sung to an appropriate musical accompaniment. [16] The favourite genre in the *Primavera* is the pastoral ballad, but the short-lined Castilian stanzas such as the *redondillas,* the *letras,* and *endechas* (or *romancillos*) are also well represented. The most popular poets in the collection were Mendoza, Liñán and Villamediana. Góngora does make his appearance, but as the author of verses like:

> En dos luzientes estrellas,
> y estrellas de rayos negros,
> diuidido he visto el sol
> en breue espacio de cielo. [17]

— which are very much in keeping with the tone of the entire volume. The only markedly different style of composition is that of the brilliant *conceptista* satirical piece, a field in which Quevedo's expertness assured him a prominent place. Like Corral's *Cancionero,* therefore, the *Primavera's* appeal is courtly, Castilian, modestly *conceptista,* and limited in its intellectual demands.

Bearing in mind Mendoza's views on poetry, his veneration of Esquilache, his coincidence with Polo and Bocángel in certain opinions about Góngora and poetic language, and his popularity with a particular audience whose profile I trace in more detail in another chapter, we may postulate the existence of a taste, even a tradition,

---

[16] See p. 195 here. Corral's *Cancionero* significantly gives musical tablature for the first four lines of seven poems, including Mendoza's "Pastores que me abraso" (see Wilson p. 143 and *passim*).

[17] See *Primavera*, ed. Montesinos, p. 79: *I have seen the sun divided into two shining stars of black rays in a small space of heaven.*

that was a product of court values: "la decencia de Palacio" made poetic flesh. Certain characteristics have already been evinced. One further point needs elaboration. Although the claim to a superior "Palace" taste may in some degree have been based on the belief that the courtly poet gave expression to certain aesthetic qualities, the choice of poetic forms and themes was also important in maintaining the sense of separateness from vulgar, and possibly indeed from learned, taste. For the court poet, with the notable exception of Villamediana, the predominant form was the pastoral ballad. But if the Count's predilection here was different, he shared Mendoza's love for the archaic *glosas,* and both shared with Esquilache a fondness for the *redondilla,* including its use as an epistolary form. Furthermore, they had certain techniques in common, so much so that at moments it is difficult to recognize the genuine voice of a particular poet. The following verse:

> De un daño no merecido
> es cordura enloquecer,
> y hay causa que en el perder
> acredita al más perdido.

happens to be by Villamediana, but it could well have been by Mendoza. [18] What unites the two poets is the fondness for placing an abstract noun in a concrete relationship, the use of paradox, and of *conceptos* based on play on different forms of the same word, in the tradition of the *Cancionero* poets. What distinguishes Mendoza's practice from Villamediana's is that he is often more daring in his conceits, and that for the Count's Platonic spirituality (even more marked in the early poetry, in the tradition of Salinas) Mendoza has substituted his own more demanding intellectualizations.

The archaic flavour in both poets is characteristic of their other courtly contemporaries: there was indeed a conscious sense of continuity. Lope de Vega, who more than once recalled the part played by the noblemen poets of the fifteenth century, drew attention (in his dedication of *La pobreza estimada* to the Prince of Esquilache) to the vogue now enjoyed by poetry at the royal court, claiming

---

[18] Juan de Tassis, Conde de Villamediana, ed. L.R.C. (Madrid, 1944), p. 189: *It is sane to go mad because of some undeserved harm, and there is a case which in the very losing accredits the most lost soul.* For Villamediana's early verse, see Juan Manuel Rozas, *Cancionero de Mendes Britto: Poesías inéditas del Conde de Villamediana* (Madrid, 1965).

that it had not enjoyed such favour since the days of King John II (1406-1454). [19] He added, however, that the earlier period had seen better poets than now "of that style" ("de aquel estilo"): Lope thus not only shows his sense of the comparability between the two groups, but associates both with a particular style of verse. We may surmise too that the conscious emulation now of the forms of the *Cancionero* was a means of drawing attention to the fact that in both periods the practisers of such poetry were noble. Such recrudescence of interest in the indigenous poetic tradition of the Middle Ages may be looked at in a wider context. It is interesting that in the same way that in the mid-sixteenth century, under the aegis of St. Gelais, French court poetry had offset the dominance of the *Pléiade,* so, in the early seventeenth, under the aegis of Voiture, it sought to counter the dominance of Malherbe. [20] The *poésie galante,* of which Voiture was master, is remarkably close in themes and manner to that of the Spanish court poets in the same period; it is characterized also by a similar medieval archaism. Renée Winegarten, in her *French Lyric Poetry in the Age of Malherbe,* has drawn attention to the feeling uttered by those who exercised the archaic manner, that subtle thoughts were better expressed in it than in the stricter technique of the classical school. [21] A corresponding gap existed in Spain between the Castilian and Italianate techniques, a gap emphasized by the continuing importance in the sixteenth and seventeenth centuries of the ability to compose impromptu (*de repente*) in the native metres. And in both France and Spain a feeling may have existed that the older tradition was better attuned to the delicate, subtle preoccupations of a court life infused by the ideal of the *Courtier.* [22] One last point suggests itself: in a period dominated

---

[19] Cf. p. 129, and see Lope de Vega, *Decimaoctava parte de las comedias...* (Madrid, 1623), f. 25v.

[20] See Bourciez, op. cit., esp. pp. 280-305, and Renée Winegarten, pp. 54-61.

[21] See Winegarten, pp. 63-75. She quotes the popularity of *le style marotique,* of which a contemporary said that in it "notre oreille est faite à sentir des finesses et des agréments que l'on ne saurait lui remplacer dans un autre style" (p. 74). See also Nathan Edelman, *Attitudes of Seventeenth-Century France toward the Middle Ages* (New York, N.Y., 1946).

[22] Lope insisted on the suitability of "nuestras coplas" for expressing "las sutilezas españolas" — quot. in Collard, p. 86. Chauvinism also played a role in the preference for the Castilian as against the Italianate — see e.g. the quots. from Lope's defence of his epic *Isidro* (1599), and Juan de Vera y Figueroa's declaration in the *Fernando* (1632) that the "Coplas Castellanas" were "capaces de cantar toda obra Eroyca" (in Frank Pierce, *La poesía épica del Siglo de Oro,* 2nd edn., revised and enlarged, Madrid, 1968, p. 225). Cf. also Pacheco's praise of Lope's *coplas,* in J. M. Asensio, *Francisco Pacheco, sus obras artísticas y literarias* (Sevilla, 1886), p. xxxviii.

by the Greco-Latin tradition, culture tended to be an exclusive commodity, of which learning rather than noble birth gave possession. Mendoza, the "lay genius" [23] with no claim to great Latinity but well tutored in the history and practice of Castilian verse, may have been representative on both sides of the Pyrenees of a type of courtier whose background and thought found more congenial expression in the comparatively unlearned tradition of the older native poetry.

When Polo de Medina confessed that he had filched the enamels (esmaltes) of Mendoza, he may well have been thinking of the smooth elegance of the latter's witty verse (the estilo donoso), for Jacinto Polo was one of the masters of satire in the mid-seventeenth century. [24] Nevertheless, the kinship between much of Mendoza's satirical verse and that of Quevedo or Góngora (to which attention was earlier drawn) makes it difficult to claim a special place for Mendoza as an inspirer of other witty satirists. One distinction, nevertheless, may be a pointer to the nature of Polo's debt — José María Cossío in assessing Polo's poetry contrasted his satirical wit with that of a late sixteenth-century imitator of Martial, Baltasar de Alcázar. [25] In the latter, wit proceeds from the depiction of a real event or situation; in Polo from "the wit in the image", and the poetic perspectives which it opens up. Again, argued Cossío, Polo's humour, unlike Quevedo's, is not cruel, but "humorous play" (a "juego de donaire"). Mendoza's kind of wit belongs essentially to that of Polo rather than of Baltasar de Alcázar; unlike Quevedo, he is also rarely cruel in his satire. Mendoza's insistence that the poeta de bien did not slander [26] may have reflected his interpretation of how a courtier should practise the art of satire, and his sense of Palace decorum may explain his poetry's almost total freedom from

---

[23] Tamayo y Vargas in his Junta de libros (1624) [BNM MSS 9752-53] ranged Antonio de Mendoza alongside Cervantes as an "ingenio lego" — ref. in Américo Castro, El pensamiento de Cervantes (Madrid, 1925), p. 113. Alfonso de Batres in an academy vejamen refers to Mendoza as a "raton de sola vna lengua" (Academia burlesca, ed. J. M. Blecua, Valencia, 1952, p. 123).

[24] Salvador Jacinto Polo de Medina, El buen humor de las Musas (Madrid, 1637), f. 31. The author, in referring to various influences on his work, says "Ya dandole à la broza / de mis versos esmaltes de Mendoça."

[25] Polo de Medina, Obras escogidas, ed. J. M. de Cossío, pp. 50-56.

[26] See p. 212. Montalbán may have borne this same lack of grossness in mind when he says of Mendoza that nobody else "con mas gala, con mas viveza, con mas verdor, y con mas aseo ha escrito las burlas y las veras en nuestro idioma" (Primero tomo de las comedias [ed. Alcalá, 1638], f. 131ᵛ).

grossness and obscenity. Even when occasionally he is being trans-
parently allusive, he draws over his subject a discreet veil of poetry:

> hielo blando y jazmín vivo
> tu cuerpo, brinco de amores. [27]

The *vejamen* of a contemporary academy has preserved a significant
moment. Mendoza is on record as having censured the "common-
ness" ("ciuilidad") of some poet's *concepto*. [28] Likewise in some
witty *redondillas* on Madrid street-names the poet thought that he
should first make excuses for taking as his subject such "vulgarities"
("civilidades"). [29] A wit that was decorous and in good taste is what
links Mendoza with Polo, as well as with Bocángel and Pedro de
Quirós. The latter, a Sevillian poet, who died in 1665, wrote with
an elegant and delicate wit so akin to that of Mendoza that Quirós
almost seems his spiritual heir:

> Zagala, yo vi tu pie;
> Si digo lo que sentí,
> En mí mucho fuego fué
> La poca nieve que vi. [30]

The decorousness of Don Antonio and these other contemporaries
(to whose names one would wish to add Esquilache and Salinas) is
not only a distinctive feature of the Spanish courtly tradition of that
time, but contrasts with palace poetry elsewhere — the poets of the
Cancionero, like those of the early Tudor court, or the French court
in the time of Voiture, were fond of obscenities and scurrility. It
may well be that in Mendoza and others the *précieux* spirit regis-
tered more in an inhibition of thought than one of language.

A psychological approach to *amour courtois* poetry was implicit
in the convention from the very beginning, but usually the poet had
been more concerned with stating his passion than with tracing its

---

[27] *MOP*, III, 175: *your body is soft ice and live jasmin, a gambol of love.* Such coy
idealization sometimes leads to preciosity, e.g. in a pastoral *romance* (*MOP*, II, 386-387),
or with probable ironic intent in a *loa* (*MOP*, III, 29-37): "que donde pongo / el
zapato, breve engaste / de un jazmin de cinco dedos / todo tiembla" (p. 30).

[28] *Academia*, ed. Blecua, p. 123.

[29] *MOP*, II, 289-292. The subject could only produce "vulgares conceptos."

[30] *Poetas líricos de los siglos XVI y XVII* (I), BAE, XXXII, p. 423: *Shepherdess, I
saw your foot. If I tell you what I felt, that little ball of snow was in me a great fire.*

effects with exactness, or verisimilitude. In the Spanish tradition
the great exceptions are Garcilaso and Ausias March. The former's
"grave and passionate voice," admired and imitated by Camoens,
continued to influence Spanish poets at the beginning of the seventeenth century. [31] Luis Rosales observed that the line of "Garcilasan
sensibility" descended as far as poets such as the Count of Villamediana, and that it continued, now a combination of conceptist and
traditional Castilian, right down until the end of the century. Villamediana's subtle understanding of love's convolutions is often the
subject of his sonnets: "cuando me trato más, menos me entiendo"
he says in one poem, thus declaring a dedication to an understanding
of the processes of love in himself. [32] In some of the love sonnets, as
was earlier noted, Mendoza similarly attempted the task of self-under-
standing. But the logical extension of Petrarchanism was, as Rosales's
statement implies, better served in some ways by the *Cancionero*
tradition: the shorter metres and brusque expression set a premium
on clear-cut, witty distinctions, on strong contrasts as against the
graduated light and shade of the Italian hendecasyllable. Here too
Villamediana scored, though the Count of Salinas at moments was
also capable of transferring to the Castilian forms the passionate
spirituality which marked his sonnets, while investing them with a
concision uncharacteristic of his sometimes turgid Petrarchan eloquence. One may instance here the ending of a Salinas poem "Arded coraçon Arded":

> Este fuego desigual
> ningun rremedio rreciue
> que como en el alma bibe
> tiene dolor ynmortal. [33]

Mendoza's own *conceptismo* of love (like that of Villamediana) is
derived from this strange compound of court gallantry, Petrarchanism, and Platonism; it is characterized also at times by the
word-play of the old *Cancioneros*. That Mendoza's style was thought

---

[31] See Luis Rosales's introduction to Vivanco and Rosales, *Poesía heroica del Imperio*,
II, xvii-xix, and his "La poesía cortesana," pp. 290-291, and p. 293 *et seq.*

[32] Villamediana, *Poesías*, ed. L. R. C., p. 4: *The more time I spend in my own
company, the less do I understand myself.*

[33] BNM *MS* 3700, "Poesías varias," f. 45: *This great fire has no remedy, for as
it lives in the soul, it suffers an immortal pain.*

to be similar to Salinas's is suggested by the fact that in one manuscript, one of Don Antonio's best-known poems, "Quien ama correspondido," is ascribed to Salinas. [34] The attribution may also signify that both poets were reckoned likely authors of a piece that anatomizes succinctly and with wit the "leyes de amor" that were an important aspect of palace life, and the basis of its poetry.

But Mendoza (again like Villamediana) sought to explore further the *concepto*'s ability to tease out the nature of love, and in a few of his poems he managed to conjoin the intimacy and directness of a Garcilasan poem with the alembications and paradoxes of *conceptismo,* as may be judged by the opening verses of a beautiful ballad:

> A las voces de un silencio
> su pena fía un dolor,
> para que muera un callar
> basta descubrir la voz.
>   ¡Qué en vano el amor se encubre,
> qué inútilmente calló!,
> pues el no querer decirlo
> dice más bien que es amor.
>   Ni aun callar puede el silencio,
> ni que vos, Celinda, sois
> la causa, pues ya lo dicen
> callar, morir, y amar yo. [35]

A different quality is expressed in some *décimas* making play with the lover's inability at the same time both to hear and see his lady. The poem ends thus:

> Yo os oigo y veo, mas cuando
> en cada acción me suspendo,
> no sé si es la que estoy viendo
> la que estoy luego escuchando,
> que hablando vos, yo adorando
> en vos las obras de Dios,
> por no repartirme en dos,
> sin veros os oigo, y luego

---

[34] BNM *MS* 3884, "Poesías varias, Tomo I," f. 371: see *MOP*, II, 380-381. The MS version contains some extra verses.

[35] *MOP*, I, 201-202: *A sorrow entrusts its pain to the voices of silence. For silence to die it is enough just to find one's voice. How in vain does love conceal itself! How uselessly did it keep silent, for the refusal to admit proclaims rather that it is love. Silence cannot even keep silent, nor refuse to say that you, Celinda, are the cause, for this is already announced by my silence, my death, and my love.*

> no viéndoos ya dudo ciego,
> si la que escucho sois vos.
>   Este dudar y dejar
> de veros a un tiempo mismo
> pudieran ser un abismo
> de confusión y pesar.
> Pero no ha dado lugar
> venir tanto a suspender
> el alma todo su ser
> que aun no es posible sentir
> en la gloria del oír
> el tormento de no ver. [36]

This is a poetry of slow motion, in which the flashing of the conceits has not disturbed the poet's watchfulness over his subject. In such verses too Mendoza comes near to the spirit, even to the quasi-scientific manner, of John Donne: it is truly a metaphysical poetry. The manner is found in Villamediana as well, and will pass into Bocángel's sonnets: Mendoza's own achievement is usually to have preserved an even balance between the cleverness of the saying, and the truthfulness of the said. It is a tragedy of the latter part of Philip IV's reign and that of Charles II that Antonio de Solís, [37] the poet who in turn was heir to Bocángel, as the latter had been to Mendoza, inherited the frivolity and gallantry of manner of the court without bringing to them any of the intellectual penetration and subtlety of feeling with which his predecessors had frequently infused their verse, to the delight of the company and the enrichment of the poetic tradition. Gracián's regret in mid-century that the "royal lute" lay neglected was probably the greater for the feeling that Mendoza had been the last great representative of the courtly tradition in Spain.

---

[36] *MOP*, II, 305-306: *I hear and see you, but when both these actions are in suspense, I do not know whether the lady I am looking at is the one also that I am listening to, for when you speak (while I am also adoring God's works in you), so as not to divide myself into two, I listen to you without seeing you, and then no longer seeing you I doubt in my blindness whether you are the one I am listening to. This doubt, and at one and the same time ceasing to see you, could be an abyss of confusion and sadness. But things have not reached such a pitch that the soul's whole being has been so suspended that it is not yet possible to feel in the glory of hearing, the torment of not seeing.*

[37] Antonio de Solís, *Varias poesías sagradas y profanas*, ed. Manuela Sánchez Regueira (Madrid, 1968). The vol. was published in 1692. Solís's earliest composition to appear in print was in Polo de Medina's *Academias del jardín* (1630).

VIII

A POET AND HIS AUDIENCE

L I K E any other poet Mendoza had both an immediate and a more remote audience. The former was composed primarily of those he served: his King and Queen, the royal favourite, the noble families of the court. At an intermediate distance were the literary academies whose members were drawn from the court itself and those outside. And beyond these were the public at large, whose knowledge was circumscribed by the availability of printed texts, and whose estimate of the author was possibly inflated by consideration of his social and political prestige.

Of these circles the most important was the least numerous. In part this was because the appeal of some poems was limited by the ephemeral nature of the occasions they commemorated, or the purely personal function they served. But the poet's audience was also limited by choice, or fashion, since he showed little interest in having his poems printed, or circulated in manuscript on any scale. With the exception of *Querer por solo querer* (considerable sections of which are lyric poetry), no published collection of his poems appeared, and only towards the end of his life did he arrange for the compilation of the *Palacio* manuscript, a comprehensive collection presumably intended for circulation at court. [1] Two other large compilations of his poems were also, in all likelihood, aimed at a palace audience: *Palacio de las Musas y Musas de palacio* one declared itself; whilst the manuscript which eventually served as the basis of the text of *El Fénix castellano* (1690) had been in the possession of Archbishop Luis de Sousa, an avowed admirer of Mendoza's work, who had been also a member of the Portuguese Council of State. [2] But what is significant is that these collections belong to the very last years of the poet's career, or to the period not long after his

---

[1] For this and the other MSS mentioned, see *MOP*, I, xxxiv-xlviii, and the List of Manuscripts and Books here.

[2] See *FC*, prelims., ff. II-III, and *MOP*, I, xxxii.

death. Apparently therefore a comprehensive view of his poetry was not available, even to the courtly reader, in the twenties and the early thirties when his reputation was at its height.

What of a more limited selection? At least four manuscripts gave Mendoza's contemporaries some impression of his work. [3] Two of them (BNM *MSS* 17678 and 17723) appeared late, no earlier than 1636. A third compilation (BNM *MS* 3700) forms part of a collection by various hands of the seventeenth century, but the only clue to the date of the Mendoza section is that one of the poems had appeared in a printed collection of 1621. The fourth manuscript, *Romances de D. Antonio de Mendoza* (Hisp. Soc. Am. *MS* B2413), bears a close relation to the selection in *MS* 3700, but once more the only clue to dating lies in the identical poem, pointing to 1621 as a *terminus a quo*. Since the chronological evidence of the two latter manuscripts is inconclusive, it is impossible to reach firm conclusions about the availability of Mendoza's poems. But always remembering the not unlikely contingency that more manuscript material lies undiscovered, one may hazard these suggestions: that towards the end of the thirties or soon afterwards the desire had grown to read Mendoza's poems in manuscript; but that during the greater part of the poet's lifetime his reputation must largely have been created by the performance of his poems *viva voce*.

One of Mendoza's poems must be put in a separate category. His *Life of the Virgin* was not printed until 1666, when it appeared in Seville. But an unfinished draft existed as early as 1628, and the evidence, discussed elsewhere, shows that the poem was read in manuscript both during the remaining years of the poet's life and in the period between his death, and eventual publication. Subsequently, the poem went through numerous editions in the latter part of the seventeenth century, and well into the eighteenth. [4]

Mendoza's shyness about getting into print is confirmed by some remarks in the prologue to *Querer por solo querer*, which are sufficient indication of how (at least publicly) he viewed his art. [5] A

---

[3] The bibliography of MSS and printed sources is discussed in *MOP*, I, xviii-xxxii. For other MSS not mentioned, see List of Manuscripts and Books.

[4] See ch. on *Vida de Nuestra Señora*.

[5] See *Querer por solo querer* (1623), prologue: "La ambicion de la Emprenta es vna Culpa, que no le basta arrepentirse." His reason, however, is in part prudence: "Vn dia es siempre Maestro de otro; contra lo que se escriue oy, estara lo que mañana se sabe mas."

deliberate amateurism was indeed, as Luis Rosales remarked, the hall-mark of the palace poet. [6] Professional men of letters like Lope de Vega, or even Gabriel Bocángel, on whose shoulders Mendoza's mantle would eventually fall, could publish their verse with impunity. With the aristocratic poet things were different: poetry for the palace poets was not an art but an ideal of life, [7] and the social pressures to which they responded are implied in a statement made by Gracián and attributable to the Count of Orgaz, that the man who did not know how to write a *copla* was a fool, and the man who wrote two, a madman. [8]

The double standard that acknowledged the art but denied its practice is clear too from Lope de Vega's remarks in the prologue to the San Isidro *Justa poética* of 1620. [9] The age of the *Cancionero* poets, he averred, had produced a goodly number of "admirals," dukes, counts, and kings who practised poetry. The equivalents of these poets, equal in genius and culture, were still to be found in Spain, but were shown less approval by people who knew nothing about the subject. We may judge that Lope's words imply the contemporary palace poet's sense that he stood in a hallowed tradition, but that he needed a measure of courage to stand against the charge of ridicule. Mendoza certainly acquiesced in the view that he should not appear so serious about his poems as to get them printed, an attitude he presumably shared with Salinas, and Villamediana; or indeed with Esquilache, whose works only appeared at the end of a long and fruitful career. [10]

Some of Mendoza's poems did find their way, however, into the popular lyric collections of his day, among them some of his best-known compositions, if we may judge by the regularity of their occurrence in the manuscripts. The most important collection to give currency to some of Antonio de Mendoza's verses was Arias Pérez's

---

[6] Luis Rosales, "La poesía cortesana," p. 329.

[7] Ibid., p. 329.

[8] See *El discreto* (1646), in *GOC*, ed. E. Correa Calderón (Madrid, 1944), p. 350 — the editor draws attention to the probable source of Gracián's ref., cf. similar advice in Alonso Núñez de Castro, *Libro historico politico: solo Madrid es Corte*, 2nd impression (Madrid, 1669), pp. 159-160 and p. 198. On the print-shy poet in England, see J. B. Leishman, "Donne and Seventeenth-Century Poetry," in *Seventeenth-Century English Poetry: Modern Essays in Criticism*, ed. W. R. Keast (New York, N. Y., 1962), pp. 75-91.

[9] Lope de Vega, *Justa poética en honor de San Isidro...*, in *Obras escogidas*, II, p. 1574; also Rennert and Castro, p. 270 *et seq*.

[10] Francisco de Borja, Príncipe de Esquilache, *Obras diuinas, y humanas en verso* (Madrid, 1648).

Primavera y flor in its varying editions. [11] The first, of 1621, had contained five of his poems, only two of which were to become very well-known, a *letra* "No corras, arroyo, ufano," and a ballad "Poca tierra y muchas flores." The 1623 edition included another poem, the famous "Con sus trapos Inesilla," whilst the 1641 edition brought in another popular *jácara*, the "Villana de Leganés." In the intervening period (during which the *Primavera y flor* was reprinted several times) one ballad appeared in a Portuguese collection, *Maravillas del Parnaso y flor de los mejores romances* (1637), and another in a Zaragozan collection, *Romances varios de diversos autores* (1640). [12]

The *Primavera y flor* has been recognized, however, as more than the means by which the poems of Mendoza and others reached a wider reading public; these volumes, it has been argued, were the repositories of texts intended primarily for singing at aristocratic gatherings. [13] Whether this was so may still be open to doubt, but we do know from other evidence that in Mendoza's case the provision of lyrics for song-writers was a significant part of his contribution to the cultural life of his age, and an important channel for communication with a wider audience.

Lope de Vega, in commenting on the Spaniards' special aptitude for vocal and instrumental music, called the voice "the soul of the words," [14] a remark that many of his contemporaries would have endorsed, since poetry for them was quite often associated with musical setting, and to some extent, as we shall see, the very identity of a poem was sometimes determined by the needs of the composer rather than those of the poet. If in the early seventeenth century in Spain the art of music did not reach those heights of excellence and originality attained during the years of Philip II, there could be no

---

[11] Pedro Arias Pérez, *Primavera y flor de los mejores romances* (Madrid, 1621). The subsequent edns. and revisions are discussed by J. F. Montesinos in his edn. (Valencia, 1954), pp. 275-284.

[12] *Maravillas del Parnaso* (Lisboa, 1637), facsimile edn., de Vinne Press (New York, 1902), f. 89v, and *Romances varios* (Zaragoça, 1640), p. 89. There appears to have been an earlier edn. of 1636 (see James O. Crosby, *En torno a la poesía de Quevedo*, Madrid, 1967, pp. 172-173, Note 46).

[13] *Primavera*, ed. Montesinos, p. xxxviii *et seq.* Jack Sage (King's College, London) has privately expressed his doubt whether the *Primavera* was primarily intended as a source for the song-writers.

[14] "La voz, que era el alma de la letra:" see Lope's dedication of his *Carlos Quinto en Francia* to Gabriel Díaz, *Maestro de Capilla* at the monastery of the Incarnation, in *Parte decinueve* (Madrid, 1625), ff. 261-262.

doubt of its popularity. [15] Philip IV's court was especially fond of music. Juan Ruiz de Robledo in the *Laura de música eclesiástica* praised the monarch's musical prowess, for Philip under the guidance of his *Maestro de Cámara*, Mateo Romero *(Capitán)*, had learnt both the theory and practice of the art, having indeed "admirably composed many works of Latin and Romance" which he himself conducted. [16] The King's favourite too was given to good music, a conclusion fairly drawn from the curious fact that as a sufferer from insomnia Olivares would get his servants to sing him to sleep. [17] The King's secretary shared the enthusiasm of monarch and favourite, witness some verses written in celebration of the court musicians' part in a play performed in the *Retiro* on St. John's Eve 1638:

> Qué de músicas y tonos
> de Gabriel y el Capitán,
> mas para toda garganta
> es mi devoción Juan Blas.

Mendoza here referred to three eminent composers of the day who served the royal family: Mateo Romero, the King's teacher as we have seen, and a writer of rare invention, distinguished by the purity of his musical style; Gabriel Díaz, *maestro de capilla* at the monastery of the Incarnation, to whom Lope de Vega dedicated one of his plays; and Juan Blas, Mendoza's favourite, immortalized by Lope in a commemorative elegy in 1631, and described by him on another occasion as an Orpheus painting a divine world. [18]

---

[15] See Rafael Mitjana, "La Musique en Espagne," *Encyclopédie de la Musique et Dictionnaire du Conservatoire*, ed. Albert Lavignac, Part One (*Histoire de la Musique: Espagne-Portugal*), Paris, 1920, pp. 1913-2351 (the 17th century is discussed on pp. 2035-2114); Jesús Bal, *Treinta canciones de Lope de Vega* (Madrid, 1935), esp. p. 97 *et seq.*; José Subirá, *La música en la casa de Alba: Estudios históricos y biográficos* (Madrid, 1927), pp. 49-82.

[16] See text, not always dependable, in Higinio Anglés and José Subirá, *Catálogo musical de la Biblioteca Nacional de Madrid*, I (*Manuscritos*), Barcelona, 1946, 182-187. The original MS, itself a copy made for Barbieri of an Escorial MS (iiij &-7), has the signature M1287. Mendoza in his account of the Feast of Aranjuez praised the excellent musical standards achieved by the *maestro* of the Chapel Royal (*MOP*, I, 25).

[17] Marañón, p. 394. An account of a palace *fiesta* of 1631 shows the favourite fussily engaged in perfecting the musical arrangements (in Casiano Pellicer, *Tratado histórico sobre el origen y progresos de la comedia...*, Madrid, 1804, II, 171-174).

[18] *MOP*, III, 70: *What music and songs of Gabriel and* Maestro Capitán, *but for every kind of embellishment* [and throat?] *my choice goes to* Juan Blas. Mendoza's fondness for music is shown too in his account of the Feast of Aranjuez, where he praises Juan Blas, Palomares and Álvaro de los Ríos, declaring also that Spain produces the most outstanding voices in the world (*MOP*, I, 25). On Romero, see Mitjana, op. cit., pp. 2049-2050, and Felipe Pedrell, *Cancionero musical popular español*, III (Valls, 1922), 43-44;

Was Mendoza like his monarch also a musical performer? He
may have been. In an occasional poem he offers a lady his guitar;
his early connexions with Lope and Vicente Espinel may have increased his appreciation of that instrument; and it may be significant
that Gracián described Mendoza's neglected genius as that abandoned "royal lute." [19] Allowance having been made for the fact that
such language was found in the verses of other poets too, Mendoza's
fondness for musical metaphor may yet echo his predilections: some
lines from *Querer,* recalling a poem by Góngora, describe the stream
which spreads its music afar as an "instrumento sonoro /　en trastes
de crystal, clavijas de oro;" and in an unpublished poem, declaring
his readiness to take up verse again, he likens his abandonment of the
Muse to the Psalmist hanging his harp on the willow tree — but
the present poet's instrument is a fretted one, like a guitar: "el corvo,
el ocioso leño / cuios rotos trastes / pulsan susurros del viento." [20]
There is nothing to suggest that Mendoza, like Thomas Campion,
was also a composer who performed his own songs, though an
account of an academy meeting depicts "el canoro Antandro" singing
his own poem to the accompaniment of a mustachioed guitarist. [21]
The poet may in some degree, therefore, have exemplified what had
been said by Castiglione, that music was not only an adornment but
a necessity in the ideal courtier.

What proportion of Mendoza's poems was usually sung? His
pastoral ballads (with their division into four-line stanzas in the style
of the *romancero nuevo*) were particularly suitable, and settings for
some of them were indeed made. Many of his other compositions
— in particular his *letras, jácaras, seguidillas, madrigales,* and even
his sonnets — may on occasion have reached their audience through

Lope in his dedication paid respect to Díaz's musical genius (see note 14); on Juan
Blas, see *Historia de la música española* (Barcelona, 1953), pp. 312-314, Mitjana, op. cit.,
pp. 2071-2083, and Jesús Bal, *Treinta canciones,* pp. 102-103.

[19] See Hisp. Soc. Am. *MS HC*: 371/224, f. 48ᵛ; for Espinel and Gracían, see
p. 21, and pp. 55-56 here. On Lope's musical prowess, see Barbieri, "Lope de Vega, músico," *Gaceta musical barcelonesa,* numbers for 27 December 1863 - 13 March 1864, and
Treinta canciones, p. 97 *et seq.*

[20] *Querer* in *FC,* pp. 374-375: *sonorous instrument, pegs of gold upon frets of crystal,*
echoing Góngora's more ambitious exercise in metaphor (ed. Millé, p. 576, No. 390 of
otras composiciones de arte mayor); *the curving and idle wood, where broken frets move
to the wind's murmur,* in Hisp. Soc. Am. *MS HC* 371/224, f. 113, where on f. 75 the
poet also writes, with seeming direct experience: "y no enmienda diestra mano / imper-
fecciones del plectro."

[21] Quot. in Sánchez, *Academias literarias,* p. 321, Note, Anastasio Pantaleón's account
of the *Academia de Madrid.* The identification with Don Antonio, though not certain, is
quite likely.

the medium of music, though one must always bear in mind that at this period musical composition was not dominant enough an art for a poet to think instantly of his poem as something that would be set to music.

Mendoza's popularity as a writer of song lyrics can no longer be accurately gauged — the collection of the Chapel Royal, in which one might expect to find many of his songs, was destroyed in the Alcázar fire of 1734; and a similar fate overtook another potential repository when a number of the *tonos* of Mateo Romero, *Maestro Capitán,* were destroyed by fire in the music library of the Portuguese King, João IV. [22] The remaining evidence may well reflect insufficiently the extent of Mendoza's musical collaboration, but certainly even by the extant material we may judge that he had considerable appeal as a lyricist. The *Cancionero de Sablonara,* of around 1625, made up of 78 songs, included two with *letras* by Mendoza, a number which may reflect the author's modest, but growing, reputation at court, where these songs were sung; the collection was made up of the best songs for two, three and four voices that the editor Claudio de la Sablonara had been able to find at the palace. [23] The *Cancionero poético-musical de 1645* almost certainly reflects the advance in the poet's popularity, for in this collection of 118 songs (by composers including Mateo Romero, Padre Correa and Cristóbal Galán) at least six, if not seven, are settings of lyrics by Mendoza: Lope de Vega in comparison rates only a modest two. [24] This collection may also reflect in part the resurgence of interest in Mendoza at the end of his career and just after his death, an interest still reflected, perhaps anachronistically, in the large volume BNM *MS M1262,* a manuscript kept in the Carmelite Convent in Salamanca, but presumed to have been copied in Madrid in 1655-56. Of

---

[22] For these losses, see Mitjana, op. cit., pp. 2071-2083, and José Subirá, *Historia de la música teatral en España* (Barcelona, 1945), p. 79.

[23] *Cancionero de Claudio de la Sablonara,* ed. Jesús Roca (Madrid, 1916), No. 1, and No. 38. I am grateful to Jack Sage for his help in assessing Mendoza's representation in the *cancioneros* of the period. He has not found any of Don Antonio's *letras* in the Italian collections (see also C. V. Aubrun, "Chansonniers musicaux espagnols du XVIIᵉ siècle," *BH,* LI [1949], 268-290 and LII [1950], 313-374), including the *cancionero* of the Biblioteca Marziana in Venice, nor in the *Cancionero de Olot*; nor in *Tonos a lo divino y a lo humano, Recogidos por el Lizenziado D. Geronimo Nieto Madaleno,* MS 477 of the Borbón-Lorenzana collection in the Biblioteca Pública de Toledo (see Francisco Esteve Barba, *Catálogo de la colección Borbón-Lorenzana* (Madrid, 1942). See Appendix I for an account of Mendoza's songs, and their whereabouts.

[24] See Andrés Ortega del Álamo, *Dos canciones de Lope de Vega en un Cancionero poético musical del siglo XVII* (Valencia, 1962).

these 226 songs (the names of whose authors are not given) the words of eight are by Mendoza, though sometimes in a slightly different guise from the poems found in the *Obras poéticas;* but significantly too a number of the other lyrics are attributable to him on stylistic grounds, even though they do not form part of the established canon of his works. The manuscript indicates the names of composers only sparingly, but three of the Mendoza poems have settings by Padre Correa, and one by Machado. One other *cancionero* should be mentioned, BNM *MS* 4103, a Jesuit-inspired collection of the lyrics of songs of the day, put together after 1680, possibly in Valencia. [25] A poet who had by that time been dead forty years, and who was apparently in Gracián's estimation neglected by the early sixteen-fifties, should not be well represented. In reality the collection included the *letras* of one of Mendoza's best-known poems, "Compitiendo con las selvas," and another probably by him, "Ya es turbante Guadarrama," which like its companion certainly deserved to be remembered.

The occasions when Mendoza's pieces reached their public in musical setting varied. The least usual probably were the great public occasions, such as the religious celebrations during Epiphany 1624 when, presumably at the Chapel Royal, some *letras* by the poet, in an unusual setting by the *Maestro Capitán,* were performed by the "best singers in the world." [26] The nature of another occasion may only be guessed at, since the copyist of the Paris manuscript of Mendoza's poems extracted only the *estribillo* of an obviously patriotic poem whose text he had seen in a "musical copybook" in a drawer of the royal palace. [27]

More characteristic certainly were the meetings of the literary academies in the more elaborate of which music played an important

---

[25] See Jack Sage, "Valentín de Céspedes — Poet, Collector or Impostor?" *Homage to John M. Hill* (Indiana University, 1968), 85-112. The continuing attraction of Mendoza as lyricist is suggested by *Romances varios. De differentes authores. Nuevamente Impressos por un Curioso* (Amsterdam, 1688): "Compitiendo con las selvas" is found on pp. 38-39. Jack Sage has evidence that this is predominantly a collection of song-lyrics.

[26] See Real Ac. de la Historia, *Papeles variados de Jesuitas,* CLIII, No. 35: *Copia de vna carta de Andrés de Mendoza,* an *impreso,* no place, Andrés de Parra, 1624. The lyrics may have been those of an unpublished *romance, Villancico para la fiesta de Reyes* in *PMS,* p. 527: "O corteses, o tiranos."

[27] *PMS,* p. 536, an unpublished *estribillo* "Que bien que pelea." The lines are described as "Sacadas de un quaderno Musico de las gavetas del Rey." Another poem (*MOP,* II, 127-128) is described simply as a "Romance para la guitarra."

part. In one quite extraordinary academy Mendoza may have participated, since the president was his friend Luis Vélez. [28] It was held on 28 February 1627 in the Madrid home of that celebrated and rich eccentric Juan de Espina, who had invited musicians and dancers, as well as fifty-three guests of both sexes. The distinguished company was entertained in part by the usual poetic fare, but music too made a striking contribution, performed by a group of "the most illustrious musicians," including performers on sackbut, flute, trumpet, clarion and percussion. A *fiesta* that included a procession of mules cannot be regarded as altogether typical, but other evidence suggests that other academy contests sometimes had music. For instance Gabriel del Corral's *La Cintia de Aranjuez* (1629) refers to a poetic competition arranged "with music and dancing *(sarao)*," whilst Luis Vélez in his *Diablo cojuelo* (1641) describes what purports to be a Sevillian academy, where at the end of the evening "one of the veiled ladies took out a guitar, which she had tuned without anyone noticing it, and with two other ladies sang with three voices a most excellent ballad by Don Antonio de Mendoza." [29] We do not know whether that *fiesta* actually took place, or whether Luis Vélez was merely evoking a characteristic festivity. If the latter, then significantly he associated the musical entertainment with the name of Mendoza.

The private entertainment, though it may have afforded the most characteristic occasion for the musical performance of Antonio de Mendoza's poems, is necessarily the least well documented. For this reason the evidence of an evening probably quite removed from any historical reality assumes importance. This was a *fiesta* described in Castillo Solórzano's *Tiempo de regocijo y Carnestolendas* (1627), at which a literary patron entertained his guests:

> The ladies took their seats, and near them their fathers and brothers. When the inquiries after each other's health had been made, Don Enrique, anxious

---

[28] See BNM MS 2359, an *impreso* wrongly foliated as f. 167 of a bound volume: *Relación de la fiesta que hizo don Iuan de Espina, Domingo en la noche, ultimo dia de Febrero, Año 1627.*

[29] Gabriel del Corral, *La Cintia de Aranjuez, prosas y versos* (Madrid, 1629), f. 29v; and Luis Vélez de Guevara, *El diablo cojuelo*, Clás. Cast. (Madrid, 1918), pp. 249-250 (the editor argues that the Sevillian academy actually existed): "Sacando una guitarra una dama de las tapadas, templada sin sentillo, con otras dos cantaron a tres voces un romance excelentísimo de don Antonio de Mendoza." Alonso de Castillo Solórzano (in *Las harpías en Madrid y coche de las estafas*, Barcelona, 1633, f. 70v) described an academy "full of poets, musicians and the greatest gentlemen of the court" at which

for his *fiesta* to begin, asked for silence so as to give ear to eight musicians who, with their instruments, occupied one part of the room. And to their gentle embellishments they sang with gentle voices this *romance,* which had been composed in praise of the singular beauty of Doña Ana, Don Enrique's daughter. [30]

The text does not suggest that Mendoza was the author of this *romance.* But this was certainly a characteristic evening of entertainment, in which Mendoza might have fulfilled the role we have seen him perform at court, as well as in the households of the palace entourage. The roles played here by patron, poet, musicians and music, as well as by the lady who was the object of the poet's praise, characterize the context of a large portion of Mendoza's art.

How responsive was Don Antonio's poetry to the possible demands of musical setting? Francisco Pacheco spoke aptly of Lope de Vega's contribution: "and not only has he perfected poetry, but music owes him like gratitude, since the variety of his verses, and the smooth flow of his thoughts, have given it material with which it may sustain itself with abundance and the most felicitous results." [31] Lope recognized the interdependence of the two arts in his famous *Elogio* on the death of the musician Juan Blas de Castro:

> Y dilatabas tú mis pensamientos
> con dulce voz que el aire suspendía. [32]

But how true would it be for Mendoza, or for Lope, that in writing their poems they anticipated the conditions of musical setting? José María de Cossío, when discussing the relationship between words

---

"a quatro coros cantaron primorosos tonos, en bien escritas letras, por los mismos Academicos." Later, reference (f. 78) is made to the performance of "una letra escrita por el Presidente, y puesta en tono por el insigne maestro Capitan."

[30] Alonso de Castillo Solórzano, *Tiempo de regozijo y Carnestolendas de Madrid* (Madrid, 1627), f. 4: "Ocuparon sus assientos las damas, y cerca dellas sus padres y hermanos. Y despues que se huuieron preguntado por sus saludes, Don Enrique deseoso de que se començasse su fiesta, les pidio que prestassen silencio a ocho musicos que ocupauan una parte de la sala con varios instrumentos: a cuyas suaues diferencias cantaron con suaues vozes este Romance, que se auia hecho en alabança de la singular hermosura de Doña Ana, hija de don Enrique."

[31] "Y no solo la Poesia ha perficionado, pero la Musica le debe igual agradecimiento, pues la variedad de sus versos, y la blandura de sus pensamientos le ha dado materia en que con felicissimo efecto y abundancia se sustente" (in J. M. Asensio, *Francisco Pacheco,* p. xxxviii).

[32] *and you broadcast (as well as expanded) my thoughts with a sweet voice that kept the air suspended* (in *Obras sueltas,* IX, Madrid, 1777, p. 387). He died in 1631 (see Subirá, *Historia de la música española,* pp. 312-314).

and music, commented on the slackness of musical rhythm in comparison with a prosodic one, mentioning how "broken harmonies, irregular correspondences, a neglect of, or disdain for, precise symmetries, contribute to the vagueness and lightness of the really musical line." [33] It would be tempting to claim that the subservience in Mendoza of strict prosody to an overall sinuous rhythm was due to the anticipation of a musical setting. But the evidence on the whole would be against this view. In the first place, as was suggested earlier, a possible musical setting would not have been in the forefront of the poet's mind. Secondly, the musical evidence suggests that as yet the composer aimed at an overall expressiveness rather than following the meaning of the words stanza by stanza. One increasingly popular form in seventeenth-century Spanish poetry did, in contrast, offer the composer the opportunity to express the meaning in a more individual way — this was the *romance* that included long *estribillos* in a different metre. [34] Mendoza was certainly fond of writing in this form, and though the combination may indicate that the poem (as distinct from a *romance* by itself) was intended to be sung, nothing suggests that as a genre it was more "musical" than the poet's other compositions.

But the very term "poem" has a certain ambiguity, greater possibly where musical setting was concerned. What we have in many cases is a gesture towards a poem, one version in its direction: what a reader saw, or an audience heard spoken or sung, was marginally or fundamentally different from the experience of a reader or audience on a different occasion. Assuming for the moment that Mendoza wrote a ballad of perhaps ten or twelve *cuartetas,* he might reckon that the song-writer would select for performance only three or four stanzas; [35] or more generously in the case of BNM *MS M 1262* composers might use seven or eight stanzas. But if we return to the full "original" version, what is striking is the Protean nature of the descendant texts: Mendoza's poems, like the traditional

---

[33] José María Cossío, "Dos corrientes rítmicas," *Notas y estudios de crítica literaria. Poesía Española. Notas de asedio* (Madrid, 1936), p. 36.

[34] See Miguel Querol Gavaldá (editor), *Romances y letras a tres vozes (siglo XVII), Monumentos de la Música Española. XVIII,* I (Barcelona, 1956), 14-17. Also Jesús Bal, *Treinta canciones,* pp. 100-101.

[35] See Jesús Bal, p. 101: "dos o tres estrofas bastan para cada canción," a judgment sometimes supported by *Romances y letras,* though six *cuartetas* of a ballad are at times given there.

romancero, live in their variants, and one can rightly refer to better, or weaker, versions of the same piece. The fact is easily grasped, but what is less comprehensible is the method of composition behind it. Are we to assume that Mendoza separately, and at different times, wrote distinct versions of the same "idea" of a poem, and that we get in the varying texts a differing blend stanzaically of the old and new? Or did he originally compose a matrix consisting of a very large number of strophes from which different versions were subsequently derived by selection? Perhaps he combined both methods.

Certainly two other factors would help determine a poem's eventual identity: in the case of the *Primavera y flor,* or of the manuscript collections of music, the editor's judgment would be decisive in the selection of verses; and in the case of the committal of poems to paper, the vagaries of an amanuensis's memory, as Rodríguez-Moñino has pointed out, often determined the shape in which a poem reached posterity in an apparently definitive form. [36] Another conclusion, important for the study of Mendoza as of his contemporaries; the poem's unity, especially in the case of the ballad, was stanzaic rather than organic, which explains not only the omission in various texts of certain strophes, but also the fact that their transposition, when it occurs, hardly affects the poem overall.

Mendoza enjoyed another, and different, audience, that of the public theatre. Here it was as a composer of lyrics that he was appreciated, though again it is difficult to be sure of the degree of his success. A modern music critic has commented how, for instance, in the seventeenth century in Spain, "the ballad floods the theatre," and by 1689 Ignacio de Camargo, who listed the various types of song in use in the stage entertainment of his day, claimed that music was then at a pinnacle of achievement. The effect of the combination of words and music was such, he said, as to hold an audience spellbound. [37] Already in Mendoza's time music was very important: it provided incidental entertainment, such as the brief introductory compositions (the *cuatro de empezar*), the *loa,* the *jácara,* and the interlude, whilst quite often the *comedia* would end with

[36] See A. Rodríguez-Moñino, *Poesía y Cancioneros (Siglo XVI),* Madrid, 1968, pp. 26-29. James O. Crosby, in "A New Edition of Quevedo's Poetry," *HR,* XXXIV (1966), 331, drew attention to the remarkably fluid nature of Quevedo's texts.

[37] Querol, op. cit., p. 14, and Ignacio de Camargo, *Discurso theológico sobre los Theatros, y comedias de este siglo* (Salamanca, 1689), pp. 55-56.

song and dance. [38] But in addition music began to play a role in the *comedia* itself, and here its significance is only now being realized, as for instance in the study of the plays of Calderón.

In Mendoza's case a distinction should be made between the role of music in his romanesque plays, and in his interludes and social comedies. In *Querer por solo querer,* for instance, music was probably important, though we do not know what specific lyric sections were sung rather than spoken — if Villamediana's *Gloria de Niquea* formed a precedent in this as in other respects, musical intervention would have been frequent, since the *Maestro Capitán* had been very busy with vocal and instrumental accompaniment for the Count's spectacle play. [39] As for Mendoza's interludes and social comedies, the dependence on music probably varied from case to case. In the interlude we find place for song at the end, for instance in the *Entremés de Getafe,* where a delightful *letra* sums up the mood of the whole work. And in *Cada loco con su tema* the author provides himself with an excuse for introducing a musician onto the stage, making him announce that they are going to sing a "new and famous *letrilla*": the text begins "Pastores de Manzanares / Yo muero por Isabel." [40] We cannot be sure that the text was Mendoza's, though it presumably was. While allowing for the appropriate degree of ballyhoo, it may still be significant, if the song was Mendoza's, that the announcement betrays a note of self-congratulation, as though the poet were drawing attention to the popularity the piece now enjoyed.

But the poem may well have been somebody else's: a common feature of the use of song material in the plays of the period. A recent study has shown Calderón's frequent use of such extraneous lyric material, a fact that suggests that other playwrights in greater or lesser degree may have done the same. [41] In Calderón the use varies from quotations sung in their own right, to instances where the snatch of song (or poem) is made the basis on which the author expends his wit or lyrical power. In either case the dramatist presumably drew on material which he believed he shared with

---

[38] J. Subirá, *La participación musical en el antiguo teatro español* (Barcelona, 1930), p. 23, and his *Historia de la música teatral en España* (Barcelona, 1945), p. 52 *et seq.*

[39] See Subirá, *Música teatral,* p. 71, and *Relación, passim,* in *MOP,* I.

[40] See *BAE,* LXV, 469. The composer was Mendoza's favourite, Juan Blas.

[41] See Edward M. Wilson and Jack Sage, *Poesías líricas en las obras dramáticas de Calderón, passim.* See also Jack Sage, "Calderón y la música teatral," *BH,* LVIII (1956), 274-300.

the audience. Calderón frequently used Antonio de Mendoza's poetry in these ways. On occasion a considerable fragment, possibly even in actual performance the whole poem, was sung — a popular song like "Compitiendo con las selvas" got a hearing no less than seven times in Calderón's dramatic works; another of Mendoza's ballads, "Montañas de Cataluña," possibly in the setting by *Maestro Capitán,* found expression just once. [42] But the short snatches are really more significant, for all that they appear trivial, or incidental. Calderón, for instance, was fond of referring to Don Antonio's *romance* in which this stanza occurred:

¡Qué me queréis desdichas!
que los pesares tienen
condición de cobardes
en venir tantos siempre. [43]

And on one of the three occasions when he used this, he alluded to the author and paraphrased the reference. Furthermore Calderón felt so sure that the audience would recognize the allusion that he did not bother to give Mendoza's name, but merely said:

... ¡Qué bien aquel
gran cortesano decía! [44]

It would be wrong to assume that Calderón took for granted that the whole of his audience would recognize at once who the author of this *romance* was: however, he probably counted upon such recognition by a minority in-group. In contrast, such a reference, as well as the inclusion of this type of poetic material in a *comedia,* signals the way in which, gradually, in the course of the seventeenth century, courtly poetry and courtly music spread and became fashionable with the masses. [45] This fact, apart from marking out

---

[42] Wilson and Sage. Nos. 34 and 160.

[43] *MOP*, I, 207: *Oh misfortunes, what do you want with me? For woes are of cowards' estate in always coming in large numbers.*

[44] *How well that great courtier put it* (No. 125). Another favourite was the line "milagros y basiliscos" (*MOP*, II, 367), which Calderón invoked five times, in one instance adding "con licencia del romance" (see No. 102).

[45] I am grateful to Jack Sage for this invaluable comment, as well as for other help in the preparation of this chapter. Mendoza, he added, "like the Prince of Squillace, the Count of Salinas etc., acquired a faceless, ironically folk-like fame for the many, but a distinct reputation with the few in the know."

further the boundaries of Mendoza's potential audience, may provide one of the reasons why, despite Gracián's pessimism, Mendoza's name would be perpetuated into the later part of the century.

IX

MENDOZA'S *ENTREMESES*

MENDOZA'S contemporaries join with modern critics in praising his *entremeses*. What may be presumed to have been his first exercise in the genre, or possibly in any dramatic form, was presented at the *Fiesta* of Lerma in 1617, when its great wit and satirical humour were praised. [1] A few years later, Tirso de Molina, referring to a performance of one of his own plays in Toledo, some time probably between 1618 and 1621, recalled with appreciation the *entremeses* by Mendoza that had spiced the occasion. [2] And a *loa* by the poet himself, datable to this same span of years, shows him blandly assuming that his audience is well acquainted with *Miser Palomo,* the protagonist of his best-known *entremés*. [3] Indeed, a modern critic of the genre has suggested that such was the "spectacular triumph" of *El ingenioso entremés de Miser Palomo* that it was the first interlude ever to be published separately in its own right; certainly its remarkable popular success was the reason for its publication in 1618. [4]

Emilio Cotarelo and Eugenio Asensio, who in our time have appraised Mendoza's contribution to the *género chico,* agree about its importance. Cotarelo gave only a brief account, but stated

---

[1] See Pedro de Herrera, *Translacion del Santissimo Sacramento,* f. 33: "un entremes de don Antonio de Mendoça en que con mucha agudeza satirizaron en donayre (por diferentes figuras) diuersas inclinaciones y costumbres de gente ociosa cortesana." The description suggests that the interlude was his *Miser Palomo* — see below.

[2] See p. 42.

[3] *MOP,* III, 45-46. The date of the *loa* is discussed in Eugenio Asensio, *Itinerario del entremés desde Lope de Rueda a Quiñones de Benavente* (Madrid, 1965), p. 120 and Note, and by me in "A Chronology." Asensio has suggested (p. 115) that Palomo is a proverbial figure, celebrated also by Quevedo in a *letrilla* "Yo me soy el rey Palomo."

[4] Asensio, p. 110. *El Ingenioso entremes d'El Examinador Miser Palomo, compuesto por Don Antonio de Mendoza, gentil-hombre del Conde de Saldaña, y representado en esta ciudad de Valencia por Sancho de Paz, en este año de 1618* (Valencia, 1618). The *autor de comedias* who published the work comments: "Lo que me ha obligado a imprimir este ingenioso Entremes ha sido el saber que en diez y nueve veces que lo he representado en esta ciudad, muchos a quien no he querido dar traslado dél, lo han ido sacando, ya de memoria o ya escribiéndolo, mientras yo lo representaba" (see ref. in José Gallardo, *Ensayo de una biblioteca española de libros raros y curiosos,* Madrid, 1863-1889, III, col. 745, No. 3039).

plainly his view that the three pieces which represent Mendoza's published production, were "so many jewels of our literature." [5] Asensio likewise recognized the achievement in these interludes, according them a separate chapter in his *Itinerario del entremés* as well as a significant place in the development of the genre.

Before evaluating these interludes one must ask what the present corpus represents. Asensio has assumed that the three published pieces are only the residue of a larger output. [6] This may well have been the case, though caution is urged by Mendoza's own admission of his infrequent incursions into the theatre. [7] Furthermore, the three interludes were written before Mendoza took up his duties at court, and the only known references to his association with the *género chico* belong likewise to those years, indeed to the period from 1617 to 1621. It could well be, therefore, that the present pieces represent almost the totality of his contribution, and that they were an exercise he abandoned at an early stage in his career.

It had been wellnigh impossible, until Sr. Asensio published his book, to make a proper estimate of the *entremeses* tradition. Cotarelo before him had amassed a great amount of material of one sort or another, but had made little attempt to outline the artistic development of the genre. That deficiency being now supplied, the tradition itself, and Mendoza's part in it, may be more clearly seen. [8] Originally a free dramatic form, drawing frequent inspiration from folklore and anecdote, and reflecting largely, but not exclusively, the language and situations of everyday life, the *entremés* ultimately assumed a more formal place in the theatre, alongside the *comedia*, as part of the staple entertainment. The resultant symbiosis between *comedia* and interlude was to affect the latter's development; "the contrast pushes it [the *entremés*] towards contemplating the world not as the great theatre of noble actions, but as the jungle of instincts in which the strong and the astute triumph, or as a vast cage of madmen." And whereas the *comedia* is moral, the interlude

---

[5] E. Cotarelo, *Colección de entremeses* (I), NBAE, XVII, pp. LXXI-LXXII.

[6] Asensio, p. 122. The ch. extends from p. 111 to p. 123.

[7] See final lines of *Más merece*, FC, p. 340. The other two interludes were also produced in 1621 or before (see my "A Chronology"). The possibility of other *entremeses* coming to light is shown by the finding of an unknown interlude, attributed to Mendoza, in the Hisp. Soc. Am. collection — see below.

[8] I have followed Asensio's outline closely in the following account.

adopts an attitude which Asensio again neatly described as a "moral holiday." [9]

Lope de Rueda, the creator of the interlude as an artistic form, left as his inheritance a collection of picturesque types, various recipes for humour, and a subtle understanding of everyday language. Cervantes, the next great exponent of the interlude, continued the convention of writing in prose, and of dealing with what had become traditional themes of the *entremés* (the old man married to the young girl, the sexton, the picaresque types, etc.). His original contribution lay, however, in the novelistic focus he brought to the genre, and he did not exercise a particular influence on those who followed. The way ahead was indeed being adumbrated with the evolution of a different kind of interlude, in which the comedy of stock character and situation, and of crude, rapid action, gave way to an interest in the delineation of social types, especially those of a ridiculous nature. Such preposterous characters (called *figuras*) were fit targets for satire, and when paraded before an audience, made even the minimal plot, or action, of the older *entremés* superfluous.

Antonio de Mendoza's specific contribution to the genre was made at this point of transformation in the interlude's history. Whereas the interludists had hitherto shown a preference for prose without excluding poetry as an occasional alternative (either sporadically, or throughout), Mendoza now chose a specifically verse *entremés,* which he tied so delicately, yet inexorably, to lyrical expression that he set the style for subsequent practitioners of the *género chico.* And in his two *entremeses de figuras* he not only provided authoritative examples of this form, but helped also to establish a lasting relationship between the genre and the life of Madrid. "The city square of Madrid," declared one of his associates in the art, "is an admirable theatre, and for those who put on an interlude, there is none better nor more entertaining." [10]

What may plausibly have been Mendoza's first *entremés de figuras, Miser Palomo,* turned to advantage a technique long

---

[9] Asensio, p. 36: "El contraste le empuja a contemplar el mundo no como el gran teatro de nobles acciones, sino como la selva de instintos en que el fuerte y el astuto triunfan, o como una vasta jaula de locos;" and p. 35: "vacaciones morales."

[10] See Salas Barbadillo's *Los mirones de la corte,* in Cotarelo, No. 65, I, 256: "...la plaza de Madrid es teatro admirable, y para representantes de un entremés ningunos mejores ni más entretenidos" (quot. in Asensio, p. 83).

14

exploited in the traditional *entremés,* the surgery consultation with a doctor (quack or otherwise). [11] Mendoza made his doctor, an extravagant Italian gentleman, to be an expert in social therapy, who sets up his consulting room in a tavern kept by a helpfully witty hotelier, and there meets in turn with different court types, all suffering in one way and another from a social malady. Mendoza was not unique in giving an old technique this new form of life: Quiñones de Benavente, in his *Entremés del doctor Sánalotodo,* has a doctor who dispenses advice on matters of love, courtesy, and sundry social ailments; in Salas Barbadillo's *El comisario contra los malos gustos,* it is a lawyer who gives counsel; whilst in the same author's *El cocinero de amor,* advice is proferred in culinary, rather than medical, terms. [12] These three pieces, however, may well all be later than *Miser Palomo,* and indeed could have been influenced by the formula's success in Mendoza's piece.

But the already existing *entremés* tradition could certainly have provided some precedents for *Miser Palomo.* Cervantes's *El juez de los divorcios* had set up a similar framework of professional or juridical consultation as a means of making social or moral comment, but so interested was that author in the liveliness of his characters and their interaction that the moralist's role was relegated to the background. Furthermore, Cervantes's exemplary novel *El Licenciado Vidriera,* which appeared in 1613, provided a parallel situation, in which a mad *figura* pronounces judgment on the citizens who flock to hear him. [13]

However, the anonymous *El hospital de los podridos* is much nearer *Miser Palomo.* [14] The setting is a hospital set up to control and cure a plague of melancholy raging at court, an epidemic attributable to different social causes — one courtier has been driven into a depression by the habits of the poets, another by envy at a neighbour's success. This interlude uses another technique paralleled in *Miser Palomo:* either voluntarily, or under prompting from the

---

[11] Cotarelo, No. 82 (I, 322-327). He reproduces the text of the Valencia edn. of 1620.

[12] Cotarelo, Nos. 296 (II, 703-705), 67 (I, 261-266) and 69 (I, 271-276). Quiñones Benavente's career as *entremesista* may have begun as early as 1616, but it is only from 1625 onwards that we hear of him in that role (see Asensio, p. 124 *et seq.*). *El comisario* appeared in 1622 (Cotarelo, I, 261-266), as did also *El cocinero* (II, 271-276).

[13] Cotarelo, No. 1 (I, 1-5). For the *Licenciado*'s connexion with the *entremés de figuras,* see Edwin B. Place, "Notes on the Grotesque: the 'Comedia de figurón' at home and abroad," *PMLA,* LIV (1939), 412-421.

[14] Cotarelo, No. 23 (I, 94-98).

medical authority, the patient condemns himself out of his own lips, while giving the doctor the opportunity to comment, and suggest treatment. And yet, however relevant *El hospital,* profound differences separate it from *Miser Palomo.* The former, despite its lightness of tone, is characterized by a profound moral discontent: the latter adopts the same tone, but is light-hearted equally in its satire. Again, *El hospital* has prose dialogue, and though the work is not a notable example of the colourful use of everyday language, it belongs evidently to that tradition in Spanish letters; Mendoza, in contrast, has chosen verse, which he infuses with a lyrical *élan* that makes of it an equivalent of the lively speech of the prose *entremés.*

When the interlude opens, Miser Palomo arrives with a commission to examine the mental and moral health of the court: his intention to report on the "Sabandijas del arca de la corte, / donde se acoge tanto vagamundo / como en diluvio universal del mundo." [15] Various types come before him, wittily confess their weaknesses, and as wittily have their cures propounded by the doctor. We recognize the types: the courtier not satisfied with his progress in the art of being a gentleman, the braggart who has killed a bear by blowing on him, and the nitwit who always says the wrong thing. Certainly the comparative lack of moral earnestness is plain, in contrast to *El hospital,* whose primary target is human weakness in its universal form; yet Mendoza's attitude is not one of moral indifference, for he is riled by the pretentiousness and hypocrisy of much that passes for culture at court, and when the doctor is told that an *hombre de bien* has presented himself for examination, the patient is dismissed with the words: "De lo que no se usa no hay examen" ("There is no examination for what is no longer in use"). Indeed, the undertone of the piece is serious, and almost at variance with the predominant urbanity of a satire that aims at making its audience feel vulnerable, but never under attack.

In writing a Second Part to *Miser Palomo* Mendoza probably wanted to repeat the success he had enjoyed. [16] The sequel offers

---

[15] I, 322: *vermin of the courtly Noah's Ark, where as much vagabondry gathers as in a universal deluge.*

[16] Cotarelo, No. 83 (I, 327-332). The episode of the *discreta* and her husband, not found here, is contained in *Entremés famoso del Doctor Dieta* (Cadiz?, 1646): [BNM copy, shelf-mark R12451]. Cotarelo has reproduced the text of the Valencia edn. of 1628.

us the doctor of the First Part under a new name, "el licenciado Dieta," who had come to cure more court maladies. His patients this time include a purveyor of calumnies, a blue-stocking who reads Latin and Italian to the neglect of her home, and a woman who cannot bring herself to love the men of her day. Despite the similarity in structure and aim, this piece is very different from its predecessor: indeed its moral tone is as keen as that of *El hospital de los podridos*. For instance, the woman who cannot bring herself to love is not just a *figura* to be ridiculed: society, implies Mendoza, is so ridden with vice as to inhibit the genuine display of love. Then with an even sharper twist to the satirist's knife, the suggestion is made that this apparently admirable woman might herself succumb eventually to the temptation of greed. She admits to liking money, whereupon Palomo (or Dieta) retorts:

> Sanaréis, sanaréis: buscad un hombre
> callado (si le hubiere en las boticas),
> y exprimidle entre dudas y esperanzas,
> que salga este licor provechísimo,
> que es el amor finezas y regalos. [17]

Mendoza's vision of society in this interlude is pessimistic: men mock maidenhood as though it were a sick joke, they are themselves "stuffed with deceit and falsehood," and over beauty hangs the perpetual threat of the passage of time — the latter preoccupation will be heard again in Mendoza's early *comedias*. And if we take the view that satire (as in the present case) is capable of changing men's ways, the author seems anxious to forestall, and destroy, such a hopeful viewpoint, for the interlude opens with a conversation between two courtiers, who comment skittishly on the news that this man Dieta can cure any spiritual ailment. Plutarch, Seneca, and the rest tried it, one of them says, but "in all ages truths have been luckless." Oddly enough, in his present catalogue of disillusion, Mendoza makes only one name stand for something positive, that of the poet, or rather the *poeta de bien,* who avoids sharp satire; his office, we are assured, is a divine one.

---

[17] *You'll get better, you'll get better: look for a quiet man (if such is to be had in the chemists' shops), and squeeze him between doubts and hopes, so that this most beneficial liquid may pour forth, since love is all little gifts and presents.*

It is characteristic, therefore, of Mendoza to refuse to be cruelly, vindictively satirical, a fact that distinguishes his interludes from Quevedo's, even though some resemblance may still be found between the two poets' work in this genre. This gentler form of satire helps establish more clearly the literary tradition onto which Mendoza's interludes abut: not that of Quevedo's *Buscón* or Mateo Alemán's *Guzmán de Alfarache* (though the *entremés de figuras* merges at its bitterest end into the picaresque genre), but those forms of social comment in which the satirical mingles with the *cuadro de costumbres* — Mendoza stands nearer, therefore, to Castillo Solórzano or to Juan de Zabaleta, nearer also to Mendoza's own social comedies like *Los empeños del mentir*.

The *Entremés de Getafe* is a Mendozan *jácara* in dramatic form. [18] The scene is a hot, dust-laden village on the road to Madrid from Toledo: Getafe indeed is an "Aranjuez to hell itself." On such an evening the carter's curses, which open the interlude, seem more appropriate than the tenderness of the young muleteer's song:

> A Madrid caminando
> vengo de Illescas;
> tengo el alma quedita
> dale morena. [19]

In fact much of the interlude's success will depend on this double vision of country life: Mendoza seems willing to admit Getafe's plebeian vulgarity, yet cannot resist its charms. So when we meet Francisca, the beautiful village-girl, the desire to carp is tempered by a willingness to praise. She may be common (and petty-minded) in her claim to be the flower not just of Getafe, but of all Castile; yet she remains inviolate, for her beauty and verve transcend the standards of mere *bienséance*. Mendoza does not pretend here to be the moralist we saw in the Second Part of *Miser Palomo;* nevertheless, he makes plain that the snobbish norms governing court society are far less wholesome than the values for which Francisca stands. Here we see in miniature the contrast between town and city standards which is the subject of his *comedia Cada loco con su tema*.

---

[18] Cotarelo, No. 84 (I, 332-335). Cotarelo reproduces the text of BNM *MS* 3922.
[19] *I am on my way to Madrid from Illescas: no troubles on my mind: gee up, brownie!*

In the interlude the accepted social "virtues" are made incarnate in Don Lucas, a court fop and womanizer, who finding himself in Getafe, comes straight away to the conclusion that it is "the flea's own country, and the flies' ancestral home." One glimpse of Francisca, however, makes him change tack, if not mind. He must woo this beauty, who seems easy prey to a moneyed man of the court. He offers her the title of "la metresa de don Lucas" with all its rich appanage, only to find that Francisca considers her present fortune of beauty and freedom to be greater. In the middle of a fruitless seduction, Lucas's wife, Doña Clara, appears, ready to recognize her husband's advances for what they are, and Francisca for what she is not. Her snobbish attack on the *villana* ends with a challenge to Lucas that he must choose between the two ladies. Francisca's reply opens wittily with a line from a popular song: "Mirad con quién y sin quién" ("Just see with whom and without whom"). She then gives the reasons for her own sure triumph: Doña Clara is merely "Lady Yesterday's face," whereas Francisca is a wonder of the world, a view mightily confirmed by her carter swain, who comes on the scene.

But the dramatic movement of the piece is not in a single direction. Lucas is more than a fop: he has a quick wit too, and an astonishing capacity for changing course: one glimpse of the girl makes him cease his carping criticism of Getafe, one glimpse of the carter's strength encourages a realist's view of his own physical prowess. And though his wooing of Francisca fails, as a display it is impressive. The carter likewise is a character with a modicum of complexity: he begins as the clumsy strong man, whose love for Francisca is rejected, but before the conclusion he is her "querido Alonso Andrés," whose presence and strength determine that the action will end to his advantage. Francisca too, for all that she represents the assertiveness of youth, ultimately voices Mendoza's characteristic doubt: in a final lyric (part of the conventional song and dance finale of many interludes) Francisca affirms those qualities of village life which she embodies, but the burden of the song, in contrast, invokes and hammers out time's ultimate threat:

> no hay que dudar,
> y acudir con tiempo,
> no hay que dudar. [20]

---

[20] *Don't stop to think, and come on time, don't stop to think.*

This is probably the best of Mendoza's interludes. It bears traces of the *entremés de figuras* in that Lucas and Clara could both have figured on Doctor Palomo's list. But it is also closer to the older form of *entremés* with its nucleus of action, its mirroring of everyday life, and its interaction of character. Above all, it is a vindication of the poetic interlude — the lyrical style varies from the crudeness of the carter's oaths to the mock-Gongorine curse on Getafe, from the preponderant *estilo donoso* typical of many of Mendoza's poems, to the feather-weight loveliness of the closing song:

¿Cuántos hombres le bastan a una muchacha?
No le bastan todos, si los engaña.
¿Y si bien ama?
Uno solo, mozuela,
cabe en el alma. [21]

But whichever style the author chooses in turn, he is at triumphant ease in it.

Asensio makes the point that the *Entremés de Getafe* looks to the future: [22] the relation between Lucas and Francisca anticipates that between the *petimetre* (fop) and the *maja* (a beauty of the popular classes) in the interludes of Ramón de la Cruz in the eighteenth century. The piece anticipates too a development in Mendoza's own dramatic art: Lucas, even more than Palomo, will predominate in a form of dramatic entertainment more firmly dedicated to social satire, because he manages to combine incongruity with wit and intelligence.

And Mendoza will also take forward with him into the later plays the habit of fashioning characters like Lucas (or even Francisca), that are morally ambivalent, as capable of calling forth our admiration as our criticism, and who occupy the confusing divide between the hero and anti-hero. Finally, having sharpened his talent here for the vivid depiction of place and atmosphere, Mendoza will display it even more effectively in the social comedy to which he would become attracted.

---

[21] *How many men are enough for one girl? Not even all, if she deceives them. And if she truly loves? There is room in the heart, my girl, for only one.*

[22] Op. cit., p. 121.

One unpublished interlude, attributed to Mendoza, lies in the Hispanic Society of America collection in New York. [23] It is arguably his: a verse interlude, it offers the same free and varied use of the hendecasyllable line (with frequent recourse to rhymed couplets) as Mendoza's other *entremeses;* though it lacks the lyricism of the *Getafe* interlude and fails to include at the end of the text the *letras* of the intended final song which might have been a surer guide to the master's hand, the piece's style is fluent, witty, and assured in the manner of the *Palomo* interludes; furthermore, certain features recall the *Entremés de Getafe,* and in particular that work's self-assertive heroine Francisca, who by a superior wit and force of character lords it over the male gallant.

The interlude, which has no title, might be described as a potential sequel to the *Entremés de Getafe.* Don Lucas here has finally made Francisca his "metresa," and set her up in what he would like to think is the appropriate style. The protagonists are in fact called Señor Turrada and his *amada,* Lucía. The piece begins stridently with Lucía telling her lover that the affair is over, since for two months now and more he has failed to provide her with food and other necessaries. She furthermore accuses him of jealousy, eavesdropping, creating trouble, and of misinterpreting everything she says or does:

> si suena en la cocina algun ruido
> dice que esta el galan alla escondido
> si algo enfadada reçio quiero ablalle
> que lo ago porque me oygan en la calle   f. 342
> si llama vn pobre y pide vna limosna
> Voto a Cristo que viene a disfraçado
> y que me quiere dar algun recaudo. [24]

In other words, Lucía continues, her lover keeps watchful solicitude over everything, except food. When Turrada in reply protests his love, his cares and his desires, Lucía tells him that these will not

---

[23] Hisp. Soc. Am. *MS B2331,* ff. 341-346ᵛ, "Entremes de D. Antonio de Mendoza" (see *Hisp. Am. Cat.* I, 189).

[24] *If there is a noise in the kitchen he says a gallant is hidden there; if somewhat indignant I wish to give him a piece of my mind, he says I am doing it so that people in the street can hear me; if some poor man calls asking for alms, then by Heaven, he is in disguise and is wanting to give me a message.*

bring her the things she needs. Try buying a piece of tunny-fish for one desire, or fob off the servant with one care for remuneration! The first part of the interlude ends with a characteristic Parthian shot from Lucía: when Turrada threatens to "give her cause for jealousy" *(dar celos)*, Lucía counters that this is the only thing that he *can* give her.

The subsequent change of scene and character marks also a shift towards more traditional interlude material. We meet the Mayor and *regidor* (an officer of the law), the latter berating the former for being a simpleton and a drunk. The reason for such complaint (and whether it is justified) becomes plain when the Mayor explains what has happened. It was a feast day, and the prisoners in his charge at the local gaol were demanding Mass. The Mayor had protested, saying that he could only arrange for the verger to come and say *Tenebrae,* whereupon the prisoners further insisted on their religious rights and obligations:

> dexenos yr a oyr missa
> que luego nos volueremos
> que tamuien somos Cristianos
> los pressos como los sueltos.
> yo dixe enttonçes pues vaian
> oygan missa y buelban luego
> y abriendo de par en par
> la puerta todos los sueltto
> sin dexar tan sola vn alma. [25]

This strange apologia is interrupted by a drunken Turrada, who has decided to use the forces of the law to straighten out matters between himself and Lucía. He will make her jealous by getting the Mayor to impersonate a woman to whom he can pay court in Lucía's hearing. The Mayor at first will not countenance the scheme, but changes his mind after the promise of wine, sausage and other delicacies, with bread thrown in for good measure! In the final scene, after dark and presumably under Lucía's window, Turrada and the Mayor play out their deception, the Mayor dressed

---

[25] *Allow us to go and hear Mass. We shall come back straightaway, for we prisoners are as much Christian men as those who go free. Whereupon I said, well off you go to Mass and come back at once, and opening the door wide I freed them all without leaving a single soul behind.*

up as a woman. Turrada flirts with the "recien muger" ("newly-made woman"), Lucía's jealousy is aroused, and she comes out to assert her prior claim to Turrada. On trying to unmask the "lady" she discovers it is a bearded man. Turrada explains the deception and his object of winning Lucía back by making her jealous. The lady thereupon becomes more incensed, and is about to break off relations with her lover once more when the law dramatically intervenes: the Mayor commands them both to be taken off to prison, a turn of events that may only be averted by the intercessions of musicians and singers pleading on the lovers' behalf. The interlude ends, we may presume, to the sound of that song.

The theme of the kept woman gives the interlude a special interest for the light it throws on what must have been a common phenomenon of Mendoza's Spain. That the theme has been exploited in an *entremés* rather than a *comedia* reflects that greater freedom which Asensio saw as a characteristic of the interlude tradition. At the same time the treatment of the material here maintains a marked decorum, since the text is free of the bawdiness which characterized other interludes in their dealings with aspects of sexual life: this may be a further indication that the piece was the work of a palace poet. One further fact merits attention: the piece by its very existence has added a further third to Mendoza's meagre contribution to the genre of the *género chico*, revealing the *entremesista* this time in closer contact with more popular and traditional forms of comedy, that have their roots ultimately in medieval farce. If the piece could be considered as the earliest of Mendoza's experiments with the *entremés* (though like its fellows it shows no signs of immaturity), it may well mark a stage where the author was moving from the exploitation of one type of broad farce (as represented in the episode with the Mayor and *regidor*) to an interest in a more *costumbrista* setting and the delineation of court *mores*. One important factor distinguishes the present interlude from its companions: it is morally neutral, recording the scene for the amusement it affords, not for any critical judgment that the author wishes to offer.

The piece, if slight, has considerable artistic value. It is primarily good theatre, from the raucous exchange at the beginning between the two lovers, to the absurdly comic second scene, in which, using a technique developed to even greater effect in the *Palomo* interludes, the Mayor's defence of his actions over the prisoners serves effectively to condemn him; and to the last scene, where Mendoza allows his hectoring female to reassert her dominance over the male. The dialogue, unlike that of the other interludes, is not heightened by lyricism, but has gusto and wit. The characters too succeed in suggesting universal types: one might even want to see in Lucía something of that authoritarian second wife, Doña Clara, of whom Don Antonio complained. Certainly the two lovers are recognizable, both within and outside the bounds of matrimony, as predatory creature and victim, and it is characteristic of the author that he should have introduced a piquant irony into his treatment of the theme of the kept woman by emphasizing that a Francisca, even when she accepts a Don Lucas's favours, does not become subject to the will and whim of her lover, but remains a woman who triumphs by her beauty, spirit and wit.

For Eugenio Asensio the three published interludes occupy a crucial position in the development of the genre. [26] The First Part of *Miser Palomo* represented the final triumph of the verse *entremés*, setting also the prosodic pattern for the future interlude, namely the hendecasyllabic *verso suelto* with considerable use of rhyming couplets for witty effect, or simple emphasis. More important, perhaps, the exploitation of lively colloquial language in the prose *entremés* gave way to a "splutter of witticisms." This interlude finally, claims Asensio, set the fashion for the *entremeses de figuras* in which puppetlike figures were displayed for the sake of social criticism, rather than to engage in dramatic action, or conflict.

Asensio's appraisal of Mendoza's achievement may be right, yet there is so much we still do not know about the genre, as a great deal of the material has disappeared. [27] On the face of it, Asensio attributes an excessive importance to three pieces, one of whose significant qualities is their survival. A comparison with Quiñones de Benavente, the great master of the interlude, may help to get Mendoza's contribution into a more modest perspective. We know

---

[26] Asensio, esp. p. 68 and pp. 122-123.

[27] The point is emphasized by Asensio's discussion of a ref. by Tirso to an outstanding *entremesista* (pp. 128-131). Tirso's text names fourteen interludes, presumably as the best instances of this author's work, but their identity is very uncertain (Cotarelo, I, lxxv-vi, Asensio, pp. 129-131; the latter will only recognize three). Tirso also refers to this young *entremesista* as the composer already of 300 interludes.

that the younger man began his career in close proximity to Mendoza, so that it is not unlikely that he was influenced by someone who was making a reputation for himself in this genre. And such a conclusion is suggested too, if we look at the cases where the two *entremesistas* wrote in the same vein — for instance, Quiñones's *Las civilidades,* with its Doctor Alfarnaque dispensing advice on courtly language, seems out of the same box as the *Miser Palomo* pieces. But Quiñones's range is far wider — a morality piece like *El Tiempo;* a vignette of contemporary customs grafted onto the stock of an older comedy tradition in *Los cuatro galanes;* or a more straightforward *entremés de figuras* in *El enamoradizo.*[28] This suggests that, whatever Quiñones may have taken from Mendoza, there was already an abundant and varied tradition on which the master could draw. If influence there was, it was most likely in the use of language. It is rare for Quiñones to display the same fondness as Mendoza for the witty style, but there are moments when he chooses the *estilo donoso* — at the opening of *El Tiempo,* for instance, the old enemy is thus described:

> este bulto barbiluengo,
> graduado de fantasma,
> consultado en esqueleto,
> dos alas por acicates.[29]

But example — if example were needed — could be found for such expression in the comic verse of Quevedo or Góngora. In consequence, even in this aspect of Mendoza's interludes it would be unwise to go further than suggesting that he had shown Quiñones de Benavente how effective such a style was in this genre.

If, out of what now remains of the *entremés* tradition, one is looking for the more positive influence of Mendoza, it is on the work of his old friend and associate Salas Barbadillo. Here, in *El tribunal de los majaderos,*[30] *El comisario de los gustos,* and *El cocinero del amor,* Salas wrote in very similar vein, in the same period probably as Don Antonio, or shortly afterwards. Even in this case, however,

---

[28] Cotarelo, Nos. 214 (II, 507-509), 220 (II, 519-522) and 269 (II, 629-631).

[29] Cotarelo, II, 507: *This long-bearded rag-bag, qualified as ghost, put forward for skeleton with two wings for spurs.*

[30] Cotarelo, No. 66 (I, 257-261).

the doubt remains that these may all have been exercises in a new vogue, and that influence might as easily have flown from Salas to Mendoza as in the other direction — indeed both sets of interludes could have come about independently. But when we make comparisons of quality, no such doubts are entertained: Salas's hand is heavy, and despite his wit he is humourless. By contrast, in Mendoza's pieces, which are so full of humour, the author has left the mark of a serious man's point of view: we recognize here more than in any other part of his work the man who could condemn the society in which he lived as "this vile and common republic." [31]

---

[31] Quot. in Matías de Novoa, *Historia de Felipe IV*, in *Colección de documentos inéditos* (Madrid, 1875-1883), LXIX, 39 ("esta miserable y mecánica república como dice D. Antonio de Mendoza").

X

QUERER POR SOLO QUERER

"T H I S Seat ... contains amongst many other Miracles of amoenity a Garden, which Tagus embraces with two Currents, sometimes in suspence, sometimes hasty, shaping it an Isle, and serving it for a Wall, over which the Trees are one way delightful Battlements, another, they are flow'ry Margents. Amidst the intricacy of the matted Hearbs, of the Galleries of Flowers, of the Meandrian Wildernesses, of the diversified Plats, of the Crystal Fountains (Competitors in Plenty and Novelty) there is reserv'd a most beautiful Space, which hath the openness of a Market-place, and wants not the pleasantness of a Forrest." [1]

Mendoza thus picturesquely described the setting, and probably the actual spot, where his play *Querer por solo querer* would be performed at the palace of Aranjuez, sometime in 1622, during the two spring months that the court spent there; [2] a performance given by a very special cast, the *meninas* (the young noblewomen of the court), and giving pride of place to María de Guzmán, the daughter and favourite of the Count of Olivares.

If setting is a significant (and easily overlooked) factor in the making of a spectacle play such as *Querer por solo querer,* so too is its aristocratic audience, which helped determine the sort of entertainment it should be. Mendoza felt that a court art, whether dramatic or lyrical, should differ from that offered the vulgar throng. In his prose account of the *Fiesta de Aranjuez,* performed for the King's birthday in 1622, Mendoza insisted that dramatic enter-

---

[1] *Relación*, in MOP, I, 6: "Este sitio ... contiene entre muchos milagros de amenidad, un jardín, que el Tajo le ciñe en dos corrientes, ya suspenso, ya presuroso, formándole isla, y sirviéndole muro, en que los árboles son una vez deleitosas almenas, y otras floridas márgenes. Entre los lazos de los artesones de hierba, de las galerías de flores, de la confusión de las calles, de la diversidad de los cuadros, de la hermosura de las fuentes, competidas en la copia, y la novedad, se reserva un bellísimo espacio, que tiene el desembarazo de plaza, y no le falta la beldad de floresta." In addition to Mendoza's prose account of the earlier occasion at Aranjuez, two verse *relaciones* are found: see ch. I, Note 42. I quote Fanshawe's translation (pp. 2-3).

[2] The exact date is uncertain: see my "A Chronology," and ch. I, Note 43. Mendoza notes the brief stay of the court there: "los dos mejores meses" (*Relación*, MOP, I, 7). For the original performance, see ch. I, p. 29.

tainments on these occasions should not be known by the common name of *comedia*, but as *invención*, a genre which is not measured by the usual precepts for plays, to wit a fable all of one piece, but is made up of a loose variety, in which the eyes play a more important role than the ears, and the display consists more in what is seen than in what is heard. [3]

Such words at once suggest the author's fair acquaintance with this type of entertainment of which indeed there was a long tradition, inspired in part by Italian experience, in part by Flemish love of display. [4] But if the reign of Charles V and Philip II had provided instances of court spectacle, it was the reign of Philip III that gave Spanish court plays their great impetus. Two occasions stand out, both entertainments provided by the royal favourite in the park of his estate in Lerma, on the Arlanza. We cannot be sure that Antonio de Mendoza was present at the first Lerma *fiesta* of 1614, when Lope de Vega's *El premio de la hermosura* was performed by the ladies of the court and members of the royal family, [5] but in the view of a contemporary critic, the play showed how a dramatist should write for a court occasion of this kind. [6] As spectacle the piece was certainly impressive, conjuring up mountains, caves, an enchanted castle, and a magnificent riverscape dominated by a boat large enough for thirty people, which would be wrecked during the action. With its combination of the chivalresque and the exotic, the play was deemed to bring alive all the fantasies of the books of chivalry. Lope had furthermore sought to furnish an entertainment in keeping

---

[3] *MOP*, I, 7 and 21-22: "no se mide a los precetos comunes de las farsas, que es una fábula unida, esta se fabrica de variedad desatada, en que la vista lleva mejor parte que el oído, y la ostentación consiste más en lo que se ve, que en lo que se oye." See also C. V. Aubrun, "Les Débuts du drame lyrique en Espagne," in *Le Lieu théâtral à la Renaissance: Études ... réunies et présentées par Jean Jacquot avec la collaboration d'Élie Konigson et Marcel Oddon* (Paris, 1964), pp. 423-444. The article is largely an analysis of Mendoza's prose *relación*, basic portions of which are reproduced (436-442). Aubrun calls Mendoza "cet excellent critique" (p. 427).

[4] See Shergold, *A History of the Spanish Stage*, esp. pp. 236-263.

[5] Shergold, pp. 252-255. Mendoza's presence may be indicated in a *loa* (*MOP*, III, 39) which alludes to precedents for the appearance of court ladies on stage: "Del Príncipe y las Infantas / vimos una Farsa en Lerma..." Court ladies and members of the royal family certainly took part in the 1614 festivity (Shergold, p. 252, and Note 6 below).

[6] See *Relacion de la famosa comedia del "Premio de la hermosura y amor enamorado" que el Príncipe, nuestro señor, la cristianísima Reina de Francia y serenísimos infantes don Cárlos y doña María, sus hermanos, y algunas de las señoras damas representaron en el Parque de Lerma, lúnes 3 de Noviembre de 1614 años*, in *Colección de libros españoles raros ó curiosos*, VI (Madrid, 1873: *Comedias inéditas de Frey Lope Félix de Vega Carpio*, vol. I), pp. 479-494, and Lope de Vega Carpio, *Decimasexta parte de las comedias...* (Madrid, 1621), dedication.

with the custom, propriety and intention *(propósito)* of the ladies in the cast. Furthermore the verse itself, we are told, possessed an eminence, a decency, and a decorum which declared them to be Lope's, the only man who could adequately write for players such as these. Lope's text certainly attests a straining after appropriate decorum, but the result is an extraordinary stiffening of the verse. [7] The important thing then, as later, was the concept of a specifically noble entertainment in which decorum ruled over setting, subject, spectacle, cast, mode of performance, as well as form of expression.

Mendoza helped provide the entertainment at the second Lerma *fiesta* in 1617. [8] The main piece of the occasion was by another close associate of his, Luis Vélez de Guevara. The text of *El caballero del sol* has not survived, but the *relaciones* of the festival give a clear picture of this spectacle play, which, as distinct from *El premio de la hermosura,* would have afforded Antonio de Mendoza a chance to witness what the stage engineer could now accomplish in effecting complete scene changes, in this instance a representation of Naples giving way suddenly to a mountain panorama. [9] And another play at this festival would have shown Mendoza the part that horror could play in a spectacular dramatic art: in the battle between the pigmies and the cranes, the real and the false, we are told, became indistinguishable, and the spectacle was thought to compare with the "fantastic monstrosities of Hieronymus Bosch." [10]

The magnificence of the *Fiesta de Aranjuez,* held on 15 May 1622, [11] was a more immediate source of inspiration. Firstly, that vernal atmosphere, which Mendoza captured so well in one of his verse *relaciones* of that Festival, [12] he would later make his own accomplice in the representation of *Querer por solo querer.* Secondly, the Festival would have revealed to him the flexibility of a large playing area, as well as indicating the enlargement of dramatic

---

[7] *Decimasexta parte,* f. 6: "Esta que veys es digna / del premio de hermosura y gentileza / tan perfeta y diuina, / que luego que formó naturaleza / su rostro se detuuo, / rompio la estampa y admirada estuuo."

[8] See Shergold, pp. 255-258, and here, pp. 23-24.

[9] Shergold, p. 256.

[10] Pedro de Herrera, *Translacion del Santissimo Sacramento,* f. 59ᵛ.

[11] See Mendoza's *relaciones,* and Shergold, 268-270, and 272-274.

[12] *FC,* pp. 387-388: "Aqui tienen los Abriles / su verde florido assiento, / ya Babilonia de flores / en tantos jardines bellos."

horizons that could be assured by royal munificence. More specifically, the *Fiesta* consisted of two entertainments; the first, Villamediana's *La gloria de Niquea* on a theme out of *Amadis;* the second,
a play by Lope de Vega on the Jason legend, *El vellocino de oro.* [13]
The staging for both of these was memorable: Lope's play with
its examples of simulated motion, Villamediana's with its discovery
scenes, and its flying dragons; some of these elements, as we shall
see, reappear in such a way in *Querer por solo querer* that it is a
fair presumption that he was making use of the same devices. In
his prose account of the occasion Mendoza, like the critic of the
1614 *Fiesta* at Lerma, did not fail to ask whether the entertainment
satisfied the criteria appropriate to a palace art, and it was his
impression that Villamediana's play had been written "with attention
to the Palace's Sovereignty," its verses displaying the rightness
(atino) which should characterize court poetry. [14] Other elements,
however, whose appropriateness Mendoza does not discuss, must
surely have impressed him too; as in the earlier court entertainments
the authors drew on chivalresque and mythological material, and
expressed peculiarly aristocratic sentiments, which projected an
idealized simulacrum of palace society. And the colours, the sump-
tuousness of costume, the richness of the musical accompaniment
(aspects which Mendoza emphasized in his criticism) afforded the
monarchy a chance to display its peacock's tail. But Mendoza was
aware too of an aesthetic aspect to the *ostentación* — in his *Querer*
por solo querer, as the magic castle swung into view, one of the
characters would remark that the vision made "such a beautiful
consonance, that it is a music of the eyes." [15] It would be wrong
in this instance to talk of Wagnerian synaesthesia, but it is worth
remembering that, in *Querer* itself, as in the other palace spectacles,
the overall aim was a totality of effect, in which the senses,
ambiguously and ambivalently stimulated, enriched the artistic
impression conveyed by painter, poet, and musician.

---

[13] Juan de Tassis, Conde de Villamediana, *Obras,* ed. Dionisio Hipolito de los Valles
(Zaragoza, 1629), 1-54, and Lope de Vega Carpio, *Parte decinueve* (Madrid, 1625),
ff. 219v-235. The prologue and *acotación* of *La Gloria* are now available in Villamediana,
Obras, ed. Juan Manuel Rozas (Madrid, 1968), pp. 359-374. Some details in Mendoza's
prose *Relación* suggest a knowledge of Villamediana's prologue.

[14] *Relación, MOP,* I, 9: "escribióse con atención a la soberanía de Palacio."

[15] *FC,* p. 354. For ease of ref., I note the page numbers in the *FC* text rather than the
edn. of 1623: "tan hermosa consonancia, / que es musica de los ojos."

It is partly because of this complex artistic aim that *Querer* presents a problem of genre. Is it *invención,* or is it *comedia?* The author uses the latter term, even though he deliberately turns away from some of the conventions of the stage play: there is no *Senado* to appeal to, he has eschewed the conventional marriage at the conclusion, his *figura del donayre* is more a cynical commentator than the usual *gracioso,* and even the play's inordinate length seems intended as a mark of distinction. [16] At the same time, this is no *invención:* despite the paucity of dramatic development, the main interest lies still in dialogue and the shock of contrary opinions, whereas, in comparison, *La gloria de Niquea* and *El premio de la hermosura* had largely made of dialogue a framework into which the changing spectacle preferred by the stage devices or machines could be fitted.

To retell in detail a plot as complicated as that of *Querer* would baffle rather than enlighten. It tells of three eastern princes, and their love for Princesses Zelidaura and Claridiana. Felisbravo, having seen Zelidaura's portrait, determines to seek her and win her love; the second prince, Claridoro, is already one of Zelidaura's suitors, but loves in vain; and the third, Floranteo, is in love with the other princess, Claridiana, though he too is unrequited. Claridiana, because of the terms of her father's will, lies under a spell in her castle, and may only be released when a suitor both wise and brave presents himself. Even though their own amorous inclinations lie elsewhere, Claridoro and Felisbravo, between them, fulfil the conditions of disenchantment, thus releasing Claridiana. Cupid, however, decrees that she shall marry the one who loves her most, a title that easily falls to her devoted suitor, Floranteo. The Princess refuses to recognize him, thus provoking a popular revolt in Floranteo's favour.

Felisbravo's search for Zelidaura, the unknown lady of the portrait, is the other mainspring of the action. When the prince does find her, both, for one reason or another, assume a false identity, a situation further complicated by Claridiana's interest in the prince, which awakens Zelidaura's jealousy. Felisbravo takes the side of Claridiana in her attempt to restore her authority at home, but

---

[16] See *FC,* p. 424. The *loa* (pp. 341-343) reflects a similar desire to make of this occasion something "different". For the *figura del donayre,* see J. F. Montesinos, *Estudios sobre Lope,* pp. 13-70.

no sooner is her enemy defeated than another threat impends, an invasion by Zelidaura's army seeking jealous vengeance on the other princess. At this moment Mars intervenes, decreeing that because of their beauty both ladies should be called to the cult of Diana. The princes protest, but are fated to love henceforth without hope.

Such an exotic plot, with its atmosphere of fantasy, invited spectacular effects, but the intrigue owed something too in some of its details to the devices used in former court entertainments. Like the *Gloria de Niquea* the play was preluded by a masked ball; which was then followed by a *loa,* and a song of praise for the *Fiesta de Aranjuez.* And Villamediana's play on that earlier occasion may also have helped inspire the first spectacular effect in *Querer,* when Claridiana's enchanted castle is "discovered": the other play too had its enchanted princess. A duel between Felisbravo and Claridoro over possession of Zelidaura's portrait is suddenly interrupted by the noise of firecrackers, and the contestants are separated by a bridge, swung down from above, along which Floranteo enters, accompanied by giants and "many horrible figures." Inside, a staircase is revealed, all adorned with arms, whilst a black giant, armed with a club and breathing fire, is seen to jump out of a serpent's mouth. Later, a second drawbridge falls, "discovering" frightening cliffs on which horrible animals stand, belching flame. When the princes finally bring about the disenchantment, the castle itself is lowered to stage level, and glass doors open to reveal Princess Claridiana on her throne. By a magic sleight of hand the act closes with the removal from sight of protagonists, bridges, and everything. [17]

The second act did not attempt wonders such as these, but in the final act the stage engineer's art is again displayed, the occasions being the arrival of Mars in his chariot, and the final vision of Diana's temple. [18] Mars' entry belongs as much to the tradition of court hieroglyphics and the symbolic processions of the period as to the

---

[17] *FC*, p. 354 *et seq.*, and pp. 362-367. Shergold draws attention to the similarity of conception between *Querer* and the *Gloria de Niquea* (p. 271), suggesting that the same scenery was used on both occasions. He specifies the serpent's jaws, and notes the similarity between the "discovery" of Niquea and that of Claridiana. This view receives corroboration from one detail: the "gloria de Niquea" was a huge glass sphere with a building inside (Shergold, p. 270), and Claridiana's castle was likewise "más Sphera que Palacio" (*FC,* p. 354).

[18] *FC*, pp. 423-425.

dramatic tradition, but the *Gloria de Niquea* likewise had been heralded by the pageant-wagons of April and the waters of the Tagus. Mendoza's temple of Diana too echoes the earlier occasion, when Mars' temple had been "discovered" in Lope's *El vellocino de oro*. [19] In *Querer* we see a troupe of nymphs come out of Diana's magnificently decorated temple, and finally we see her on her throne. As the play ends, proclaiming that the purest love is a love beyond hope, the goddess, along with the chaste princess and some of the nymphs, are raised to heaven, whilst, to the sound of trumps and drums, the opposing armies of Zelidaura and Claridiana withdraw, leaving the stage empty for more jousting on the dancing place, a tourney performed in men's costume by some of the court ladies.

In this play the characters possess little dramatic interest in the usual sense. The male protagonists, taken from the books of chivalry, and compounded with the swains of the pastoral novel, have only one distinguishing mark, a varying degree of constancy. The princesses similarly are stereotypes, their originals to be sought in the disdainful *desamoradas* (frigid maidens) of the pastoral novel, the legend of the Amazons, and that of the chaste Diana. However, in the princesses' case the intermittent flashes of jealousy and passion, as well as the desire to pursue an individual, independent destiny, give them a relative depth of dramatic experience, and anticipate thus certain important themes in Mendoza's later theatre. It may well be that in *Querer* a cast of noblewomen severely restricted the author's ability to exploit the effects of sexual passion, since his actresses' behaviour might have been deemed indecorous. A similar inhibition may also explain the inconclusive way in which the play ends, with no prince getting possession of either lady — certainly in one of the verse *relaciones* of the *Fiesta de Aranjuez* Mendoza had drawn attention to the fact that in the *Gloria de Niquea* the "generous lovers" had been satisfied with love for its own sake, and had not sought the marriages found in vulgar *comedias* (FC, p. 452). The complications of plot in *Querer* serve likewise an end different from that in the stock *comedia,* or indeed in Mendoza's other plays. Plot is not used to awaken dramatic

---

[19] See *Relación, MOP,* I, 12-14. For *El vellocino,* see Shergold, p. 273, and FC, pp. 455-456.

interest, or to effect shifts in the action, as much as to create focal points for discussion, or for lyrical patterning. Thus, Claridoro's attempt to get Zelidaura to return his affection seems primarily an excuse for a prolonged debate on the true nature of courtly love and its demands; Felisbravo's discovery of Zelidaura's portrait, and later the Princess's trick of stealing it from the sleeping prince, though they mark developments in the plot, are primarily opportunities for lyrical contributions to one conventional topic, rapturous comment on a lady's picture, and to another more original one, reflexions on the fact that a man in love should actually lie asleep.

Such divergences from the more ordinary *comedia* prompt the question by what criteria the artistic value of *Querer por solo querer* should be judged. Mendoza evidently sought to achieve a spectacular effect in which poetry played a significant role, but how did he envisage achieving that "rightness" in verse which he deemed essential? We may presume that he sought to provide, on the stage, a range of sentiments, topics, arguments and exemplary actions, appropriate to an aristocratic audience; and he also introduced, in poetic form, interchanges of opinion about love which, as suggested in an earlier chapter, formed, at a less coherent level, a staple for much formal, and informal, intercourse at court. In general, therefore, the characters are courtiers writ large, whose life, dominated by courtly love and knightly war, is an idealizing mirror held up to palace *mores*.

Courtly love is treated in an unexceptional way, though an attempt is made to portray it in its various aspects; love's ardent pursuit of woman, or its willingness to love unto death, love's constancy in the man, matched by the lady's coldness and disdain. In all this only one theme brings us close to an everyday problem in a gallant society; woman's right not to be loved, if that is her wish. A theme from pastoral, this probably found its most poignant expression in the Marcela of *Don Quixote*. Mendoza's treatment of it is original: he creates a dialogue between suitor and lady through which we sense many a court lady's protest at a code of gallantry which reduces her to a beautiful object on which she must lavish her art. When Zelidaura finds herself caught up in the love game, she can only laugh:

> Enfado, y risa me dan
> las noticias del oir
> lo que llamavan servir,
> y fineza en un galan. [20]

Martial sentiments are also much to the fore. These take two forms: they reflect the problems of the characters themselves, as in the case where Felisbravo must choose between the call of love and a soldier's honour; [21] or they express indirectly the warlike aspirations of the audience, as happens at the very opening of the play, when a general returns to Felisbravo's court after a naval battle in which the prince's forces have won. Felisbravo represents Philip IV — a point to which I shall return — and the play's opening cry "invicto señor" has therefore a special relevance. The language of the general's speech is brutal and chauvinistic, echoing the self-assertion of a court at the beginning of a new and promising reign, as well as the hope that after the renewal of hostilities in what would be known as the Thirty Years War, the problem of the Germanies would be settled to the dynasty's satisfaction. Indeed the plot itself, with its forever warring princes, may be a distant echo of that long struggle. [22]

Yet war is also seen at moments with sardonic irony. The warlike protagonists are after all nothing more than girls, as the *gracioso* Rifaloro points out. [23] But there is more to it than this: love here, because of the nature of the struggle between the princely contestants, becomes, even more than usual, a mode of war. Mendoza implies that, barbarous as war is, love is much more fierce. The bloodthirsty general of the opening scene utters later a sonnet not only condemning the barbarous law of war, but asserting that love is a worse alternative:

> No quiero amor, màs quiero dar despojos
> a la dura violencia de una espada,
> que a la blanda sobervia de unos ojos. [24]

---

[20] *FC*, p. 353. *News of what they called "serving" and courtly behaviour in a gallant provoke in me laughter and annoyance.*

[21] *FC*, p. 412.

[22] The truce was finally broken at the end of 1620 (see C. V. Wedgwood, *The Thirty Years War*, pp. 94-125).

[23] *FC*, p. 421.

[24] *FC*, p. 421. See ch. v, Note 81.

The heroic ideal is treated with equal irony. Zelidaura invites her suitor to fight for her, if he wishes to do anything at all, but Claridoro prefers the maudlin death of the tortured lover:

> La vida la guardo aqui
> para empresa más amada,
> y a cada instante ocupada,
> señora, en morir por ti. [25]

Such a choice, even for purposes of debate, is a comic reflection of a society which had abandoned heroism for *bienséance,* with the poet drawing attention to the gap between a perfunctory belligerency, and the humdrum pursuit of gallantry.

Such irony, when it breaks surface, reminds us of Mendoza, the quizzical satirist of the *entremeses.* Indeed, in *Querer por solo querer* the irony is primarily expressed through a character in some ways reminiscent of *Miser Palomo.* Rifaloro, the "criado de donaire," [26] is a figure of disillusion. His role at first sight is an ambiguous one, for Mendoza claims to have given him "wit with decorum," and Rifaloro should not proffer insults or tell straight truths, since the latter, we are told, coming from so lowly a fellow, would only lose their lustre. [27] But we soon realize that the unexceptionable, harmless fellow is really a sharp-tongued observer of human foibles. For instance his first reaction to Claridiana's castle is that it will be no different from any ordinary royal court in its proliferation of vices and weaknesses, which he then enumerates. The voice of a Doctor Dieta is again heard to ask: "Is there not one single good man?" [28] And Rifaloro probes also the court orthodoxy of gallantry. When Felisbravo outlines the heavenly nature of a love from which all desire is banished, Rifaloro counters pungently:

> Finissimo Bachiller
> este galan mentir,
> todos lo saben dezir,
> y nadie lo sabe hazer. [29]

---

[25] FC, p. 353: *I preserve my life here for a more beloved enterprise, given over every instant to dying for you, my lady.*

[26] FC, p. 355, in the stage direction, a "comic servant."

[27] FC, pp. 356-357: "un donayre con decoro" (p. 356).

[28] FC, p. 387: "No ay hombre de bien ninguno?"

[29] FC, p. 356: *He is a most well-mannered Bachelor of Arts that gallant lie: they all know how to say it, and no-one how to do it.*

Rifaloro, a character who has wandered out of an interlude into a play, will appear again in Mendoza's later *comedias* in yet a different guise. He remains hitherto on the margin, content to comment on, rather than to participate in, or manipulate, the action.

Mendoza saw his play too as a means of eulogizing his King and Queen, and reminding them of the kingly virtues and duties. Felisbravo, who here represents Philip IV, [30] speaks words of counsel to a monarch:

> Los ojos del Rey severos
> en lo apacible templados
> fabrican fuertes soldados,
> y hazen justos Consejeros. [31]

Elsewhere the appropriateness in a monarch of the pursuit of love is given great emphasis:

> ... juntos siempre anduvieron
> buen Principe, y buen amante. [32]

The speech is presumably intended as a compliment to Fileno, Belisa's young husband, though Mendoza's ambiguity is deep enough for him to be making a sly dig at the King's prowess as extra-marital lover. The Queen herself is clearly represented by Zelidaura, Princess of Tartary, an identification made easier by the allusion at the beginning of the play to her beauty, youth, and the present occasion of her birthday:

> Que a su cara, y pocos años
> florida licencia piden,
> para lo verde, y lo bello
> los Mayos, y los Abriles. [33]

---

[30] At the beginning of the play Felisbravo is addressed as a prince who has reigned for one year (*FC*, p. 348) — Philip IV acceded in March 1621, approximately a year before the play was performed. And Philip's age at accession is later referred to in words addressed to Felisbravo (p. 349): he was fifteen.

[31] *FC*, p. 348: *The King's severe gaze, tempered in gentleness, makes strong soldiers and just counsellors.*

[32] *FC*, p. 355: *A good prince and a good lover have always been found together.*

[33] *FC*, p. 348: *For April and May seek from her face and tender years a flowery licence for the green and the beautiful.* The play was in celebration of the Queen's birthday; in "pocos años" there is a play on *años* = years, and *años* = birthday.

Mendoza's willingness to use his play as a political instrument is shown not only in the vague reference above to the need for a good king to choose just counsellors, but in explicit mention of the "two ministers" who are praised for their good governorship of affairs — a clear reference to the Count of Olivares and his uncle Baltasar de Zúñiga, the King's prime advisers up to Zúñiga's death in October 1622. [34] At a deeper level, of course, the whole play is in part a political exercise, demonstrating the wealth and power of the régime, bolstering the prestige of the new King, and at the same time providing for him and the whole court an entertainment that was in every sense royal.

Querer por solo querer, by its very length, should have been a monumental bore. Perhaps Mendoza hoped to disarm criticism on that account by admitting that the play was inordinately long, and suggesting that this was due to the young and noble actresses' demands for material. [35] Long it certainly is — so long, claimed Rifaloro, that it could serve as the life of a Mr. Somebody — and the sameness of the material has led to some repetitiousness. [36] Despite such shortcomings, it remains a remarkable work, displaying a high standard of lyrical verse, and a mastery over many varied verse forms. [37] Furthermore, the dialogue's suppleness and wit, along with the swift interchanges of points of view, electrify scene after scene. Making use of a technique later exploited by Calderón, Mendoza casts into the debating arena a notion, or image, which characters seize upon in turn, and develop to their own ends. A splendid instance is the dialogue between Floranteo and Claridiana, in which the latter recalls the peace of mind she enjoyed when under a spell, since she was free from the preoccupations of having suitors. How good it would be to find someone who actually loved without hope, but she could only find the nightingale, "tender

---

[34] *FC,* p. 356. For Zúñiga's mysterious and sudden death, see Marañón, p. 51.

[35] *FC,* p. 387.

[36] e.g. Claridiana, who at the end of Act One bemoans that her fate depends on her father's whim (*FC,* pp. 366-367), returns to her theme at length in the following Act (pp. 369-370).

[37] In addition to the more usual *romance, redondilla* and *quintilla* forms, we have a large number of *décimas,* more than the usual number of sonnets, *octavas,* and two different sextets (one 7.7.7.7.7.11. with rhyme scheme abbacc [see *FC,* pp. 373-375]; the other 7.7.11.11.7.11. with rhyme scheme abbacc (p. 406). *Querer's* lyrical value is emphasized when Gracián called it "aquel gran poema" (*GOC,* p. 428).

gallant of the dawn," who day in day out unstintingly paid court
to his love, with no thought for reward:

> Que en voz doliente, y medrosa
> parece que le dizia:
> no te quiero para mia,
> que te busco por hermosa. [38]

No sooner does this lyrical spiral end than Floranteo takes up in
turn the example of the nightingale, seeking now to demonstrate
the human lover's superiority. Argument succeeds argument in man's
favour, the most original and persuasive being the nightingale's inability to love an absent lover:

> Del aurora la presencia
> ama solo el ruyseñor,
> pero en la fè de un amor
> lo distante no es ausencia. [39]

Gracián, who understandably called the play "that emporium of
conceits," paid special tribute to Mendoza's subtlety in this kind
of conceitful outbidding. [40] Part of the audience's delight probably
sprang from its inability to anticipate the ingenious, and unexpected,
direction that the argument would take.

But this is not the only kind of lyricism: there are numerous set
pieces of considerable beauty, sonnets including the memorable
"Amable soledad," some beautiful *décimas* including his "Soledad,
no hay compañía," and some *octavas* beginning "Bella ninfa del
sol, deidad de nieve" which rightly called forth Gracián's praise. [41]
And among the variety of verse forms introduced, mention should
be made of an unusual sextet to which the poet imparts a sinuous
tenderness:

> En acentos suaves
> su musica dilata
> arroyuelo de prata,

---

[38] FC, p. 372: *For in a fearful and plaintive voice it seems he said to her: I do not
seek you to be mine, I seek you for your beauty.*

[39] FC, p. 372: *It is the dawn's presence only that the nightingale loves, but in love's
faith, that which lies distant is not absence.*

[40] Agudeza, in GOC, p. 320: "aquel emporio de conceptos."

[41] FC, p. 405. For Gracián's comment, GOC, pp. 253-254.

de las alegres aves
instrumento sonoro
en trastes de crystal, clavijas de oro. [42]

In comparison with the spectacles that later, from time to time, entertained and astounded palace audiences, *Querer por solo querer* appears primitive. Mendoza's stage devices titillated the fancy, but were not inextricably linked to the plot, or the play's development. They did not achieve either those "mudanças totales del Teatro" that were later so much praised. [43] A measure of the gap between Mendoza's conception and the more sophisticated spectacles may be had by a comparison with two outstanding instances of the latter. First, Calderón's *El mayor encanto amor* (1635), which was staged on the lake of the *Buen Retiro*. Working in close collaboration with the famous stage engineer Cosme Lotti, Calderón introduced into Circe's island all manner of miracle and metamorphosis, including real ships and real sea. Nevertheless, Calderón made all these visual elements subordinate to the plot, so that the audience's capacity to marvel at the miracles of theatrical engineering was not marred by any feeling that the changes of scene were gratuitous and uncalled for. The second outstanding example is different in that the emphasis was unashamedly on visual spectacle rather than on plot or words. The occasion was a play by Antonio de Solís, performed in the Coliseum of the *Buen Retiro* in the late sixteen-fifties. *Triunfos de Amor y Fortuna* was built around a continuous series of *mutaciones* (changes of scene), ten in all, and these ranged from the richly adorned Royal Hall of Love to a maritime scene including a seaport dominated by the Colossus of Rhodes, and a vision of Venus in her conch shell. [44]

Querer por solo querer, however, although a much more modest entertainment in comparison with inventions such as those described, did mark an advance on earlier palace spectacles. In particular it took the *comedia* as a viable basis for a lavish, dignified, and poetic spectacle. Furthermore, the pre-eminence it gave to verse helped retrieve the balance lost in works like the *Gloria de Niquea,* and

---

[42] *FC*, pp. 373-375. *A silvery stream in smooth accents spreads out its music, being the gay birds' sonorous instrument, pegs of gold upon frets of crystal.*

[43] Alonso Núñez de Castro, *Solo Madrid es Corte* (Madrid, 1658), f. 8: *total scene changes.*

[44] See Shergold, pp. 280-284, and pp. 320-324. See also Antonio de Solís y Ribadeneyra, *Triunfos de Amor y Fortuna. Fiesta real...* (n.p., no date).

so made Calderón's task easier. Nevertheless, as I hope to have shown, *Querer* deserves considerable praise in its own right. A contemporary critic in discussing the *comedia de tramoyas* acknowledged only Mendoza as the master of this genre, [45] and although this judgment may relate in part to works of Mendoza's that are lost, it does remind us of *Querer's* considerable qualities both as a fount of lyricism and as a "beautiful consonance" that charmed the eye. It is greatly to the play's credit that its poetry, removed from the totality of effect provided by scenic splendour and musical offering, is still capable of recreating for us much of the beauty expended on a spring evening three centuries ago.

---

[45] See p. 58.

XI

THE COMEDIAS

MENDOZA'S experience with the stock *comedia* of his day cannot of course be separated from his achievements in the *entremés* on the one hand, and the spectacle play *Querer por solo querer* on the other. Continuity, rather, is maintained along two lines of development, the *entremés* widening into the social comedy of the author's later plays, the spectacle play developing into a form of romanesque entertainment based, like *Querer*, on a preoccupation with courtly love and the standards of *bienséance*. These however are not two distinct genres, for we find in some plays a mingling of both.

Perhaps Mendoza's earliest *comedia* was *El premio de la virtud y sucesos prodigiosos de D. Pedro Guerrero*, a surmise however that can only be based on the play's untidiness and primitive construction. [1] The hero of this *comedia de santo* was archbishop of Granada at the time of the Morisco uprising, and representative too at the Council of Trent. The play is a straightforward account of his career first as a poor peasant, then as servitor at Salamanca, and later as canon of a provincial college, until finally he displays as archbishop an uncompromising attitude towards the Moriscos. The story ends with the announcement that he is going to Trent, and the audience is promised a second part. The plot is loosely threaded on two strands: first the character and destiny of Fernando de Válor, the Morisco prince, who foresees his death at the hands of Pedro Guerrero, then but a lad in the fields; and second, the Christian self-denial of the hero who displays, throughout, a peasant's true humility. A chronicle type of subject makes for a loose construction with little dramatic momentum, but Mendoza has given the play unity, and an end towards which the action may be impelled. First, the account of Pedro's humble beginnings is linked to the

---

[1] *El premio de la virtud, y sucessos prodigiosos de D. Pedro Guerrero. Comedia famosa, de Don Antonio de Mendoza* (n.p., no date) [BNM copy, shelf-mark T-20666]. For the arguments in favour of the likely order of composition of this and the other *comedias*, see my "A Chronology."

encounter with Fernando, thus foreshadowing the end to which we may look forward. Second, in the cave scene after a hunt, Fernando, having seen a crown inscribed with the words "I shall be thine," only to find it turn to dust, witnesses his own funeral. Finally, the mysterious prophecy, hinted at earlier, begins to come true, though the play's end stops short of its complete fulfilment. Pedro Guerrero's character is carefully delineated, but the rehearsal of his virtues leads only to boredom. What occasionally awakens interest is the use of visual techniques: in the cave scene Fernando de Válor's symbolic crown emits a flame as he puts it on his head, and thereafter turns to dust as it falls to the floor. We have not only the spooky cortège of Fernando's own funeral, but a pageant of figures representing those bishops of Granada who helped encompass the downfall of the Moors. The audience presumably enjoyed too the display of music and dancing which at one point is given in celebration of the Morisco prince. But such moments of colour are infrequent, as are the intermittent signs of an instinct for the theatre. All in all, this is a bad play.

Más merece quien más ama must have been put together at about the same time as *Querer por solo querer*, with which it shares not only a romanesque plot, and a fondness for the discussion of problems of etiquette, but even common details of character and action. [2] In both plays we have two princesses jealous of each other because of their love for the same man; in both a princess who, though spurning love and preferring manly pursuits, is overcome by passion; and a princely suitor who, loving only for love's sake, is eternally faithful to his lady.

As in *Querer por solo querer*, succession to a kingdom is a point of departure. Here Fidelinda, a Diana who spends her time hunting, is so stubborn in her dislike of men that, despite her numerous suitors, she has allowed two years to go by without observing her father's command that she should marry within a year of his death. Her sister Felisbella, "less mad, and more likeable," will inherit her kingdom unless she obeys. [3] Fidelinda, being vain as well as cold,

---

[2] *FC*, pp. 297-340. The play was twice performed before Their Majesties by Avendaño and company between 5 October 1622 and 5 February 1623 (see Shergold and Varey, "Some Palace Performances"). The play first appears in print in *Doze Comedias nuevas de Lope de Vega Carpio, y otros Autores. Segunda parte* (Barcelona, 1630) — see La Barrera, p. 707.

[3] *FC*, p. 297: "menos loca y màs amable."

is moved to envy and hate when she hears of a Prince Felisardo who spurns the love of all mortal women. By accident she discovers Felisardo wounded, and without realizing his identity falls in love with him. He likewise falls in love with her without knowing who she is. We now meet the fourth protagonist, Rosauro: despairing of ever winning her love, he becomes a humble gardener, so as to be near Fidelinda, who, through confusion over a portrait she has seen, concludes that this Rosauro must be the disdainful Felisardo in disguise, and makes him at once the object of her scorn and cruelty. In consequence Felisardo (whose life Rosauro had earlier saved) feels that his friend is being badly treated, with the result that his own feelings towards Fidelinda cool. Fidelinda, unable to imagine how any man could spurn her, angrily accuses her sister of causing Felisardo's disdain. Felisbella protests at her sister's tyranny, and denies any affection for the prince. But in reality, Felisardo's disdain for Fidelinda has had the effect of awakening the sister's affection, a development that foreshadows the play's conclusion.

Rosauro, despite Fidelinda's obsessive hatred, maintains so steadfast a love for her that a rebellion in the kingdom in the other sister's favour still finds him at Fidelinda's side — a situation closely paralleled in *Querer por solo querer*. In that revolt Felisbella, aided by Felisardo, proves successful. Fidelinda, though supported now only by Rosauro, is still unwilling to recognise his worth, nor will she mitigate her wrath at his presumption in having loved her. Fidelinda discovers too late that her constant prince is Rosauro not Felisardo (as she has for so long supposed), and that she has furthermore suffered the indignity of defeat at the hands of the real Felisardo. She confesses her esteem for Rosauro, but admits that now, because of the demands of her honour, she cannot love him. She calls on Rosauro instead to help her wreak revenge on Felisardo. When Felisbella's forces come to capture Fidelinda, Rosauro appeals to Felisardo, and he, mindful of his debt to Rosauro, places himself at the feet of the defeated princess, who forces him to confess his presumption. And to punish Felisardo for that presumption, she now gives her hand to Rosauro. Felisbella for her part says she no longer loves Felisardo, since she had loved in him the proud man, not the man thus humbled. Notwithstanding, Rosauro decrees that Felisbella must marry Felisardo since the latter, though knowing how to be proud, had shown humility. And thus the play ends.

The audience's principal interest must lie with Fidelinda. Noble in her incapacity to love, she, like Claridiana in *Querer*, refuses to allow another's will to challenge her freedom of choice:

> Mi padre obligarme pudo
> a que yo, yo sujetasse
> a dueño indigno una vida
> nunca victoria de nadie? [4]

She also disregards her suitors' warning that the years will rob her of beauty, and thus of the chance to win a husband. That threat leaves her unafraid, because she feels sure of the continuance of her own identity:

> Quando de mis ojos, no
> viva la luz generosa,
> dexarè de ser hermosa;
> pero siempre serè yo. [5]

Fidelinda's presumption, and its eventual consequences, are echoed in the *gracioso's* warning:

> à bellezas, glorias breves,
> nieve al Sol, y flor al ayre! [6]

and by Felisbella, who points out to her sister the madness of "denying that she is mortal." Fidelinda, however, asserts the validity of youth's experience for its own sake, without regard for the future:

> Ay tema tan loca, y vana?
> Si oy hermosa, y moça soy,
> porque he de mirarme oy
> con los ojos de mañana? [7]

The *Getafe* interlude contains a similar suggestion that life's force may run counter to the wisdom of morality. [8] But however sure

---

[4] *FC*, p. 299: *Could my father have obliged me, me, to tie to an unworthy master a life that has been conquered by no-one?*

[5] *FC*, p. 301: *When the generous light in my eyes dies down, I shall cease to be beautiful; but I shall still be myself.*

[6] *FC*, p. 298: *to beauty, brief glory, snow in sunshine, and flower in the breeze.*

[7] *FC*, p. 300: *Was ever so mad and empty a whim? If today I am beautiful and young, why must I look upon myself with tomorrow's eyes?*

[8] See pp. 213-214 here.

the author may be of the rightness of this view he obviously realizes that in Fidelinda's case she is riding for a fall. The play's outcome bears this out, for her pride has made her lose her kingdom, and choose Rosauro, who is not the man she loves. Yet, with a characteristic irony Mendoza makes her choose out of wisdom, and of her own free will. Fidelinda's real punishment has come much earlier in the play, when, after having maintained all her life a disdainful aloofness from love, she begins to yield to it. And it is a punishment administered not by morality but by nature. When she finds the wounded Felisardo and begins to fall in love with him, her self-respect breaks down as she realizes her frailty:

> Que sirve ser yo quien puedo
> dar al Sol desconfiança,
> y atar la misma esperança
> entre cadenas de miedo?
> Si en fin soy muger tambien? [9]

But the deepest struggle rages between her passion for Felisardo and the memory of her former nature. Overwhelmed by a love which she cannot really believe and which causes fear at every step, she is plagued by the thought that she is forced to be the first to avow her love. Thus what in her novelistic stereotype was a convention becomes the deep-felt utterance of a real woman:

> Callar quisiera el dolor,
> y hazer los cuidados sabios,
> mas que importa en mis agravios,
> mas que importa en mis antojos,
> si dan vozes en los ojos,
> que estèn mudos en los labios? [10]

But if Fidelinda's new-found passion is a form of madness, what shows her to be really mad is her treatment of Rosauro. Felisbella points out to her sister how mistaken she is in assuming this man to be Felisardo. She replies: "it is he, and if not I would that

---

[9] FC, p. 310: *What serves it to be the one who can make the Sun diffident, and tie Hope herself with chains of fear, if after all I am also a woman?*

[10] FC, p. 317: *I would prefer to keep my pain a secret, and make love's cares discreet, but what avails it to my honour [and the offence done it] and to my whims [in not loving], that those cares remain silent on my lips, if they shout aloud in my eyes?*

everything I despise bore that name." [11] The action of the play now moves into its second phase, in which Fidelinda's relation with Rosauro assumes a greater importance than her love for Felisardo, and in which the seeds of her jealousy for Felisbella begin to grow. Unfortunately, an accumulation of complex improbabilities in the last act effectively buries the development one would have hoped for, though finally, after the beginning of the rebellion, Fidelinda is faced with the terrible ordeal of a love unsolicited, undeserved, yet constant. The conclusion, nevertheless, is not completely satisfactory, since it neither emphasizes the wrongness of Fidelinda's presumption, nor brings nearer the threat of her mortality. All it effectively does is to reward constancy at Fidelinda's expense.

Because of Fidelinda's predominance, the other characters pass through a relative eclipse. Felisardo suffers particularly, since though he is the male equivalent of Fidelinda, his qualities cannot be given due emphasis as they would merely duplicate those of his female counterpart. Notwithstanding, he has his moments of interest, particularly when his decision to withdraw his growing affection for Fidelinda appears as a reversion to his natural coldness. Unfortunately his final act of humility at Fidelinda's feet is felt more as a sudden, and unprepared, reversal of fortune than as a merited punishment for presumption. Felisbella does not, fortunately, suffer an equal eclipse. She serves as an effective foil to Fidelinda, and is in some degree custodian of Fidelinda's conscience. Furthermore her fearsome wit and independence of judgment make her much more than a foil to her sister.

Rosauro is the only other character to arouse strong interest. His gallantry does not always combine well with apparent saintliness, but in the last scenes where he suffers moral degradation at the hands of Fidelinda rather than mere discourtesy, he becomes a striking figure, his constancy in hopeless love, though in the direct line of Arnalte in Diego de San Pedro's novel, is reminiscent also of the constancy in faith of Calderón's *El príncipe constante*. Precisely because of his success in this role, his sudden change of fortune and transformation into the ultimate arbiter of the action seem out of keeping with the mood of the play at that point.

---

[11] *FC*, p. 316: "el es, sinò / quanto aborreciere yo / quiero que tenga este nombre."

Despite the lack of a uniformly effective lyricism, and the length and over-elaboration of some of the speeches, the dialogue in general is witty, smooth, and agile. The play contains too some good passages: Rosauro's portrait of the sleeping princess, for instance, is one of the finest examples of the *pintura* genre. With what elaborate attention does the poet define the gesture of the sleeping woman's hand as it rests against her cheek, and the ardour with which the speaker regards the scene!:

> descuido bello en atencion ayrosa,
> y en la tregua del sueño que se atreve,
> mostrava nuevo ardor de mis antojos,
> despierta el alma en los dormidos ojos. [12]

Such language is reminiscent of the later frieze-like *enargeia* of Gabriel Bocángel.

Although the play is sustained by the analysis of the psychology of love, and by its lyrical *élan,* Mendoza's interventions as arbiter of etiquette are significant too. In one scene Rosauro and Felisardo hold a formal disputation on the respective merits of *confianza* and *desconfianza* in the gallant; Felisbella's remonstrations with her sister's suitors are in their way a discussion of the appropriate approach by a gallant to his lady, and her suitable response; and there are incidental pieces of advice — Fidelinda counsels how an elder sister should treat her junior, or again upbraids Felisbella for failing to show generosity towards a rejected suitor. Mendoza certainly wrote here with the "sovereignty of the palace" in mind. But his analysis of courtly attitudes and ideals reflects in turn that psychological subtlety which is the play's finest quality.

No hay amor donde hay agravio must also probably be counted among Mendoza's earlier *comedias.* [13] Its location in Zaragoza, and more particularly the attempt to introduce the atmosphere of the banks of the Ebro, suggest that it may have been written in that area, especially as Mendoza usually preferred to set his realistic plays in Madrid. But if circumstantial evidence points therefore

---

[12] *FC,* p. 307: *a lovely carelessness in attitude of alert attention, and in that truce from sleep which dares to be declared, she showed what proved new ardour of my love, her soul awake in her sleeping eyes.*

[13] *FC,* pp. 181-217. The play first appears in print in *Flor de las mejores doze Comedias de los mayores Ingenios de Espana* (Madrid, 1652), D1-F2v.

to the play having been composed during the royal *jornada* to Aragon in 1625-26, the play's weak construction, and its dependence on overlong lyrical speeches, indicate either that it was very hastily put together, or alternatively that it was written at a much earlier moment in Mendoza's career. The language suggests the second surmise — it lacks the well-balanced conceits of the author of *Más merece*, and is characterized by a rather heavy Gongorine manner, including for Mendoza the unusual exploitation of the *bimembre* tendency in the hendecasyllable line, which Góngora so much favoured. The language all in all recalls someone writing in the sixteen-tens when Góngora's influence was at its height, and when Mendoza's style was as yet labile. The degree of lyricism, as well as the interest in the discussion of etiquette, again suggest the preoccupations of *Querer* or *Más merece*, a conclusion that confirms the view that *No hay amor* belongs either to the early twenties, or more probably to an even earlier date.

Violante, the heroine of the play, is unofficially betrothed to Juan, but is in fact deeply in love with Enrique, Juan's life-long friend, who returns that love. Juan contrives to make Violante's reputation suspect if he does not marry her at once, and this he is obliged to do by Violante's guardian, Don Lope. Juan, having now discovered the former attachment between Enrique and Violante, begins to suspect that their love still persists. Those suspicions are confirmed, and since Enrique's behaviour suggests that he at least is not guilty, Juan resolves only to kill his wife. Enrique, however, intervenes at the very moment when Juan is about to murder Violante, so that eventually both he and Violante die at the hand of the avenging husband.

In what is basically an exercise in the casuistry of the honour code, Mendoza, like other playwrights, has sought circumstances that would test to the utmost a husband's right to avenge his outraged honour. The author, however, rather than concentrate on the usual parade of fateful peripecies, has presented the issues in a way most favourable emotionally to the guilty lovers. Thus the play opens poignantly with a love scene between Violante and Enrique, who is about to leave on a journey. The audience straightaway identifies itself with their tender emotions, being tempted almost to make the assumption that they are already man and wife. For this reason, even though it later becomes clear that Juan (and not Enrique) is Violante's betrothed, we carry our original prejudice in favour of Enrique into the situation where Juan becomes Violante's husband. In Juan's case, the prominence given to the scene in which he compromises Violante stamps him on our sensibilities as her attempted seducer, even though his primary role in the play will be that of honour-obsessed husband. By these means Mendoza, with some originality, has successfully identified us emotionally with Violante's conviction that she has been required, overnight and by a quirk of destiny, to make her proper husband Enrique into an adulterer, and her seducer into her vengeful spouse. One further complicating circumstance determines our emotional reactions: in a long lyrical section, Enrique, in trying to excuse to Juan his continuing presence (when supposedly away on business), transforms the recent scene of love with Violante into a fictitious account of the seduction of a local beauty, Aurora. The depth of his affection must therefore be suspect, and he appears to the audience (as indeed he wishes to appear to Juan) as a womanizer. In consequence the audience responds ambiguously in the latter half of the action, being prone to feel that Enrique assumes rather naturally his present role of potential seducer of a married woman.

Violante stands at the centre of the action. She is not the innocent victim of some of the other honour plays, trapped in ambiguities not of her own devising. She is, rather, wilful and vulnerable, sure of her love for Enrique, suspicious of any emotion or stance that is not unequivocally one of affection for her. And when the honour code suddenly forces her into the false role of Juan's wife, she is unwilling to play it, even though perfectly aware of her dilemma:

> No soy màs, que mi passion,
> pues me vence, y me atropella,
> ni tampoco al honor santo
> dexo cerrada la puerta.
> Alli mi valor me llama,
> aqui mi amor me averguença. [14]

---

[14] FC, p. 200: *I am reduced to my passion, which conquers and tramples me down. Nor do I leave the door closed to holy honour. Thither my valour (and worth) call me, and hither my love puts me to shame.*

But subsequently, though she again has her moments of self-assertion, she becomes the plaything of an action which is dilatory and mechanical.

The play's ambiguity necessarily extends to our response to its conclusion. The deaths of wife and lover produce little cathartic effect — no sense of desolation at Violante's end, since she was not guiltless; nor of *terrible exemplo,* since we are in sympathy with her predicament. The sub-plot directs our attention to how we are ultimately to view the action. Clarín, Juan's servant, carries on a love-affair whose basis is not love, but expediency and venality. Clarín too views his master as the irresponsible, unreflecting youth who blunders into matrimony "as though marrying were taking two swigs of red wine." [15] And in any case, opines Clarín, a married man is like a bull tied down hands and feet for everything except his work. These cynical views help us to draw certain conclusions: that Juan as lightly doffs his seducer's guise to assume that of husband, as he dons thereafter the guise of avenging spouse; that Enrique, another "toro ayroso" ("lively bull") may be deeply in love with Violante but likes to see and to project himself as a man who has a way with the women; and finally that Violante herself suffers because she is guided by her feeling where she might have exercised a more realistic discretion. In a world where, as Clarín indicates, beauty is merely a commodity put up for sale in "pleasure's auction," [16] Violante's scruples of sentiment are merely finicking.

Mendoza has sought to give his play unity by its lyricism. The heroine's name has floral associations, the key scenes take place in a garden, and many of the key images are taken from the world of flowers. On the one hand, the flower is the symbol of love's primal power: it is the "clavel ingerto en açucena" which is the sensual hieroglyph of Aurora's hand held to her lips; the temptation of the "golden vessel" in which Juan with insect-like urge to self-destruction would suck the poison from the flower; the rose of Enrique's passion seeking always to face the light of the sun in his beloved's eyes. [17] And then, in contrast, we have the *flor ajada,* the bruised flower, whose present state is almost a necessary corollary of its

---

15 *FC,* p. 206: "como si el casarse fuera / beber dos tragos de aloque."

16 *FC,* p. 205: "la almoneda del gusto." Clarín goes on to make the point that love is a feudal fief to whom only men pay their tribute.

17 *FC,* p. 196: *carnation grafted on to lily;* p. 188, and p. 183.

fragile beauty. This, the symbol of the threat to Violante's honour when Juan enters her house, is, ironically, again the symbol of that honour as later threatened by Enrique and Violante's love; [18] and the untimely cutting of the flower's head by the passing ploughshare was the famous simile used by Virgil in describing how death eventually put an end to the friendship of Nisus and Euryalus, a comradeship to which that of Juan and Enrique is here compared. [19]

The difficulty therefore is to preserve the flower's beauty, since passion is by its nature violent. The play comes nearest to offering a solution through its emphasis on the virtue of self-control, *vencerse*. Violante invokes it, but fails eventually to attain it; it is a quality which Enrique does attain at one point when he places, for the moment, his honour above his passion, but he was unable to display such control in his passion for the fictitious Aurora, nor, in the long run, in his feelings for Violante. [20] In a very different situation, self-control permits Juan to overcome his love for Violante, and decide to slay her because of the offence to his honour. [21] But once again we return to the play's ambiguous answer. In Enrique, as in Violante, self-control could have led to harmony, but only at the expense of love; an awful dilemma which Mendoza throws into relief in an exchange between the lovers at the climax of a very moving scene, when Enrique has announced his decision to place honour first. Enrique refers to the triumph of male honour, Violante to the genuineness of real affection:

> ENR: Y el triunfo de ser quien soy?
> VIOL: Yo tambien no soy la misma?
> quieresme Enrique? [22]

In the other case, Juan's action did bring about the re-establishment of honour, but his achievement of self-control led at the same time to the destruction of both love and friendship.

The play's weakness lies partly in its inability to make the underlying issues clear, partly in the defective construction of the last

---

[18] *FC*, p. 188, and p. 201.

[19] *FC*, p. 194. See Virgil's *Aeneid*, Book IX.

[20] *FC*, p. 200, p. 203, and pp. 194-198.

[21] *FC*, p. 204.

[22] *FC*, p. 203: *ENR. And the triumph of my own identity? / VIOL. Am I still not the same woman? / Do you love me, Enrique?*

act, to which I have alluded. But these defects are to some extent offset by the quality of some of the lyrical verse. The long monologue describing Aurora bathing, though not completely successful, does contain some beautiful lines, but probably the most effective lyrical scene is that when Juan threatens Violante's honour. Juan, invoking the fascination of the flower for the insect, thus explains why he has entered the garden:

> A gustar bella Violante,
> en vaso de oro veneno:
> a mirar entre las flores
> mi esperança, a ser incendio
> de una llama, que me abrasa
> en el màs ardiente fuego. [23]

No hay amor donde hay agravio, even more than the other *comedias* so far discussed, is better in its parts than its entirety. What is so far lacking is over-all control and a single artistic aim, qualities that indeed Mendoza was to acquire in his later stage career, after a comparatively long absence from the theatre. In 1625 he certainly tried his hand at play-writing, but only to scribble one act of a play in which Quevedo and Mateo Montero also collaborated. The next certain reference to a performance of a play by Mendoza was around 1630, when *Cada loco con su tema* was performed. The explanation of this silence may well have been the royal secretary's heavy duties, and of course the *jornada de Aragón* kept the court away from Madrid from autumn 1625 until mid-May of the following year. Perhaps some of the reasons for this neglect of his dramatic talent are echoed by Salas Barbadillo, at some time before October 1630. Through the mouth of Apollo, the author expresses regret that Mendoza, who had been so successful in the *comedia de tramoyas,* should now abandon the Muses, but consoles himself with the thought that he is now "occupied in being minister to a more benign and brightly shining Apollo," a clear reference of course to King Philip. [24]

---

[23] *FC*, p. 188: *To taste, lovely Violante, poison in a golden cup; to look at my hope lying among flowers, to be the conflagration kindled from a flame that consumes me in most ardent fire.*

[24] Alonso de Salas Barbadillo, *Coronas del Parnaso*: Mendoza now "se ocupa en ser ministro de mas benigno y luziente Apolo" (f. 34). The *aprobación* is dated October 1630.

Mendoza's later drama contrasts with that of the earlier period. The romanesque themes appeal less, there is less desire to create a specifically poetic drama, and instead there emerge new interests and emphases. Mendoza's *graciosos* had always tended to cast a cold eye on the paraphernalia of the romanesque *comedia*. The author too repeated, half-approvingly, Lope's dictum "es cosa de risa el arte," and that the playwright may do as he likes as long as he pleases the public. [25] Perhaps a growing weariness with the princesses of his plays and with "decoro de Palacio" made Mendoza yearn for a less reverent form of art. Certainly he was to return to the comedy vein so brilliantly exploited in the *entremeses,* and never entirely absent from the romanesque *comedias*. By turning to immediate social problems and situations, he enables Miser Palomo again to set up shop, and comment devastatingly on the foibles of his age. Mendoza perhaps had always felt that attraction, for in a *loa* of about 1619 he made the time-honoured distinction between *burlas* and *veras,* jest and truth, in which the former is likened to a surfeit of greens that gripe the stomach, whereas truth is a food that feeds the whole body and even satisfies the soul. [26]

The form of his later *comedia* is also in contrast with the earlier one. The "thousand equivocal paths" of plot [27] are abandoned in favour of a more straightforward intrigue. His approach to character is also different, for he now prefers broader lines, as well as the exaggerated types of the *comedia de figurón,* to those more detailed, and indeed profound, studies of human nature in his romanesque plays. Though in such an account profit is at the expense of a corresponding loss, the newer style is more generally in keeping with Mendoza's talent and, more importantly, offers him a better chance to bind his plays into an artistic whole.

In one sense Mendoza's greatest discovery in his later social comedies was Madrid, and *Cada loco con su tema,* probably the earliest

---

[25] See e.g. *Más merece, FC,* p. 314, or *Querer, FC,* p. 417. Lope's view is referred to in *Más merece, FC,* p. 315: *art is something to laugh about.*

[26] *MOP,* III, 44-49: "Las veras son las viandas / que todo el cuerpo alimentan / y aun al alma satisfacen" (p. 45). The same distinction is made again in *Cada loco con su tema* (*BAE,* XLV, p. 464), with which the *loa* is apparently linked — see Asensio (p. 120 and Note, also p. 127 and Note), who dates the *loa* to about 1619.

[27] *FC,* p. 314: "mil caminos / equivocos."

of these, already breathes the atmosphere of the court, conveying the author's feeling that the place was special, different:

> que tienen, advertid,
> Otro *saber* (sic) diferente　　[*sabor* BNM MS]
> De otro clima y de otra gente
> Estos aires de Madrid. [28]

But this play is also essentially Mendoza: not only his talent, but also his social role as a provincial *hidalgo*, with a claim to nobility but comparatively little money, whose fairly rigid moral standards he finds neglected at court. A version of *Cada loco* already existed in the period 1619-22, and the final draft, whenever it was made, still bears numerous traces of an earlier form: the reference to a *rey santo* smacks more of Philip III in his declining years than of the young Philip IV; the fun at the expense of *culteranismo* would be more topical in the decade of the *Soledades* than later; and it might seem doubtful that a poet would still, some years later, be using lyrical material found in *Más merece*. More basically, the play's moral attitude suggests in greater measure the critical outsider than the man who by the mid-twenties was enjoying considerable court privileges. Despite all this, however, *Cada loco* was, in some degree, rewritten around the period 1629-30, and contemporary references also give the impression that the play was then enjoying considerable public favour.

In *Cada loco* the author again exploited the possibilities of the relation between two sisters of opposing character; but for a world of princesses he substitutes a comfortable city interior. Isabel, a

---

[28] *BAE*, XLV, p. 458: *for this Madrid air has, you notice, a different tang from that of another climate and another people.* The text of the *comedia* (sometimes known as *El Montañés indiano*) extends from pp. 457-476. For the possibility of an earlier version of this play, and the date of the first palace performance, see my "A Chronology." Shergold and Varey, "Some Palace Performances," pp. 218-219, argued that the royal performance given by Antonio de Prado's company may have occurred not in February 1629 but (owing to a confusion in the palace accounts) in 1630, or even 1631. However, the autograph MS of the play (BNM *MS Res.* 93) bears the date 29 August 1630, which would be six months later than a supposed palace performance on 27 February. The 1631 interpretation would have the advantage of conforming with the local licence to perform noted on the MS, and dated in Valencia, 6 May 1631. The text of the poem (*MOP*, I, 181-186) refers to the great success at the palace, of Montalbán's *De un castigo dos venganzas*, probably about 1630, and acknowledges that in comparison Mendoza's own "Montañés" had done less well (see Victor Dixon, "Juan Pérez de Montalbán's *Para Todos*," *HR*, XXXII, 1964, 46-47). Significantly, the text of the poem in Palacio *MS* 2802 (f. 131) adds the date 1631 to the title. These details tend to strengthen the argument for autumn 1630 as the likely date of first performance of *Cada loco*. A printed version of the play did not appear until the *Obras líricas* (1728), *Cada loco con su tema y el Montañés Indiano*, pp. 421-464. I cite here the *BAE* text, having checked the quotations against the autograph manuscript.

discreet young lady, and her rather foolish sister Leonor, are the daughters of a rich *indiano* who has returned from Peru to settle in the Spanish capital. The father intends to marry one of them to his nephew from the northern province of La Montaña, a worthy man "of small estate and much honour," who at the play's opening is about to arrive in Madrid to claim his bride. Neither girl is attracted to the match: Isabel, having forgotten one American suitor, now has hopes of a handsome gallant, Don Juan; Leonor (whose only measure of human worth is whether a man rides, or goes on foot) will only be content with the noblest, and richest, suitor in all Spain. The girls' rebellion against the half-hearted tyranny of the father, Hernán, is strengthened by a maiden aunt, Aldonza, who considers it foolish that either of the sisters, having but recently arrived from America, should so soon exchange the giddy attractions of Madrid for a remote province where she would reign over "a court of chestnut trees, a Babylon of ilexes." [29] Isabel's gallant meanwhile is already getting ready to lay siege to her, his plan hinging on persuading his companion Bernardo to be suitor to Doña Aldonza. A message from Isabel, conveying the news of the *Montañés*'s suit, helps Bernardo make up his mind to aid his friend. Now, a third gallant appears in the person of Julián, a silly young fop, whom Leonor baits by dropping her glove. The amorous tangle is complicated further by the arrival of two other suitors, the provincial relation, new to the corruption of the capital; and in addition another *ingénu,* the Peruvian suitor Don Luis, with whom Isabel was originally in love. The first act ends to the clash of swords, as Luis and the *Montañés* challenge each other after having quarrelled in front of Isabel's house.

The second act thrives on the ensuing duel. The *Montañés* is persuaded by Juan and Bernardo that he has badly wounded Don Luis, and should flee from the law, whilst Don Luis is advised by them to keep away from the house because the *Montañés* is wounded. The way is thus left open for the gallant and Bernardo to use their persuasions on Isabel and Aldonza. Julián too continues his suit, but, without realizing his error, he woos an *escudero* at the window in place of Leonor. And after guitar and song, again the

---

29 p. 458: "una corte de castaños / y Babilonia de encinas."

sound of fighting; the act ends as the *Montañés* tries to clear the street of unwelcome rivals.

In the final act, Juan and Bernardo's plans come to their fruition, though hardly by the means they intended. Juan, having persuaded Isabel of his deep affection, is told that she is now betrothed to the *Montañés*. Isabel does not understand why Juan reacts so coolly to her subsequent declaration of love — her gallant in fact knows that for lack of money he cannot by litigation gain a woman who is now officially the *Montañés*'s betrothed. The play ends, therefore, not through the subtlety of Juan and Bernardo who have hitherto manipulated events, but through the quiet guile of Isabel, who informs the father that her honour has been compromised by Juan. Leonor gets as her deserts Julián, who is assured enough income by his father-in-law to keep a horse. And Luis in the closing minutes of the play utters his loudest condemnation of the court, retiring brideless, but with the assurance of Juan's friendship. Bernardo finally refuses the hand of Aldonanza, but offers to take her as his mother-in-law!

A rollicking play, much of the amusement derives from using events in such a way as to catch the characters unawares. Thus when we expect to see the country cousin, we are confronted with the American one, whom the father has long been trying to avoid; and in the same scene Isabel, having heard of the arrival of her former gallant, finds herself in the embrace of this *hombrón* (hulking fellow), a phrase that has considerable influence on what the *Montañés* subsequently thinks of his city cousins. Again the *Montañés*, having come to Madrid to wed, is forced to hide from the law in his future father-in-law's house. Or again Julián, having come to serenade Isabel, not only says sweet nothings to an *escudero*, but gets from him a declaration of affection that maintains his faith in his own success as a lover right into the last act.

A very funny comedy of action, it is not for that reason less a comedy of manners in an *hidalgo* setting. The family belongs to a province (Mendoza's own) where honour is placed above riches. However, the acquisition of wealth, the key to Madrid's pleasures and privileges, [30] has changed matters: Leonor, Isabel and Aldo-

---

[30] e.g. Bernardo's words: "Que cualquier persona rica / Caballero se fabrica / Del polvo de su dinero" (p. 473).

nanza are mainly concerned with gaining the advantages which an inflated social status gives them; the father, more a realist, knows what people are after, and his purpose in marrying one of his daughters to a poor relation is to gain someone "who will gently temper in the blood of a relative the greed of an heir." [31] By bringing in the country cousin, Mendoza sets the more traditional alongside the new, and he further conveys through the Peruvian, Luis de Peralta (who reacts with an even greater horror to the unethical standards of the capital), a sense that even in distant Peru, society is more civilized. The play's message seems a variation on that of Quevedo's *Epístola censoria;* Spain's moral greatness lies, if not in the past, then in her provinces and empire. And however personal a declaration Don Luis de Peralta's farewell speech may be, it presumably reflects in some degree the author's own condemnation of Madrid:

> No quiero en la corte nada,
> Donde es tan vil, tan incierta
> La amistad, y donde vive
> la ventura tan soberbia. [32]

By placing so many of his characters on the fringe of a society to which they do not belong, Mendoza has made their satirical position ambivalent. They may, as with Leonor or Aldonanza, imply criticism of that society's standards through an adherence to them in a most ludicrous way; or they may, like the *Montañés,* react vigorously against those standards by asserting their own. But at moments the blade of satire is double-edged. Thus the *Montañés's* inability to adapt himself to the court is only partly a condemnation of Madrid life, it is in part a funny comment on the primitive ways of rural society; Don Luis's long eulogy of Peruvian life likewise may have ironic overtones, despite its service here as a wholesome contrast to Madrid.

Where then does the truth lie? The proper standards are in fact presented on a different plane of character, that of Juan and Bernardo, whom Mendoza, with sheer perversity, has also made unscrupulous meddlers. However, like the characters of the *commedia dell'arte* they initiate improper action, but are not sullied by it;

---

[31] p. 471: "Quien templará mansamente / En la sangre de pariente / La codicia de heredero."
[32] p. 476: *I want nothing in the court, where friendship is so cheap and uncertain, and where good fortune lives a life of such splendour.*

the most inexcusable rogues, they contrive to appear the moral superiors of those whom they dupe. Certainly they remain the audience's prime moral guide. Juan, a poor nobleman forced by financial circumstance to use devious paths and urged on by a sense of devilment, is never ultimately willing to stoop to evil in any significant action. So, having embarked in fun upon the courtship of Isabel, he finally decides that since he loves her he will not win her as legitimate wife "by the bastard means" so far employed. [33] Bernardo points out to Leonor that Juan is above the kind of nobility that inheres merely in outward symbol:

> Él es un hombre
> Que de nada, que no es culpa,
> Ni se corre ni disculpa. [34]

When Leonor counters, declaring that though true nobility deserves respect it has become impotent, Bernardo replies:

> ¿Cómo que no pueden nada?
> ¿No ves que lo mandan todo?
> Un señor es de temer,
> Que manda, y no es importuno;
> Que nunca falta á ninguno
> Mil doblones que ofrecer. [35]

This then is the play's message, an appropriate one for a society dominated by often ill-gotten gains, and by a snobbery caused by an inability to distinguish between the true and the false.

What makes *Cada loco* such a delightful play is the fact that the characters, with the possible exception of Julián the fop, transcend their satirical function. Isabel, for instance, though sharing with her sister and aunt an unreflecting admiration for the capital, is in fact a sensible, clear-sighted creature, capable of distinguishing the kind of gallant she wishes to marry from the "mud jewel, placed in a diamond case" for whom Leonor would fall. [36] Isabel, fur-

---

[33] p. 468: "Por camino tan bastardo."

[34] p. 473: *He is a man who is only embarrassed, and makes excuses, because of that which is a fault.*

[35] p. 474: *How do you say that they can do nothing? Don't you see that they control everything? A gentleman who gives orders and is not importunate is to be feared. For anyone can find a thousand doubloons to offer.*

[36] p. 459: "joya de lodo / Puesta en caja de diamante."

thermore, by her ingenuity engineers the action to her own advantage more effectively than the apparent past masters, Juan and Bernardo. As for the *Montañés,* despite his addiction to a "stupid concern for nobility" [37] his function as critic of court life invests him
with dignity, and his conviction about his own standards makes him a
figure of constancy amid moral flux. The father, Hernán, painfully
straddles the old and the new: anxious for his daughters' welfare,
weak in the face of their rebellion, credulous in the face of dupery,
he seeks primarily to wed the virtues of his family tradition to what
his wealth can buy, to become what he calls a "rico honrado" (p. 457).
But to no avail: before the end of the play he has been denounced
by his Peruvian nephew for his ill-gotten wealth, and is told that
but for the vicissitudes of fortune he would have been the country
bumpkin. Even his belief in the magic of money has proved ill-
founded: having started with the intention of finding a son-in-law
with less than the normal rapacity, he ends by getting not his own
choice, but someone to whom the prospect of wealth is but a secondary consideration. The second sister, Leonor, it could be fairly
argued, is primarily a cartoon figure. Yet her caricatural attribute,
the love of a man on horseback, becomes ultimately a trait of
character: it is her womanly need to overcome the disability of her
convictions that makes her wonder whether Juan goes on foot "out
of necessity or pleasure." [38]

Juan and Bernardo, along with Julián, belong to a different
world, dramatically speaking. Bernardo as "figura del donayre" is
in the line of the *gracioso,* yet he is different. The relation between
him and his master has been anticipated in *Más merece quien más
ama,* where the *gracioso* Burón enjoys a strangely egalitarian relationship with Rosauro, being free to chide, even to mock him.
Bernardo goes further, having almost attained his master's rank. The
two act in concert, indeed "le nerf de l'intrigue" has passed into
Bernardo's hands. Bernardo too has retained the *gracioso*'s ability to
point the play's moral or meaning, but on the other hand the
master has now assumed qualities that belonged formerly to the *gracioso:* he must be quick, ingenious, capable of turning the action
to his own advantage. What makes Juan different from Bernardo is

---

[37] p. 470: "necias hidalguías."
[38] p. 473: "Andar á pié (¡qué disgusto!) / ¿Es necesidad ó es gusto?"

that he must also play the hero. As we have seen, Mendoza gives him significant virtues. Nevertheless he remains, on the whole, a protagonist in whom dynamism has taken the place of heroic action.

Julián, clearly in the line of the *comedia de figurón* and the cardboard figures of Miser Palomo's circus, is also very similar to the hero of Moreto's *El lindo Don Diego,* but is more than the fop: the social upstart, lacking altogether in family background, he is in this sense a foil to Don Juan. He ignores disdain, rebuff, insult: indeed, his great gift is a sublime apathy, an attitude he sums up in these words: "De nada me he de podrir" ("Nothing will make me lose sleep over it"). [39] Julián represents, therefore, the utter lack of values of contemporary society, a situation made even more bizarre by Leonor's obvious admiration for Julián, until disabused of him. In Julián perhaps we sense Mendoza's ultimate resignation to the improbability of society changing for the better: self-blindness is difficult to cure.

In addition to its social satire and colourful character, *Cada loco con su tema* is characterized by a terse, witty dialogue, tenderness in the relation of the lovers, and a sense of atmosphere varying from the authentic feel of a family interior to lively street scenes, interrupted at one point by a musical interlude. Above all, Mendoza writes for the stage, and for the space around his characters: he senses where they stand, what they see, and how they will react. All these qualities together make of the play one of the jewels of the Golden Age drama.

The vigour of Mendoza's opening scenes is well displayed in *Celos sin saber de quien,* whose beginning, dramatic, witty and tinged with poetry, is above all calculated to engage our curiosity. [40] Leonor, who has seen a young man race his horse in the Prado in Madrid, falls in love with him for his skill and style. She says to her maid:

> Marcela, el amor se ygyala
> con la poluora (amor ciego)

---

[39] p. 474. The mental state is of course that referred to in *El hospital de los podridos* (see p. 210 here).

[40] I quote the text of *Zelos sin saber de quien, Comedia famosa de don Antonio de Mendoza* (n.p., no date): BM copy, shelf-mark 11728 c 78 — the Museum catalogue suggests "Madrid? 1700?" The text is unfoliated, and I give references here by signatures.

que antes que en la vista el fuego
pone en la herida la vala.

When Marcela reminds her that she already has a suitor, Leonor assures her that the old one "is not so gallant, and more mine." [41] Diego, the rejected lover, enters, reflecting sorrowfully on the news that his father intends to marry him to some other woman. "I am with marriage," he says, "as though I were already married:" only Leonor could ever reconcile him to the married state, were she but to requite his affection. [42] But for Leonor, Diego is merely a man who has his uses, the most pressing being to help her discover who the mysterious horseman is. Diego indeed proves very useful, for he has found a picture (and accompanying letter) dropped by the rider in passing, and he now meekly accepts the task of spying out the horseman's identity.

We now begin to see the other side of the action, contrived to mirror the first. The rider is a Granadine gentleman, Rodrigo, brought to Madrid by his desire to find the lady whose picture had been sent him by a match-making friend. But if Leonor and Rodrigo stand therefore in a relation of correspondence, so do Rodrigo and a second lady, María, for the latter (the lady of the portrait) represents the Madrid side, so to speak, of the marriage deal. Intrigued by earlier reports of this Granadine gallant (whose name she does not know), María has fallen in love with him on seeing his portrait. But like Rodrigo, she does not know how to uncover her love's identity and whereabouts, since the matchmaker Don Luis has gone into hiding after a duel. However, whether we already view Leonor, or María, as the one who should eventually marry Rodrigo, the course of love is impeded by the decision made by the two fathers that Diego and María should become husband and wife: the whole action will henceforth move menacingly towards that resolution.

The main characters are caught therefore in a web of emotions: Leonor, who feels "jealousy without knowing for whom;" [43] Rodrigo, likewise teased by the knowledge that an unknown gallant — Diego,

---

[41] f. A1 recto: *Marcela, love (blind love!) is like gunpowder. It places the ball in the wound sooner than does the fire reach the eye;* and verso: "No es tan galan, y es mas mio."

[42] f. A1v: "Estoy con el casamiento, / como si fuera casado."

[43] The title of the play is found in a variant text of Mendoza's "Quien ama correspondido": see BNM MS 3884, ff. 404v-405: "Celos sin saber de quien / son celos de hombre de bien."

17

in fact — has been showing off a portrait of María to a group of friends; Diego unwilling to see his love for Leonor unrequited, and himself forced to marry María, whom he does not love; and María, in trying to engage the affections of Rodrigo (whom she has finally discovered), contending for him with a passion equal to that of her rival and complement, Leonor, yet condemned for all this to the marriage-bed of Diego.

The play's final resolution is sudden. Until almost the last moment it appears that Diego must marry María after all, despite the luckless lover's hope that Leonor will fulfil her promise to substitute her own hand for María's at the official betrothal. And Rodrigo has to wait meanwhile, sadly sure that he will lose María. In a way characteristic of Mendoza, love's true course is again made straight through the arbitrament of *gusto* and a woman's free will. The final decision, as in *Más merece quien más ama*, rests with a woman:

> Padre, porque de mi gusto
> no burlen las esperanças
> mis recatos, mis temores,
> quando tu casar me mandas.
> Yo para viuir contenta,
> para no ser desdichada,
> doy la mano a don Rodrigo. [44]

Celos sin saber de quien stands rather awkwardly between the old and the new in Mendoza's art. Its desire to mirror the life of the times; its interest in a family situation in which the relations between father and daughter, and father and son, are briefly, but tenderly, examined; its sense of contemporary Madrid, all bustle and brilliance, and for the Prado which in winter "gives audiences of the sun" [45] — these qualities all remind us distinctly of a play like *Cada loco con su tema*. But, apart from the odd gibe, the work lacks satirical intent, its mood being nearer that of *Más merece quien más ama*, of whose romanesque world the author has retained a number of essential features: the device of the portrait, which, this time, is more significant dramatically, though we do not have

---

[44] f. D4v: *Father, when you command me to be married, so that my fears and my modesty may not make mock of the hopes that my own taste cherishes, I give my hand to Rodrigo, so as to live happy and not be a miserable wretch.*

[45] f. A1v: "En inuierno el prado alto, / dâ las audiencias del Sol."

Fernando's father is also shown in a bad light since, despite Ipólita's plea that the son has become "a tyrant of my honour," Don Lope merely acquiesces in the fact that such behaviour is prevalent in Madrid. [50] As for Rodrigo, his dishonour might have come about as a consequence of his own infidelity, for not only did his dalliance with the *andaluza* seem likely to provide the opportunity for adultery, but much more important, it created in the wife an attitude of mind most receptive to temptation:

> Porque las mas recatadas
> mas firmes mas presumidas,
> sufren ser aborrecidas
> pero no ser despreciadas. [51]

But if Rodrigo to some extent merits censure, his attitude is exemplary on other accounts. His dilatoriness and circumspection have ensured at each step that his wife does not suffer unjust punishment, and by seeking out Inés's suitor, he tried to remove the most obvious threat to his honour. But Rodrigo faces the dilemma of any husband in these circumstances, that the man who is over-confident of his wife's fidelity may appear foolish, whilst the distrustful husband may appear a villain. Rodrigo, largely because of his intelligent awareness of the problem, has followed a prudent course of action. Ipólita for her part gives expression to a more subtle, and pragmatic, view of what the husband's attitude should be. In answer to a theoretical case of honour, she tells Rodrigo that honour lies in the eye of the beholder. Referring to the husband, she says:

> El la salua, ò la condena,
> que si la tiene, y señala
> por mala, para el es mala
> y quando por buena, es buena. [52]

---

[50] pp. 200-201: "tirano de la honra mia."

[51] p. 202: *Because the most modest, the most unyielding, the most conceited put up with being hated, but not with being despised.*

[52] p. 183: *He is the one who saves, or condemns her, for if he considers her a bad woman and points her out to be such, for him she is bad; and if a good one, then she is good.*

Mendoza's prime interest, nevertheless, is in his characters. Ipólita dominates the action. Another woman of passion, she is here put to the test. She cannot acquiesce in dishonour any more than Fidelinda could acquiesce in someone loving her against her wishes. She is quick, perhaps too quick, in pointing out to Inés how unwise the latter had been in naming Fernando as husband, and at the beginning of the play she displayed similar spirit on seeing Inés's open flirtation with her suitors:

> Baste,
> lo que jamas han podido
> ni libres años ni pocos,
> en mi, auian de poder
> de una ignorante muger
> unos Consejos tan locos.
> Yo musicas, abrir yo
> a estas horas mis ventanas? [53]

But she is a woman of intelligence too, a quality that helps retain Rodrigo's love for her. For her part she does not cease to feel a deep love for him despite her bitter realization that Rodrigo is deceiving her. Such conflict of feeling is given poetic expression in a beautiful soliloquy:

> No tan inquietamante
> dulce tortola en tronco, en seca rama,
> busca al esposo que con quexas llama
> quando hallandole ausente,
> se encuentran al momento
> sus alas, y sus quexas en el viento.
> No el Rey de dulces aues
> de la selua *sintio* dulce armonia   [*virtio?*]
> al cielo alegre, al parecer del dia,
> su amor en quexas Graves
> celebra entre las flores,
> infuso el mismo amor, en sus amores.
> Como yo que adorando
> mi dueño, soy ya triste, ya quexosa
> tortola, y ruiseñor con voz llorosa,

---

[53] p. 173: *That's enough! Should the madcap advice of an ignorant woman prevail over me where years of freedom and youth have failed? Me have music? Me open my windows at this hour?*

mas morire callando
leyendo mis enojos
en mis lagrimas letras de mis enojos. [54]

Rodrigo is more than the conventional husband of the honour play. If his extramarital pursuits undermine his ethical position, they add to his dramatic stature, since his pursuit of purity of honour is so obviously at variance with his moral actions. But he appears, above all and despite all, the epitome of *cordura* (prudence), an upright, suffering man who wishes to believe in his wife's innocence, yet is obliged to consider the symptoms of infidelity.

The other figure to call for comment is Chrisóstomo. He combines in a strangely effective way the fop with the figure of disillusion — a combination that Mendoza's experience in the *entremés* form may have made more natural to him. So his exchanges with Fabio and Celio, or with Motril, are reminiscent of *Miser Palomo* in style and tone of dialogue. But the *persona* of a foolish Don Juan masks a tender awareness of life's tragedy. If Chrisóstomo makes fun of women it is not from cynical disregard, but because of a sense of ultimate irrelevance, since "Each day beauty has one more enemy." [55] And admitting his passionate urge to write a play, Chrisóstomo claims to see life as a series of *comedias,* the world as a "representante / de farsas y de tragedias" (p. 184). Chrisóstomo in this same scene stated too that Lope de Vega is his friend. Mendoza by such easy identification with this character suggests we should see in him more than a hint of his creator: frivolity, even foolishness, may not always be the mark of unwisdom, but the product of a deep disillusion.

In *El marido hace mujer* the author took much of the material used in *El galán,* but presented it in a more symmetrical, indeed antiphonal form. [56] It is a mirror plot, in which two brothers of

---

[54] p. 181: *A gentle turtledove on trunk or withered branch does not so anxiously seek out her husband, to whom she calls with her laments, when on finding him absent, her wings and her sighs float in the wind at the same moment. The King of gentle birds did not at daybreak pour his gentle harmony from woods to happy heaven, celebrating his love amid flowers in grave laments, with the same love [as mine] infused in his. As I, who adoring my loved one, am now a sad, now a plaintive dove, and a nightingale with tearful voice. But I shall die in silence, reading my anger in my tears, letters of my anger.*

[55] p. 184: "Cada dia, la hermosura / tiene vn enemigo mas."

[56] The play first appears in print, *El marido haze mujer,* in *Parte treynta de comedias famosas de Varios Autores* (Çaragoça, 1636), pp. 255-290 [by signatures, Q8v-T1v]. I

different character marry two sisters, the one opposed to the match and hankering after her former lover Diego, the other prepared to accept her responsibilities. Juan, who marries Leonor, the unwilling bride, intends to combine vigilance with a tolerant good sense; Sancho, even before the marriage, begins to instruct his wife, Juana, in the laws that she must obey. Although both husbands are seeking happiness in marriage, their behaviour in the event leads to opposite conclusions; a bond characterized by "esteem, peace and pleasure;" and one that has all the characteristics of battle, for "it is war, it is siege, it is assault." [57]

Leonor is still in touch with her former gallant Don Diego, whose message to her is intercepted by the two brothers. Juan opens it, but assures his brother that the note is not for Juana. He omits to tell Sancho, however, that the note implies Leonor's continuing dalliance with her former suitor. Juan might well now have sought immediate revenge, but with a patience akin to Rodrigo's in *El galán sin dama*, he resolves to wait until the threat of infidelity is more real. Meanwhile, Sancho, convinced in his own suspicions as a result of his brother's silence, places further restrictions on Juana. In contrast, Juan continues to treat his wife with such generosity that she becomes convinced that her loyalty to him is stronger than her feelings for her former lover. Juana, for her part, becomes so disillusioned at her treatment that, almost as an act of desperation, she seeks out Diego. Undeterred by Leonor's pleading, Juana goes to the Prado accompanied by Leonor's maid, Inés. There Sancho happens to find her in conversation with Diego. Sancho, concluding that this must be Leonor, condemns his brother's laxity, and, when Juan appears, is quick to point this out. Juan at last seems convinced of his error, but will still only act on the incontrovertible evidence of his own eyes. He returns home, while Sancho — who has still not recognised her — takes the opportunity to upbraid the woman whom he believes to be his brother's wife.

---

quote the text in *FC*, pp. 218-253, where the play appears under its alternative title *El trato muda costumbre*. "Some Palace Performances" shows the play to have been represented sometime just before 30 April 1633.

[57] *FC*, p. 219: "estimacion, paz, y gusto;" and p. 220: "es guerra, es sitio, es assalto."

The last act opens. Juan, on his return home, is overjoyed to discover that his wife is there, and could not thus have been the woman in the Prado. When Juana comes back, Leonor attempts to persuade her to mend her ways, but to no avail, and the former's lingering doubts are dispelled when Sancho, back from the street, takes his wife to task for not having stopped Leonor from going to the Prado. So strong does Juana's sense of outrage now become, that she makes an assignation with Diego at her house after nightfall. Diego comes, convinced however that the call was from Leonor. Juana disabuses him, but cannot in fact bring herself to commit adultery. The two are discovered in a compromising situation, but Sancho's revenge is prevented by the arrival of Don Fernando, Juana's guardian, who, having heard reports of Sancho's inhuman behaviour, has decided that the unhappy marriage should be dissolved.

For its period the *comedia* evinces a remarkably liberal attitude to marriage. Though it accepts the honour convention, the play retains the bloodthirsty revenge only as a *deus ex machina* which will never be invoked. [58] Mendoza's real concern is with the practicalities of everyday marriage, which he views not as a sacrament but as a bond which may break when overstrained. Juana's attack on marriage at the opening of the play represents, in its extremest form, what may become of a marriage. The severity of life of the Egyptian hermit may be nothing as compared to

> ... la religion en que entra
> una muger, professando
> en la ley de un matrimonio
> las clausuras de un recato.

One factor makes marriage an even worse form of imprisonment: in the monastic life there is a period of novitiate, a chance of escape. But the marriage vow once made, may not be broken:

> romper podremos a quexas
> los Cielos, mas no los laços. [59]

---

[58] The direct inspiration of Lope de Vega's *El castigo del discreto* seems unlikely. The latter was probably composed in the period 1598-1601 (see S. G. Morley and C. Bruerton, *The Chronology of Lope de Vega's 'Comedias', with a Discussion of Doubtful Attributions*, New York, N.Y., 1940, pp. 181-182). However, Lope's friendship may have been a factor in Mendoza's liberal attitude.

[59] *FC*, p. 220: ... *the religion into which a woman enters, professing in the law of marriage the enclosed life of modesty. ... We shall with our complaints be able to shatter the Heavens, but not our bonds.*

Furthermore an unhappy marriage ("un matrimonio a disgusto") is a war which goes on until the death of one of the partners. These opinions form a background to the author's treatment of his theme. Marriage is a destiny, within which the partners should seek to discover the proper way to accommodate each other's will. Juan's attitude is superior to his brother's to the extent that it allows room for the exercise of the wife's free will, and for the creation of trust:

> La muger que màs se muestra
> flaca, quando và a perderse,
> firme suele mantenerse
> en la confiança nuestra.
> Mas si con desconfiança
> la tratamos, vengativa
> todo lo arrastra, y derriba
> hasta la misma esperança. [60]

Mendoza's attitude here is unobjectionable from an orthodox point of view, but in judging the case of Juana and Sancho he takes a surprisingly liberal stand. Juana acknowledges that her sense of virtue is too strong ever to yield to dishonour, yet she admits that in the circumstances she could never be a good wife:

> Ser mala yo es impossible,
> y ser buena su muger,
> y estas dos cosas no pueden,
> ni estar juntas, ni estar bien.
> Su suerte cada marido
> labra con su proceder. [61]

---

[60] *FC*, p. 223: *Even the most weak-willed woman, when she is about to abandon herself, is usually kept firm in our trust. But if we show her distrust, then in vengeful mood, she drags all down, even hope itself.* Mendoza's attitude may owe something to the highly influential *Civile Conversation* (1574) of Stefano Guazzo, who in discussing marriage refers reprovingly to the Romans' habit of making their wives "to bee cloistred Nunnes." In the ensuing discussion, which advocates trust, leniency and good example, Guazzo argues that the husband who makes himself responsible for the wife's honour, reduces her respect for it: "but when her honour is committed to her owne keeping, shee is carefull and jealous of it, as of that whiche is her owne" (*The Civile Conversation of M. Steeven Guazzo*, tr. George Pettie, ed. Edward Sullivan, London, The Tudor Translations, 1925, II, 1-43, quots. on p. 19 and p. 24).

[61] *FC*, p. 252: *It is impossible for me to be wicked, nor to be good whilst being married to him: these two things cannot be found together, nor work out. Every husband shapes his fate by his way of setting about things.*

And if we argue that this only affirms the importance of Sancho learning to behave differently, we fail to reckon with Mendoza's view that Sancho is incompatible with the married state. Sancho himself confesses at the very end of the action that he cannot be "a husband in peace," a point then underlined by Morón's words that "he is Sancho *a nativitate*." [62] Such a pragmatic view of marriage implies the possibility of dissolution in unfavourable circumstances. Don Fernando, in declaring his intention to put an end to the marriage, without even consulting the church authorities, jokingly promises a second part to the play in which the official outcome might be revealed: here Mendoza seems to anticipate criticism of his point of view, but determines to maintain the courage of his convictions.

If in his other *comedias* Mendoza concentrates his attention on one, or at most two, of his main characters, he has now set himself the problem of presenting virtually four different experiences and viewpoints. This has two immediate consequences: the role of sub-plot and of the *gracioso* is diminished; and more importantly, the play gains in objectivity because of the audience's lack of opportunity to identify too strongly with any one of the protagonists. Juana is the most interesting, since her experience embraces both the naïveté of innocence and the temptation of sin. But what indelibly stamps her is her *valor* (her worth, or valour), a quality asserted through the individual will. Her resentment of Sancho's tyranny is grounded not in the fact of enslavement, but in the inhibiting effects which that has on her personality: her natural worth cannot be displayed properly because it is being demanded of her under duress. She puts the point in a sonnet:

> que no es decente a generosa vida,
> que lo que obra el valor, se deva al miedo. [63]

---

[62] *FC*, p. 253: "mas ser / marido en paz, no es possible." … "El / es Sancho à nativitate." Cf. also Diego's words earlier: "El Sancho nació / de su condicion esclavo" (p. 226). Guillén de Castro's *Los mal casados de Valencia* (see *Obras*, II, Madrid, 1926, 449-490) also ends an unhappy marriage by dissolution. Castro's treatment of the theme is more frank and brutal than Mendoza's, but little interest is shown in the question of what makes for a happy marriage.

[63] *FC*, p. 237: *For a noble life deserves better than that valour's acts should be owed to fear.* [There is play here on the two meanings of *valor*.]

But in her present predicament she is able to reassert her *valor* in a different way: through it she faces successfully both her husband's tyranny and the temptation of adultery. For this reason her potential espousal of immorality never appears as a manifestation of weakness, but as a declaration of power. Even the ultimate threat of a bloody revenge is for her a moment of self-assertion, since she would welcome the prospect of death at her husband's hand. [64] Furthermore Juana's sense of self and of individual responsibility enlivens her relation with others: by her caustic exchanges with Sancho she protects her *valor,* and in her dealings with Leonor she is quick to condemn an overweening virtue which (unlike her own) has been prone to succumb to temptation. [65]

Sancho, the jealous husband, is naturally a dramatically interesting figure. Like Calderón's *Médico de su honra* he is congenitally jealous, and furthermore incapable of compromise or wisdom. Almost his first words after marriage express an intention to dispense a "severe law" to his wife, and though willing to accord that people may call him all manner of names, he remains adamant:

> Pues perdone mi muger,
> y quantos se cansen dello,
> que todo esso quiero sello,
> y nò lo que puedo ser. [66]

And the rest of the *comedia* reveals in him a devilish consistency, marked sometimes by a peevishness not necessarily incompatible with sound moral principle. Furthermore, he is an enormously active character, pursuing the demons he sees on all sides, defending his own views as well as condemning those of others. In the conviction of his own rightness, and his desire to correct the misconceptions of others, Sancho is not unlike Juana. And they share too a sense of individual responsibility, and a destiny to be fulfilled:

> Qualquiera no como nace,
> como vive tiene el nombre,

---

[64] *FC*, p. 246.

[65] See e.g. *FC*, p. 244.

[66] *FC*, p. 223: *Well begging my wife's pardon, and that of everyone else who may grow tired of it, but all this is what I want to be, and not what I can be.*

la sangre es tiempo perdido,
el marido haze muger. [67]

To some extent, therefore, the incompatibility of the husband and wife is a consequence not of their differences of character, but of their similarity. However, Sancho has more obvious faults than Juana: he is hasty in his judgments, impatient, utterly unaccommodating, and, at bottom, arrogant. He tells his brother in one of the play's early scenes:

que si estoy
necio agora, no lo soy
en cosa, ni casa agena. [68]

Such a conviction makes it impossible for him to listen to his brother's views, or to those of his wife: he is a man isolated by certainty.

Leonor and Juan make a different, yet corresponding couple. Leonor first appears as a witty, attractive woman, disillusioned by a forced marriage, yet able to accept it on condition that her husband treats her with affection and respect. She is, unlike her sister, not cynical about matrimony, and in answer to Juana's attack paints tenderly a picture of married bliss as husband and wife walk together along the banks of the Manzanares. [69] Indeed her dramatic interest is in part compounded of ambiguity. Her farewell to Diego breathes one word of hope, yet holds out no prospect of its achievement. And when she decides to go in search of him, she is perhaps impelled more by the need to warn him, than by the desire to see him again. But what in one sphere may be construed as ambiguity may in another be recognized as open-mindedness, a quality that straightaway reminds us of Juan. And it is because of this that Leonor is able so soon to recognize her husband's worth, and his superiority over any prospective lover.

---

[67] FC, p. 241: *Anyone gets his (or her) reputation not by how he is born, but by how he lives. Lineage is a waste of time, it is the husband that makes the wife.*

[68] FC, p. 222, answering Juan's charge of stupidity: *for if I am stupid now, I am not behaving thus in a matter (or in a house) that is not my own.*

[69] FC, p. 221.

But once that recognition comes, Leonor is in danger of lapsing into dullness, since her dramatic conflict has ceased. But such a fate is partly avoided by her assumption of the role of good (if ineffective) counsellor to Juana. Necessarily, however, Leonor's role diminishes in the latter stages of the play as Juana's importance increases, and although the intervention of Don Fernando brings the play to a satisfactory conclusion ideologically, it has the unfortunate effect of moving Leonor even further from the centre of the action.

Like Sancho, Juan is an active, proselytic force, plagued likewise by crises of jealousy and uncertainty. But Sancho's crises spring from an infirm mind, whereas Juan's are the consequence of applying generosity where it might very plausibly have aided infidelity rather than preventing it. And of course Juan, the upright man, experiences greater travail for being exposed to his brother's strictures, and to the apparent certainty of his wife's guilt. At the very opening of the third act, Juan's suffering is beautifully expressed in a speech reflecting on his expectation that now at last he will find proof of his wife's guilt in her absence from the house: and a glimpse of his virtuous sister-in-law only increases his envy and shame. [70] But Juan's prime quality is his tenderness. A necessary product of the play's didactic purpose, it is incarnate in Juan's attitude and actions, and is distilled in his poetic turns of phrase, as we may judge, for instance, in his words when he realizes that his wife had half yielded to the seductions of her former lover:

> Veamos si con el arte,
> y el cuidado, recogemos
> esta barquilla entregada
> a un ayre de tantos vientos. [71]

And by the end of the play such tender generosity seems amply justified: the author has proved his point.

In most ways beautifully constructed, *El marido hace mujer* has one fundamental fault. So balanced is the framework there can be little room for the anticipation of unexpected action, since the next

---

[70] *FC*, pp. 241-242.

[71] *FC*, p. 232: *Let us see whether with skill and care we may bring to safety this small bark out in such squally weather* [there is play on *ayre* = air, wind; and = air, manner].

development always seems that to which two sets of contrary pressures has inevitably led. Another weakness lies in the pivot of the action, Don Diego, the unsuccessful gallant. His equivalent in *El galán* was the colourful fop, Chrisóstomo; whereas in *Cada loco con su tema* the unwelcome gallant was the one who manipulated the action. In *El marido,* in contrast, Diego is a void, since in the main he is the recipient of Juana's attentions for motives that are hers, rather than his own.

But whatever the blemishes, the play has in its favour one outstanding merit, the excellence of its verse. Gracián was right to praise it for its wit and sententious concision. [72] It possesses in remarkable degree that comfortable, unobtrusive, poetic diction that marks its author's best work in the theatre. And since *El marido* also succeeds in conveying something of the feel of the capital, it is appropriate to quote as an instance of the quality of the poetry part of Leonor's description of the evening walk along the Manzanares:

> No has visto en Madrid el rio
> donde es tan dulce tacaño,
> y moço de tan buen ayre
> el picaro del verano,
> las emboçadas meriendas,
> sus verdes traviessos baños,
> blanca injuria de las ondas,
> fresca embidia de los ramos? [73]

But is was in *Los empeños del mentir* that Mendoza best captured the atmosphere of Madrid, [74] when in a beautiful opening scene two likeable twisters, recently arrived from abroad, paint the setting in deft strokes. Teodoro's encomium contains for instance the following lines:

---

[72] *GOC,* p. 380. He also refers to its popular success: it was "siete veces repetida con el mismo agrado." That even this number of performances was considered a long run is plain from Montalbán's pleasure at his own phenomenal success when *De un castigo dos venganzas* was performed "veinte y vn dias continuos" with a good audience present (see Victor Dixon, "Juan Pérez de Montalbán's *Para Todos,*" *HR,* XXXII [1964], p. 47).

[73] *FC,* p. 221: *Have you not seen in Madrid (where the river is so sweetly mean, and rogue summer a youth of pleasant air), the picnics in disguise, the green and mischievous bathes, white insult to the waves, cool envy of the branches* [there is play on *verde* = green, and = dirty, daring].

[74] *FC,* pp. 254-296. The play first appears in print, *Los empeños del mentir,* in *Flor de las mejores doze comedias de los mayores Ingenios de Espana* (Madrid, 1652), ff. 43-84 [by signatures, F3-H8].

> Mira estos ca[m]pos, mira estós jardines,
> que le son a Madrid, en ayres puros,
> roja atalaya en florecientes muros;
> en quien hallan los Consules màs graves,
> aplaudidos tambien de flores, y aves,
> paz al cuidado y tregua a los deseos. [75]

The germen of the play is found in this scene. Teodoro and his companion Marcelo, rascals with a fund of plausibility and cleverness, find Madrid a challenge, and determine to make their way by telling lies. They acquire goodwill and a patron through their part in saving a gullible dupe, Diego, from some assailants. And once Diego volunteers information about himself and his family, the foundation of a mighty deception is laid. Marcelo claims to be Luis Vivero, known to be on the way from Italy to marry Elvira, Diego's sister. Diego is convinced, and offers the two men hospitality. Elvira, like her cousin Doña Ana, is less ready to believe the tale, especially as Marcelo's behaviour proves atrocious. They are even more sceptical when Teodoro, who has grown tired of playing second fiddle, informs the world that he, not Marcelo, is the genuine Luis de Vivero. The family, in spite of moments of doubt and suspicion, not only accept this claim, but also the later rectification, that Teodoro is a certain Italian count, who having seen a picture of Elvira, has come in search of her. The final uncovering of the deception does not come about because of anybody's perceptiveness: the fabric of lies merely becomes too great for even Marcelo and Teodoro to sustain. The real Luis de Vivero turns up, and at first the impostors succeed in convincing the others that he is a fraud, but when Don Luis's friends and servants come on the scene, Teodoro and Marcelo realize that the game is up. The play ends generously: they get off scot-free, whilst Luis gains Elvira's hand and Diego that of his cousin Ana.

Los empeños del mentir was probably first performed not long after the victory of the Imperial troops at Nördlingen in September 1634, a long description of the battle being included in the text. [76]

---

[75] *FC*, p. 255: *Look at these fields, these gardens, which in its pure air are to Madrid a red watchtower set upon flowering walls, where the most solemn Consuls (applauded also by flowers and birds) find peace from their cares, and a truce from their desires.*

[76] See "A Chronology." The Palace Archives may have recorded the date of an early performance, but under the wrong title: a play called *Los empeños del amor* was performed on 3 June 1635 (see "Some Palace Performances").

However, there may be something to the view that *Los empeños* bore some relation to an earlier *comedia,* not extant, in which Mendoza, Quevedo and Mateo Montero had collaborated. Entitled *Quien más miente, medra más,* it had been performed on St. John's Eve 1631, Mendoza being apparently responsible for the middle act. *Los empeños,* in the corresponding second act, has some lines which, at the very least, suggest a memory of the earlier play. [77] The title too, *Quien más miente, medra más,* suggests that both plays may have exploited a similar theme, even used common material. But *Los empeños,* whatever its dependence on an earlier piece, was indubitably a new creation, for it celebrated the recently built palace of the *Retiro* (completed in 1632) as well as a festival there of which the play itself was part. [78]

Unlike most of Mendoza's other plays, *Los empeños* was written plainly for a palace audience. From its outset it praises the *Retiro* and the favourite's part in its construction, it refers incidentally to the King, the favourite, and other nobles, as well as to the festival in which it was performed. It also used the occasion to score a political success for the régime by emphasizing the part played by the King's brother, the Cardenal-Infante, and by some of the Spanish nobility, in the most recent Imperial successes in The Thirty Years War. Indeed, the very verve and good humour of the comedy seem a product of the new hope of ultimate military success adumbrated with the providential death in battle of Gustavus Adolphus three years before, confirmed by the new unity within the House of Hapsburg, and crowned with achievement in the victory of Nördlingen and the subsequent autumn. [79]

Los empeños may have owed a debt to Juan de Alarcón's *La verdad sospechosa,* though, as the outline of the plot clearly shows, the theme of the inveterate liar is differently treated in the two plays. [80] In addition to the lying protagonist, both *comedias* share a *gracioso* who is more companion than servant; and among

---

[77] *FC,* p. 270: "ni es justicia, ni ha de serlo; / que tu agora medres màs, / si yo no sè mentir menos."

[78] See *FC,* p. 290. Apart from the ref. to *Los empeños* itself, the text mentions a play by Tirso de Molina.

[79] For the background, see C. V. Wedgwood, op. cit., *passim,* and my "A Chronology."

[80] For the date of composition of *La verdad sospechosa,* see *Obras completas de Juan Ruiz de Alarcón,* ed. A. Millares Carlo, II *(Teatro),* México, 1959, p. 363: it was written before 31 March 1621.

incidental features one may mention that master and servant arrive in the capital at the beginning of both plays; that both protagonists are able to conjure up, at will, astounding lies which, because of their vividness, carry with them an air of conviction; and that the intention of such *embustes* is (in differing measure) to win the affection, and eventually the hand, of a *dama* of the court. However, Alarcón's aim and technique differ from Mendoza's in a way that helps to bring out essential features of the latter's *comedia*. For Alarcón Don García is a moral, even psychological, problem, by which the author seeks to demonstrate how a liar (especially if he does not have a good memory) creates difficulties for himself, so that eventually even the truth he tells awakens suspicion. Don García belongs to a society which will only accept him if he adheres to its standards, and the *gracioso*'s role as his master's "secretario del alma" [81] is not only to act as the link between Don García and society, but also to restore him to it. Apart from making some occasional, and superficial, comment on the universality of deceit, Alarcón's aim is not to point to the need for over-all reform, but rather to demonstrate the effects of one particular deviation from a social norm.

Mendoza's intention is very different, both at the artistic and moral level. The *embustero* (trickster) and his companion are essentially outsiders, seeking to exploit society rather than conform to it, and as if to underline the difference between them and the other characters, Mendoza has deliberately given them the characteristics, and unreality, of the figures of the *commedia dell'arte*. Furthermore, unlike Don García and his *gracioso* Tristán, they act in consort, their deliberate victim, court society. Teodoro and Marcelo could be identified with Harlequin and Scapino; the former in whom amorality is combined with a lack of viciousness, and an ability to wriggle out of difficulties; the latter, traditionally Harlequin's companion, who joins a rather brutish nature to a fondness for epigrammatic comment. [82] But the *commedia* person-

---

[81] See ibid., p. 460: *a secretary of the soul.*

[82] It is more appropriate, however, to think in terms of basic *commedia* types, than specific characters, whose roles changed with the years. See also p. 293 here. On the *commedia* and its influence, see art. in vol. III of *Enciclopedia dello spettaculo* (which also gives bibliography), Allardyce Nicoll, *The World of Harlequin: A Critical Study of the Commedia dell'arte* (Cambridge, 1963), and K. M. Lea, *Italian Popular Comedy. A Study in the Commedia dell'arte, 1560-1620, with Special Reference to the English Stage* (Oxford, 1934).

ages were essentially traditional figures, recognizable to the audience by their costume and masks, their traits of character and behaviour already known to the public: furthermore, the technique of the *Arte* consisted in improvising dialogue based on an already agreed plot. Given these differences, how did Mendoza accommodate such extraneous material to a genre which depended essentially on a set script, and on personages which, within the much looser framework of Spanish *comedia* types, evinced their character in the course of the action? Mendoza took for granted the traditional nature of the characters as well as his audience's recognition of them: this partly explains the air of unreality that surrounds Teodoro and Marcelo, as well as the lack of any need to explain, or justify, their behaviour. Also, by making the action itself largely a plaything in their hands, the dramatist introduced a form of improvisation. Whereas the traditional pantomime figures improvised upon an agreed plot, Teodoro and Marcelo here improvise the play itself, creating all the time new and different responses to the pressure of events, sometimes friendly, sometimes hostile. Their speeches, therefore, as they veer the plot in a new direction are, in an almost strict sense, improvisations. To this it may be objected that the author had already written their parts. Yet in the magic of performance they become free agents, improvising their own destiny.

Since Teodoro's gift of lying, unlike Don García's, is not a vice but the mark of a traditional *persona,* his actions do not awaken condemnation so much as wonder. Such moral neutrality is extended also to Marcelo, whose "character" indeed, in the tergiversations of the action, becomes almost indistinguishable from that of his master, except that the latter retains a veneer of gallantry and a touch of sentiment. Both are in one sense reduced to a single type; brilliant, Protean, unscrupulous, resourceful, yet essentially predictable and superficial. And at the end the two *embusteros,* saved from both our incredulity and our moral criticism, fade from the action. It is true that to have accorded Teodoro victory and Elvira's hand would have been morally dubious: more relevant is the fact that it would have been as improbable as the domestication of a creature from outer space.

It may well be that Don Diego, the dupe incarnate, also owes something to the *commedia,* in particular to Pantalone, who managed to combine the utmost gravity with a tendency always to be the butt of the action. The presence of a dupe, a common figure in Spanish Golden Age comedy, hardly of itself points to the influence of the *commedia*. But, with two companions from the *Arte* already in the play, Pantalone may have made a third pantomime figure, particularly as Diego brings to his dupery a positive panache, being well-nigh astute in his ingenuousness. He evokes in us wonder, even admiration, as he does in those who have dealings with him. That he almost displays creative genius in his gullibility is clear from the scene in which he learns of Teodoro's latest variation in identity, that of Count Fabio *incognito:* Diego reacts at once with assurance in these words to Elvira:

> y agora acordarme quiero,
> que mil vezes me escrivió,
> que un señor Napolitano
> era su amigo, mi hermano,
> y si tu retrato vió,
> no dudes, que enamorado,
> te busca. [83]

And in a play in which the *gracioso*'s traditional role has merged into that of unscrupulous protagonist, it falls to Don Diego to play the fool in a more gentlemanly guise. His stupidity and destiny as the butt of raillery may reflect a divided inheritance: on the one hand, the *gracioso* rustic of Golden Age drama, on the other, the Pantalone figure. Something of the latter heritage may be preserved in Diego's role as the one who provokes wit and sarcasm in others, in this instance primarily Elvira and Ana, who spend their time disabusing him. Ana makes perhaps the most savage, and witty, remark in the whole play. Diego, by this time used to the idea that Teodoro is Count Fabio, has to admit to his ignorance of the proposal now revealed to marry him, Diego, to a certain Doña Quitería Fracaso. Ana rasps out the words:

> Tenialo reservado
> para albricias. [84]

---

[83] *FC*, p. 284: *And now I remember, my brother wrote me a thousand times that a Neapolitan gentleman was his friend, and if he saw your picture, don't doubt but that, having fallen in love with you, he comes in search of you.*

[84] *FC*, p. 286: *He was keeping that in reserve as a reward for good news.*

The heroine, Elvira, does not appear to belong completely either to this *hidalgo* household. Unlike Juana and Leonor in *El marido hace mujer* she is under the influence of the gallant preoccupations of the court, and of romanesque comedy. Indeed, very much in the tradition of Fidelinda, or of the shepherdesses of the pastoral novel, love brings a sense of vulnerability that gives Elvira depth of character. At the beginning, when she already has wind of the marriage intended for her by her guardian, Diego, she expresses her feelings about love, in response to Ana's proposal to introduce her to a suitable match. Love, claims Elvira, cannot be arranged by counsel, or by third party. It is an inclination, and, in such a hazard, her security must depend on mastery over herself: "solo de mi tengo miedo." [85] The prospect of a forced marriage grieves her because she is above all intent on engaging her affections deliberately, and wisely. For this reason her emotional and ethical problems coincide. She is thus in conformity with herself when, after the arrival of the *embusteros*, she reacts against Marcelo because he shows a "mala traça de hombre," [86] but later, despite herself, she is attracted to Teodoro, a hazard that must test her nature. She realizes all the time that Teodoro's genuineness is suspect, and that her duty is to find out the truth about him. Faced with a conflict between her feeling and her moral sense, her affection for Teodoro ravages her. However, despite doubts about Teodoro's integrity, she is as yet unwilling (or unable) to shake off her love, on whose power she reflects in a beautiful monologue:

> Amor, que medrosa llego
> a tu nombre, ò nunca amigo
> no seas traidor conmigo!
> basta loco, y sobra ciego:
> a perdonarte me entrego,
> si me pierdo bien en ti,
> algo de la dicha, si,
> mas de la disculpa, no:
> sea lo que amare yo
> cuerdo en el, y digno en mi.
> Un hombre que vino errante
> ha de obligar a querido?

---

[85] *FC*, p. 263: *I am afraid only of myself.*
[86] *FC*, p. 265: *a bad design for a man.*

> Si ruin, le huyo marido,
> si noble, le temo amante.
> Pero siempre estoy constante
> en que no he de sufrir yo
> corto empleo; y si nació
> sin favor mi suerte alguna,
> sea baxa su fortuna,
> pero con baxeza, no. [87]

What guides her all the time is a prudent response to both feeling and good sense, along with a determination to assert her responsibility. Elvira, in one way, is a female equivalent of the good husband in *El marido hace mujer,* or of Rodrigo in *El galán sin dama:* she does not take lightly the task of making up her own mind, but persists in searching for more evidence before arriving at her judgment. More original in one sense than Juan or Rodrigo, she manages to separate out her moral, or social, judgment on Teodoro from her personal one: the two are linked necessarily, given Elvira's nature, but it is as though she looked first to the man's "buena traça," and then allowed his faults to fall into place.

It is a pity that Elvira as character should have to yield before the demands of the comedy of *embustes.* Her attempt to find firm moral bearings as lie succeeds lie, identity identity, helps bring out her essential nature, but eventually the two protagonists disappear before Elvira's role can really be fully played out: she at least merited the chance of a final encounter with Teodoro, in which to upbraid him. It is perhaps a weakness too that the feeling is almost all on one side: Teodoro admits to a fleeting attraction for Elvira, but the dramatist's plans for him lie in a different direction, and it would, in any case, have increased Teodoro's involvement in a world that can never be his.

The play's good humour and its unwillingness to castigate the *embusteros* may suggest that the author is only making a perfunctory

---

[87] FC, p. 281: *Love, how fearfully do I reach your name! You who are never friend, do not be traitor to me! Enough for you to be mad, more than enough to be blind: I submit to forgiving you (if I am well damned in you) something of the happiness, but not of the excuses [that I may make?]. May that which I love represent what is wise in him, and worthy in me. Must a man who wandered by oblige one to make him one's love? If he is a scoundrel, I flee from him as husband, if he is noble then I fear him as lover. But in one thing I always stand firm, that I will not put up with shabby treatment; and if whatever luck is mine was born without favour, let my fortune be low, but not degrading.*

moral point about crime not paying in the end. But this is to underrate his subtlety: his underlying message is that Teodoro and Marcelo succeed in their exploits because they are playing on society's weaknesses. The case is put by Teodoro when he replies to Marcelo's complaint that, by reversing the lie they had originally mounted, their genuineness would become suspect: asks Teodoro:

> tiene coto la mentira?
> la necedad tiene medio? [88]

Pleasurable deceptions have few doubters, and Teodoro avers too that he will be more easily believed than was his companion, because he is, socially, a cut above him. Furthermore, self-deception is universal:

> embusteros de si mismos
> son todos, moral me buelvo,
> que no engaña aun en nosotros,
> dentro de nosotros mesmos:
> quien no se miente a si mismo,
> sangre, discrecion, y esfuerço;
> y pues, mentir a los otros,
> si yo a mi proprio me miento:
> quantos en Madrid professan
> en exercicios diversos,
> mentir semblantes, y nombres. [89]

The view that we have a vested interest in the furtherance of our own illusions is reinforced by the reactions of the maid Teresa to the revelation that Teodoro is really Count Fabio. Her mistress is still perplexed by the desire to reach the truth, but Teresa tries to move her away from such unproductive thoughts:

> Ea, señora, que dudas?
> se Condessa, pues que puedes,

---

[88] *FC*, p. 271: *Does the lie know any boundaries? Does stupidity steer a middle path?*

[89] *FC*, p. 271: *Everyone is his own trickster! — I'm turning moralizer — What is there that does not practise deception in us even, deep down in ourselves? Who does not lie to himself about his lineage, his prudence, and his efforts? Well then, let me tell lies to others if I lie to myself! How many are there in Madrid who in their diverse callings lie about their appearance and reputation?*

> porque oy andan las mercedes
> ò reboltosas, ò mudas. [90]

And later Teresa grovels at Teodoro's feet, because she believes him a moneyed count. Diego, in contrast, is not moved by purely financial, or social, considerations, though his excessive concern with lineage and with his kinsmen's exploits (as distinct from his own) suggests an inability to distinguish between real nobility and its trappings. But above all he is gullible in a society where deception is rampant. His lady, Ana (who shares with Elvira the play's remedies for deception, namely perceptiveness and a sense of values) tells Diego:

> Donde està tu entendimiento?
> no sabes, moço ignorante,
> que en Madrid a cada instante
> se piza en un escarmiento?
> Lo que pide mayor modo,
> es una atenta cordura;
> no creer nada es locura,
> civilidad creerlo todo. [91]

The audience may have derived satisfaction from such advice. But in the play's dying moments the author offers only cold comfort. Teodoro in his farewell speech reminds them again that deception is everywhere:

> atencion, que nada vive
> sin mentir, no miente el ayre,
> miente el dia, miente el año?
> todo miente; y en el naype
> del mundo, figuras todas,
> y todos representantes
> en su teatro. [92]

---

[90] FC, p. 282: *Come, my lady, why are you hesitating? Be a Countess, since you can, for today titles are either in rebellious mood, or they've been struck dumb.*

[91] FC, p. 280: *Where is your good sense? Do you not know, you ignorant boy, that in Madrid at every instant one treads on some example to avoid? A watchful prudence is what is most called for. It is madness not to believe anything, vulgarity to believe all.*

[92] FC, p. 296: *Have a care, for nothing lives without telling a lie. Does not the air lie, or the day, or year? Everything lies, and in the world's pack all are court-cards (cutting extravagant figures), and all players on his stage* [there is play on *carta de figura* and *figura (de comedia)*].

Where falsity lies everywhere like a thick rime, man's duty, we must conclude, is to seek remedy in disillusion: Alarcón's moral, in contrast, was both more pragmatic, and less sour.

Despite the moral seriousness, *Los empeños* is, above all, a very funny play. There is fun of situation, as when Elvira and Ana search for ways of persuading Diego at least to give thought to the possibility that he is the victim of a swindle; or when Elvira, driven by a passion for truth, comes upon evidence which the audience knows (or thinks it knows) to be falsified, proving the genuineness of Teodoro and Marcelo. And there is the fun of the incredible *embustes*, with the strains they place on the swindlers themselves, as they vie with each other, in turn outraging and being outraged, their actions making increasing demands on the credulity of others.

But however hilarious the comedy, Mendoza makes it serve his moralistic ends. If falsity is ubiquitous, then it is present too in the deception that constitutes the *comedia*. Whereas in *Querer por solo querer* it had been left to the *gracioso* to comment on this fact, [93] in *Los empeños* the play's refusal to develop in a consistent way, its back-tracking, its new departures, its characters' assumption of new guises, all add up to a hieroglyph spelling out the imposture of the art form, and of the world which that form mirrors. And the action itself, so rich in humour and inventiveness, creates a continuously varying challenge to the other characters, who share the audience's bafflement at the ability of words to create what the facts belie.

The play's atmosphere is perhaps its most endearing quality. If we see Madrid in its new splendour, we get the feel also of an *hidalgo* interior. The author this time has hinted, albeit in caricature, at the family's precise social background: Elvira is described as "una dama Española, / que au[n]que de buen gesto, y garbo / no es mas q[ue] una honrada hidalga." [94] The description occurs in the forged letter addressed to a Count Vitoldo, pretending to recount his son's dalliance in Spain with Elvira. As in *Cada loco* the comedy is partly at the expense of a class teetering on the verge of nobility without quite making the grade. Elvira and Ana do not share with

[93] See p. 230.
[94] *FC*, p. 286: *A Spanish lady, who though of fine appearance and bearing is only an honest* hidalga. Cf. *Cada loco, BAE*, p. 470, the *Montañés's* praise of the *hidalgo* class.

the Leonor of the other play the latter's extravagant social snobbery, but Diego is bound to make the household appear pretentious, especially to a palace audience. Nevertheless, the *hidalgo* class has its points, and Mendoza uses them as a means of painting the contrast with his unflattering picture of the nobles. Elvira and Ana, as we saw, demonstrate in the *hidalgos* a sense of discrimination, whereas the titled nobility makes its appearance here in the guise of a supposed feckless Neapolitan count, whose family is horrified at the prospect of a match so below their station. In a strange way, Diego's household creates the impression of plausibility: even Diego, as his long self-portrait attests, cannot be very far from the reality of the court *hidalgo*, partly mirroring possibly the author's own family background:

> Mis padres fueron ilustres,
> y siguieron mis abuelos
> las dos sendas vinculadas
> a la gran sangre del Reyno:
> palacio, y la guerra, en donde
> ganaron criança, y premios,
> Pajes del Rey, y soldados,
> alta escuela de aquel tiempo. [95]

Diego's sister, Elvira, in her present bewilderment, reflects the characteristic concern of an *hidalga*, attempting to reconcile feeling with the *force majeure* of the marriage of convenience; Ana, the cousin, is joined to Diego by the bond of an established courtship, and to Elvira by a friendship that sometimes veers towards cattiness; and the maid Teresa reveals a comic anxiety to better herself by becoming servant to someone further up the social scale.

Along with *Cada loco* this play must be regarded as the highest achievement in Mendoza's career in the theatre, for in addition to the qualities discussed, it possesses a dialogue that shows them off to the greatest advantage. It can be colourful as in the opening description of the *Retiro*, even flamboyant as in the picture of the Cardenal-Infante's army. But more characteristic is its subdued tone,

---

[95] *FC*, p. 260: *My parents were illustrious, and my grand-parents followed those two paths closely linked to the kingdom's blue blood; royal service, and war, where they gained good breeding and rewards, as pages of the king and soldiers, the high school of that time.*

in which conceit heightens, without straining, the apparent normality of the spoken word. We may take as an example a passage in which Teodoro, at the beginning of the second act, appraises for Marcelo's benefit those pressures which he can bring to bear on his companion in order to make him give way to a successor:

> Si tu estàs enamorado,
> yo tambien lo estoy, Marcelo:
> es rica, y tengo codicia,
> es hermosa, y alma tengo.
> Concede con el embuste,
> que sinò, desato luego
> la maraña, y digo a vozes
> las traiciones, los desvelos,
> las costumbres, las maldades,
> con que embustero professo
> eres el horror del mundo
> y el escandalo del pueblo. [96]

Gracián could well have praised the opening section of this passage for its balanced antitheses. [97] One could go on to praise its use of rhetorical cumulation and climax. Despite all, however, it remains a subdued poetic style, heightening, suffusing, yet never overwhelming, the everyday tenour it is intended to convey.

Los riesgos que tiene un coche (or *Lo que es un coche en Madrid*) has been left till last because of lingering doubts about its authenticity. [98] These are not engendered by any uncharacteristic use of theme or character, but spring from the intuition that no single verse has upon it the undoubted stamp of Mendoza's authorship, and indeed, that it is unlike Mendoza's other plays because

---

[96] *FC*, p. 270: *If you are in love, Marcelo, well so am I. She is rich, and I am greedy, she is beautiful, and I have a soul. Admit the imposture, for if you do not, I straightaway shall untie this tangled scheme, and shout out loud the treachery, the worries, the ways, the wickedness, by which you, a professed trickster, are the horror of the world, and the scandal of the people.*

[97] Cf. *Agudeza*, *GOC*, p. 380, where he praised the author's use of "opuesta gradación" in *El marido hace mujer.*

[98] See "A Chronology." The first printed text may be *Lo que es un coche en Madrid (Los riesgos que tiene un coche)*, in *Comedias de Lope de Vega Carpio, Parte veinte y seis* (Zaragoza, 1645): see La Barrera, p. 682, who further argued that this edn. is a reprint of an original of 1632-33. Rennert, however, in his "Bibliography of the Dramatic Works of Lope de Vega Carpio," *RH*, XXXIII (1915), 34-35, indicates the problems surrounding the identity of a Part XXVI of Lope's plays. See also Rennert's "Notes on some *Comedias* of Lope de Vega," *MLR*, I (1906), 96-110. I quote the text of *Los riesgos que tiene un coche. Comedia famosa de D. Antonio de Mendoza*, in *Laurel de comedias. Quarta parte de diferentes autores...* (Madrid, 1653), ff. 116-136.

of its preference for a specifically unpoetic choice of diction. It could be argued that the play belongs to an earlier period in Mendoza's career, when his concept of the verse play was different from what we have seen in those probably written between 1630 and 1635. Yet an early play ought to show some signs of immaturity, for example in its construction. The fact is that *Los riesgos* is one of the best constructed of all Mendoza's plays (if indeed it *is* his). But to reject the play completely is not easy either, since there are in it elements reminiscent of other pieces by Mendoza, particularly aspects of the theme of deception, or the woman of sour wit bent on retrieving her honour whatever the costs. *Los riesgos* must for these reasons be discussed, even though it may ultimately prove to be by a different hand.

A Granadine lady, Ángela, having been jilted by her lover, Alonso, comes to Madrid in search of him, and eventually marries him: the play's theme seems reminiscent of *Celos sin saber de quien,* in which the heroine, of similar ingenuity and dedication, stage-manages the action so as to gain her lover from a rival. In Ángela's case she succeeds by pretending to be the wife of a coachman, Gonzalo — a strange ruse, were it not that Gonzalo is really Alonso's servant, who has been placed by his master in Octavio's house, since he, Alonso, is in love with Gerarda, Octavio's sister. By means of this fifth column, Alonso hopes to win Gerarda's love so that they may elope together; whereas Ángela, through her counter-espionage, hopes to thwart Alonso's schemes, and at the same time win Gerarda's confidence. Ángela is aided by Octavio's weakness for her, and by her knowledge of the real identity of Don Jacinto: he, Alonso in disguise, has been secreted into the coachman's room, a presence improbably helpful to Ángela, since both find themselves united in a desire to remain as *persona grata* in Octavio's household.

Angela's counter-plot to the plan for Gerarda's elopement is highly ingenious. She manages to persuade Don Diego, a bosom-friend of Alonso, that Gerarda is in love with *him,* and would like to speak to him that night. Ángela's task meanwhile is to remove Alonso from the scene, since Alonso, as we know, is the one really due to visit Gerarda; and at the same time Ángela must somehow keep Octavio out of the way. She hits on a very simple measure:

using her charm she easily persuades Octavio that it is his duty to keep Don Jacinto (Alonso) close company in order to save him from a possibly fatal duel with a person unknown, at some remote spot. This purpose Octavio achieves admirably, and by the time the two men return, Ángela has contrived to whisk the real Gerarda into a coach in which Diego waits expectant (Gerarda of course had counted on finding Alonso in it). The lady's honour thus compromised, Gerarda is forced to marry Diego, whilst Alonso, finally acknowledging himself outwitted, gives his hand in marriage to Ángela.

When M. de Hauteroche, a minor French dramatist of the late seventeenth century, drew on *Los riesgos* for his play *Le Cocher*, [99] he was obviously drawn to it primarily by its admirable stage mechanics. The action moves under two counter pressures. On the one hand, the thwarted woman of honour seeks retribution: Alonso's behaviour has been such as to challenge a woman's *ingenio* and subtlety, forces that, along with a woman's superior capacity for deception, seek to bring nearer Ángela's success. On the other hand, in a manner reminiscent of *Los empeños del mentir*, Gonzalo, who, more than his master Alonso, represents the spirit of devilish intrigue, seeks to draw on some central human weakness in order to achieve his ends. As in *Los empeños*, the schemers play on man's inability to resist self-interest: says Gonzalo, "Todo pienso que sucede / â medida del deseo". [100] But in the case of *Los riesgos* the schemers must contend with a woman, their equal in *ingenio*, who likewise knows how to bait desire in order to accomplish her ends. The action is therefore extruded under these different pressures, with the characters reacting to a constantly changing situation, as one deceit or stratagem gives way to the next. Understandably, therefore, the play's essence is humour of situation. For example, Gonzalo, having hidden Don Jacinto in his room so that he may later be with Gerarda, is forced to explain to Octavio both the strange man's presence, and the embarrassing inquiry that Jacinto makes as to "whether it is yet time." [101] And when, in due course, Octavio reacts with the remark that Don Jacinto's words were more than likely to

---

[99] See *Les Œuvres de théâtre de Monsieur de Hauteroche* (ed. Paris, 1736), II, 193-257. Also Eugène Lintilhac, *Histoire générale du théâtre en France* (Paris, 1904-11), III, 368. Hauteroche in his preface acknowledges his debt to Mendoza's *Los riesgos*.

[100] f. 127v: *I think that everything happens in accordance with desire.*

[101] f. 122: "Gonzalo, / es hora ya?"

arouse suspicion, the audience reflects how, nevertheless, it suits Octavio to accept Gonzalo's explanation, since to do otherwise would involve putting out of the house not only Gonzalo but his supposed wife, Ángela in disguise — a consequence that Octavio dearly wants to prevent. Again, at the very opening of the second act, Alonso's well-laid scheme for the abduction of Gerarda is in danger of failing because of the unexpected, and untimely, intervention of his former love — who, to make the situation even funnier, is there, lurking in the shadows, ready to do her damnedest! But if such scenes are very funny, they lose in one respect — they fail to provoke the wit with which Mendoza elsewhere laces his dialogue.

The characters in the play too lack sharpness, and that hint of depth which gives some of his other creations their liveliness. The woman of passion dominates here, the embodiment of a type that Mendoza loved to portray in the theatre. And as with the heroine of *Celos sin saber de quien*, Ángela's passion lends her both resilience and ingenuity. But such a character loses much in a comedy of intrigue — her passion engenders, rather, qualities such as ingenuity, that do not express, or even reflect, the originating feeling. And Ángela's scheming tends to make her less easily distinguishable from her maid. One characteristic however lends her depth, a sense of personal destiny: she is unwilling to blame Alonso for having preferred another woman, but attributes that preference to some "misfortune" of her own. [102] Furthermore, her dignity as a woman in love who expects fond treatment from her lover strengthens the dramatic impression made by her in a scene with Alonso, which even in details of language recalls a parallel encounter in *No hay amor donde hay agravio:*

> Quando no, por ser muger,
> â quien toda cortesia
> el hombre llega a deuer,
> por ser vos quien sois, y yo
> quien en efecto os amo,
> que en esso se incluye todo,
> deuierais con otro modo
> llegar a hablarme. [103]

---

[102] f. 126v, and cf. ff. 118v-119.

[103] f. 126v: *If not because of my being a woman, to whom man owes every courtesy, [then] because of you being who you are, and I the one who loves you (for that includes everything), you should speak to me in a different way.* Cf. p. 247.

Alonso expostulates pointing out that he was never in love with Ángela: his duel with Lisardo had not been provoked by love, but by the need to save his reputation, besmirched by Lisardo's instruction that he should leave Ángela alone. At this moment Ángela pronounces the only moving speech in the play, in which she tells how her sense of personal reputation brought her from Granada to Madrid, with only one thought in her mind; that she would never return until she had Alonso as husband by her side. [104]

Alonso's stature, in contrast to Ángela's, has grown, for the reason that his original part as the man fallen out of love has been joined to that of the *gracioso* schemer. Even that original role is made more interesting because of its links with a moral point of view much more fully presented in *No hay amor:* like Juan and Enrique there, Alonso is a *toro ayroso,* whose attitude towards love admits gallantry but not loyalty, or marriage on the basis of affection. We are never told for certain whether Alonso was ever really in love with Ángela: it is important, indeed, that he should deny the charge in the play. For him loving is a form of stamp-collecting, and for his friend Diego too, Gerarda is a new issue about which he is curious. One further significant attribute common to the two friends: their attitude to Gerarda is compounded of one other element, venality — both are very much concerned with the size of the lady's dowry. [105]

What really energizes Alonso is his relation with Gonzalo, his servant. Their ambiguous relationship in intrigue is of course reminiscent of *Los empeños* and, as in that play, their roles are reversed. Yet the parallel with *Los empeños* points up the weakness of the present *comedia.* Teodoro and Marcelo's relationship is a two-way affair, with a real creative tension between the two men. True, Gonzalo demonstrates an intermittent resentment at his enforced role as coachman, but the pique is incidental, whereas in *Los empeños* Teodoro's tiredness with an inferior role as servant is what prompts his palace revolution at the end of the first act. In the case of Alonso and Gonzalo we have much more of a Wooster-Jeeves relationship: admiration and passivity on the one hand combined with, in this instance, a not too successful ingenuity on the other. But it would

---

[104] f. 127.
[105] See esp. ff. 116v-117, and f. 129.v

19

be in any case wrong to make too much of the parallel between
Gonzalo and Marcelo, his equivalent in *Los empeños;* for Gonzalo
has in him much more of the old-fashioned *gracioso* — he is the
butt of humour, Ángela beats him about the ears, and his relation
with the maid Juana is old-fashioned to the point of his marrying
her at the play's conclusion, a resolution rejected and made fun
of in the last scene of *Los empeños.* Yet these points could be made
in a different way: that Alonso himself already displays that same
lack of gentlemanly superiority which marks Teodoro and other
heroes of the later Golden age *comedia,* whereas Gonzalo, in his
relation to his master, is, if not yet an equal, a protesting associate.

Like Alonso, Octavio gains from a mingling of roles. He is
primarily the prince of dupes, marvellously inured to the deceptions
perpetrated on him by both factions. He is also the potential schemer,
who in reality is nothing more than a pawn in Ángela's much deeper
game. And as Gerarda's guardian, he fails in his duty, because his
affection for Ángela always leads him to sacrifice honour to self-
interest: thus he is blinded by his hope of gain into refusing to see
what Don Jacinto is really up to in Gonzalo's room; and out of a
touching desire to meet any of Ángela's wishes, he later spirits himself
and Alonso from the scene at the time when Ángela is devising her
own scheme for Gerarda, his ward.

The play's virtues are those of a fast-moving entertainment,
dominated by an intrigue whose complications always seem plausible
in the hands of the participants. Thus the charge of implausibility is
not allowed to preoccupy our thoughts even in that most unlikely
development, Octavio's spiriting away of "Don Jacinto": we accept
his co-operation because we know of his love for Ángela; and later
after Jacinto's (that is Alonso's) arrival at his strange destination,
we are so amused by his fears that Octavio has penetrated his
intentions, and wishes now to dispose of him, that we forget how
improbable a ruse it has been. The play's construction, however,
reveals one notable weakness — since it opens with the protagonists
already in Madrid, much information about former events in Granada needs to be given to the audience, and it is unfortunate that
because of insufficient care, the explanations appear more in the
nature of inspired leaks. But even without that flaw the *comedia,*
despite its delicious humour, would not have been on a par with
Los empeños: the absence of social criticism (apart from the half-

hearted attack on the morals of coachmen and those that ride in coaches), and of a firm moral point of view means that *Los riesgos* lacks a cutting edge. The play, it is true, attempts, like *Los empeños*, to give its audience a sense of the capital, but in this instance atmosphere has been reduced to local geography and noises offstage. The principal lack, of course, is that of good poetry — and even as a poetic play with underlying prose rhythms, it falters because of an easy acquiescence in timid verse and rhyme patterns, and an inability to cut out superfluities. Nevertheless, it is important to emphasize that *Los riesgos* has real value as theatre. The audience will not come away from it suitably edified, in fact its notion of the virtues may have been slightly warped. But it will have been royally, and comically, entertained.

XII

MENDOZA'S *COMEDIAS*: CONCLUSIONS

M E N D O Z A' S plays in general are not very different from those of his contemporaries. Yet certain features even of the run-of-the-mill *comedias* merit discussion, especially in their relation to the dramatic tradition as a whole, whilst his romanesque plays appear to have contributed one essential feature to his theatre, the woman of passion. Furthermore, the general question arises as to the extent to which even the less courtly plays were aimed at a public thought to have rather special interests and standards.

Mendoza showed some originality in his *graciosos* or *figuras del donayre*. [1] His types vary from the more old-fashioned butt-cum-buffoon-cum-moralist of *No hay amor donde hay agravio* to the sententious and disillusioned commentator in *Querer*. But the most interesting is the emancipated *gracioso,* the ingenious companion of some of the social comedies. He was not a new figure in the theatre, and he indeed recalls the *gracioso* of some of Ruiz de Alarcón's plays. Characterized by "wit and frankness," [2] he supplies the underlying message not from the backstage immunity of sub-plot, but from the forward positions of a main action which he significantly impels. Historically Bernardo (in *Cada loco*), or Marcelo (in *Los empeños*) represents a further stage in the development of the *gracioso* from Alarcón's Clarín to Beaumarchais's Figaro; and in a more limited historical perspective, Mendoza's contribution may have been to have kept the Alarcón type of *gracioso* memorably alive in the generation which intervenes between Don Juan (whose theatre had reached its zenith by 1625), and Agustín Moreto, whose art was only to develop in the period after Mendoza's death.

But the *gracioso* as companion may not, in Mendoza's drama, be separated from the influence of the *commedia dell'arte*. We cannot

---

[1] See Montesinos's classic study, in *Estudios sobre Lope*, "Algunas observaciones sobre la figura del donaire en el teatro de Lope de Vega" (pp. 13-70).

[2] Bernardo in *Cada loco con su tema* is a "mozo / De gracejo y desembozo" (*BAE*, XLV, p. 461).

say whether he had seen performances of the *Arte* on a visit to Italy
— his *Empeños del mentir* appears to relive a recent Italian experience — or had read some of the printed scenarios. [3] It may even
be possible that he saw in Spain Italian troupes whose presence has
left no trace in the extant records for the decades following Ganassa's Spanish tour towards the end of the sixteenth century. [4] Possibly
too Mendoza's early friendship with Lope de Vega (in whose first
plays the *gracioso* may have emerged in part under the influence
of the *Arte*) [5] had led to an interest in the *commedia*'s dramatic
potential. Clearly there is no proof of direct influence in Mendoza's
case, but the circumstantial evidence is strong: Sr. Asensio in discussing *Doctor Dieta* posits a similarity between the learned Italian
doctor and Graziano, the charlatan of the *commedia;* [6] the dupe of
Mendoza's plays may owe something to the Italian Pantalone, though
of course he is a not uncommon type in the Golden Age drama. But
it is *Los empeños* that comes nearest to proving the inspiration of the
Italian improvised theatre. In addition to the apparently meaningful
reference to the *commedia dell'arte* at the end of the play, [7] there
are certain key features of the cynical protagonists and their role:
their essential character and origin are never explained to the audience, presumably because the author deems that the audience would
already be familiar with them as the equivalents of *Arte* characters,
such as, for example, the types represented by Harlequin, Scapino, or
Capitano Spavento; [8] and their final departure into the limbo whence
they sprang suggests both the author's continuous dependence on
this familiarity, and his desire to juxtapose, for artistic contrast, the
stock setting of the contemporary Spanish drama, and the more
mysterious world of the Italian *commedia*. Finally, if we put the
question whether *Los empeños* can be fully appreciated without

---

[3] See ch. I, Note 70, and also "A Chronology." Of the various printed scenarios, the
best-known were those of Flaminio Scala (Venice, 1611): see Vito Pandolfi, *La Commedia
dell'arte*, 6 vols. (Firenze, 1957-61), *passim*.

[4] See N. D. Shergold, "Ganassa and the 'Commedia dell'arte' in Sixteenth-Century
Spain," *MLR*, LI (1956), 359-368. Professor John Varey has privately mentioned to me
the gap in relevant archive sources for the early years of the seventeenth century.

[5] See Edwin B. Place, "Does Lope de Vega's *Gracioso* stem in part from Harlequin?"
HisL, XVII (1934), 257-270.

[6] Asensio, p. 118.

[7] *FC*, p. 296: "... y a muchos, / y a nosotros bien galantes / nos ha durado tres días,
/ como Comedia del arte."

[8] See e.g. Nicoll, op. cit., *passim*.

assuming the relevance of the *commedia dell'arte* the answer is that it could not.

Passing reference has been made to the *comedia de figurón* as a form of entertainment to which some of Mendoza's plays approximated. What is less than clear, however, is the relation, chronologically and otherwise, between Mendoza's art and this genre, if it may be so called. The *comedia de figurón* has about it, unfortunately, an air of false definition, so that the critic has been in danger of inventing a genre which he then invests with certain fixed attributes and a determined chronological development. [9]

A fairer hypothesis would be that, possibly under the influence of the *entremés de figuras* (like Mendoza's own *Miser Palomo*), the depiction of extravagant and ridiculous characters spread to the *comedia* proper, and that where, as in a minority of cases, the *figura* became the protagonist, we get the *comedia de figurón*, whose principal character is anti-gallant, and by definition ridiculous. However, the interest in *figuras* is more significant than the development of the *figurón*, who may have been merely an accidental, and occasional, by-product. For this reason it would be wrong to assume too much concerning the *comedia de figurón* as "genre," since it is its dramatic configuration rather than the potential attributes of the *figurón* that makes it a recognizable form; and its sporadic appearance may owe little or nothing to any desire to conform to an already existing genre.

Let us stay therefore with the term *figura*, that was used in the contemporary theatre. Where the *figura* becomes protagonist, one prime consequence flows: the audience's centre of interest is no longer simply the object of admiration or censure, but primarily one of mirth. But within the ambit of this dramatic situation, the range of variation is very great, extending from Alarcón's *La verdad sospechosa* (in which the *figura*'s glib lying is not only ridiculous, but open to severe moral censure) to the same author's *No hay mal que por bien no venga*: in this, a historical play, we find two *figuras,* a nobleman fallen on bad times who is prepared to stoop to fraud and theft in order to further his ends, and the more central

---

[9] See e.g. Edwin B. Place, "Notes on the Grotesque," *PMLA*, LIV (1939), 412-421. Asensio (p. 77 *et seq.*) traces the history of the term *figura* and its derivatives. Ignacio de Luzán's definition of the *figurón* play is appropriately vague. He refers to certain *comedias* as "las que llaman de *Figurón*, porque pintan y ridiculizan los vicios ó sandéces de alguna persona extravagante" —see *La poetica* (ed. Madrid, 1789), II, 35.

character, Domingo de Don Blas, a wayward, plain-spoken eccentric, who eventually by his true nobility, wins the affection and admiration both of characters and audience. In *No hay mal* Alarcón deliberately exploits the ambiguity of category of his protagonist, and the ambiguity of response in his audience.

If these two plays represent in a sense the two extremes to which the portrayal of the *figura* may be pushed, there is an ample middle ground where the playwright may blend mirth with social or moral comment. With Mendoza's *figuras* the principal object is laughter. Some of them are paralleled in the work of other playwrights: his fops (for instance Chrisóstomo in *El galán sin dama,* or Julián in *Cada loco*), may be found in Guillén de Castro's *El Narciso en su opinión,* and will be recreated by Moreto in *El lindo don Diego;* the *Montañés* of *Cada loco,* with his exaggerated sense of his origins, his impatience with court clothes and manners, and his ridiculous escapades, is reminiscent of the pretended *indiano* of Castillo Solórzano's *El mayorazgo figura,* or of Don Lucas in Rojas Zorrilla's *Entre bobos anda el juego.* [10] But in the parallel with Don Lucas we meet a further complication of the *figura's* role, already suggested in Alarcón's *No hay mal:* Mendoza's *Montañés,* Rojas's Don Lucas, and Alarcón's Don Domingo de Don Blas are all characters in whom the ludicrous shares an uneasy alliance with proper moral standards. At this point too the interlude becomes relevant. It is no accident that one of the characters in *Entre bobos* should comment that Don Lucas has an "excellent name for a gallant in an interlude" (the name indeed of Mendoza's ridiculous gallant in the *Entremés de Getafe*); or that Don Cosme, the "figura de figuras" in Castillo Solórzano's *El Marqués del Cigarral* has a name suggesting "a low character of an *entremés.*" [11] The explanation is that the inspiration for such creations had come in part from the interlude. Further, the dramatic richness of the *Montañés,* or of Rojas's Don Lucas, derives from interlude *figuras* like Miser Palomo, whose dominant trait is the strange combination of fool and moral judge. Mendoza's originality in the *Montañés* lies in his having created out of such a crude

---

[10] The two latter plays may be found respectively in *BAE,* XLV, pp. 289-307, and Francisco de Rojas Zorrilla, *Teatro,* Clás. Cast. (Madrid, 1917), pp. 145-280. The editor, F. Ruiz Morcuende, later averred that *Entre bobos* was the first *comedia de figurón* (see p. L of 1956 edition).

[11] Op. cit., p. 153: "Excelente nombre tiene / para galán de entremés;" *BAE,* XLV, p. 309, and Edwin Place's comment (p. 418) on the Marquis.

potential a complex character that is for ever testing the audience's power to discriminate, and determine its proper moral standards.

Perhaps the most important aspect of the interlude's influence on Mendoza was its liberating nature. Like the satirical novel of the period, the *entremés* was less tied by convention to the depiction of the life of the noble classes. [12] Thus it could develop greater range of character in a typological sense; it dealt with a broader segment of society, and it gave more place to social satire. This artistic freedom has had its effect on Mendoza's *comedia*, though it has not completely transformed it. Perhaps the most important influence has been on the role of social satire. Edwin B. Place has drawn attention in what he identifies as the early *figurón* play (which was an expansion of the interlude or its partial transformation) to the "social satire of the middle class." [13] If we interpret "middle" here as denoting an *hidalgo* class barred from the ranks of the nobility yet convinced of its superiority over the lower classes, the statement significantly applies to Mendoza's social comedies, thus declaring once more the relevance of the interlude tradition. Indeed it may well be that Mendoza was more indebted to the liberating influence of the interlude in general, and its provision of a gallery of social types, than to the depiction of *figuras* as such. He did not seek, like Alarcón or Moreto, to make of any *figura* an anti-gallant protagonist, but he shared with these major dramatists (though more with Alarcón than with Moreto) a desire to combine the depiction of the *hidalgo* class in a domestic setting, with a satirical or moralistic form of art.

In Mendoza's *comedias* the depiction of Madrid is a recurring concern. This of course is not a feature of *his* plays alone: one thinks of Lope de Vega's *El acero de Madrid,* even of Alarcón's *Las paredes oyen.* It is worth bearing in mind, however, the observation of Eugenio Asensio, that the interlude helped make Madrid a fit subject for the theatre. [14] Mendoza's elaboration of court life in *Miser Palomo* and *El Licenciado Dieta,* or his vivid evocation of a village in the neighbourhood of the court in the *Entremés de Getafe,* may well

---

[12] On the relation between the satirical novel and the *comedia de figurón,* see Place, pp. 412-417.

[13] Ibid., p. 416.

[14] Asensio, pp. 83-84.

have put a sharper edge on that sensitivity to place and atmosphere that marks him as a writer of *comedias,* as well as a composer of *jácaras.*

To some extent the vividness of his portrayal of Madrid was due to his sense of a rapidly changing society. In *El marido hace mujer* a character observes:

> en estremos
> distintos cada hora vemos,
> un vario, un nuevo Madrid. [15]

And it was a new, expanding Madrid that he eulogized in the opening scene of *Los empeños,* in representing Olivares's great achievement in the palace and gardens of the *Retiro.* [16] To some extent too *Lo que es un coche* is a humourist's reflexion upon the growing influence of the coach on the life, customs, and even the moral standards of the *madrileños.* But he also responds to the more permanent features of the city's life: one recalls the pretty picture of the evening walk along the Manzanares, or the frequent invocation of the Prado as the venue of gallants or ladies in search of pleasure, and full of the bustle and gaiety of the crowd. He is even fascinated by picturesque street scenes; like that in *Lo que es un coche,* where a queue of coaches is waiting to cross a bridge; or like the opening moment of the *Entremés de Getafe,* with the sweating muleteer egging on his train. Mendoza was attempting, if only on a small scale, to convey in dramatic terms what Castillo Solórzano, Salas Barbadillo, and later Juan de Zabaleta were doing in novelistic form: he is a minor exponent of the art of *costumbrismo.*

And his picture of contemporary life covers a range of social types, some of whom Zabaleta would again brilliantly invoke. The fops, the donjuanesque gallants, the poetasters, the snobbish young ladies as well as the discreet ones, the provincial upstarts, the returning *indiano:* these and others were part of the life of the capital. As we have had occasion to point out, Mendoza observes too the

---

[15] *FC*, p. 227: *at opposite ends we see every hour a varied and a new Madrid* [the other meaning of "extremes" is also implicit here]. Cf. also in Tirso's earlier *La celosa de sí misma* (1622-23) the same sense of a new city (*Obras dramáticas completas*, II, 1431-1492).

[16] *FC*, pp. 254-256.

fluid state of the social classes, his prime moral concern being to assert true nobility in a society where advancement was sought through the possession of wealth, and where moral standards were being eroded. If *Cada loco* deals most explicitly with the social implications of this crisis, the confused, but well-intentioned *dama* of *Los empeños,* the more determined Ángela of *Lo que es un coche,* as well as the severely virtuous Ipólita of *El galán sin dama* all represent the same struggle to maintain standards and to assert a personal *valor* in the face of a prevailing confusion.

Mendoza also goes inside the house, and like Lope in *El acero de Madrid* or Moreto in *El lindo don Diego,* gives the feel of everyday life, despite ludicrousness of situation or event: for instance, in *Los empeños,* with Diego returning from an evening's gambling, and expatiating to some newly found friends on his family fortunes, his youth, his sorrow for a dead relative, and his present intentions for an unmarried ward; or in *Lo que es un coche,* with Octavio's concern for his sister's honour, his hope that a newly acquired coach will attract a pretty girl of whom he is fond, and his involvement in the schemes and counter-schemes of his servants. These things add up to an impression of *hidalgo* life reminiscent of Molière's treatment of the French *bourgeoisie.*

Mendoza's position in the tradition of Spanish social comedy in the seventeenth century is difficult to determine. It would be tempting for instance to see in Mendoza's Chrisóstomo or Julián a link between Guillén de Castro's fop Gutierre, and Moreto's Don Diego. But Chrisóstomo may even antedate Guillén's *El Narciso,* [17] and such are the differences of emphasis and interest among all four plays that to establish a definite connexion between any of them would be rash, especially when the fop was such an obvious figure of fun. What may be put forward more realistically is the suggestion that the success of a number of Mendoza's *comedias* in the thirties and afterwards may have helped Moreto continue that tradition so splendidly.

---

[17] *El Narciso* was written in 1625 or before (see Guillén de Castro y Bellvis, *Obras,* III, Madrid, 1927, pp. XII-XIII). For discussion of the date of composition of Mendoza's *El galán sin dama,* see my "A Chronology."

Despite the possibility that Mendoza eventually grew tired of their complex plots with the resultant tendency to create confusion, [18] his romanesque *comedias, Querer por solo querer* and *Más merece quien más ama,* remain a significant achievement. Firstly, they brought into the theatre a psychological interest and a notion of dramatic character in which the stock *comedia* was deficient. Mendoza's women of passion and will (who find their way also into his more conventional *comedias,* both *de capa y espada* and social comedy), derive from the stereotypes of the pastoral novel, and thus bring with them a concern with emotional complexity that was not well served by the comedy of intrigue. The woman of passion, furthermore, in spreading her influence into Mendoza's other *comedias,* achieves a new dimension: obliged now to operate within a rapid-moving intrigue, she abandons the demonstration of passion for the deployment of an immense ingenuity, becoming in effect the female equivalent of the scheming gallant. And in *Lo que es un coche* (as indeed in *Celos sin saber de quien*) her willingness to let nothing stand in passion's way not only provokes the audience's wonder, but is the palpable reason why the usual schemers of the *comedia* fail in their object:

> Que han menester estudiar
> contra ingenio de muger. [19]

In all this the dominant factor is Mendoza's awareness of the woman character in action. The nature of his achievement is made clearer by a comparison with a later, and famous, play, Moreto's *El desdén con el desdén,* which like *Más merece* tells of disdainful princesses and their suitors. For Moreto the psychology of disdain, as also the depiction of the disdainful suitor's growing love, are the occasion for cold analysis, whereas in Mendoza the interest lies in what could be termed "dramatic" as opposed to novelistic psychology. To encounter Mendoza's heroines is to remember them.

The predilection of King Philip and his first wife for the theatre is well-known. For instance, during the months from the beginning

---

[18] The author's boredom with "Comedias confussas" is expressed in *Celos sin saber de quien,* f. B1ᵛ.

[19] f. 129: *They have to contend with the ingenuity of a woman.* Cf. also "Yo muestro de la muger / el ingenio, y sutileza" (f. 134).

of October 1622 to the beginning of February 1623 the Queen saw plays in her room no less than twice a week (among them figured *Más merece quien más ama*), a taste which continued during the remaining years of Mendoza's career. [20] We cannot say that Mendoza initially wrote for the palace stage as distinct from the public *corral,* but the evidence does indicate that out of twelve of his plays, no fewer than nine were at some time presented before Their Majesties. He may well therefore have written usually with a palace performance somewhere in mind. What effect has this had on his *comedias?* In terms of the use of staging technique, little or none, with the obvious exception of *Querer.* But in terms of content there has been a considerable effect, which may be considered under a literary, and a political aspect.

Mendoza obviously provided his audience in his romanesque plays, and to a lesser extent in his other *comedias,* with the kind of material that touched their preoccupations. Sometimes this took the form of comment aimed at the court audience's knowledge of itself and its own weaknesses: a characteristic example would be an ejaculation from *Más merece:*

> O' quantos se prometieron,
> que en Palacio no supieron
> lo que miente una esperança! [21]

Or again one recalls in *Querer* the reference by Rifaloro to the proliferation of vices at court. [22] But more characteristic of Mendoza's theatre is his aim to satisfy the courtier's interest in the game of love, and to discuss memorably in public the issues of *galanteo* that were its everyday pabulum. Moreto in *El desdén con el desdén* makes one of his princely suitors remark:

> Pues si argumento ha de ser
> desde hoy nuestro galanteo ... [23]

---

[20] See A. F. von Schack, *Historia de la literatura y del arte dramático en España,* tr. Eduardo de Mier (Madrid, 1885-87), IV, p. 122, Note, Shergold, pp. 264-297, and "Palace Performances."

[21] *FC,* p. 301: *Oh! How many made themselves promises, without knowing how often hope tells lies in the Palace!*

[22] *FC,* p. 386 *et seq.*

[23] Agustín Moreto, *Teatro,* Clás. Cast. (Madrid, 1922), p. 198: *Well then, if from today forward our gallanting must be argument...*

The words echo the prevalence of such debate in Spanish society, and its appropriateness as material for the theatre: Mendoza had similarly written with these two things in mind.

A persistent aspect of Mendoza's theatre is its political significance. Attention has been drawn incidentally to his desire to flatter his royal patrons and the *privado,* but these activities are also to be understood in a strictly political sense: they were conscious attempts to popularize the régime and its ministers, either by open allusion to their goodness and wisdom, or by drawing the audience's attention to what they had done — in *Los empeños,* for instance, the *privado's* achievement in creating a new and splendid Madrid is balanced by a eulogy of Spain's (and by implication the régime's) achievement in the battles and campaigns of the war in Germany against the Protestants. But politics might operate also at a more subtle level — in both *Querer* and *Más merece* martial glory was predominantly (if not exclusively) the subject of praise, the warring princes or the Amazonian princesses are the mirror of the real monarch in action, much as their recognition of the dues payable to glory and honour conforms to that of the Spanish court. And in addition the spectacle play was an important means of demonstrating a régime's prestige, even ultimately its military power: if the court could put on a splendid display on the stage, might it not also do so on the battlefield? We recall how Henry VIII of England in 1520 at Guisnes set up the famous Field of the Cloth of Gold by which he sought to impress ally and foe alike with the power of the Tudor régime. [24] Inevitably the function of display, formerly exercised by the joust and tourney, finds for itself more peaceful and less anachronistic forms, and it is probably more than coincidence that the reign of Philip IV and his favourite should have opened with the Fiesta at Aranjuez and with *Querer por solo querer.*

---

[24] On Guisnes and other displays, see Erna Auerbach, *Tudor Artists: A Study of Painters in the Royal Service and of Portraiture on Illuminated Documents from the Accession of Henry VIII to the Death of Elizabeth I* (London, 1954), pp. 10-13. A later exponent of political drama at court stated thus the principles on which the art should be based: "Son las Commedias de los Reies vnas historias viuas que, sin hablar con ellos, les han de instruir con tal respecto que sea su misma razon quien de lo que ve tome las aduertencias, y no el Ingenio quien se las diga. Para este decir sin decir, ¿quien dudará que sea menester gran arte?" (see F. Bances Candamo, *Theatro de los theatros de los passados y presentes siglos,* ed. Duncan Moir, London, 1970, pp. 56-58). The text was probably written between 1692 and 1693.

In the Spanish theatre, Mendoza's genius is of a secondary order. His output is limited, he lacks both the range and vision of a Calderón or a Lope, his stylistic expression, though frequently sharp and vivid, lacks the verve of Tirso de Molina, or the laconic brilliance of Alarcón. However, without doubt, his contribution was a valuable one: not only did he write the occasional brilliant *comedia* (like *Cada loco* or *Los empeños*), but even his bad plays have the merit of being interesting, with flashes of originality. Furthermore, the plays taken together present an attitude towards life that is refreshingly honest and liberal. For example, on marriage and feminine rights (an issue particularly dealt with in *El marido hace mujer*, but also touched in passing in *No hay amor donde hay agravio*) he strikes a blow for woman, pointing out that she lives in a man's world with few rights of her own, and that her cooperation, rather than her subjection, is what the good husband should seek. And again, despite his almost unavoidable involvement in the adulation of both patron and King, he conveys from time to time a sense of the corruption of his age, and asserts the values needed for the transformation of the society in which he lived.

Finally, I allude again to the moral ambiguity in Mendoza's work. Elvira, heroine of *Los empeños*, who is anxious above all to be honest with herself, her feelings, and her relations with others, may reflect the author's own preference for a personal judgment based on knowledge, experience, and intuition. Eschewing the clear-cut assertion, the unqualified certainty, the religious truth, Mendoza provided the dramatic tradition with a freshness that is a product of the very contrast with the *comedia*'s normally unambiguous moral stance. What redeems *No hay amor* is the author's use of the *comedia de honor* to explore a woman's difficulties in reconciling affection and honour, especially in a world where men determine the rules of the game; in *El marido* he rejects any namby-pamby approach, preferring to deal pragmatically with the problems that the institution of marriage creates; in his romanesque plays the possession of beauty is seen as being in itself a moral virtue, subject only to the eventual triumph of time. In all these cases Mendoza has substituted for an easy moral certainty his own fumbling intuitions; his plays are better for it.

Two particular features of the plays stand out. Firstly, their originality in transferring the *galanteo* and love interest of the pastoral novel to the stage. I have emphasized how Mendoza conceived his characters dramatically rather than novelistically. At the same time, however, he made use of lyricism to evoke the *états d'âme* produced by love or disdain, an "undramatic" method in the sense that it concentrates on the psychological potential of the moment to the neglect of any linear development of character. Yet the results have greatly contributed to the beauty of his romanesque plays, even affecting the treatment of love in his other *comedias*. The pity is that Mendoza's success in this did not help create a psychological drama in Spain in the way that Urfé's *Astrée,* based on similar bucolic material, opened up in France the possibility of the psychological novel.

Secondly, there is Mendoza's achievement in his social comedies. Essentially gay, yet at bottom earnest pieces, they avoid the portentous issues of human destiny so as to concentrate on the everyday (yet fundamental) preoccupations of social life, courtship, marriage, marital honour, the source of wealth, and so on. With these topics he has dealt memorably, evincing both a wry sympathy and a concern for moral rights. Molière wrote his *École des maris* under the influence of *El marido hace mujer,* and though he finally moved considerably away from Mendoza's interpretation of the theme, the French playwright was initially attracted to the play by its concern for how a husband should assure himself of a woman's trust: [25] thereby Molière exemplified how, in both this play and others by Mendoza, the audience probably responded to the live, human issues dealt with. And the fact that Lesage in the following century drew on *Los empeños del mentir* for part of his *Gil Blas de Santillane* brings out Mendoza's ability to convey to posterity a sense of period and place, which the twentieth-century reader or theatre-public is still in a position to enjoy. [26]

---

[25] See E. Martinenche, "Les Sources de *L'École des Maris,*" *Revue d'Histoire Littéraire de la France,* V (1898), 110-116.

[26] See especially Eugène Lintillac, *Lesage* (Paris, 1893), p. 84. *Los empeños del mentir* certainly inspired the episode of the deception of Jérôme de Moyadas in *Gil Blas,* Book V, as well probably as the play *Crispin rival de son maître.*

XIII

MENDOZA'S POSTHUMOUS REPUTATION: A POST-SCRIPT

I N Mendoza's last years, when the court was at Zaragoza, a nun with whom the poet flirted regaled her lover with this remark:

> Mendoza tan sazonado
> que puedes tener aguero
> de la sal que en tus escritos
> cada dia estas vertiendo. [1]

Such appreciation of his abundant wit presumably continued even after his death; it was seen earlier how the manuscript collections suggest a revival of interest in his work during this period. That the poet's memory remained alive for quite some time is shown by the lament uttered by Francisco de Trillo y Figueroa in the *Poesías varias* (1652), that with Mendoza's passing the knife-edge of wit at court had been blunted. During the same decade Enríquez Gómez recalled Mendoza's prodigious success at court earlier in Philip IV's reign. In 1658 Alonso Núñez de Castro remembered Mendoza the dramatist, whom he rated among the best exponents of the *comedia*. And in the same year a *censura* written on a manuscript of Cubillo de Aragón's *El señor de Noches Buenas* insists that the play was not Cubillo's but by "that great courtier and man of the palace, Don Antonio de Mendoza:" the censor defends the attribution on the evidence of the play's decorum and urbanity, prime characteristics of Don Antonio. [2]

---

[1] Hisp. Soc. Am. *MS* B2505, f. 7ᵛ: *Mendoza so seasoned that one may mark an omen by the salt of the wit which every day you pour into your verse.* That the poem is associated with this period in Zaragoza rather than an earlier one is suggested by the context of the MS, which contains poems by Luis de Ulloa, the poet of Toro, and an epitaph to Mendoza's tomb (f. 8). See also p. 47 here.

[2] Francisco de Trillo y Figueroa, *Obras*, ed. A. Gallego Morell (Madrid, 1951), p. 120; for Enríquez Gómez, see ch. II, Note 4; Alonso Núñez de Castro, *Solo Madrid es Corte* (Madrid, 1658), f. 8 *et seq.*; the *censura* is found on BNM *MS* 17301, a copy of *El señor de Noches Buenas* (see Julián Paz, *Catálogo de las piezas de teatro que se conservan en el departamento de manuscritos de la Biblioteca Nacional*, Madrid, 1934-35, I, 509,

Such specific recognition of Mendoza's name is mirrored in the printed sources, and that over a wider period. At least seven of his plays were printed in the period 1644-90, some, such as *El galán sin dama* and *No hay amor donde hay agravio,* more than once. Juan de Vera y Villarroel, who in the seventies recovered *Más merece quien más ama* from obscurity and produced it in the theatre, asked the audience to give due applause to "el grande Mendoza." [3] Again the fact that Molière imitated *El marido hace mujer* in *L'École des maris,* first produced in 1661, or that the Seigneur de Hauteroche's *Le Cocher,* written in 1682, should be based on *Los riesgos que tiene un coche,* [4] suggests that Mendoza's plays were available as source material, even in France, until quite late in the century: in the former case Molière may have had to hand the *Primera parte de comedias escogidas...* (1652), which contained *El marido hace mujer.* It is worth mentioning in contrast that despite the great success of Mendoza's *entremeses,* their popularity seems to fade after the years 1646 and 1647, when two, if not three of them, were reprinted in Cadiz. A large collection of *entremeses* and *bailes, Tardes apacibles de gustoso entretenimiento* (1663), which included a fair sample of pieces by Mendoza's contemporaries, has nothing by him, and the same applies to a number of smaller compilations published in the course of the later seventeenth century, and at the beginning of the eighteenth. [5]

It is more difficult to determine the popularity of Mendoza's lyric poetry during these years, apart from the obvious success enjoyed both in manuscript and in print by the *Vida de Nuestra Señora.* Some of his poems were presumably read in manuscript, others were sung, thus continuing for a minority of initiates the

---

No. 3350). Date of *censura*, 23 January 1658; the censor, Juan Navarro de Espinosa, refers to "aquel gran cortesano y palaciego."

[3] In *Primavera numerosa de muchas armonías luzientes, en doce comedias fragantes...* (Madrid, 1679), ff. 197ᵛ-213ᵛ [=Bb5ᵛ-Eeᵛ]. The play carries the double attribution of Mendoza and Juan de Vera y Villarroel. The final lines state: "Y para el grande Mendoza / oy D. Iuan de Vera os pide / aplauso, pues le merece / ..."

[4] For the popularity of Spanish plays in France in the years 1660-1700, see e.g. ch. on "Lesage et l'Espagne" in Léo Clarétie, *Lesage romancier, d'après de nouveaux documents* (Paris, 1890), esp. Note 2 on p. 160.

[5] *Tardes apacibles de gustoso entretenimiento, repartidas en varios Entremeses, y Bayles entremesados, escogidos de los mejores Ingenios de España...* (Madrid, 1663). There is fair representation of pieces by Juan Vélez, Calderón, Moreto, and Jerónimo Cáncer, though there are none by Quiñones de Benavente. The other collections include *Flor de entremeses* (1657), *Migajas del ingenio* (no date), *Arcadia de entremeses* (1723), and those described by Montaner (pp. 136-189).

20

kind of success enjoyed during the poet's lifetime. Nevertheless, the oral transmission of his poetry must have weakened by mid-century, as people's memory of the poems faded. It is because of this inevitable process possibly that Gracián referred in 1653 to Mendoza as a forgotten and neglected poet. [6] The Aragonese writer's subsequent attempts to revive interest in Mendoza through the publication of Alfay's *Poesías varias de grandes ingenios españoles* (1654), which contained some thirteen pieces by Don Antonio, are ironically a reflection of the need now for the printing of a poetry that in its heyday had been transmitted effectively by other means. Likewise, Miguel Manescal's comment in 1690 on the obscurity into which the Castilian Phoenix had fallen reflects the same need to promote Mendoza's reputation by methods which the poet in his lifetime had shunned.

It follows therefore that whereas the publication of some of Mendoza's poems in the earlier *Primavera y flor* series had been only marginally a gauge of the poet's popularity, the appearance of his pieces in lyric collections from 1645 onwards would in increasing degree represent his true reputation. That he was not a popular poet in the widest sense is suggested by the fact that in the various editions of the *Romances varios de diversos autores* that appeared between 1655 and 1664 (each one with new revisions and additions), only two poems of this master of the ballad are included. [7] Where collections catered for a more sophisticated and courtly taste, the position was different. Mention has already been made of the Alfay collection; the *Delicias de Apolo, recreaciones del Parnaso* (1670) contained eight poems, among them a number that are redolent of the atmosphere of court pastimes; whilst eight appeared also in the *Varias hermosas flores del Parnaso* (1680), an anthology whose introduction contained a high-flown eulogy of Mendoza as "el Galán de las Musas." [8]

---

[6] See p. 56 here.

[7] *Romances varios de diversos autores* (Madrid, 1655); Sevilla, 1655; Zaragoça, 1663; Madrid, 1664. A later collection bears a slightly different title, *Romances varios. De diferentes authores. Nuevamente Impressos por un Curioso* (Amsterdam, 1688); this is, in fact, a different compilation, which does, however, contain one of Mendoza's poems (pp. 38-39).

[8] *Delicias de Apolo. Recreaciones del Parnaso ... Hechas de varias poesías de los Mejores Ingenios de España* (Zaragoza, 1670), including the text of the *Vida* (pp. 1-45); *Varias hermosas flores del Parnasso. Que en quatro floridos, vistosos quadros, plantaron junto a su cristalina fuente: D. Antonio Hurtado de Mendoza; D. Antonio de Solís; D.*

What happened to Mendoza's reputation after the turn of the century? The appearance of *El Fénix castellano* must have boosted Mendoza's fortunes, especially in a Spain that was still able to produce and to enjoy the poetry of Antonio de Solís. Indeed Manescal's appeal to the reader is on the grounds that Mendoza was "the most polished, the most elegant, and the most courtly cultivator of the Castilian Muses." [9] That such taste lasted well into the eighteenth century is shown by the decision of Francisco Medel del Castillo to republish the *Fénix castellano* in an amended and augmented form. In the dedication of the new volume, *Obras líricas* (1728), he referred to Mendoza's "witty and discreet genius," and expressed the hope that with the patronage of the Marquis of Estepa the poetry would attain the success it deserved. The same courtly standards inform Antonio de Zamora's *aprobación,* which commends Mendoza's modesty, discretion, elegance, and "the natural liveliness with which he expresses his conceits." [10] Lastly, one of the major manuscript collections of Mendoza's poems (however uncertain some of the attributions may be) was the product of the eighteenth century: I refer to Hisp. Soc. Am. *MS HC: 371/224, Varias Poësias a diferentes asump[to]s. Compuestas Por el Discreto de Palacio D[o]n Antonio Mendoza.*

For as long as the appreciation of a courtly wit lasted, Mendoza would not be entirely forgotten. The extent to which a fundamental change of taste would affect his reputation is suggested by the difference between the views of two sensitive eighteenth-century writers. On the one hand Francisco Nieto de Molina, still attuned to the taste of the previous age, spoke in the prologue of *El fabulero* (1764) of his favourite seventeenth-century poets. Lope, Quevedo, Góngora, Montalbán, and Esquilache he placed in a special category. But among the next rank of poets he singled out for praise "las [poesías] delicadas de Mendoza." [11] The other view reflects, on the

---

Francisco de la Torre y Sebil; D. Rodrigo Artes y Muñoz; Martín Iuan Barcelo: Iuan Bautista Aguilar, y otros ilustres poetas de España (Valencia, 1680). The eulogy is in prelims., f. III.

[9] *FC,* prelims., f. II: "el màs polido, el màs asseado, y el màs cortesano cultor de las Musas Castellanas."

[10] Antonio Hurtado de Mendoza, *Obras líricas, y cómicas, divinas, y humanas, con la celestial ambrosia del admirable poema sacro de María Santíssima...* (Madrid, 1728), prelims., f. IIIᵛ: "del agudo y discreto Ingenio;" and f. IV, *aprobación* dated 30 May 1728: "la viveza natural con que expressa sus conceptos."

[11] Quot. in Cossío's *Fábulas mitológicas,* p. 813.

other hand, an attitude of mind in which a constricting classicism
has rendered virtually impossible the appreciation of a poetic wit
founded in the miraculous, often arbitrary, conjunction of words,
symbols, and ideas. The 1789 edition of Ignacio de Luzán's *Poética*
gave some account of Spanish poetry during the period from Boscán
onwards. He did not name Mendoza, presumably not thinking him
worthy of mention. The explanation of the omission is clear from
Luzán's views on Góngora, to whom is imputed the responsibility
for the spread of bad taste. Góngora's style was "extraordinarily
pompous and hollow, full of extravagant metaphors, word-play,
antitheses, puns, and transpositions new and strange in our language." [12] Thus what could have passed as a description of
Mendoza's style too, may be taken as an unuttered condemnation
of it. The uncongeniality for Luzán of such writing is given further
emphasis by his criticism of Gracián's *Agudeza* because it had given
standing to a depraved style. One final comment: Luzán condemned
too the tendency of seventeenth-century poets to write *romances,
décimas,* and other forms that required the short Castilian metres,
commenting that the greatness of good poetry could not be contained
in such small limits. [13] Such an opinion offers another basic reason
why he, and possibly others, were unable to respond to Mendoza's
Muse.

It was easier for Mendoza's plays to be accepted in the eighteenth
century. Even Luzán has a good word for them, for he cites Mendoza's name along with that of ten other playwrights whom he
considered not as good as Calderón, but occasionally approaching
him in quality. [14] And in the same decade, when the Count of
Aranda commissioned Bernardino de Iriarte to examine what native
Spanish plays might be described as maintaining proper artistic
standards, of the seventy *comedias* recommended out of the total
of six hundred studied, three by Mendoza (as compared with twenty-
one by Calderón and only three by Lope) were deemed to have
passed the test, a substantial proportion in fact of his total production

---

[12] Ignacio de Luzán, *La poetica, ó reglas de la poesia en general, y de sus principales
especies* (ed. Madrid, 1789), I, 31: "estilo sumamente pomposo y hueco, lleno de metáforas
extravagantes, de equívocos, de antítesis, de retruecanos, y de unas transposiciones del
todo nuevas y extrañas en nuestro idioma." The original, and considerably different, edition
of 1737 had used similar language (pp. 81-82).

[13] Ibid., p. 32.

[14] *Poetica,* II, 30.

for the theatre. [15] And if we look to the theatre in France during the first half of the eighteenth century, the vogue for Spanish plays, already a noteworthy feature of the second half of the previous century, continued; Mendoza being one of the Golden Age dramatists whose work was presented to the public. [16]

The dichotomy that clearly emerges by the end of the eighteenth century is fundamental to Mendoza's subsequent reputation: as a playwright he was *persona grata,* as a poet he was not. The revival of interest in Golden Age drama with the advent of the Romantic movement could only strengthen the appreciation of Mendoza's *comedias:* it did nothing unfortunately for the appreciation of his poetry. We shall conclude this brief survey therefore with a consideration of Mesonero Romanos's appraisal of Mendoza in the mid-nineteenth century, since this both demonstrated the existing dichotomy, and probably by its appearance in the influential *Biblioteca de Autores Españoles* helped give the judgment, however unfair, an air of unquestionable authority. When Mesonero collected and edited the two large volumes of plays by Lope de Vega's contemporaries, he included three of Mendoza's *comedias, El marido hace mujer, Los empeños del mentir,* and *Cada loco con su tema.* The preface to the second volume (1858) contained a *critique* of Mendoza's work, covering what Mesonero knew of the plays (which certainly also included *Más merece* and *Querer*), as well as what he had read of the poetry, apparently in Manescal's edition. Mesonero accorded that Mendoza's plays were excessively florid in taste, but he had kind remarks to make about all the pieces chosen, especially *El marido hace mujer,* adding that many years earlier, "struck by the ingenious artifice, the truth and energy of the characters displayed, and even by the purity, sobriety and correctness of its style," he had adapted this *comedia* for stage presentation, bringing it into line with the requirements of classical style (a form of adaptation this which was already popular in Spain in the eighteenth century). [17] Mesonero, however, was much more severe

---

[15] Emilio Cotarelo, *Iriarte y su época* (Madrid, 1897), p. 65 *et seq.*, report on 20 August 1767.

[16] See Clarétie, op. cit., pp. 159-161.

[17] *Dramáticos contemporáneos a Lope de Vega* (II), BAE, XLV, xxvii-xxx, quot. on p. xxix: "prendado ... del ingenioso artificio, de la verdad y energía de los carácteres en ella desplegados, y hasta de la pureza, sobriedad y correccion de su estilo." For the text of the adaptation, see Ramón de Mesonero Romanos, *Trabajos no coleccionados,* II (Ma-

on Mendoza's poems, condemning their author for "that exaggeration and mannered style characteristic of the school of Góngora, that subtlety of conceits, that smartness of phrase, which, bordering frequently on the incomprehensible and obscure, was and always is ridiculous in the eyes of reason and sensible criticism." [18] It is fortunate that Mesonero's dogmatic assertion was not as definitive as he believed. Otherwise the Castilian Phoenix could never arise again from the ashes of a dead judgment.

---

drid, 1905), 245-306. For the history of the earlier classical adaptations, see *Historia general de las literaturas hispánicas*, IV, Primera parte (Barcelona, 1956), 122-124.

[18] Ibid., pp. xxvii-xxviii: "aquella exageracion y amaneramiento propios de la escuela gongorina, de aquella sutileza de conceptos, de aquel discreteo de la frase, que, rayando muchas veces en lo incomprensible y tenebroso, era y es siempre ridículo a los ojos de la razon y de la critica sensata."

MENDOZA AS A WRITER OF LYRICS FOR SONGS

The following list includes references both to Mendoza poems for which settings were made by seventeenth-century musicians, and to pieces in collections which we may presume to have served as the repository of song-lyrics. The doubt concerning the purpose of certain of these collections is shown by the case of Arias Pérez's *Primavera y flor* — see Chapter VIII here. It is also worth bearing in mind that in such collections not all poems may have been thought of as song-lyrics.

Primavera y flor de los mejores romances, ed. J. F. Montesinos, to which page reference is here made:

1621 edition: p. 32 — "Cantemos civilidades" (*MOP*, II, 289)
  p. 36 — "Mal segura zagaleja" (*MOP*, II, 265)
  p. 45 — "Hermosa zagala" (*MOP*, I, 170)
  p. 104 — "No corras, arroyo ufano" (*MOP*, II, 281)
  p. 104 — "Poca tierra y muchas flores" (*MOP*, I, 172)
1636 edition: p. 221 — "Con sus trapos Inesilla" (*MOP*, I, 176)
1641 edition: p. 238 — "Villana de Leganés" (*MOP*, II, 341)

Cancionero de Claudio de la Sablonara, ed. Jesús Roca:

No. 1 — "A la dulce risa del alba" (*MOP*, II, 252)
No. 38 — "Jacinta de los cielos" (*MOP*, II, 274)

Cancionero of Don Joseph del Corral (see study by E. M. Wilson in *HR,* XXXV [1967], 141-160). That Don Joseph was an amateur musician is suggested by the use of a recognized musical tablature (that of Luis de Brizeño's *Metodo mui facilissimo para aprender a tañer la guitarra a la española,* Paris, 1626) for seven out of the fifty and more poems. The collector (in what is in any case a no longer complete text) may therefore have included other pieces too because of their suitableness as song-lyrics:

No. 2 — "Poca tierra y muchas flores" (*MOP*, I, 172)
No. 5 — "Abril destos montes verdes" (*MOP*, II, 295)
No. 38 bis — "Pastores, que me abraso" (*MOP*, I, 180) [This piece bears musical tablature.]
No. 43 — "Desposaron a la niña" (*MOP*, II, 271)

Cancionero poético-musical de 1645, described by Andrés Ortega del Álamo. The manuscript is not yet available for general study. The *tabla de los tonos* extends from f. 8 to f. 9 in Sr. Ortega's account:

"Aquel laurel que pisa" (*MOP*, III, 120)
"Gerarda, una zagaleja" (*MOP*, II, 371)

"Los primores de una fea" (*MOP*, II, 150)

"Montañas de Cataluña" (*MOP*, II, 44)

"Qué alegre de veros triste" (*MOP*, II, 320) [The song is attributed to Correa — f. 7ᵛ.]

"Qué regaloncito está/ el cachorrillo de Venus" (*MOP*, II, 369) [Cf. the *tabla*'s "Que regalonsillo esta/ el heredero de Venus."]

"Ya es turbante Guadarrama" (*MOP*, II, 381) [The poem is only probably by Mendoza. The song attribution is to Correa.]

Also "Leves plumas que volaron/ por tantas Celias y Filis" (*MOP*, II, 239) [This is adapted as an *a lo divino* version: "Leues plumas que bolaron/ por orizontes felises." The song is found among the "Tonos a lo divino" at the end of the manuscript.]

BNM *MS M* 1262, *Libro de tonos*, copied in Madrid in 1655-6 (see *Catálogo musical de la Biblioteca Nacional de Madrid*, vol. I: *Manuscritos*). I refer to the folio number of each piece, and catalogue index:

f. 225ᵛ — "Flores, que más floreciente" (*MOP*, II, 159) [No. 199 of Section 136. The song is attributed to Padre Correa.]

f. 8ᵛ — "Heridas en un rendido" (*MOP*, II, 172) [No. 2 of Section 136. No indication of composer.]

f. 226ᵛ — "Oh qué bien descoge al viento" (*MOP*, II, 128) [No. 200 of Section 136. No indication of composer, but the *MOP* text adds to the title: "Pusole Machado" — the present setting might be his.]

f. 67ᵛ — "Ola pastor, que en la orilla" (*MOP*, II, 326) [No. 57 of Section 136. The song is attributed to Padre Correa.]

f. 151ᵛ — "Qué alegre de veros triste" (*MOP*, II, 320) [No. 135 of Section 136. The song bears a note at the end in a different hand: "En los de Correa," an attribution confirmed by the Correa setting in the *Cancionero de 1645* above.]

f. 91ᵛ — "Qué festivo el arroyuelo" (*MOP*, II, 100) [No. 81 of Section 136. No indication of composer.]

f. 148 — "Qué linda, qué sola y triste" (*MOP*, II, 386) [No. 132 of Section 136. No indication of composer.]

f. 185ᵛ — "Villana de Leganés" (*MOP*, II, 341) [No. 162 of Section 136. No indication of composer. The text is significantly different not only from *MOP* (which reproduces *Palacio MS* 2802), but also from the *Primavera y flor* version (ed. Montesinos, p. 238).]

BNM *MS M* 3881/31, a box of *sueltos* (see *Catálogo musical*, I, No. 30 of Section 138):

"Apostemos, niña, que acierto" (*MOP*, II, 99, and III, 158) [The setting is described as a "Solo de Marín." The text of the song is more closely akin to the *letra* and *glosa* of III, 158 than to II, 99. Nevertheless, with the exception of the opening stanza of the gloss, this is a different poem, though in the same style and vein. It also gives the impression of being an authentic Mendoza poem, though the poet's name is not given.]

Fitzwilliam Museum, Cambridge, *MS MU* — 4 1958, a volume of *tonos* by José Marín, compiled by Miguel Martín, a court musician. This manuscript, which belonged to Barbieri, later passed into the hands of the late Professor J. B. Trend. Barbieri in a note stated that Fray Martín García de Lague, who copied the MS, was organist of the Cathedral of Cuenca in 1695:

    p. 49 — "Turbéme, Cintia, turbéme/ de veros y hablaros" (*MOP*, II, 339)
          [Cf. MS's "Turbeme Çelinda hermosa/Turbeme de veros oy..."]
    p. 75 — "Apostemos, niña, que acierto" (*MOP*, II, 99, and III, 158)

[I am indebted to Jack Sage for an account of this manuscript, and the Mendoza references.]

BNM *MS* 4103, *Algunas poesías de Valentín de Céspedes* (see Jack Sage, "Valentín de Céspedes — Poet, Collector or Impostor:" this shows the collection to have been probably a Jesuitic collection of fashionable songs, put together after 1680):

    p. 231 — "Compitiendo con las selvas" (*MOP*, I, 196)
    p. 235 — "Ya es turbante Guadarrama" (*MOP*, II, 381) [The poem is only
          probably by Mendoza.]

Hisp. Soc. Am. *MS MC* 380, 824a (see *Hisp. Am. Cat.*, No. XLI, 36, vol. I, 290):

Carpetilla 56 — "Qué linda, qué sola y triste" (*MOP*, II, 386) [The song is attributed to Manuel Correa.]

Hisp. Soc. Am. *MS B* 2449 (see *Hisp. Am. Cat.*, No. XVIII, vol. I, 138-139). This *cancionero* of 32 songs (with music given only for some) contains:

    No. 28, p. 54 — "De mí mismo huyendo voy" (*MOP*, II, 268)

Romances varios. De differentes authores. Nuevamente Impressos por un Curioso. Jack Sage (op. cit.) argues that this is demonstrably a collection of lyrics of songs in the main, perhaps in its entirety:

    p. 38 — "Compitiendo con las selvas" (*MOP*, I, 196) [This version has only
          four stanzas.]

A P P E N D I X II

THE ATTRIBUTION OF CERTAIN PLAYS TO ANTONIO DE MENDOZA

At least four plays have been attributed to Antonio de Mendoza which are probably not his:

1. *Dolería del sueño del mundo*

Medel del Castillo's *Índice* (1735) attributed this play to Mendoza. It was in fact written by Pedro Hurtado de la Vera, an edition having been published in Antwerp in 1572 (see Gallardo, *Ensayo*, III, 252).

2. *Don Juan de Espina, Segunda parte*

Don Juan de Espina en Milán. Comedia famosa. Segunda parte (Madrid, Antonio Sanz, 1730) was a play about a famous eccentric of Mendoza's period, whom the poet almost certainly knew. Don Juan, a rich priest and great collector of *objets d'art* and curios, enjoyed after his death in 1643, a considerable reputation as a necromancer, the role in which, significantly, he is cast in the present *comedia*. [1]

Medel's *Índice* attributed this play to Mendoza, whilst Faxardo's *Índice*, covering plays printed up to 1716, makes no mention of it. The Chamber accounts do not mention it either, but there could be some significance in a title, *Los disparates de Don Juan el clérigo*, performed on 2 July 1630, [2] though no grounds exist for supposing that this is to be identified with either part of the *Don Juan* plays under discussion, or that the author was Antonio de Mendoza.

The earliest reference to the play seems a manuscript copy, Biblioteca Nacional, Madrid, *MS* 16921, which bears these words on its title-page: "Primera Jornada de la Comedia de Don Juan de espina en Milan. Para el Señor Juan Antonio Matías. Se represento en Madrid, año de 1713." At the top of the page, in another ink, appear the words: "de Mendoza," but at the top of each *jornada* is written: "De Don Joseph de Cañizares." The attribution to Cañizares is strengthened by what I have to say about the second *Juan de Espina* play.

3. *Don Juan de Espina en su patria*

The printing-house of Antonio Sanz also issued in 1730 *Don Juan de Espina en su patria*. Any doubt about its connexion with the *Segunda parte* is dispelled by the protagonist's leave-taking in the final scene: "Yo me parto mañana/ a Milán siendo esta/ de mi vida y circunstancias/ primer parte, la segunda/ la celebre alla la fama." Don Juan's promise is also a strong indication that both parts are by the same hand, probably that of José de Cañizares.

4. *El señor de Noches Buenas*

The earliest printed version of this play seems to be that in *Flor de las mejores doze comedias de los mayores Ingenios de Espana* (Madrid, 1652, f. 204 *et seq.*), where it is attributed to Antonio de Mendoza. However, when Álvaro Cubillo de Aragón's *El enano de las Musas* appeared in Madrid in 1654,

---

[1] See Emilio Cotarelo, *Don Juan de Espina: Noticias de este célebre y enigmático personaje* (Madrid, 1908).

[2] See Shergold and Varey's "Some Palace Performances," p. 223. The performance was apparently given on 2 July 1630, though there are grounds for assuming a clerical error, in which case a more likely date would be 2 July 1632.

the playwright included this *comedia* in the collection, and asserted his right to it: "Que aunque se imprimió por Don Antonio de Mendoza deuió de ser malicia de algun emulo mio" (p. 353). In dedicating the volume, Cubillo expressed his admiration for Mendoza, and regret that his own "disparates" had been attributed to a man as great as the palace poet. Despite this, Cubillo's claim was rejected by the censor in some comments written in January 1658 on Biblioteca Nacional, Madrid, *MS* 17301, a copy of this particular play; he argued for Mendoza's authorship on the grounds that the text displayed the "decoro y urbanidad" of which the great *palaciego* was master. [3]

Despite the authoritative tenor of the censor's remarks, the evidence points to Cubillo rather than to Mendoza as author. Cubillo referred in 1654 to the circumstances of the *estreno:* "Estrenóla en Granada Bartolome Romero, y en Madrid Roque de Figueroa" (p. 353). The Chamber accounts bear out what is said of the Madrid performance, since a play of this title was performed for His Majesty by Roque de Figueroa on 1 June 1634. [4] One internal reference helps to date the composition of the *comedia,* an allusion to the war being waged against "el infiel de Suecia," that is to say Gustavus Adolphus — this suggests that the *comedia* was possibly written in the period 1630 to 1632, the latter being the year in which Gustavus died. [5] This span of years would make adequate allowance for the earlier *estreno* in Granada, as well as correspond with the culmination of Gustavus's military career.

One other point strengthens Cubillo's case. The action of the play is laid in Valencia, whereas almost all of Mendoza's plays are set in Madrid; and the play's allusions strongly suggest that it was aimed at an audience at some distance from the capital — a factor that would fit an *estreno* in Granada, where Cubillo worked from 1622 to 1640. [6] The authorship of the *comedia* must remain doubtful, but on balance Cubillo seems the more likely candidate.

APPENDIX III

THE DATE OF COMPOSITION OF CERTAIN MANUSCRIPT COLLECTIONS CONTAINING MENDOZA'S POEMS

This is not an exhaustive survey, but an attempt to provide a *terminus a quo* for the major collections of Mendoza's poetry. The conclusions suggested here have been used in Chapter VII in discussing the poet and his audience. For the content of the Biblioteca Nacional, Madrid, and Palacio Real collections, see *MOP,* I, xxxiv *et seq.* I refer in brackets to dated poems which point to the earliest date for the compilation of the manuscript.

---

[3] See Julián Paz, *Catálogo de las piezas de teatro,* I, 509, and p. 304 here.

[4] See "Some Palace Performances," p. 237.

[5] For the Gustavus reference, see Álvaro Cubillo de Aragón, *Las muñecas de Marcela, El señor de Noches Buenas,* ed. A. Valbuena Prat (Madrid, 1928), p. 205.

[6] Op. cit., the editor's introduction, p. x.

BNM *MS* 17723	1636 or afterwards (see *MOP*, II, 139).
BNM *MS* 17678	1636 or afterwards (see *MOP*, I, 155). A reference also to Lope de Vega's death in 1635 (see *MOP*, II, 108).
BNM *MS* 3700	There is no clear indication of date among the Mendoza poems in this collection of *poesías diversas*. But "No corras, río ufano" (*MOP*, II, 281) and "Don Repollo y Doña Berza," both attributed here to Mendoza, appeared in *Primavera y flor* (1621) — see Montesinos edn., p. 66 and p. 104. Some of the poems, by Vélez de Guevara, the Count of Saldaña, Lope de Vega, and Antonio de Mendoza, seem related to the period of the Saldaña group in the first and second decades of the century.
The Sousa manuscript on which the *Fénix castellano* text was based	A reference to a performance of *El marido hace mujer* in 1643 (*MOP*, I, 326) suggests a *terminus a quo*, but my "A Chronology" casts doubt on this date. More certain are two references to May 1637 (*MOP*, II, 137 and 151); and another, to October 1637 (*MOP*, II, 156 does not give a date, but Palacio *MS* 2802, at Décima 135, gives the date in its title, even though the text itself has been crossed out). Suggested date, after late 1637.
The Paris manuscript, *Palacio de las Musas*	In addition to the uncertain date (see above) of the performance of *El marido* (*MOP*, I, 326), we have two references to 1636 (*MOP*, I, 155, and II, 118), and two to 1637 (*MOP*, II, 137 and 151). Suggested date, 1637, or afterwards.
Biblioteca de Palacio *MS* 2802, *Poesías de Mendoza*	One poem is dated October 1641 (*MOP*, III, 120). Otherwise a number of poems are dated 1638 (e.g. III, 68, 134, and 165). The argument that this collection — there are 300 folios of text — may have accumulated over the years can be rejected: a poem dated May 1637 (*MOP*, II, 151) appears on f. 13. Suggested date, after late 1641. Otherwise 1638 or later.
Hisp. Soc. Am. *MS* 2413 (*Hisp. Am. Cat.*, No. CLXI, vol. II, 249)	The content closely resembles the Mendoza selection in BNM *MS* 3700, the inclusion of "No corras" and "Don Repollo" indicating a date in 1621 or earlier as a *terminus a quo*.
Hisp. Soc. Am. *MS HC*: 371/224, *Varias poësias ...*	The present manuscript is of the eighteenth century (see *Hisp. Am. Cat.*, II, 251), but its sources are obviously earlier. Some of the material is almost

certainly spurious. The manuscript is unique in that no poem appears in other collections, thus making dating more difficult. A reference (f. 101) in the title of one poem to the death of Philip IV in 1665 suggests that one of the original sources was compiled after that date: but it is also possible that the later amanuensis miscopied the reference to the King, confusing Philip IV with Philip III.

APPENDIX IV

SOME OF MENDOZA'S MOST POPULAR POEMS, AS JUDGED BY THEIR APPEARANCE IN MANUSCRIPT AND PRINTED COLLECTIONS

1. *A Cintia he visto, pastores* (*MOP*, II, 94)
   1. BNM *MS* 17678, f. 41.
   2. Palacio *MS* 2802, f. 23.
   3. *PMS*, p. 391.
   4. *Fénix castellano* MS.

2. *Afuera que Mariflo-res* (*MOP*, I, 197)
   1. BNM *MS* 17678, f. 22.
   2. Palacio *MS* 2802, f. 139.
   3. *PMS*, p. 192.
   4. *Fénix castellano* MS.

3. *Afuera que una mu-chacha* (*MOP*, II, 85)
   1. Palacio *MS* 2802, f. 19.
   2. *PMS*, twice, with different variants, p. 311 and p. 385.
   3. *Fénix castellano* MS.

4. *Compitiendo con las selvas* (*MOP*, I, 196)
   1. BNM *MS* 17678, f. 11.
   2. *PMS*, p. 189.
   3. *Fénix castellano* MS.
   4. *Romances varios. De differentes authores* (Amsterdam, 1688), p. 38.
   5. Alfay collection, ed. J. M. Blecua, p. 108.
   6. BNM *MS* 4103 (The Valentín de Céspedes collection), p. 231. See also Gallardo, *Ensayo*, II, No. 1803 for this MS.
   7. Often used by Calderón (see Wilson and Sage, p. 24).

5. *Con sus trapos Ine-silla* (*MOP*, I, 176)
   1. BNM *MS* 3795, f. 312, without attribution.
   2. BNM *MS* 3700, f. 65ᵛ.
   3. *PMS*, p. 86.
   4. *Fénix castellano* MS.
   5. *Primavera y flor* (1636), ed. Montesinos, p. 221.

6. *Romances varios. De diversos autores* (Zaragoza, 1640), p. 89. J. M. Hill in *Poesías germanescas*, No. CVI, also gives the variants in the Madrid, 1655, and Madrid, 1664 editions.

6. *Desdicha, hermosu-*   1. BNM *MS* 3672, f. 437.
    ra, y novio (MOP,   2. BNM *MS* 3796, f. 367ᵛ.
    I, 157)   3. Biblioteca de Luis Valdés, *MS de Varios*, "Romance de Quevedo."
                             4. Palacio *MS* 2802, f. 105ᵛ.
                             5. *PMS*, p. 276.
                             6. *Fénix castellano* MS.
                             7. Alfay collection, p. 7, attribution to Mendoza.
                             8. Hisp. Soc. Am. *MS* B2502, f. 27ᵛ (see *Hisp. Am. Cat.*, No. XX, vol. I, 143), attribution to Mendoza.

7. *El alba Marica* (also   1. BNM *MS* 3795, f. 213, attribution to Mendoza.
    Allá va Marica) [1]   2. BNM *MS* 3922, f. 87ᵛ, attribution to Mendoza.
    (MOP, II, 195)   3. Biblioteca de Luis Valdés, *MS de Varios*, "Romance de Quevedo."
                             4. BNM *MS* 3700, f. 130ᵛ, without attribution.
                             5. *PMS*, p. 288, attribution to Mendoza.
                             6. Hisp. Soc. Am. *MS* B2413, f. 12ᵛ (*Hisp. Am. Cat.*, No. CLXI, vol. II, 250).
                             7. *Cancionero de 1628*, ed. Blecua, p. 287, attribution to Góngora. But a contemporary hand has written below: "De Mendoça."
                             8. Alfay collection, p. 54.
                             9. Gallardo, *Ensayo*, III, 769, attribution to Pedro de Mendoza. The text comes from a Cabildo de Córdoba MS, *Poesías de varios*, f. 93, a seventeenth-century manuscript.

8. *Montañas de Cata-*   1. Palacio *MS* 2802, f. 157.
    luña (MOP, II, 44)   2. *PMS*, p. 109.
                             3. *Fénix castellano* MS.
                             4. *Cancionero poético-musical de 1645*, f. 5ᵛ.
                             5. Used by Calderón (see Wilson and Sage, p. 125).

9. *No corras, arroyo*   1. BNM *MS* 3700, f. 82ᵛ.
    ufano (MOP, II,   2. Hisp. Soc. Am. *MS* B2543, f. 50ᵛ (*Hisp. Am. Cat.*, No. XXXIII, vol. I, 245), anonymous.
    281)

---

[1] This very popular ballad has been attributed to Mendoza, Quevedo, and Góngora. The evidence of the manuscripts supports the attribution to Mendoza: see Francisco de Quevedo, *Obras completas*, I (*Poesía original*), ed. Blecua, p. cxxiii, and Ignacio Aguilera, "Sobre tres romances atribuidos a Quevedo," *Boletín de la Biblioteca Menéndez Pelayo*, XXI (1945), 494-523.

3. Hisp. Soc. Am. *MS* B2413, f. 4 (*Hisp. Am. Cat.*, No. CLXI, vol. II, 249).

4. *Primavera y flor* (1621), ed. Montesinos, p. 104.

10. *Oh qué bien descoge al viento (MOP, II, 128)*
 1. BNM *MS* 17723, f. 29ᵛ.
 2. BNM *MS* 17678, f. 49ᵛ.
 3. Palacio *MS* 2802, f. 8.
 4. *PMS*, p. 333.
 5. *Fénix castellano* MS.
 6. BNM *MS* M1262, *Libro de tonos*, f. 226ᵛ.

11. *Pastores, que me abraso (MOP, I, 180)*
 1. BNM *MS* 2202, f. 135.
 2. BNM *MS* 17678, f. 5.
 3. Palacio *MS* 2802, f. 130ᵛ.
 4. *PMS*, p. 92.
 5. *Fénix castellano* MS.
 6. Alfay collection, p. 87.
 7. Hisp. Soc. Am. *MS* B2502, f. 5ᵛ (*Hisp. Am. Cat.*, No. X, vol. I, 142).
 8. *Cancionero* of Don Joseph del Corral, No. 38 bis.

12. *Pinceles dulces de pluma (MOP, II, 148)*
 1. BNM *MS* 17678, f. 51ᵛ.
 2. Palacio *MS* 2802, f. 12ᵛ.
 3. *PMS*, p. 371.
 4. *Fénix castellano* MS.

13. *Poca tierra y muchas flores (MOP, I, 172)*
 1. *PMS*, p. 5.
 2. *Fénix castellano* MS.
 3. *Primavera y flor* (1621), ed. Montesinos, p. 104.
 4. *Cancionero* of Don Joseph del Corral, No. 2.
 5. Hisp. Soc. Am. *MS* B2413, f. 13ᵛ (*Hisp. Am. Cat.*, No. CLXI, vol. II, 250).

14. *Qué festivo el arroyuelo (MOP, II, 100)*
 1. BNM *MS* 17768, f. 44.
 2. Palacio *MS* 2802, f. 19ᵛ.
 3. *PMS*, p. 331.
 4. *Fénix castellano* MS.
 5. BNM *MS* M1262, *Libro de tonos*, f. 91ᵛ.

15. *Risueña fuentecilla (MOP, II, 36)*
 1. BNM *MS* 17719, f. 245.
 2. Palacio *MS* 2802, f. 156.
 3. *PMS*, p. 127.
 4. *Fénix castellano* MS.

16. *Villana de Leganés (MOP, II, 341)*
 1. Palacio *MS* 2802, f. 24ᵛ.
 2. *Primavera y flor* (1641), ed. Montesinos, p. 238.
 3. BNM *MS* M1262, *Libro de tonos*, f. 185ᵛ.

APPENDIX V

SIR RICHARD FANSHAWE'S TRANSLATIONS OF ANTONIO DE MENDOZA

A volume appeared in London in 1671 containing translations both of Mendoza's *Fiesta que se hizo en Aranjuez,* under the title *Fiestas de Aranjuez: Festivals represented at Aranvvhez before the King and Queen of Spain, In the Year, 1623* ...; and also of his "Dramatick Romance," under the title *Querer Por Solo Querer: To Love only for Love Sake* ... The translator's name is given simply as Sir R. F., an abbreviation for Sir Richard Fanshawe, diplomat and translator, who in the latter guise had rendered into English Guarini's *Pastor Fido* and Camoens's *Lusiads.* Sir Richard had revealed his identity in an opening poem (f. A2):

> Time was when I, a Pilgrim of the Seas,
> When I, 'midst noise of Camps, and Courts Dis-ease,
> Purloin'd some Hours, to Charm rude Cares with Verse,
> Which flame of FAITHFUL SHEPHERD did rehearse:
> But now restrain'd from Sea, from Camp, from Court,
> And by a Tempest blown into a Port,
> I raise my Thoughts to Muze on Higher Things,
> And Eccho Arms and Loves of Queens and Kings.

Fanshawe here refers to the strange circumstances in which presumably both the Mendoza translations were penned. An ardent Royalist he served Prince Charles (later King Charles II) after Charles I's execution. Fanshawe later followed Charles to the Battle of Worcester (1651), where the Royalist attempt to overthrow Cromwell failed. Fanshawe was taken prisoner and put in gaol, only to be released later on bail. He eventually accepted Lord Strafford's offer of asylum at Tankersley Park in South Yorkshire, in the vicinity of Barnsley. Tankersley Hall no longer stands, having been demolished apparently as early as the seventeenth century. It was here that *Querer por solo querer* was translated. The date, as the title-page of the translation of the play shows, was 1654. The two works would only appear posthumously.

Fanshawe's contacts with Spain were spread over a long period of years: indeed, he died in Madrid in 1666, having spent the last two years of his life as Ambassador to the Spanish Court. He had been in Madrid too in 1650, on a secret mission from Prince Charles, but it is more likely that Fanshawe's admiration for Mendoza went back to an earlier time, for he first visited Madrid in 1628, and then spent the years 1635 to 1638 there as secretary to the English Ambassador, Lord Aston.

Fanshawe on the title-page referred to his translation as a paraphrase, a fairer description, for though he sometimes followed his original closely, he more often took liberties with the text. The quality of the rendering varies considerably, though at many points the translator has been singularly successful in carrying the *conceptos* over into the English version. Perhaps the most inspired rendering is his version of the sonnet "Brama el mar de los aires ofendido" (*MOP*, II, 191):

> Lash'd by the Winds, the Ocean raves, and craves
> To be a Star, and not an Element:
> The Winds cry Freedom from their horrid Caves,
> Not clogs of Mountains can their scape prevent.
> The Mountains crack; the crouded Air upheaves
> The Pillars of the Rocking Firmament:
> For none, to that which smart or loss receives,
> Forbids a sigh, a tear, or a lament.
> I only (a dead mark of Fortune's spight)
> Stand on the highest pinacle of Grief
> Firm as a Diamond, silent as Night.
> O Smart well disciplin'd, without Relief
> For a poor Lover to support his woe!
> So much a sorrow doth to custom owe.   (pp. 127-128)

[On Fanshawe, see *DNB*, and the introduction to Sir Richard Fanshawe, *Shorter Poems and Translations*, ed. N.W. Bawcutt (Liverpool, 1964). This volume includes a number of examples of his translations from seventeenth-century Spanish poetry.]

LIST OF MANUSCRIPTS AND BOOKS

I

ANTONIO DE MENDOZA: A SELECT LIST OF WORKS

MANUSCRIPTS[1]

(other than individual plays)

Real Academia de la Historia *MS* 12-2-2, *B-101, Discurso sobre los Grandes i Titulos de Castilla. Por Don Antonio de Mendoza, Comendador de Zurita en la Orden de Calatraua, Señor de la Villa de Villar del Olmo y Casa de Coalla en Madrid, de la Camara del Rey Felipe 4, su Secretario de ella y dela Santa y General Inquisicion,* ff. 1-32 [On f. 32ᵛ we have the following note: "Este papel le hizo Don Antonio de Mendoza, secretario de la Camara del Rey Phelipe quarto de España. Copiele de su original que me entrego el Dr. don francisco de Aloyciga su deudo, que estaua en su cassa, en cuyo poder entraron los mas papeles que tenía." According to the Library Catalogue the *Discurso* is also found in BNM *MS* 3071, a copy of the *Nobiliario* of Francisco de Mendoza (see below). The confusion may have been due to the similarity of the names, and of the titles.]

BNM *MS* 3991, *Tomo de varios, Nº 12,* ff. 140-145, *Papel que se escriuió al Señor Conde Duque Persuadiéndole que no permitiesse que escribiese en su Vida Don Juan de Vera. De Don Antonio de Mendoça.* [Other manuscript copies may be found in BNM *MS* 10858, ff. 3-8; BNM *MS* 7371, ff. 63-65; and Bibliothèque Nationale, Paris, *MS Espagnol* No. 422, *Mélanges historiques et littéraires. XVI siècle* (sic). *II,* ff. 6-12. See also below my "Una carta inédita".]

Biblioteca de Palacio *MS* IX/4637, *Varias fortunas de don Antonio Hurtado de Mendoza,* ff. 1-98. [The assumption has been made in *MOP,* I, xxxiv, that the name in the title is that of the author: it is in fact the name of one of the protagonists. The work, of doubtful interpretation, may be a satire on Antonio de Mendoza and the Count-Duke of Olivares.]

British Museum, *Eg. MS* 338, ff. 172-202ᵛ, *Las Señas del S. Infante Don Carlos que esté en el Zielo.* The title leaf bears the signature of Don Antonio Hurtado de Mendoza. [This document is a memoir on the life of Prince Charles, brother to Philip IV, who died in 1632.]

British Museum, *Eg. MS* 335, ff. 125-131, *Papel de D.ᵐ Antonio Hurtado de Mendoza de la horden de Calatraba y Comendador de Zurita en ella Sec[reta]rio q[ue] fue de la R[ea]l Camara de Palazio del Señor Rey Dᵐ Felipe Quarto y del Consexo Supremo de Ynquisicion en que expresa lo que es el oficio de Secretario de la R[ea]l Camara y como se debe servir.* [A note

---

[1] This list incorporates for the sake of completeness those manuscripts included in the bibliographical description in *MOP,* I, xvii-xlviii.

at the end (f. 131) indicates that the text must have been written in 1632 or shortly afterwards.]

Bibliothèque Nationale, Paris, *MS Espagnol* No. 418, *Palacio de las Musas y Musas de palacio, en las poesias de D. Antonio Hurtado de Mendoza, Comendador de Zurita de la Orden de Calatrava, Secretario de Camara de su Magestad, y de Justicia en la suprema Inquisicion*, pp. 1-541.

Biblioteca de Palacio *MS 2802, Poesías de Mendoza*, ff. 1-300. [See *MOP*, I, xxxix-xliv.]

Hisp. Soc. Am. *MS HC: 371/224, Varias Poësias a diferentes asump[to]s. Compuestas Por el Discreto de Palacio D.ⁿ Antonio Mendoza*, ff. 1-134. [See *Hisp. Am. Cat.*, No. CLXII, vol. II, 251. This collection is discussed in my forthcoming "A New Manuscript of Poems..."]

BNM *MS 17723, Mendoza. Poesías*, and on f. 1, *Obras de don Hvrtado de Mendoça*, ff. 1-82. [See *MOP*, I, xxxi-xxxii.]

BNM *MS 17678*, ff. 1-53, a collection of Mendoza's poems. [See *MOP*, I, xlv-xlvii.]

Hisp. Soc. Am. *B2412, Obras De Don Antonio de Mendoza*, ff. 1-136. [See *Hisp. Am. Cat.*, No. CLX, vol. II, 248.]

Hisp. Soc. Am. *B2413, Romances de D. Antonio de Mendoza*, ff. 1-14. [See *Hisp. Am. Cat.*, No. CLXI, vol. II, 249.]

The following manuscripts in the Biblioteca Nacional, Madrid, also contain significant poetic material by Mendoza: 3773, 3700, 3795, 3797, 2376, 2244, 3991, 4144, 5913, 3892, 4101, 17522, 3912, 17719, 12971, 3672, and 3657 (see *MOP*, I, xxxiv-xlviii, *passim*). Also BNM *MS 3890, Poesías varias*, f. 118, BNM *MS 3922, Parnaso español. 14*, ff. 87-90, and in Francisco de Quevedo, *Obra poética*, ed. J. M. Blecua, I (Madrid, 1969), pp. 3-38, section on MSS.

Vida de Nuestra Señora MSS.

BNM *MS 6700, El maior romance. escribiolo Don Antonio Hurt[a]do de Mendoza Secretario de Phelipe quarto el Grande Dirigiendole a Maria Santissima Nuestra Señora Conceuida sin mancha de pecado original desde el primer instante de su ser natural*, ff. 1-174. [See *MOP*, I, xxix.]

Biblioteca de Palacio *MS 1506, La Vida de Nvestra S[eño]ra Escripta por Don Antonio Hurtado de Mendoza Secretario de Camara de su Mag[esta]d. En Barcelona, el año de M.DC.LIII*, ff. 1-60 [See *MOP*, I, xxix-xxx.]

Hisp. Soc. Am. *MS B2414, Vida de Nuestra Señora que en un romance escrivia Don Antonio de Mendoça*, ff. 1-103. [See *Hisp. Am. Cat.*, No. CLIX, vol. II, 246.]

Bodleian *MS Add. A. 137*, ff. 163-215, *Obra posthuma, Vida de N[uest]ra Señora Por D. Antonio Hurtado de Mendoça ... Sacala a Luz D. Antonio de Salcedo Hurt[ad]o de Mendoça, Marques de Legarda, su Sobrino. Año de 1666.*

BNM *MS 2244, Varios enigmas y versos*, f. 279 *et seq.* [See *MOP*, I, xxx.]

BNM *MS 3920, Parnaso español. 10*, f. 27 *et seq.* [See *MOP*, I, xxx.]

BNM *MS 17666, Varias poesias curiosas de diferentes autores*, f. 131 *et seq.* [See *MOP*, I, xxx-xxxi.]

BNM *MS* 3797, *Poesías manuscritas*. 3, f. 71 *et seq.*, *Vida de Nuestra Señora y San José*. [See *MOP*, I, xxxi.]

BNM *MS* 18976, ff. 1-46. — incomplete. [See *MOP*, I, xxxi.]

BNM *MS* 17723, *Mendoza. Poesías*, ff. 44-82 — incomplete. [See *MOP*, I, xxxi.]

The Bodleian Library, Oxford, *MS Add.* A. 151, ff. 79-83, *Vida de la virgen nuestra señora compuesta por Don Antonio de Mendoça* — incomplete.

Hisp. Soc. Am. *MS B2505, Cancionero*, ff. 11ᵛ-21, *Vida de Nuestra señora scrita por D. Antonio de Mendoza* — incomplete. [See *Hisp. Am. Cat.*, No. XXIII, vol. I, 152.]

Hisp. Soc. Am. *MS B2412, Obras De Don Antonio De Mendoza*, f. 120 *et seq.*, *Vida De Nvestra Senora Por D. Antonio de Mendoza* — incomplete. [See *Hisp. Am. Cat.*, No. CLX, vol. II, 248.]

Hisp. Soc. Am. *MS HC 411, 27, Varias poesías manuscritas*, ff. 80 bis-105, *Romançe de la vida de n[uest]ra Señora Por Don Antonio de Mendoca* — incomplete? [See *Hisp. Am. Cat.*, No. XXV, vol. I, 162.]

PRINTED WORKS

(other than individual plays)

Fiesta que se hizo en Aranjuez a los años del Rey Nuestro Señor D. Felipe IIII. Escrita por D. Antonio de Mendoça (Madrid, 1623). [*Querer por solo querer* (see below) appeared in the same volume. The prose *relación* has been reproduced by C.V. Aubrun in his "Les Débuts du drame lyrique en Espagne," pp. 436-442 (see below).]

Fiestas de Aranjuez: Festivals represented at Aranvvhez before the King and Queen of Spain, In the Year, 1623. To Celebrate The Birth-Day of that King, Philip IV. Written in Spanish by Don Antonio de Mendoza (London, 1670). [This work, separately paginated, appeared in the same volume as the translation of *Querer por solo querer* (see below). For a discussion of these translations, see Appendix V.]

Convocación de las Cortes de Castilla, y Iuramento del Principe nuestro señor, Don Baltasar Carlos, Primero deste nombre, Año de 1632 (Madrid, 1632).

Convocación de las Cortes de Castilla y Iuramento del Principe nuestro Señor D. Baltasar Carlos, Primero deste nombre, Año 1632. Escriviola por orden desu Magestad D. Antonio Hurtado de Mendoça ... Al Excelentíssimo Señor El Conde Duque (Madrid, 1665).

Convocación de las Cortes de Castilla, y Juramento del Príncipe, N[uestro] Señor, Don Balthasar Carlos, Primero de este nombre. Año de 1632. Escribiòla, por orden de su Magestad, Don Antonio Hurtado de Mendoza, Secretario de su Camara, y del Consejo de la Suprema y General Inquisicion, Cavallero del Habito de Calatrava y Comendador de Zurita. ... Reimpresso en Madrid, por Joachin Ibarra, 1760 (Madrid, 1760).

Ceremonial que se observa en España para el juramento de príncipe hereditario ... (Madrid, 1789).

Ceremonial observado en España para el Juramento del Príncipe Heredero, según se verificó en 1632 en la época de los monarcas austríacos, según relación escrita de orden de S.M., Por el Secretario de la Cámara D. Antonio Hurtado de Mendoza (on p. 1), but with the original title of 1632 on p. 3, in *Noticia del ceremonial antiguo para el juramento del Principe de Asturias y para los bautismos de personas reales* (Madrid, 1850). [The editors in an *advertencia* explain why they are publishing three descriptions of the ceremony attending the birth, baptism, etc. of an heir to the throne. One is the *Convocación,* the second the *jura* of the Prince of Asturias in 1789, the third the royal baptisms of 1817. The present occasion, not made quite explicit, is the awaited arrival of a child to Queen Isabel.]

Vida de Nuestra Señora

Vida de Nuestra Señora. Que en vn Romance escriuia Don Antonio Hurtado de Mendoza, Comendador de Zurita, de la Orden de Calatraua, Secretario de Camara de su Magestad, y de Iusticia en la Suprema Inquisicion. Sacale a luz D. Antonio de Salcedo Hurtado de Mendoza, Marques de Legarda, sobrino de el Autor (Seuilla, 1666). [See *MOP,* I, xx-xxi. The 1666 edition is reproduced in *MOP,* I, 43-141.]

Vida de Nuestra Señora, que en vn romance escrivia Don Antonio Hvrtado de Mendoza, Comendador de Zurita, de la Orden de Calatrava, Secretario de Camara de su Magestad, y de Justicia en la Suprema Inquisicion. Al Senor D. Francisco Calderon y Romero, Oydor de la Real Audiencia, y Chacilleria (sic) *de Mexico* (Mexico, 1668). [See *MOP,* I, xxi-xxii, and José Toribio Medina, *La imprenta en México (1539-1821),* Santiago de Chile, 1907-11, II, 410, No. 996.]

Vida de Nuestra Señora, in *Delicias de Apolo. Recreaciones del Parnaso ...* (Zaragoza, 1670), pp. 1-45.

Vida de Nuestra Señora María Santíssima de Don Antonio de Mendoza Comendador de Zurita de la Orden de Calatraua Secretario de Camara del Rey Filipe Quarto, y de Iusticia en la Suprema Inquisicion. Obra póstuma, Que sale à gozar repetidos aplausos de la turquesa de mas legitimos, y correctos Originales. Consagrada al Excelentissimo Señor D. Antonio Pedro Álvarez, Ossorio, Gómez, Dávila, y Toledo, Marques de Astorga, de Velada, y San Roman, Conde de Trastamara ... (Nápoles, Por Iuan Francisco Paz, 1672). [On ff. a3-a7 there is a dedication to the Marquis by his Chaplain, Juan Antonio García; on ff. a7^{v}-a8, an *aprobación* by P.F. Niceforo Sebasto, of the Order of the *Ermitaños de San Agustín,* dated Naples, 5 August 1671. The *aprobación* says that the *Vida* "muchas veces es merecedora de auerse impresso, especialmente en la Ciudad de Seuilla, donde se imprimiò" (f. a7^{v}), and expresses the hope that "nuestra Italia logre de las elegantes, y espirituales fatigas de tan docto, erudito, y eminente Autor en todas las facultades" (f. a8). British Museum copy, shelfmark: 11451 aaa 27.]

Vida de Nuestra Señora María Santíssima de Don Antonio de Mendoza Comendador de Zurita de la Orden de Calatraua Secretario de Camara del Rey Filipe Quarto, y de Iusticia en la Suprema Inquisicion. Obra póstuma, Que sale à gozar repetidos aplausos de la turquesa de mas legitimos, y correctos Originales. Consagrada al Ilustriss[imo] y Reuerendiss[imo] Señor Don Ioan Montero de Espinosa, Prior de la Real de Bari, Señor de las Villas de Rutillano, y San Nicandro, &. (Nápoles, Por Iuan Francisco Paz, 1672). [The dedication on the title-page shows this to be a different edition from the volume above. The formal dedication (ff. a3-a4^{v}), again to Ioan

Montero, is by Fr. Ioan Antonio García, of the *Convento de Carmelitas Españoles de Napoles*, dated 15 October 1672. Fr. Ioan wrote (f. a3): "La recomendacion, que traen consigo las obras del Autor, motiuò mi deseo à leer este Romance, y lo que començò curiosidad, acabò en admiracion. No poca me causò el saber, que de diez mil tomos (aunque faltos, y llenos de errores) que se imprimieron en Seuilla quatro años ha, no se hallauan." [See *MOP*, I, xx, and xxii-xxiv. Biblioteca Nacional, Madrid, copies, shelf-marks: R-13221 and 3-64810.]

Vida de Nuestra Señora, que en un romance escriviò Don Antonio Hurtado de Mendoza, Comendador de Zurita de la Orden de Calatrava, Secretario de Camara de su Magestad, y de Iusticia en la Suprema Inquisicion. Aora nuevamente Añadida. A la protección, y amparo de mi Señora Doña Manuela Carnizer Sanez de Villanueva, Señora del lugar de Miana en el Reyno de Aragon (Madrid, 1682). [The author of the additions — now 804 stanzas instead of 786 — is D. Joseph Carios Garcés y de la Sierra. See *MOP*, I, xxiv.]

Vida de Nuestra Señora. Escriviala Don Antonio Hurtado de Mendoza. Continuábala Don Agustín López de Reta. Y añade dos romances, a Christo en el Sacramento, y à Christo en la Cruz. Y una Parafrasis del Padre Nuestro. Dedicala a la muy ilustre Señora Doña Leonor de Arbizu, y Ayanz (Pamplona, 1688). [The author of the additions is Agustín López de Reta, who also claims to have restored to the text "su genuina pureza, sacada de exemplares mas limados, que alcançò la curiosidad diligente de mi amigo D. Luys (Lopez Cerain)", quot. in *Motivos de esta impression*. See *MOP*, I, xxiv-xxviii. Biblioteca Nacional, Madrid, copy, shelf-mark: R-7459.]

Other appearances of the *Vida de Nuestra Señora* include: *El Fénix castellano* (1690) [see below], pp. 141-180; Antonio de Bordazar, *Vida* "Aora nuevamente añadida y enmendada" (Valencia, 1710) [see Salvá, I, 249 and *MOP*, I, xxviii]; J. Mareli, *Vida* (Milan, 1723) [see Salvá, I, 249 and *MOP*, I, xxviii]; *Obras líricas y cómicas* (1728) [see below], pp. 1-92.

Obras poéticas

El Fénix castellano, D. Antonio de Mendoça, Renascido de la gran Bibliotheca d'el Ilustrissimo Señor Luis de Sousa, Arçobispo de Lisboa, Capellan Mayor, del Consejo de Estado d'el Serenissimo Rey de Portugal Don Pedro II. A la excelentissima Señora D. Mariana de Sousa Marquesa de Arronches, Condessa de Miranda, & c. (Lisboa, 1690).

Obras líricas, y cómicas, divinas, y humanas, con la celestial ambrosìa del admirable poema sacro de María Santíssima, último suave divimo (sic) *aliento de aquel canoro Cisne, el mas pulido, mas asseado, y el mas Cortesano Cultor de las Musas Castellanas. D. Antonio Hurtado de Mendoza, Comendador de Zurita, del Orden de Calatrava, Secretario de Camara, y de Justicia de la Magestad del Rey Don Phelipe IV. en la Suprema Inquisicion. Segunda impression, corregidas, y enmendadas de los muchos yerros que en la primera havia cometido el descuido de la Imprenta. Añadidas algunas obras, que segun la Bibliotheca de Nicolas Antonio refiere, se tienen por ciertas, y verdaderas del Autor. Dirigidas por mano de Don Ambrosio Cano al Ex[celentísi]mo Señor Don Juan Bautista Centurion Ursino Arias Fernandez de Cordova Mendoza Carrillo y Albornoz, hijo Primogenito del*

Ex[celentísi]mo Señor Marques de Estepa, y Almuña, &c. (Madrid, no date). [The *aprobación* is dated 1728, the *tassa* November 1728. *MOP*, I, xxxiii-xxxiv, alludes to the exaggerated claims made for the correctness of this edition. The major addition is *Cada loco con su tema* (pp. 421-464), and the *Miser Palomo* interlude (pp. 465-474).]

Obras poéticas, ed. Rafael Benítez Claros (Madrid, 1947-8), 3 vols.

G.A. Davies, "Antonio Hurtado de Mendoza — Poemas y fragmentos inéditos," *Boletín de la Biblioteca de Menéndez Pelayo,* XXXIII (1957), 21-38.

Discursos de Don Antonio de Mendoza, secretario de cámara de Don Felipe IV. Publícalos con una introducción y notas el Marqués de Alcedo, académico correspondiente de la Historia (Madrid, 1911).

ENTREMESES AND COMEDIAS [1]

(Manuscript copies and early appearances in print)

1. *El entremés de Miser Palomo*

A. *El Ingenioso entremes d'El Examinador Miser Palomo, compuesto por Don Antonio de Mendoza, gentil-hombre del Conde de Saldaña, y representado en esta ciudad de Valencia por Sancho de Paz, en este año de 1618* (Valencia, 1618). [See Gallardo, *Ensayo*, III, 745, No. 3039. He prints the editor's note: "Lo que me ha obligado a imprimir este ingenioso Entremes ha sido el saber que en diez y nueve veces que lo he representado en esta ciudad, muchos a quien no he querido dar traslado dél, lo han ido sacando, ya de *memoria* o ya escribiéndolo, mientras yo lo representaba. Y por parecerme que no le podian haber copiado tan cabal, que no tuviese algunos versos ménos y muchos no cabales, he querido que salga el verdadero original a volver por sí, y a manifestar su autor; cuyo ingenio es digno de perpetua alabanza."]

B. *El ingenioso entremés del examinador Miser Palomo. Compuesto por don Antonio de Mendoza Gentil hombre del Conde de Saldaña. Impresso con licencia en Valladolid, en casa de Francisco Fernandez de Cordoua, Año de 1619* (Valladolid, 1619). [This *suelto* is numbered 16 in a bound collection of *entremeses*, British Museum shelf-mark: 11726 aa 1, 1-41.]

C. *El ingenioso entremés del examinador Miser Palomo, compuesto por don Antonio de Mendoza, Gentilhombre del conde de Saldaña* (Valencia, 1620). [See Salvá, *Catálogo*, I, 454, and Cotarelo, *Colección de entremeses (I)*, 322.]

D. F. J. de Velasco published a *suelto* edition (see La Barrera, *Catálogo*, p. 634). [No year or place is indicated, but the printer seems the one responsible for the 1646 and 1647 editions of *El Doctor Dieta* (see below). See also Joaquín Montaner, *La colección teatral de Don Arturo Sedó*, p. 135, which gives Cádiz, 1647.]

E. In *Obras líricas* (1728), pp. 465-474.

---

[1] The works appear here in the order presented in my "A Chronology," that is approximately the order in which they were written.

2. *Segunda parte de Miser Palomo*, or *El Doctor Dieta*

A. BNM MS 3922, *Parnaso Español 14*, ff. 105-113ᵛ, *Entremes del medico de espiritu segunda parte de Miçer Palomo, figuras, el medico, dos cortesanos, la desamorada, su tio, el Vano, el maldiçiente, la leyda, su marido, el poeta, el amigo de flacas, el q[ue] todo lo sabe, la firme, el criado del medico, la ama, y musicos.*

B. *Segunda parte del entremés de Miser Palomo y Médico de espíritu, compuesto por don Antonio de Mendoza, Gentilhombre del Conde de Saldaña* (Valencia, 1628). [See Salvá, *Catálogo*, I, 454, Cotarelo, *Entremeses (I)*, p. 327, and Montaner, op. cit., p. 100. The Catalogue of the Biblioteca Nacional, Madrid, refers to a copy, but I have failed to trace it. The reference to Mendoza as "Gentilhombre del Conde de Saldaña" suggests an original edition after March 1619, and before 1621.]

C. *Entremés famoso del Doctor Dieta. Por Don Antonio de Mendoza* (n. p., no date). [Biblioteca Nacional, Madrid, copy, shelf-mark: R-12451. The Catalogue suggests Cádiz, 1646, cf. similar suggestion in Montaner, p. 134, but with alternative date, 1647. The first assumption, if correct, makes this edition identical with D below. This edition contains the episode of the *discreta* and her husband, not found e.g. in B above.]

D. F. J. de Velasco published an edition in Cádiz, 1646 (see La Barrera, *Catálogo*, p. 618). Either this, or E below, is the *Doctor Dieta Entremes Famoso del* referred to by Montaner (p. 134).

E. F. J. de Velasco published another edition, Cádiz, 1647 (see La Barrera, *Catálogo*, p. 618).

3. *Entremés de Getafe*

A. BNM MS 3922, *Parnaso Español 14*, ff. 97-103ᵛ, *Famosso entremes de Getafe, conpuesto por don Atonio* (sic) *de Mendoza*. [This is the text reproduced by Cotarelo in *Entremeses (I)*, pp. 332-335.]

B. *Famoso Entremés de Getafe. Compuesto por D. Antonio de Mendoza* — 1620? [See Montaner, p. 100.]

C. *Entremés de Getafe* (Valladolid, 1621). [The name of the author is not given. British Museum copy, numbered 13 in a bound collection of *entremeses*, shelf-mark: 11726 aa 1, 1-41. The text is gravely defective, and also differs considerably in detail from A above.]

D. *La Villana de Getafe. Y carreteros de Madrid. Entremes Famoso Anónimo* (Cadiz, 1646?) — see Montaner, p. 129.

4. *An unpublished interlude*

Hisp. Soc. Am. MS B2331, ff. 341-346ᵛ, *Entremes de D. Antonio de Mendoza.* [See *Hisp. Am. Cat.*, No. XXVIII, vol. I, 181.]

5. *El premio de la virtud*

A. *El premio de la virtud, y sucessos prodigiosos de D. Pedro Guerrero. Comedia famosa, de Don Antonio de Mendoza* (n. p., no date) [Biblioteca Nacional, Madrid, copy: shelf-mark T-20666.]

B. Medel's *Índice* cites a play with this name, attributing it to Pedro Guerrero. The compiler may, therefore, have been looking at an edition in which Mendoza's name was not given: the confusion with the protagonist's name would thus be more easily explained.

6.   *No hay amor donde hay agravio*

A. *No hay fe donde hay oprobio ni amor donde hay agravio,* MS in Sedó collection (see Montaner, p. 48).

B. *Comedia famosa No ay amor donde ay agravio: De don Antonio de Mendoça,* in *Flor de las mejores doze Comedias de los mayores Ingenios de Espana* (Madrid, 1652), f. 25 [=D1] — f. 42ᵛ [=F2ᵛ].

C. *No ay amor donde ay agravio, Comedia famosa de Don Antonio de Mendoza* (Zaragoza, 1674).

D. In *El Fénix castellano,* pp. 181-217.

E. In *Obras líricas,* pp. 261-297.

F. Medel's *Índice* attributes this title to Gaspar Saravia y Mendoza. An edition may possibly exist with such an attribution.

7.   *Más merece quien más ama*

A. Without attribution in *Doze comedias nuevas de Lope de Vega Carpio, y otros autores. Segunda parte* (Barcelona, 1630), f. 2 *et seq.* [This is a composite volume of *sueltos* already in print, as the variety of signatures indicates. But *Más merece,* which comes directly after the volume's title-page (f. 1), seems part of the 1630 printing, and might be the play's original appearance in print. See also La Barrera, *Catálogo,* p. 707.]

B. *Comedia famosa, Más merece, quien más ama. De Don Antonio de Mendoza, y de Don Iuan de Vera y Villarroel,* in *Primavera numerosa de muchas armonías luzientes, en doce comedias fragantes, Parte quarenta y seis, impressas fielmente de los borradores de los mas célebres plausibles ingenios de España* (Madrid, 1679), f. 197ᵛ [= Bb5ᵛ] — f. 213ᵛ [=Ee1ᵛ]. [The final lines of the *comedia* run: "Y para el grande Mendoza/ oy D. Iuan de Vera os pide/ aplauso, pues le merece,/ y a él perdón, que se os rinde." Vera y Villarroel, not born until the thirties of the seventeenth century, could hardly have collaborated in writing the play: he was presumably just presenting it.]

C. In *El Fénix castellano,* pp. 297-340.

D. In *Obras líricas,* pp. 377-420.

8.   *Querer por solo querer*

A. BNM *MS* 3661, f. 1 *et seq., Comedia famosa, Querer por solo querer, De D. Antonio de Mendoza. Fiesta que se represento en el Real Palacio de su Magestad.*

B. A manuscript copy of *Querer por solo querer* is in the possession of The Dolphin Book Co. Ltd., Oxford. The volume, unfoliated and lacking a title-page, consists of 51 folios. It is in a seventeenth-century hand. The text diverges both from that of the 1623 printed edition, and from that of the *Fénix castellano:* its filiation is probably different from both.

C. BM *Harleian MS* 3386, *La Gran Comedia de querer por solo querer de Don Antonio de Mendoça*, ff. 1-131. [The title-page is on f. 1, and leads straight into the text of the play. The dedication is missing. The MS is in a seventeenth-century hand.]

D. BM *Add. MS* 32133, *To Love only to Love*. [The manuscript lacks a title-page, so that there is no indication of the title of the work, or its authorship. The spine of a recent binding, however, bears the words: *Sir R. Fanshawe. To Love only to Love,* an identification borne out by the contents. There are 78 folios.]

E. The Bodleian Library, Oxford, *MS Add. A.* 151, ff. 108-130, ACTO PRIMERO DE *querer por solo querer* DE DON ANTONIO DE MENDOZA: (the words in capitals have been added to the original title and are in a different ink). [The text gives the whole of the first act with certain omissions, and part of the second, as far as "por la puerta de una ofensa". On f. 108 the following note occurs: "esta comedia copié en el año 1663, que no estava impresa y no se hallava manuscrita. despues se ha impreso en el año 1669 en Madrid. está en el libro intitulado: Minerva comica q[ue] haze la parte treinta y una" — see H below.]

F. *Querer por solo querer, comedia que representaron las Señoras meninas, a los años de la Reyna Nuestra Senora. Escriuiola D. Antonio de Mendoça* (Madrid, 1623). [This appeared in the same volume as *Fiesta que se hizo en Aranjuez* (1623) — see above.]

G. *Querer por solo querer. Comedia que representaron las Señoras meninas a los años de la Reyna nuestra Señora. Escrivióla Don Antonio de Mendoça* (Lisboa, 1639). [British Museum copy, shelf-mark: 11726 bbb 1.]

H. *Comedia famosa. Querer por solo querer. De Don Antonio de Mendoza,* in *Parte treinta y una de comedias nuevas, escritas por los mejores ingenios de España* (Madrid, 1669), pp. 1-72.

I. *Querer Por Solo Querer: To Love only for Love Sake: A Dramatick Romance. Represented at Aranjuez before the King and Queen of Spain, To celebrate The Birth-day of that King, by the Meninas ... Written in Spanish by Don Antonio de Mendoza, 1623. Paraphrased in English, Anno 1654. Together with the Festivals of Aranwhez* (London, 1671). [The translation of the play had been printed privately by William Godbid in 1670, when it appeared in a volume bearing the title *Fiestas de Aranjuez: Festivals represented at Aranvvhez before the King and Queen of Spain ...* The text of the play directly followed, even though the title-page made no reference to it. In 1671 the same title-page was used again, still bearing the 1670 date. It was introduced, this time in the appropriate place, before the text of the *Relación,* being inserted between signatures Y4 and Z1. A copy of the rare 1670 text of the play forms part of the Grenville collection, British Museum shelf-mark, G. 11507.]

J. In *El Fénix castellano*, pp. 341-425.

K. In *Obras líricas*, pp. 177-260.

9.   *Cada loco con su tema* or *El Montañés indiano*

A. BNM *MS Res.* 93, *Comedia autógrafa en tres jornadas titulada Cada loco con su tema de Don Antonio de Mendoza. Madrid 30 de agosto de 1830* (corrected to 1630), the text beginning on f. 6. The play is foliated by *jornada*, thus: I, ff. 1-18; II, ff. 1-17; III, ff. 1-18. At the end of the play (III, f. 18) the following note occurs: "Laus Deo, en Madrid, a 29 de agosto de 1630. Don Antonio de Mendoça (signature)." Underneath, in a different hand, is written a *licencia* to perform the play in Valencia: "no tiene esta comedia cosa contra/ la fe ni contra las buenas costumbres. pareçeme que muy bien/ se le puede dar licencia al autor para que se repre/sente: enpredicadores (sic) de Valencia, mayo 6 de 1631/ el Pre[benda]do fr Phelipe de Salazar/ calificador del S[an]to off[ici]o".

B. In *Obras líricas*, pp. 421-464. [In the table of contents there is added to the title "y el Montañés Indiano". I know of no printed version earlier than this of 1728. The play seems to have lain in manuscript until then.]

10. *El marido hace mujer* or *El trato muda costumbre*

A. BM *Add. MS 10334, Comedias Españolas. Vol. III*, f. 1-51ᵛ, *La famosa comedia del marido hace mujer conpuesta por don antᵒ de mendoza. año de 1692.*

B. *El marido haze muger*, in *Parte treynta de comedias famosas de Varios Autores* (Çaragoça, 1636), p. 255 [= Q8ᵛ] — p. 290 [= T1ᵛ]. [H. A. Rennert, in "Notes on some *Comedias* of Lope de Vega," *MLR*, I (1906), p. 101, Note, referred to a play of this title in vol. XXX of a collection of *Diferentes* (Huesca, 1636).]

C. *El trato muda costumbres* (sic), in *Comedias de Lope de Vega, Parte veinte y ocho* (Zaragoza, 1639) — see La Barrera, *Catálogo*, p. 683. [The play is attributed to Lope. Rennert, in his "Notes," pp. 101-102, raises doubts about the existence and identity of Part XXVIII, pointing out that the sole authority for these rests with the testimony of Faxardo's *Índice*. See also my "A Chronology."]

D. *Comedia famosa. El trato muda costumbre. De D. Antonio de Mendoza*, in *Primera parte de comedias escogidas de los mejores de España* (Madrid, 1652), ff. 223ᵛ-241ᵛ.

E. *El trato muda costumbre*, in *El Fénix castellano*, pp. 218-253.

F. *El marido hace muger, y el trato muda costumbre*, in *Obras líricas*, pp. 298-333.

G. *Comedia famosa, El trato muda costumbre. De Don Antonio de Mendoça* (n.p., no date). [This *suelto*, foliated 1-18, bears "Num. 119" on f. 1. Two Biblioteca Nacional, Madrid, copies, shelf-marks: T-6435 and T-14838, the latter being a volume of *Comedias de varios autores* of which this play forms part.]

H. *Comedia famosa, El trato muda costumbre. De Don Antonio de Mendoza*, unfoliated [signatures: A1-D3], no date, but colophon [D3ᵛ] states: "Impressa en Valladolid, Imprenta de Alonso del Riego". [This *suelto* is numbered 14 in a bound collection of plays, British Museum shelf-mark: 11728 h 11, 1-14.]

I. Faxardo's *Índice* alludes to two *suelto* editions, in Valencia, and Madrid, the latter at the house of León.

11. *Los empeños del mentir*

A. *Comedia famosa de los empeños del mentir. De don Antonio de Mendoça,*
   in *Flor de las mejores doze Comedias de los mayores Ingenios de Espana*
   (Madrid, 1652), f. 43 [=F3] — f. 84 [=H8].
B. In *El Fénix castellano,* pp. 254-296.
C. In *Obras líricas,* pp. 334-376.

12. *El galán sin dama*

A. *El galán sin dama,* MS in Sedó collection (see Montaner, p. 48).
B. *Comedia famosa. El galán sin dama,* without attribution, in *El mejor de los
   mejores libro que ha salido de Comedias nuevas* (Alcalá, 1651), pp. 170-
   206. [On f. 5^v of the preliminaries there is a separate list of the *ingenios*
   in the volume, including "D. Antonio de Mendoza, el Galan sin dama." A
   second edition, under the imprint of María de Quiñones, appeared in Madrid in 1653 — see La Barrera, *Catálogo,* p. 709.]
C. Faxardo's *Índice* refers to a play of this title, attributed to Calderón, in
   Part VI of *Varios:* by the latter, Faxardo usually meant the series *Comedias
   escogidas de los mejores ingenios de España* (1652-1704). In fact *El galán*
   does not appear in Part VI — see La Barrera, *Catálogo,* p. 689.
D. Faxardo referred to a number of *suelto* editions, attributed to Calderón,
   published in Valencia, Seville, and Madrid (at the house of León).
E. *Comedia famosa, El galán sin dama. De Don Pedro Calderón de la Barca*
   (n.p., no date). [Salvá (I, 605), noting in his collection an edition attributed
   to Calderón, refers to the play's rejection by Vera Tassis, Calderón's editor.
   See Pedro Calderón de la Barca, *Primera parte de comedias verdaderas,*
   ed. Juan de Vera Tassis y Villarroel (Madrid, 1726), in prelims., "Tabla
   de las comedias verdaderas de Don Pedro Calderón."]

13. *Celos sin saber de quien*

Zelos sin saber de quien, Comedia famosa de don Antonio de Mendoza (n.p.,
no date), ff. 1-16. [British Museum copy, shelf-mark: 11728 c 78. The
Catalogue, without giving reasons, suggests Madrid? and 1700? for this
suelto.]

14. *Los riesgos que tiene un coche* or *Lo que es un coche en Madrid*

A. *Lo que es un coche en Madrid,* attributed to Lope in *Partes extravagantes,
   Comedias de Lope de Vega Carpio, Parte veinte y seis* (Zaragoza, 1645), a
   reprint of an original edition of 1632-33. [See La Barrera, *Catálogo,* p. 682.
   But H. A. Rennert (in "Bibliography... of Lope de Vega," *RH,* XXXIII
   (1915), 34-35 and 40, as well as in "Notes on some *Comedias* of Lope de
   Vega," *MLR,* I (1906), 98-100) questioned the authoritativeness of these
   assertions, though he was prepared to accept them on the basis of cor-
   roborative evidence. The matter is discussed more fully in my "A Chronology".]

B. *Los riesgos que tiene un coche. Comedia famosa de D. Antonio de Mendoza,* in *Laurel de comedias. Quarta parte de diferentes autores. Dirigidas a Don Bernardino Biancalana* (Madrid, 1653), ff. 116-136.

C. *Comedia famosa. Los riesgos que tiene un coche. De Don Antonio de Mendoza* (n.p., no date), signatures: A1-E1ᵛ.

D. *Comedia famosa. Los riesgos que tiene un coche. De Don Antonio de Mendoza* (Madrid, 1750), signatures: A1-E2ᵛ. [British Museum copy, along with other plays, in vol. V of *Colección de Comedias sueltas con algunos Autos y Entremeses de los mejores ingenios de España, desde Lope de Vega hasta Cornella, hecha y ordenada por I. R. C.* (= J. R. Chorley), shelf-mark: 11728 h 11, 1-14.]

E. *Lo que es un coche en Madrid. Comedia famosa de Lope de Vega Carpio* (n.p., no date), ff. 1-18ᵛ. [British Museum copy, no. 14 of a volume of *sueltos,* shelf-mark: 11728 h 10, 1-22.]

F. *Comedia famosa. Los riesgos que tiene un coche. De Don Antonio de Mendoza* (Valencia, 1792), pp. 1-34.

G. Faxardo's *Índice* notes a *suelto* edition attributed to Calderón. And Medel's *Índice* mentions two plays entitled *Los riesgos que tiene un coche,* attributing one to Calderón, and the other to Mendoza.

II

GENERAL WORKS

MANUSCRIPTS

Archivo Histórico Nacional

(a) Calatrava. *Pruebas de Caballeros, legajo* 1255: *Hurtado de Mendoza y de la Rea, Antonio,* 1623.
Pruebas de Caballeros (Casamientos), legajo 17, No. 500: *Ocón Coalla de Pineda, Clara,* 1631.

(b) Santiago. *Pruebas de Caballeros, legajo* 917 — 3998: *Hurtado, Bernardino,* 1622. [Brother of Antonio de Mendoza.]
Pruebas de Caballeros, legajo 917 — 3991: *Hurtado, Juan,* 1629. [First cousin of Antonio de Mendoza.]

(c) Alcántara. *Pruebas de Caballeros, legajo* 934: *Mendoza y Briceño, Jerónimo de,* 1628. [Son of Antonio de Mendoza and Doña Luisa.]
Pruebas de Caballeros, legajo 1082: *Ocón y Coalla, José Antonio de,* 1633. [Son of Antonio de Mendoza and Doña Clara.]

(d) Inquisición. *Inquisición, legajo* 1185, No. 20: *Hurtado de Mendoza Rea, Antonio, y su mujer, Briceño de la Cueva y Figueroa, Luisa,* 1620. [The date is incorrect: it should read 1625. This is an inquiry into the *genealogía y limpieza* of Mendoza and his first wife before the granting of his appointment as official of the Holy Office.]
Inquisición: Consejo Supremo: Personal, juramentos prestados por empleados, Book I (No. 1338), for period 1574-1635.

(e) Títulos del Reino. *Títulos del Reino: Sección de Consejos Suprimidos, legajo 4735, No. 21, Doña Clara Ocón, viuda de Don Antonio Hurtado de Mendoça,* 8 March 1645. [This is an attempt to press for a decision over an earlier request for a title for the family, made in a *memorial* of 28 September 1644.]

Archivo de Simancas

Archivo de Simancas, *Quitación de Cortes,* 8°: *Antonio Hurtado de Mendoza,* 24 November 1641. [His nomination to the Secretaryship of the *Cámara de Justicia.*] And at Zaragoza, 24 July 1643 [grant for an increase in salary].

Archivo de Palacio

Legajo 9079 — M. 57: Mendoza, D. Antonio de, Ayuda de la Guardarropa de S. M., Ayuda de Cámara de S. M., Secretario de S. M., 1621, and 1628.

Legajo 8962 — I. 4: Infantado, Duque del, Mayordomo Mayor de S. M., Caballerizo Mayor de S. M., 1621.

Legajo 8956 — H. 19: Hurtado de Salcedo y Mendoça, Antonio, 1642.

Cuentas del Secretario de la Cámara, legajo 6764 (1621-1638). The accounts for 1621 and 1622 have disappeared. [See also Shergold and Varey, "Some Palace Performances" below.]

Legajo 666: Comedias (1622-1626).

Archivo de Protocolos

Legajo 2034, Escribano, Santiago Fernández, 1623, ff. 345-346. [Mendoza's first marriage: *Poder* for marriage by proxy.]

Real Academia de la Historia

Papeles variados de Jesuitas, vols. XCIII, CXI, CXIX, CXXIX, CXXXII, CXLVI, and CLIII. [Some of the letters in this collection have been published: see *Cartas de algunos padres* below.]

Biblioteca Nacional, Madrid

Diario de lo sucedido en Madrid entres (sic) *años de 636, 637 y 638 por semanas y dias,* in BNM MS 6746, ff. 1-281.

FAXARDO, JUAN ISIDRO. *Índice de todas las comedias impresas hasta el año de 1716,* BNM MS 14706, ff. 1-61.

LEÓN PINELO, ANTONIO DE. *Annales o historia de Madrid de el nacimiento de Cristo Señor Nuestro hasta el año de 1658,* BNM MS 1764, ff. 1-379.

MENDOZA, FRANCISCO DE. *Nobiliario de los Grandes y Títulos de España,* BNM MS 11459, ff. 1-486.

Sucesos del año 1623, BNM MS 2354, ff. 1-388.

Sucesos del año 1627, BNM MS 2359, ff. 1-169.

Sucesos del año 1637, BNM MS 2368, not properly foliated. [A collection of miscellaneous items, manuscript and printed.]

TAMAYO DE VARGAS, TOMÁS. *Junta de libros, la maior que España ha visto en su lengua hasta el año de MDCXXIV*, BNM MS 9752, paginated 1-258, and MS 9753, foliated 1-100.

British Museum, London

BM *Eg*. MS 335, f. 317ᵛ, 12 March 1623, the granting by the King of *merced* of the Royal Secretaryship to Antonio Hurtado de Mendoza.

PRINTED WORKS

ACADEMIA BURLESCA. *Academia burlesca en buen retiro a la Magestad de Philippo Quarto el Grande (Manuscrito. Madrid, 1637)*, ed. J. M. Blecua, in *Libros raros de poesía de los siglos XVI y XVII* (Valencia, 1952).

AGUILAR, JUAN BAUTISTA DE (ed.). *Varias hermosas flores del Parnaso* (Valencia, 1680).

AGUILAR Y PRADO, JACINTO. *Co[m]pendio histórico de diversos escritos* (Pamplona, 1629).

AGUILERA, IGNACIO. "Sobre tres romances atribuidos a Quevedo," *Boletín de la Biblioteca de Menéndez Pelayo*, XXI (1945), 494-523.

ALABASTER, WILLIAM. *The Sonnets of William Alabaster*, ed. G. M. Story and Helen Gardner (Oxford, 1959).

ALARCOS, EMILIO. "Los sermones de Paravicino," *RFE*, XXIV (1937), 162-197, and 249-319.

ALCEDO, LE MARQUIS D'. *Olivares et l'alliance anglaise* (Bayonne, 1905).

ALENDA Y MIRA, JENARO. *Relaciones de solemnidades y fiestas públicas de España* (Madrid, 1903).

ALFAY, JOSÉ (ed.). *Poesías varias de grandes ingenios españoles* [Zaragoça, 1654], ed. J. M. B[lecua], (Zaragoza, 1946).

ALMANSA Y MENDOZA, ANDRÉS DE. *Cartas de Andrés de Almansa y Mendoza, Novedades de esta corte y avisos recibidos de otras partes, 1621-1626*, in *Colección de libros españoles raros y curiosos*, vol. XVII (Madrid, 1886).

ALONSO, DÁMASO. *La lengua poética de Góngora (parte primera, corregida)* [Madrid, 1950].

———. *La poesía de San Juan de la Cruz: Desde esta ladera* (Madrid, 1942).

ALONSO CORTÉS, NARCISO. *La muerte del Conde de Villamediana* (Valladolid, 1928).

———. *Noticias de una corte literaria* (Valladolid, 1906).

ÁLVAREZ DE COLMENAR, JUAN. *Les Délices de l'Espagne et du Portugal* (Leide, 1707), 5 vols.

ANGLÉS, HIGINIO, AND SUBIRÁ, JOSÉ. *Catálogo musical de la Biblioteca Nacional de Madrid, I (Manuscritos)*, [Barcelona, 1946].

ÁNGULO Y PULGAR, MARTÍN. *Epístolas satisfatorias* (Granada, 1635).

ANTOLOGÍA DEL ENTREMÉS. *Antología del entremés (Desde Lope de Rueda hasta Antonio de Zamora): siglos XVI y XVII*, ed. Felicidad Buendía (Madrid, 1965).

ANTONIO, NICOLÁS. *Bibliotheca Hispana Nova* (ed. Matriti, 1783-8), 2 vols.

ARCADIA DE ENTREMESES. *Arcadia de entremeses. Escritos por los ingenios mas clasicos de España* (Madrid, 1723).

ARGENSOLA, LUPERCIO AND BARTOLOMÉ LEONARDO DE. *Rimas*, ed. J. M. Blecua (Zaragoza, 1950-1), 2 vols.

ARIAS PÉREZ, PEDRO (ed.). *Primavera y flor de los mejores romances*, ed. J. F. Montesinos (Valencia, 1954).

ARTIGAS, MIGUEL. *Catálogo de los manuscritos de la Biblioteca Menéndez y Pelayo* (Santander, 1930).

———. *Don Luis de Góngora: Biografía y estudio crítico* (Madrid, 1925).

ASENSIO, EUGENIO. *Itinerario del entremés desde Lope de Rueda a Quiñones de Benavente con cinco entremeses inéditos de D. Francisco de Quevedo* (Madrid, 1965).

ASENSIO, J. M. *Francisco Pacheco, sus obras artísticas y literarias* (Sevilla, 1886).

ASTRANA MARÍN, LUIS. *La vida turbulenta de Quevedo* (Madrid, 1945).

ATKINSON, W. C. "On Aristotle and the Concept of Lyric Poetry in Early Spanish Criticism," in *Estudios dedicados a Menéndez Pidal*, vol. VI (Madrid, 1956), 189-213.

AUBRUN, C. V. "Chansonniers musicaux espagnols du XVIIe siècle," *BH*, LI (1949), 268-290, and LII (1950), 315-374.

———. "Les Débuts du drame lyrique en Espagne," in *Le Lieu théâtral à la Renaissance: Études ... réunies et présentées par Jean Jacquot avec la collaboration d'Élie Konigson et Marcel Oddon* (Paris, 1964), 423-444.

AUERBACH, ERNA. *Tudor Artists: A Study of Painters in the Royal Service and of Portraiture on Illuminated Documents from the Accession of Henry VIII to the Death of Elizabeth I* (London, 1954).

AULNOY, MME D'. *Relation d'un voyage d'Espagne où est exactement décrit l'Estat de la Cour de ce Royaume, & de son gouuernement*, new edn. (Paris, 1668).

BAHNER, WERNER. *La lingüística española del siglo de oro* (Madrid, 1966).

BAL, JESÚS (ed.). *Treinta canciones de Lope de Vega, puestas en música por Guerrero, Orlando de Lasso, Palomares, Romero, Company, etc., y transcritas por Jesús Bal* (Madrid, 1935).

BANCES CANDAMO, FRANCISCO ANTONIO DE. *Theatro de los theatros de los passados y presentes siglos. Prólogo, edición y notas de Duncan W. Moir* (London, 1970).

BARBIERI, FRANCISCO ASENJO. "Lope de Vega, músico," *Gaceta musical barcelonesa*, 27 December 1863 — 13 March 1864, *passim*.

BAROZZI, NICOLÒ, AND BERCHET, GUGLIELMO (ed.). *Relazioni degli stati europei lette al Senato dagli Ambasciatori Veneti nel secolo decimosettimo*, series on *Spagna* (Venezia, 1856-60), 2 vols.

BARRERA Y LEIRADO, CAYETANO DE LA. *Catálogo bibliográfico y biográfico del teatro antiguo español* (Madrid, 1860).

BELMONTE BERMÚDEZ, LUIS DE. *La aurora de Cristo* (Sevilla, 1616).

BENÍTEZ CLAROS, RAFAEL. "Una curiosa *jinojepa* del siglo XVII," *Revista de Bibliografía Nacional,* VII (1946), 355-358.

——. *Vida y poesía de Bocángel* (Madrid, 1950).

BERGMAN, HANNAH E. "'Juan Rana' se retrata," in *Homenaje a Rodríguez-Moñino. Estudios de erudición que le ofrecen sus amigos o discípulos hispanistas norteamericanos,* vol. I (Madrid, 1966), 65-73.

——. *Luis Quiñones de Benavente y sus entremeses* (Madrid, 1965).

BERTAUT, FRANÇOIS. *Journal du voyage d'Espagne fait en l'anne'e mil six cens cinquante neuf* ... [Paris, 1669], in *RH,* XLVII (1919), 1-317.

BOCÁNGEL Y UNZUETA, GABRIEL. *Obras,* ed. R. Benítez Claros (Madrid, 1946), 2 vols.

BODENSTEDT, SISTER MARY IMMACULATE. *The Vita Christi of Ludolphus the Carthusian* (Washington, 1944).

BONILLA, ALONSO DE. *Glossas a la Inmaculada Concepción* (Sevilla, 1615).

——. *Nombres y atributos de la impecable siempre virgen María* (Baeça, 1624).

——. *Nuevos conceptos espirituales* (Baeça, 1615).

BORJA, FRANCISCO DE, PRÍNCIPE DE ESQUILACHE. *Obras diuinas, y humanas en verso* (Madrid, 1648).

BOURCIEZ, ÉDOUARD. *Les Moeurs polies et la littérature de cour sous Henri II* (Paris, 1886).

BOURDEILLE, PIERRE DE. *See* BRANTÔME, PIERRE.

BOUVIER, RENÉ. *Philippe IV et Marie d'Agréda. Confidences royales* (Paris and Limoges, 1939).

BRANDI, KARL. *The Emperor Charles V: The Growth and Destiny of a Man and of a World-Empire,* trans. C. V. Wedgwood, 2nd impression (London, 1949).

BRANTÔME, PIERRE. *Œuvres complètes,* ed. L. Lalanne (Paris, 1864-82), 11 vols.

BRUNEL, ANTOINE DE. *Voyage d'Espagne curieux, historique et politique. Fait en l'année 1655* [Paris, 1665], in *RH,* XXX (1914), 119-375.

BUXTON, EDWARD JOHN MAWBY. *Elizabethan Taste* (London, 1963).

CALDERÓN DE LA BARCA, PEDRO. *Comedias,* ed. Juan Eugenio Hartzenbusch, in *BAE,* vols. VII, IX, XII, and XIV.

CAMARGO, P. IGNACIO DE. *Discurso theológico sobre los theatros, y comedias de este siglo* ... (Salamanca, 1689).

CÁNCER Y VELASCO, JERÓNIMO DE. *Obras varias* (Madrid, 1651).

CANCIONERO. *Cancionero antequerano. 1627-1628,* ed. Dámaso Alonso and Rafael Ferreres (Madrid, 1950).

——. *Cancionero castellano del siglo XV,* ed. R. Foulché-Delbosc (Madrid, 1912-15), 2 vols.

——. *Cancionero de 1628, Edición y estudio del Cancionero 250-2 de la Biblioteca universitaria de Zaragoza,* ed. J. M. Blecua (Madrid, 1945).

——. *Cancionero de Nuestra Señora en el qual ay muy buenos romances, canciones y villancicos (1591),* ed. Antonio Pérez Gómez (Valencia, 1952).

——. *Cancionero de romances impreso en Amberes sin año,* ed. R. Menéndez Pidal (Madrid, 1945).

CANCIONERO. *Cancionero general*, ed. A. Rodríguez-Moñino (Madrid, 1958). See also *Suplemento ... que contiene todas las poesías que no figuran en la primera edición y fueron añadidas desde 1514 hasta 1557* (Valencia, 1959).

CÁNOVAS DEL CASTILLO, ANTONIO. *Estudios del reinado de Felipe IV* (Madrid, 1888-9), 2 vols.

——. *Historia de la decadencia de España* (Madrid, 1910).

CARDUCHO, LUIGI. *Diálogos de la pintura entre maestro y discípulo* (Madrid, 1629).

CARRARA, ENRICO. *La poesia pastorale* (Milano, 1909).

CARTAS JESUITAS. *Cartas de algunos padres de la Compañía de Jesús sobre los sucesos de la monarquía entre los años de 1634 y 1648*, in *Memorial histórico español* (Madrid, 1851-1918), vols. XIII-XIX.

CARVAJAL Y ROBLES, RODRIGO DE. *Fiestas de Lima por el nacimiento del Príncipe Baltasar Carlos* [Lima, 1632], ed. Francisco López Estrada (Sevilla, 1950).

CASCALES, FRANCISCO. *Cartas filológicas*, ed. Clás. Cast. (Madrid, 1930-41), 3 vols.

CASTELLO, ALBERTO. *Rosario della gloriosa vergine Maria* (Venezia, 1522).

CASTIGLIONE, BALTASAR. *El Cortesano*, trans. Juan Boscán, Austral, 2nd edn. (Buenos Aires, 1946).

CASTILLO SOLÓRZANO, ALONSO DE. *Donayres del Parnaso* (Madrid, 1624).

——. *Donayres del Parnaso. Segunda parte* (Madrid, 1625).

——. *Jornadas alegres* (Madrid, 1626).

——. *Las harpías en Madrid y coche de las estafas* (Barcelona, 1633).

——. *Tardes entretenidas* (Madrid, 1625).

——. *Tiempo de regozijo y Carnestolendas de Madrid* (Madrid, 1627).

CASTRO, AMÉRICO. *El pensamiento de Cervantes* (Madrid, 1925).

CASTRO Y ANAYA, PEDRO. *Auroras de Diana* (Madrid, 1631).

CASTRO Y BELLVIS, GUILLÉN DE. *Obras*, ed. E. Juliá Martínez (Madrid, 1925-7), 3 vols.

CEJADOR Y FRAUCA, JULIO. *La verdadera poesía castellana. Floresta de la antigua lírica popular* (Madrid, 1921-4), 5 vols.

CERVANTES, MIGUEL DE. *Obras completas*, ed. Rudolph Schevill and Adolfo Bonilla (Madrid, 1914-41), 18 vols.

——. *Obras completas*, ed. Aguilar (Madrid, 1962).

CIOCCHINI, HECTOR. *Góngora y la tradición de los emblemas* (Bahía Blanca, Cuadernos del Sur, 1960).

CLARAMONTE, ANDRÉS DE. *Letanía moral* (Sevilla, 1613).

CLARÉTIE, LÉO. *Lesage romancier, d'après de nouveaux documents* (Paris, 1890).

CLARKE, DOROTHY CLOTELLE. *A Chronological Sketch of Castilian Versification together with a List of its Metric Terms* (Berkeley, California, 1952).

——. "A Note on the *décima* or *espinela*," *HR*, VI (1938), 155-158.

——. "Sobre la *espinela*," *RFE*, XXIII (1936), 293-304.

Coe, Ada M. *Catálogo bibliográfico y crítico de las comedias anunciadas en los periódicos de Madrid desde 1661 hasta 1819*, The Johns Hopkins Studies in Romance Literature and Languages, IX (Baltimore, Md., 1935).

Collard, Andrée. *Nueva poesía: conceptismo, culteranismo en la crítica española* (Madrid, 1967).

Corral, Gabriel del. *La Cintia de Aranjuez, prosas y versos* (Madrid, 1629).

Correa Calderón, E. "Gracián y la oratoria barroca," in *Strenae. Estudios de filología e historia dedicados al Profesor Manuel García Blanco* (Salamanca, 1962), 131-138.

Cossío, José María de. *Fábulas mitológicas en España* (Madrid, 1952).

——. *Notas y estudios de crítica literaria. Poesía española. Notas de asedio* (Madrid, 1936).

——. *Notas y estudios de crítica literaria. Siglo XVII.* ... (Madrid, 1939).

Coster, François. *Libellus Sodalitatis: Hoc est Christianarum Institutionum Libri quinque, In gratiam Sodalitatis B. Virginis Mariae* (Antuerpiae, 1588).

Cotarelo y Mori, Emilio. *Bibliografía de las controversias sobre la licitud del teatro en España* (Madrid, 1904).

——. *Catálogo descriptivo de la gran colección de "Comedias Escogidas" que consta de cuarenta y ocho volúmenes, impresos de 1652 a 1704*, in *Bol. Ac. Esp.*, XVIII (1931), 232-280, 418-468, 583-636, 772-826, and XIX (1932), 161-218.

——. *Colección de entremeses, loas, bailes, jácaras y mojigangas* (Madrid, 1911), 2 vols., in *NBAE*, vols. XVII and XVIII.

——. *Don Francisco de Rojas Zorrilla: Noticias biográficas y bibliográficas* (Madrid, 1911).

——. *Don Juan de Espina: Noticias de este célebre y enigmático personaje* (Madrid, 1908).

——. "Dramáticos españoles del siglo XVII: Álvaro Cubillo de Aragón," *Bol. Ac. Esp.*, V (1918), 1-23, 241-280.

——. *El Conde de Villamediana — estudio biográfico-crítico* (Madrid, 1886).

——. *Iriarte y su época* (Madrid, 1897).

——. "Luis Vélez de Guevara y sus obras dramáticas," *Bol. Ac. Esp.*, III (1916), 621-652, and IV (1917), 137-171, 269-308, and 414-444.

Cotarelo Valledor, Armando. "El teatro de Quevedo," *Bol. Ac. Esp.*, XXIV (1945), 41-104.

Covarrubias Orozco, Sebastián de. *Emblemas morales* (Madrid, 1610).

Crane, T. F. *Italian Social Customs of the Sixteenth Century and their Influence on the Literatures of Europe* (New Haven, Conn., 1920).

Crashaw, Richard. *The Poems English Latin and Greek of Richard Crashaw*, ed. L. C. Martin, 2nd edn. reprinted (Oxford, 1966).

Croll, Maurice W. "Attic Prose in the Seventeenth Century," *Studies in Philology*, XVIII (1921), 79-128.

——. "Juste Lipse et le mouvement anticicéronien à la fin du XVIe et au début du XVIIe siècle," *Revue du Seizième Siècle*, II (1914), 200-242.

CROLL, MAURICE W. "The Baroque Style in Prose," in *Studies in English Philology: A Miscellany in Honor of Frederick Klaeber,* ed. K. Malone and M.B. Rund (Minneapolis, Minn., 1929), 427-456.

CROSBY, JAMES O. "A New Edition of Quevedo's Poetry," *HR,* XXXIV (1966), 328-337.

——. *En torno a la poesía de Quevedo* (Madrid, 1967).

——. "Quevedo and the Court of Philip III: Neglected Satirical Letters and New Biographical Data," *PMLA,* LXXI (1956), 1117-1126.

CUBILLO DE ARAGÓN, ÁLVARO. *Las muñecas de Marcela, El señor de Noches Buenas,* ed. A. Valbuena Prat (Madrid, 1928).

——. *El enano de las Musas. Comedias, y obras diversas* (Madrid, 1654).

CURTIUS, ERNST ROBERT. *European Literature and the Latin Middle Ages,* trans. Willard R. Trask (London, 1953).

——. "Mittelalterlicher und Barocker Dichtungstil," *MPh,* XXXVIII (1941), 325-333.

DANIÉLOU, JEAN. *From Shadows to Reality: Studies in the Biblical Typology of the Fathers,* trans. Dom Wulstan Hibberd (London, 1960).

DARBORD, MICHEL. *La Poésie religieuse espagnole des Rois Catholiques à Philippe II* (Paris, 1965).

DAVIES, G. A. "Antonio Hurtado de Mendoza: Biographical Notes," *BHS,* XXXIV (1957), 79-88.

——. "Una carta inédita de Antonio Hurtado de Mendoza al Conde-Duque de Olivares," *His,* XIX (1959), 82-91.

——. "A Chronology of Antonio de Mendoza's Plays," to appear in *BHS,* XLVIII (1971), p. 97 *et seq.*

DELEITO Y PIÑUELA, JOSÉ. *El declinar de la monarquía* (Madrid, 1947).

——. *El Rey se divierte* (Madrid, 1935).

——. *La mala vida en España* (Madrid, 1948).

——. *Sólo Madrid es corte* (Madrid, 1942).

——. *También se divierte el pueblo* (Madrid, 1944).

DELICIAS DE APOLO. *Delicias de Apolo. Recreaciones del Parnaso ... Hechas de varias poesías de los Mejores Ingenios de España* (Zaragoza, 1670).

DICCIONARIO. *Diccionario de la lengua castellana. Compuesto por la Real Academia Española* (Madrid, 1726-39), 6 vols.

DIXON, VICTOR. "Apuntes sobre la vida y obra de Jerónimo de Villaizán y Garcés," *Hispanófila,* XIII (1961), 5-22.

——. "Juan Pérez de Montalbán's *Para Todos,*" *HR,* XXXII (1964), 35-59.

DONNE, JOHN. *The Divine Poems,* ed. Helen Gardner (Oxford, 1952).

DRAMÁTICOS CONTEMPORÁNEOS. *Dramáticos contemporáneos a Lope de Vega,* ed. R. Mesonero Romanos, 2 vols., in *BAE,* vols. XLIII and XLV.

DUQUE DE ESTRADA, DIEGO. *Comentarios del desengañado ó sea Vida de D. Diego Duque de Estrada escrita por él mismo,* in *Memorial histórico español* (Madrid, 1851-1918), vol. XII.

EDELMAN, NATHAN. *Attitudes of Seventeenth-Century France toward the Middle Ages* (New York, 1946).

ELIOT, T. S. *Selected Essays,* 2nd edn., reprinted (London, 1945).

ELISIO, BALTASAR. *Limpia concepción de la Virgen Señora Nuestra* (Madrid, 1618).

ELLIOTT, J. H. *Imperial Spain 1469-1716* (London, 1963).

——. *The Revolt of the Catalans: A Study in the Decline of Spain (1598-1640)* (Cambridge, 1963).

ENRÍQUEZ GÓMEZ, ANTONIO. *Sansón Nazareno. Poema heroico* (Ruán, 1656).

ENTRAMBASAGUAS, JOAQUÍN DE. *Estudios sobre Lope de Vega* (Madrid, 1946-58), 3 vols.

——. "Un olvidado poema de Vélez de Guevara," *Revista de Bibliografía Nacional,* II (1941), 91-176.

——. *Vida de Lope de Vega* (Madrid, 1942).

ESCUDERO Y PEROSSO, FRANCISCO. *Tipografía hispalense* (Madrid, 1894).

ESPINEL, VICENTE. *Diversas rimas,* ed. Dorothy Clotelle Clarke (New York, 1956).

ESPINOSA, PEDRO DE. *Obras,* ed. Francisco Rodríguez Marín (Madrid, 1909).

ESQUILACHE, PRÍNCIPE DE. *See* BORJA, FRANCISCO DE.

ESSEN, ALFRED VAN DER. *Le Cardinal-Infant et la politique européenne de l'Espagne 1609-1641,* vol. I *(1609-34),* [Bruxelles, 1944].

ESTEVE BARBA, FRANCISCO. *Catálogo de la colección Borbón-Lorenzana* (Madrid, 1942).

FARIA Y SOUSA, MANUEL. *Fuente de Aganipe o rimas varias* (Madrid, 1644-6).

——. *Muerte de Jesús. Llanto de María* (Madrid, 1624).

——. *Noches claras* (Madrid, 1624).

FERNÁNDEZ-GUERRA Y ORBE, LUIS. *Juan Ruiz de Alarcón y Mendoza* (Madrid, 1871).

FLOR DE ENTREMESES. *Flor de entremeses y sainetes de diferentes autores (1657),* 2nd edn., ed. M. Menéndez Pelayo (Madrid, 1903).

FLORESTA ESPAÑOLA. *Floresta española de apotegmas, ó sentencias, sabia y graciosamente dichas, de algunos Españoles: Recogidas Por Melchor de Santa Cruz* (edn. Madrid, 1777).

FORSTER, L. W. *The Icy Fire* (Cambridge, 1969).

FREEMAN, ROSEMARY. *English Emblem Books* (London, 1948).

GALLARDO, BARTOLOMÉ JOSÉ. *Ensayo de una biblioteca española de libros raros y curiosos* (Madrid, 1863-89), 4 vols.

GARCÍA CARRAFA, ALBERTO AND ARTURO. *Diccionario heráldico y genealógico de apellidos españoles y americanos* (Madrid, 1919-47), 62 vols.

GARCÍA DE LA HUERTA, VICENTE. *Theatro español ... Catálogo alphabético de las comedias, tragedias, autos, zarzuelas, entremeses, y otras obras correspondientes al theatro español* (Madrid, 1785).

GARCÍA MERCADAL, J. *España vista por los extranjeros* (Madrid, no date), 3 vols.

GARCILASO DE LA VEGA. *Obras de Garci Lasso de la Vega con anotaciones de Fernando de Herrera* (Sevilla, 1580).

GERBI, ANTONELLO. "Diego de León Pinelo contra Justo Lipsio," in *Fénix* (Lima), II (1945), 188-231, and 601-612.

GERHARDT, MIA. *La Pastorale: Essai d'analyse littéraire* (Assen, 1950).

GIULIAN, ANTHONY A. *Martial and the Epigram in Spain in the Sixteenth and Seventeenth Centuries* (Philadelphia, 1930).

GOLDSCHMIDT, E. PH. *Medieval Texts and their First Appearance in Print* (London, 1943).

GÓNGORA Y ARGOTE, LUIS DE. *Obras completas,* ed. Juan and Isabel Millé y Giménez (Madrid, 1943).

——. *Obras de Don Luis de Góngora Comentadas,* ed. García de Salcedo Coronel (Madrid, 1636-44), 3 vols.

——. *Obras poéticas,* ed. R. Foulché-Delbosc (New York, 1921), 3 vols.

——. *Soledades de D. Luis de Góngora Comentadas,* followed by *El Polifemo de Don Luis de Góngora Comentado,* ed. García Salcedo Coronel (Madrid, 1628).

GONZÁLEZ PALENCIA, ÁNGEL (ed.). *La Junta de Reformación. Documentos procedentes del archivo histórico nacional y del general de Simancas (1618-1625),* [Valladolid, 1932].

——. "Noticias biográficas del Virrey poeta, Príncipe de Esquilache (1571?-1658)," *Anuario de Estudios Americanos,* VI (1949), 73-160.

GRACIÁN, BALTASAR. *Obras completas,* ed. Arturo del Hoyo (Madrid, 1960).

——. *El Criticón,* ed. M. Romera-Navarro (Philadelphia, 1938-40), 3 vols.

GRACIÁN DANTISCO, LUCAS. *Galateo Español. De lo que se deue hazer, y guardar en la comun conuersacion para ser bien quisto y amado de las gentes* (ed. Barcelona, 1595).

GREEN, OTIS H. *Courtly Love in Quevedo* (Boulder, Colorado, 1952).

——. "On the 'Coplas castellanas' in the *Siglo de Oro*: Chronological Notes," in *Homenaje a Rodríguez-Moñino. Estudios de erudición que le ofrecen sus amigos o discípulos hispanistas norteamericanos,* vol. I (Madrid, 1966), 213-219.

——. "Se acicalaron los auditorios: An Aspect of the Spanish Literary Baroque," *HR,* XXVII (1959), 413-422.

——. *Spain and the Western Tradition* (Madison, Wisc., 1963-6), 4 vols.

GUAZZO, STEFANO. *The Civile Conversation of M. Steeven Guazzo,* trans. George Pettie and ed. Edward Sullivan (London, 1925), 2 vols.

GUTIÉRREZ CORONEL, DIEGO. *Historia genealógica de la casa de Mendoza,* ed. Ángel González Palencia (Madrid, 1946).

HAFTER, MONROE Z. *Gracián and Perfection: Spanish Moralists of the Seventeenth Century* (Cambridge, Mass., 1966).

HALEY, GEORGE. *Vicente Espinel and Marcos de Obregón. A Life and its Literary Representation* (Providence, R. I., 1959).

HATZFELD, HELMUT. "A Clarification of the Baroque Problem in Romance Literatures," *Comparative Literature,* I (1949), 113-139.

HAUTEROCHE, MONSIEUR DE. *Les Œuvres de théâtre de Monsieur de Hauteroche* (ed. Paris, 1736), 3 vols.

HENNESY, JOHN POPE-. *The Portrait in the Renaissance*: The A. W. Mellon *Lectures in the Fine Arts. 1963*, No. 12 of Bollingen Series XXXV (New York, 1966).

HERRERA, PEDRO DE. *Descripción de la Capilla de N[uestr]a S[eñor]a del Sagrario que erigió en la S[an]ta Iglesia de Toledo el Ill[ustrísi]mo S[eñ]or Cardenal D. Bernardo de Sandoual y Rojas, Arçob[is]po de Toledo* (Madrid, 1617).

——. *Translacion del Santissimo Sacramento a la Iglesia Colegial de San Pedro de la villa de Lerma; con la Solenidad, y Fiestas, que tuuo para celebrarla el Excellentissimo Señor don Francisco Gomez de Sandoual y Roxas* (Madrid, 1618).

HERRERO GARCÍA, MIGUEL. "Génesis de la figura del donaire," *RFE*, XXV (1941), 46-78.

——. *Ideas de los españoles del siglo XVII*, revised edn. (Madrid, 1966).

——. *La vida española del siglo XVII* (Madrid, 1933).

——. *Madrid en el teatro* (Madrid, 1963).

HESSE, EVERETT W. "Court References in Calderón's *Zarzuelas*," *HR*, XV (1947), 365-377.

HILL, JOHN M. *Poesías germanescas* (Bloomington, Indiana, 1945).

HOWELL, JAMES. *Epistolae Ho-elianae: The Familiar Letters of James Howell*, ed. Joseph Jacobs (London, 1892), 2 vols.

HUIZINGA, JOHAN. *The Waning of the Middle Ages* (London, 1952).

HUME, MARTIN. *Spanish Influence on English Literature* (London, 1905).

——. *The Court of Philip IV. Spain in Decadence*, new edn. (London, no date).

HYMA, ALBERT. *The Christian Renaissance: A History of the "Devotio Moderna,"* 2nd edn. (Hamden, Conn., 1965).

INSERNI, FRANK M. *Vida y obra de Jerónimo de Villaizán* (Barcelona, 1960).

JÁUREGUI, JUAN DE. *Discurso poético* (Madrid, 1624).

JIMÉNEZ PATÓN, BARTOLOMÉ. *Mercurius Trimegistus, sive de triplici eloquentia sacra Española, Romana* (n. p., 1621).

JONCH, E. DE. "Erotica in Vogelperspectief. De dubbelzinnigheid van een reeks 17de eeuwse genrevoorstellingen," *Simiolus*, III (1969), 22-74.

JOVER, JOSÉ MARÍA. *1635: Historia de una polémica y semblanza de una generación* (Madrid, 1949).

JUDERÍAS, JULIÁN. *Don Francisco de Quevedo y Villegas: la época, el hombre, las doctrinas* (Madrid, 1922).

KENNEDY, RUTH LEE. "*Escarramán* and Glimpses of the Spanish Court in 1637-38," *HR*, IX (1941), 110-136.

KING, WILLARD F. *Prosa novelística y academias literarias en el siglo XVII* (Madrid, 1963).

KINKAID, WILLIAM A. *Life and Works of Luis de Belmonte Bermúdez (1587?-1650?)*, in *RH*, LXXIV (1928), 1-260.

LANDO, ORTENSIO. *Quatro libri de dubbi con le solutioni a ciascun dubbio accommodate* (Venezia, 1552).

LAPESA, RAFAEL. *Trayectoria poética de Garcilaso* (Madrid, 1948).

——. "Poesía de cancionero y poesía italianizante," in *Strenae. Estudios de filología e historia dedicados al Profesor Manuel García Blanco* (Salamanca, 1962), 259-279.

LATHUILLERE, ROGER. *La Préciosité. Étude historique et linguistique*, vol. I (*Position du problème - les origines*), [Genève, 1966].

LAYNA SERRANO, FRANCISCO. *Castillos de Guadalajara* (Madrid, 1933).

LEA, K. M. *Italian Popular Comedy. A Study in the Commedia dell'arte, 1560-1620, with Special Reference to the English Stage* (Oxford, 1934).

LEDESMA, ALONSO DE. *Conceptos espirituales* (edn. Madrid, 1602).

——. *Epigramas y Hieroglificos a la vida de Cristo* (Madrid, 1625).

——. *Juegos de Noche Buena moralizados a la vida de Christo, martirio de Santos, y reformacion de costumbres. Con unas enigmas hechas para honesta recreacion* (Madrid, 1611).

——. *Romancero y monstro imaginado* (Lerida, 1616).

——. *Segunda parte de los conceptos Espirituales, y Morales. Compuesta por Alonso De Ledesma, natural de Segouia* (Barcelona, 1607).

LEFRANC, ABEL. *Grands Écrivains de la Renaissance* (Paris, 1914).

LEISHMAN, J. B. "Donne and Seventeenth-Century Poetry," in *Seventeenth-Century English Poetry: Modern Essays in Criticism*, ed. W. R. Keast (New York, 1962).

LEÓN, LUIS DE. *The Original Poems*, ed. Edward Sarmiento (Manchester, 1953).

LINTILHAC, EUGENE. *Histoire générale du théâtre en France* (Paris, 1904-11), 5 vols.

——. *Lesage* (Paris, 1893).

LIÑÁN DE RIAZA, PEDRO. *Rimas* (Zaragoza, 1876).

LOARTE, GASPAR. *Instruction and Advertisements, How to Meditate the Misteries of the Rosarie of the most holy Virgin Mary. Written in Italian by the Reuerend Father Gaspar Loarte D. of Diuinitie of the Societie of Jesus. And newly translated into English* (n. p., no date). [The British Museum Catalogue suggests Rouen?, 1600?]

——. *Meditationes de Rosario Beatae Virginis* (Venezia, 1573).

LÓPEZ, DIEGO. *Declaración magistral sobre las emblemas de Andres Alciato con todas las Historias, Antiguedades, Moralidad, y Doctrina tocante a las buenas costumbres* (Najera, 1615).

LÓPEZ DE VEGA, ANTONIO. *Heraclito i Democrito de nvestro siglo* (Madrid, 1641).

——. *Paradoxas racionales*, ed. Erasmo Buceta (Madrid, 1935).

LORENZ, CHARLOTTE M. "Seventeenth-Century Plays in Madrid from 1808-18," *HR*, VI (1938), 324-331.

LUDOLPH OF SAXONY. *Vita Jesu Christi e quattuor evangeliis et scriptoribus orthodoxis concinnata per Ludolphum de Saxonia ex ordine Carthusianorum* (Parisiis et Romae, 1865).

LUZÁN, IGNACIO DE. *La poetica, ó reglas de la poesia en general, y de sus principales especies* (ed. Madrid, 1789), 2 vols. [The earlier edition (Zaragoza, 1737) is virtually a different work, though it bears the same title.]

MAGENDIE, MAURICE. *La Politesse mondaine et les théories de l'honnêteté, en France, au XVIIe siècle, de 1600 à 1660* (Paris, 1925), 2 vols.

——. *Le Roman français au XVIIe siècle de l'"Astrée" au "Grand Cyrus"* (Paris, 1932).

MALE, ÉMILE. *The Gothic Image: Religious Art in France of the Thirteenth Century*, trans. Dora Thussey (London, The Fontana Library, 1961).

MALVEZZI, VIRGILIO. *Historia de los primeros años del reinado de Felipe IV*, ed. D. L. Shaw (London, 1968).

——. *Sucesos principales de la Monarquía de España en el año de mil seiscientos i treintainueve* (Madrid, 1640).

MANTUANO, EL BACHILLER. See VEJÁMENES LITERARIOS.

MARAÑÓN, GREGORIO. *El Conde Duque de Olivares* (*La pasión de mandar*), revised edn. (Madrid, 1945).

MARAVILLAS DEL PARNASO. *Maravillas del Parnaso y flor de los mejores romances graves, burlescos, y satiricos etc.* (Lisboa, 1637), facsimile edn. by de Vinne Press (New York, 1902).

MARINO, GIAMBATTISTA. *Marino e i Marinisti*, ed. Guido Ferrero (Milano-Napoli, 1954).

MARTINENCHE, E. "Les Sources de *L'École des Maris*," *Revue d'Histoire Littéraire de la France*, V (1898), 110-116.

MARTZ, LOUIS L. *The Poetry of Meditation: A Study in English Religious Literature of the Seventeenth Century*, 2nd edn. (New Haven, Conn., 1962).

MAURA GAMAZO, GABRIEL AND AMEZÚA, AGUSTÍN G. DE. *Fantasías y realidades del viaje a Madrid de la condesa d'Aulnoy* (Madrid, 1943).

MAY, T. E. "An Interpretation of Gracián's *Agudeza y arte de ingenio*," *HR*, XVI (1948), 275-300.

MAZZEO, JOSEPH A. "A Critique of some Modern Theories of Metaphysical Poetry," *MPh*, L (1952-3), 88-96.

——. "A Seventeenth-Century Theory of Metaphysical Poetry," *RR*, XLII (1951), 245-255.

——. "Metaphysical Poetry and the Poetic of Correspondence," *JHI*, XIV (1953), 221-234.

——. "Universal Analogy and the Culture of the Renaissance," *JHI*, XV (1954), 299-304. See also Mazzeo's *Renaissance and Seventeenth-Century Studies* (New York, 1964) for this and earlier essays.

MEDEL DEL CASTILLO, FRANCISCO. *Índice general alfabético de todos los títulos de comedias que se han escrito por varios autores, antiguos y modernos* [Madrid, 1735], in *RH*, LXXV (1929), 144-369.

MEDINA, JOSÉ TORIBIO. *La imprenta en México* (*1539-1821*), [Santiago de Chile, 1907-11], 8 vols.

MEDRANO, SEBASTIÁN FRANCISCO DE. *Favores de las Musas Hechos a Don Sebastian Francisco de Medrano ... Recopilados por Don Alonso de Castillo Solorzano intimo amigo del Auctor* (Milán, 1631).

MELE, E. AND BONILLA, ADOLFO. "Un cancionero del siglo XVII," *Revista de Archivos, Bibliotecas y Museos,* XXIX (1925), 180-216, and 241-261.

MÉNDEZ BEJARANO, MARIO. *Diccionario de escritores, maestros y oradores de Sevilla y su actual provincia* (Sevilla, 1922-5), 3 vols.

MENDOZA, DIEGO DE. *Obras del insigne cavallero Don Diego de Mendoza,* ed. Juan Díaz Hidalgo (Madrid, 1610).

MENDOZA, FRAY ÍÑIGO DE. See RODRÍGUEZ-PUÉRTOLAS, JULIO.

MENDOZA ESCOBAR, ANTONIO DE. *Historia de la Virgen Madre de Dios, María, Poema Heroyco* [Valladolid, 1618], facsimile edn. by Hispanic Society of America (New York, 1903), 2 vols.

MENÉNDEZ PELAYO, MARCELINO. *Historia de las ideas estéticas en España,* ed. Enrique Sánchez Reyes (Santander, 1946-7), 5 vols.

MENÉNDEZ PIDAL, RAMÓN. *Romancero hispánico: (hispano-portugués, americano y sefardí),* [Madrid, 1953], 2 vols.

MESONERO ROMANOS, RAMÓN DE. *Trabajos no coleccionados. Publicados por sus hijos* (Madrid, 1903-5), 2 vols.

MIGAJAS DEL INGENIO. *Migajas del ingenio. Colección rarísima de entremeses, bailes y loas* (Zaragoza, no date), ed. E. Cotarelo y Mori (Madrid, 1908).

MILÁN, LUIS. *Libro intitulado El Cortesano compuesto por D. Luis Milan. Libro de motes de damas y caballeros por el mismo,* in *Colección de libros españoles raros ó curiosos,* vol. VII (Madrid, 1874).

MIROLLO, JAMES V. *The Poet of the Marvelous. Giambattista Marino* (New York, 1963).

MITJANA, RAFAEL. "La Musique en Espagne," in *Encyclopédie de la Musique et Dictionnaire du Conservatoire,* ed. Albert Lavignac, 1ère Partie (*Histoire de la Musique: Espagne-Portugal*), [Paris, 1920], pp. 1913-2351.

MOIR, DUNCAN. "Lope de Vega's *Fuenteovejuna* and the *Emblemas morales* of Sebastián de Covarrubias Horozco (with a few remarks on *El villano en su rincón*)," in *Estudios y ensayos sobre el teatro antiguo hispánico. Homenaje a William L. Fichter,* ed. A. D. Kossoff (Brown University Press).

MONGRÉDIEN, G. *Les Précieux et les précieuses* (Paris, 1939).

MONREAL, JULIO. *Cuadros viejos* (Madrid, 1878).

MONTANER, JOAQUÍN. *La colección teatral de Don Arturo Sedó* (Barcelona, 1951).

MONTEMAYOR, JORGE DE. *Los siete libros de la Diana,* ed. E. Moreno Báez (Madrid, 1955).

MONTESINOS, JOSÉ F. "Algunos problemas del *Romancero nuevo,*" *RPh,* VI (1952-3), 231-247.

——. *Estudios sobre Lope* (México, 1951).

——. "Notas a la primera parte de *Flor de romances,*" *BH,* LIV (1952), 386-404.

MOREL-FATIO, ALFRED. *L'Espagne au XVIᵉ et au XVIIᵉ siècle. Documents historiques et littéraires* (Bonn, 1878).

MORETO, AGUSTÍN. *Teatro*, Clás. Cast. (Madrid, 1922).

MORLEY, S. G. AND BRUERTON, C. *The Chronology of Lope de Vega's 'Comedias', with a Discussion of Doubtful Attributions* (New York, 1940).

MOSQUERA DE BARNUEVO, FRANCISCO. *La Numantina* (Sevilla, 1612).

MOURGUES, ODETTE DE. *Metaphysical, Précieux and Baroque Poetry* (Oxford, 1953).

MUÑOZ CORTÉS, MANUEL. "Aspectos estilísticos de Vélez de Guevara en su 'Diablo Cojuelo'," *RFE*, XXVII (1943), 48-76.

MUÑOZ MORILLEJO, JOAQUÍN. *Escenografía española* (Madrid, 1923).

MYROURE. *The Myroure of our Ladye*, ed. J. H. Blunt, Early English Text Society (London, 1873).

NADAL, OCTAVE. *Le Sentiment de l'amour dans l'œuvre de Pierre Corneille*, 4th edn. (Paris, 1948).

NELSON, JOHN C. *Renaissance Theory of Love: The Context of Giordano Bruno's 'Eroici furori'* (New York, 1958).

NICOLL, ALLARDYCE. *Stuart Masques and the Renaissance Stage* (London, 1937).

———. *The World of Harlequin: A Critical Study of the Commedia dell' arte* (Cambridge, 1963).

NIEVA CALVO, SEBASTIÁN DE. *La mejor muger, madre y virgen. Sus excelencias, vida, y grandezas, repartidas por sus fiestas todas. Poema sacro del licenciado Sebastián de Nieua Calvo* (Madrid, 1625).

NOTICIAS. *Noticias de Madrid (1621-27)*, ed. Ángel González Palencia (Madrid, 1942).

NOVELISTAS ANTERIORES. *Novelistas anteriores a Cervantes*, in *BAE*, vol. III.

NOVOA, MATÍAS DE. *Historia de Felipe III*, in *Colección de documentos inéditos*, vols. LX and LXI (Madrid, 1875).

———. *Historia de Felipe IV*, in *Colección de documentos inéditos*, vols. LXIX, LXXVII, and LXXX (Madrid, 1878-83).

NÚÑEZ DE CASTRO, ALONSO. *Libro historico politico, solo Madrid es Corte, y el Cortesano en Madrid*, 2nd impression with additions, Domingo García Morrás (Madrid, 1669). [The original edn. appeared in Madrid, Andrés García de la Iglesia, 1658.]

OCHOA, EUGENIO DE. *Catálogo razonado de los manuscritos españoles existentes en la Biblioteca Real de París* (Paris, 1844).

OÑA, TOMÁS DE. *Fenix de los ingenios, qve renace de las plavsibles cenizas del certamen qve dedico a la venerabilissima imagen de N[uestra] S[eñora] de la Soledad en la celebre translacion a sv svmptvosa capilla* (Madrid, 1664).

ORTEGA DEL ÁLAMO, ANDRÉS. *Dos canciones de Lope de Vega en un Cancionero poético musical del siglo XVII* (Valencia, 1962).

OWST, G. R. *Literature and Pulpit in Medieval England* (Cambridge, 1933).

PANDOLFI, VITO. *La Commedia dell' arte* (Firenze, 1957-61), 6 vols.

PANTALEÓN DE RIBERA, ANASTASIO. *Obras*, ed. Joseph Pellicer y Tovar (Madrid, 1634).

PAPELL, ANTONIO. *Quevedo, su tiempo, su vida, su obra* (Barcelona, 1947).

PARKER, ALEXANDER A. "La 'Agudeza' en algunos sonetos de Quevedo: contribución al estudio del conceptismo," in *Estudios dedicados a Menéndez Pidal*, III (Madrid, 1952), 345-360.

PAZ Y MELIA, ANTONIO. *Sales españolas o agudezas del ingenio nacional: Segunda serie* (Madrid, 1902).

PAZ, JULIÁN. *Catálogo de las piezas de teatro que se conservan en el departamento de manuscritos de la Biblioteca Nacional* (Madrid, 1934-35), 2 vols.

PEDRELL, FELIPE. *Catàlech de la Biblioteca Musical de la Diputació de Barcelona* (Barcelona, 1908-9), 2 vols.

——. *Cancionero musical popular español* (Valls, 1918-22), 4 vols.

PELLICER, CASIANO. *Tratado histórico sobre el origen y progresos de la comedia y del histrionismo en España* (Madrid, 1804), 2 vols.

PELLICER Y TOVAR, JOSEPH. *Anfiteatro de Felipe el Grande* (Madrid, 1631).

——. *Avisos históricos, que comprehenden las noticias y sucesos mas particulares, ocurridos en nuestra Monarquía desde el año de 1639*, ed. A. Valladares de Sotomayor, in *Semanario Erudito*, vols. XXXI-XXXIII (Madrid, 1790).

——. *El fénix y su historia natural* (Madrid, 1630).

——. *Lecciones solemnes a las obras de Don Luis de Góngora y Argote* (Madrid, 1630).

PÉREZ, DIEGO. *Relación de las fiestas que el Marqués del Carpio hizo al Rey Nuestro Señor* (Sevilla, 1624).

PÉREZ DE GUZMÁN, JUAN. "Las academias literarias del siglo de los Austrias," *La Ilustración Española y Americana*, XXXI (1880), 106-107, 123-126, and 139-142.

PÉREZ DEL BARRIO ÁNGULO, GABRIEL. *Dirección de secretarios de señores, y las materias, cuydados y obligación que les tocan* (Madrid, 1613).

——. *Secretario y consejero de señores, y ministros* (Madrid, 1667).

PÉREZ DE MONTALBÁN, JUAN. *Para todos. Exemplos morales humanos y divinos* (ed. Huesca, 1633).

——. *Primero tomo de sus comedias* (ed. Alcalá, 1638).

PÉREZ PASTOR, CRISTÓBAL. *Bibliografía madrileña* (Madrid, 1891-1907), 3 vols.

——. "Nuevos datos acerca del histrionismo español," *BH*, at intervals between 1906 and 1914, Index in vol. XVII (1915), 36-53. [See also his *Nuevos datos acerca del histrionismo español en los siglos XVI y XVII, Primera serie* (Madrid, 1901), and *Segunda serie* (Bordeaux, 1914).]

PICARD, ROGER. *Les Salons littéraires et la société française 1610-1789* (New York, 1943).

PIERCE, FRANK. *La poesía épica del Siglo de Oro*, 2nd edn., revised and enlarged (Madrid, 1968).

PIFERRER, FRANCISCO. *Nobiliario de los reinos y señoríos de España* (Madrid, 1855-60).

PINHEIRO DA VEGA, TOMÉ. *Fastiginia o Fastos geniales,* trans. Narciso Alonso Cortés (Valladolid, 1916).

PITOLLET, CAMILLE. "Lettre Espagnole: Le Roi d'Espagne Philippe IV fut-il auteur dramatique?" *La Renaissance d'Occident,* VII (1923), 787-795.

PLACE, EDWIN B. "Does Lope de Vega's *Gracioso* stem in part from Harlequin?" *HisL,* XVII (1934), 257-270.

———. "Notes on the Grotesque: the 'Comedia de figurón' at home and abroad," *PMLA,* LIV (1939), 412-421.

POESÍAS VARIAS DE GRANDES INGENIOS. *See* ALFAY, JOSÉ.

POETAS LÍRICOS. *Poetas líricos de los siglos XVI y XVII,* ed. Adolfo de Castro, 2 vols., in *BAE,* vols. XXXII and XLII.

POLO DE MEDINA, SALVADOR JACINTO. *El buen humor de las Musas. Lo compuso Salvador Jacinto Polo de Medina, natural de Murcia* (Madrid, 1637).

———. *Obras en prosa y en Verso Recogidas por vn aficionado svyo* (Zaragoça, 1664).

———. *Obras escogidas,* ed. J. M. de Cossío (Madrid, 1931).

POURRAT, PIERRE. *Christian Spirituality,* trans. W. H. Mitchell and S. P. Jacques (London, 1922-27), 3 vols.

PRAZ, MARIO. *Studies in Seventeenth-Century Imagery,* vol. I (London, 1939), vol. II: Bibliography (London, 1947).

———. *The Flaming Heart: Essays on Crashaw, Machiavelli, and Other Studies in the Relations between Italian and English Literature from Chaucer to T. S. Eliot* (New York, 1958).

PSEUDO-BONAVENTURE, THE. *Meditations on the Life of Christ,* ed. Isa Ragusa and Rosalie B. Green (Princeton, N. J., 1961).

PUJOL, E. "Les Ressources instrumentales et leur rôle dans la musique pour vihuela et pour guitare au XVIe siècle et au XVIIe," in *La Musique instrumentale de la Renaissance: Études réunies et présentées par Jean Jacquot* (Paris, 1955).

QUEROL GAVALDÁ, MIGUEL. *La música en las obras de Cervantes* (Barcelona, 1948).

——— (ed). *Romances y letras a tres vozes (siglo XVII), Monumentos de la Música Española.* XVIII, vol. I (Barcelona, 1956).

QUEVEDO Y VILLEGAS, FRANCISCO DE. *Obras completas. I. Poesía original,* ed. J. M. Blecua (Barcelona, 1963).

———. *Obras completas: Obras en prosa,* ed. Luis Astrana Marín, 2nd edn. (Madrid, 1941).

———. *Obras completas, verso,* ed. Luis Astrana Marín (Madrid, 1932).

RAJNA, P. "L'Episodio delle questioni d'amore nel *Ficolo* del Boccaccio," *Romania,* XXXI (1902), 28-81.

———. "Una questione d'amore," *Raccolta di studii critici dedicata ad Alessandro d'Ancone* (Firenze, 1901).

RAMÍREZ, ALEJANDRO. *Epistolario de Justo Lipsio y los españoles* (1577-1606), [Madrid, 1966].

TERRY, ARTHUR (ed.). *An Anthology of Spanish Poetry, 1500-1700* (Oxford, 1965-68), 2 vols.

THOMAS, LUCIEN-PAUL. *Góngora et le Gongorisme considérés dans leurs rapports avec le Marinisme* (Paris, 1911).

THURSTON, GEORGE. "Our popular Devotions. II — The Rosary," *The Month,* XCVI (1900), 403-418, 513-527, 620-637, and XCVII (1901), 67-79, 172-188, 286-304, 383-404.

TIRSO DE MOLINA. *Comedias,* ed. Emilio Cotarelo (Madrid, 1906-7), 2 vols.

——. *Obras dramáticas completas,* ed. Blanca de los Ríos (Madrid, 1946-62), 3 vols.

TORRE, FRANCISCO DE LA (ed.). *Agudezas de Iuan Oven traducidas en metro castellano, ilustradas con adiciones y notas por Don Francisco de la Torre* (Madrid, 1674).

TORRENTE BALLESTER, G. *Sor María de Agreda. Selección por Gonzalo Torrente Ballester* (Madrid, 1942), 2 vols.

TREND, J. B. "Escenografía madrileña en el siglo XVII," *Revista de la Biblioteca, Archivo y Museo del Ayuntamiento de Madrid,* III (1926), 269-281.

TRILLO Y FIGUEROA, FRANCISCO DE. *Obras,* ed. Antonio Gallego Morell (Madrid, 1951).

TUVE, ROSEMOND. *A Reading of George Herbert* (London, 1952).

——. *Elizabethan and Metaphysical Imagery: Renaissance Poetic and Twentieth-century Critics* (Chicago, 1947).

UNDERHILL, JOHN GARRETT. *Spanish Literature in the England of the Tudors* (New York, 1899).

URIBE, P. ÁNGEL. "La Inmaculada en la literatura franciscano-española," *Archivo Ibero-Americano,* 2ª época, XV (1955), 201-495.

VALBUENA PRAT, ÁNGEL. "La escenografía de una comedia de Calderón," *Archivo Español de Arte y Arqueología,* VI (1930), 1-16.

VALDENEBRO Y CISNEROS, JOSÉ MARÍA. *La imprenta en Córdoba. Ensayo bibliográfico* (Madrid, 1900).

VAREY, JOHN E. "L'Auditoire du *Salón Dorado* de l'*Alcázar* de Madrid au XVIIe siècle," in *Dramaturgie et Société. Rapports entre l'œuvre théâtrale, son interprétation et son public aux XVIe et XVIIe siècles,* ed. Jean Jacquot, Élie Konigson and Marcel Oddon (Paris, 1968), 77-92.

——. "La mayordomía mayor y los festejos palaciegos del siglo XVII," *Anales del Instituto de Estudios Madrileños,* IV (1969), 145-168.

VARIAS HERMOSAS FLORES. *Varias hermosas flores del Parnasso. Que en quatro floridos, vistosos quadros, plantaron junto a su cristalina fuente: D. Antonio Hurtado de Mendoza; D. Antonio de Solís; D. Francisco de la Torre y Sebil; D. Rodrigo Artes y Muñoz; Martín Iuan Barcelo: Iuan Bautista Aguilar, y otros ilustres poetas de España* (Valencia, 1680).

VEGA CARPIO, LOPE FÉLIX DE. *Colección de las obras sueltas* (Madrid, Antonio de Sancha, 1776-9), 21 vols.

——. *Colección escogida de obras no dramáticas,* in *BAE,* vol. XXVIII.

VEGA CARPIO, LOPE FÉLIX DE. *Decimaoctava parte de las comedias* (Madrid, 1623).

——. *Decimasexta parte de las comedias* (Madrid, 1621).

——. *Epistolario,* ed. A. G. de Amezúa (Madrid, 1935-43), 4 vols.

——. *Iervsalén conqvistada, epopeya trágica* (Madrid, 1609).

——. *Ivsta poetica, y alabanzas ivstas que hizo la insigne villa de Madrid al bien-auenturado San Isidro en las fiestas de su Beatificacion* (Madrid, 1620).

——. *La Circe con otras Rimas y Prosas* (Madrid, 1624).

——. *La Filomena con otras diversas Rimas, Prosas, y Versos* (Barcelona, 1621).

——. *Obras,* ed. Real Academia Española (Madrid, 1916-), vol. 1-.

——. *Obras completas,* ed. J. de Entrambasaguas, I *(Obras no dramáticas. I),* [Madrid, 1965].

——. *Obras escogidas,* ed. Federico Carlos Sáinz de Robles (Madrid, 1946), 2 vols.

——. *Parte decinueve, y la mejor parte de las comedias* (Madrid, 1625).

——. *Pastores de Belén: Prosas y versos divinos* (ed. Brusselas, 1614).

——. *Poesías líricas,* ed. J. F. Montesinos, Clás. Cast. (Madrid, 1925-6), 2 vols.

——. *Relacion de las fiestas que la insigne villa de Madrid hizo en la canoni-zacion de su bienaventurado hijo, y patron, San Isidro* (Madrid, 1622).

VEJÁMENES LITERARIOS. *Vejámenes literarios por D. Jerónimo de Cáncer y Velasco y Anastasio Pantaleón de Ribera* (Madrid, 1919).

VÉLEZ DE GUEVARA, LUIS. *El diablo cojuelo,* ed. F. Rodríguez Marín, Clás. Cast. (Madrid, 1918).

——. *Elogio del Iuramento del Serenissimo Principe Don Felipe Domingo, Qvarto deste nombre* (Madrid, 1608).

VERA Y FIGUEROA, JUAN DE. *Fragmentos históricos de la vida de D. Gaspar de Guzmán, Conde de Olivares* (1628), in *Semanario Erudito,* II (Madrid, 1787), p. 145 *et seq.*

VERA Y MENDOZA, FERNANDO LUIS DE. *Panegírico por la poesía,* ed. M. Cardenal de Iracheta, in *Revista de Bibliografía Nacional,* II (1941), 302-342.

VOSSLER, KARL. *La poesía de la soledad en España,* trans. Ramón de la Serna y Espina (Buenos Aires, 1946).

WARNKE, FRANK J. *European Metaphysical Poetry* (New Haven, Conn., 1961).

WEDGWOOD, C. V. *The Thirty Years War* (London, Penguin Books, 1957).

WHINNOM, KEITH. "El origen de las comparaciones religiosas del Siglo de Oro: Mendoza, Montesino y Román," *RFE,* XLVI (1963), 263-285.

——. "The Supposed Sources of Inspiration of Spanish Fifteenth-Century Narrative Religious Verse," *Symposium,* XVI (1963), 268-291.

WILLIAMS, ROBERT H. "Satirical Rules of Etiquette," *HisL,* XIII (1930), 298-299.

WILLIAMSON, GEORGE. *The Senecan Amble: a Study in Prose Form from Bacon to Collier* (London, 1951).

WILSON, E. M. "A Key to Calderón's *Psalle et sile*," in *Hispanic Studies in Honour of I. González Llubera*, ed. Frank Pierce (Oxford, 1959).

——. "Samuel Pepys's Spanish Chap-books," *Transactions of the Cambridge Bibliographical Society*, II (1954-8), 127-154, 229-268, and 305-322.

——. "Spanish and English Religious Poetry of the Seventeenth Century," *Journal of Ecclesiastical History*, IX (1958), 38-53.

——. "The *Cancionero* of Don Joseph del Corral," *HR*, XXXV (1967), 141-160.

—— AND SAGE, JACK. *Poesías líricas en las obras dramáticas de Calderón* (London, 1964).

WINEGARTEN, RENÉE. *French Lyric Poetry in the Age of Malherbe* (Manchester, 1954).

ZABALETA, JUAN DE. *El Dia de Fiesta por la tarde. Parte secunda del Dia de Fiesta* (Madrid, 1660).

——. *El Dia de Fiesta, Primera parte. Que contiene el Dia de Fiesta por la mañana* (Coimbra, 1666).

ZONTA, GUISEPPE. "Arbitrati reali o questione giocose," *Studi Medievali*, III (1908-11), 603- 637.

——. "Rileggendo Andrea Cappellano," *Studi Medievali*, III (1908-11), 49-68.

INDEX

270, 302, 308; and music, 204-206; *Jácaras, Las,* 123 n. 26; *Mayor encanto amor, El,* 235; *No hay burlas con el amor,* 106 n. 71; *Príncipe constante, El,* 242; *Psalle et Sile,* 176; *Secreto a voces, El,* 91; *Troya abrasada,* 82.

Camargo, Ignacio de, 203.

Camoens, Luis de, 94, 144, 189.

Campion, Thomas, 197.

Cáncer y Velasco, Jerónimo de, 62-63.

Cancionero BNM *MS* 4103, a Jesuit-inspired collection of song-lyrics, 199, Appendices I and IV.

Cancionero de Baena, 92.

Cancionero de Sablonara, 198, Appendix I.

Cancionero poético-musical de 1645, 198, Appendices I and IV.

Cancionero poetry, 80-83, 89, 92, 98 n. 41, 102 n. 54, 105, 128-130, 150, 181, 185-186, 188, 189, 194.

Cantillana, Countess of, 45 n. 13.

Cardenal-Infante. *See* Austria, Fernando de.

Cardona y Borja Ruiz, Felipe de, Admiral of Aragon, 19 n. 7, 47 n. 17.

Carpio, Marquis del, 32 n. 52.

Carrillo de Sotomayor, Luis, 146 n. 79.

Cartagena, Pedro de, 81, 82.

Castello, Alberto, 159.

Castiglione, Baltasar, 87-89, 91, 95, 102, 186, 197.

Castillejo, Cristóbal de, 181.

Castillo Solórzano, Alonso de, 200, 213, 295, 297.

Castro y Bellvis, Guillén de, 295, 298; *Mal casados de Valencia, Los,* 269 n. 62; *Narciso, El,* 295, 298.

Catalina Clara, Doña, 100.

Cervantes Saavedra, Miguel de, 21, 23, 209; *Don Quixote,* 94, 144 n. 72; *Galatea, La,* 91, 94; *Gitanilla, La,* 120; *Juez de los divorcios, El,* 210; *Licenciado Vidriera, El,* 210; *Viage del Parnaso, El,* 21.

Charles V, Emperor, and King of Spain, 17, 96, 223.

Charles II, King of Spain, 191.

Charles Stuart, Prince of Wales, 25, 141.

Chauvinism and poetry, 186 n. 22.

Chivalry and chivalresque, 87, 94, 223, 225-228.

Civile Conversation, The, 268 n. 60.

Collado del Hierro, Agustín, 72-73.

Comedia de figurón, 249, 256, 294-296.

———— *de santo,* 237.

———— *de tramoyas,* 58, 236, 248.

Commedia dell'arte, 253-254, 276-278, 292-294.

Concepto, Gracián's definition of, 67; and rhetorical figure, 86, 146, 149; in Christian tradition, 76 *et seq.,* 86.

Concepto por correspondencia y proporción, 135.

———— *por desemejanza,* 146.

Córdoba, Sebastián de, 78.

Corral, Gabriel del, 73 n. 34, 91, 200.

Corral, Joseph del, 183-184, Appendices I and IV.

Correa, Padre Manuel, 198, 199.

Cossío, José María de, 187, 201.

Costumbrismo, 213, 218, 297.

Cotarelo y Mori, Emilio, 14, 207, 208, 211 n. 16.

Court hieroglyphics, 71, 227.

———— spectacle, 223.

Courtier, The, of Castiglione, 87 *et seq.,* 95, 186.

Covarrubias Orozco, Sebastián de, 68, 69, 142.

Crane, T. F., 13, 90 n. 10, 92.

Crashaw, Richard, 79, 160, 161 n. 21, 163, 165, 167, 174.

Crotalón, El, 92.

Cruz, Ramón de la, 215.

Cubillo de Aragón, Álvaro, 60, 124, 304, Appendix II.

Culteranismo, 167, 180, 182, 250.

Culterano and *conceptista,* 64-66, 103, 105, 106.

Curtius, Ernst Robert, 67.

Darbord, Michel, 77.

Davies, John, of Hereford, 169.

Desrealización, 114.

Device, 71-72, 89.

Díaz, Gabriel, 195 n. 14, 196, 197 n. 18.

Díaz de Zurbano, Sancho, 26.

Lotti, Cosme, 62, 235.
Love, courtly, 87, 125, 130, 141, 180, 184, 188-191, 229.
———, game of, 97-102, 110-111, 229, 238.
———, psychology of, 188-190, 243, 299, 303.
———, questions of, 89-93, 101.
Lucan, 157 .
Ludolph of Saxony, 162-166, 177, 178.
Luján, Micaela de, 19.
Luzán, Ignacio de, 294 n. 9, 308.

Machado, Manuel, 199.
Madrid, sense of, 121, 209, 249-250, 256, 258, 271, 273-274, 283, 291, 296-297.
Madrigal, 131-132, 197.
Magendie, Maurice, 97 n. 35.
Maja, 215.
Malherbe, François de, 186.
Malón de Chaide, Pedro, 78.
Manescal, Miguel, 154, 167 n. 41, 306, 307, 309.
Manrique, Jorge, 82.
Manrique, María, 45.
Manzanarian idyll, 94-95, 97, 109 *et seq.*, 184.
Marañón, Gregorio, 53.
March, Ausias, 189.
Marguerite, Queen of Navarre, 88, 89.
Marino, Giambattista, 81 n. 66, 168.
Marot, Clément, 111.
Martial, 72, 73, 75, 76, 133, 137, 153, 175, 187.
Martz, Louis L., 158-159, 161, 166, 175-178.
Mazzeo, Joseph A., 68, 72, 80, 81 n. 66, 86.
Medel del Castillo, Francisco, 307.
Medieval court, Christ's, 171.
Medinaceli, Duke of, 60.
Medina de Ríoseco, Duchess of, 48, 98.
Medina de Ríoseco, Duke of, Admiral of Castile, Juan Alfonso Enríquez de Cabrera, 31, 39, 47-48, 54-55, 128.
Medina Sidonia, House of, 47.
Medina de las Torres, Duke of, Marquis of Toral, Ramiro Felipe Núñez

de Guzmán, 32 n. 50, 44, 45-46, 47, 48.
Meditation, 158, 160, 161-162, 165, 175-178.
Medrano, Sebastián Francisco de, 25, 60, 183.
Mendoza, Antonia de (*Antandra*), 91, 99-100, 138.
Mendoza, Antonio de; and language of society, 107; and marriage, 259, 263, 267-269, 302; and musical performance, 197-203; and other writers, 20 *et seq.*, 48-59, 275; and politics, 37, 39, 40-41, 43-44, 52-53, 141; and politics in the theatre, 225, 230, 232-233, 253, 275, 297, 301; and society, 212, 213, 221, 230-231, 246, 249, 252-254, 255-256, 262-263, 265, 281-283, 296, 297-298, 300, 302; and song-writers, 195 *et seq.*, 199 n. 25, 202, 204, Appendix I; and theatre music, 203 *et seq.*, 225, 238, 251; on language of poetry, 179-181, 182, 183.
Mendoza's first marriage 28, 30-31; his second marriage, 33-34, 38, 259; his palace coterie, 45-48; his poems in the public theatre, 203-206; his reputation as a playwright, 48-49, 305, 308-310.
Mendoza's works: A) COLLECTIONS: Manuscript collections of poems, 192-193, Appendices III and IV, List of MSS and Books; *Fénix castellano, El*, 12, 14, 154, 156, 192, 307; *Obras líricas, y cómicas*, 156, 307, 327-328; *Obras poéticas*, ed. R. Benítez Claros, 12, 13, 199; B) PLAYS: *Cada loco con su tema*, 14, 17 n. 2, 21 n. 15, 24, 26, 107, 180, 204, 213, 248, 249-256, 258, 260, 273, 283, 284, 292, 295, 298, 302, 309; *Celos sin saber de quien*, 256-260, 286, 288, 299; *Doctor Dieta, El* (see *Miser Palomo*, Part Two); *Empeños del mentir, Los*, 19, 21, 37 n. 70, 48, 213, 273-285, 287, 289-290, 292-293, 297, 298, 301, 302, 303, 309; *Entremés de Getafe, El*, 204, 213-215, 216, 240, 295, 296, 297;

Entremés, Hispanic Society of America, 208 n. 7, 216-219; *Galán sin dama, El,* 49 n. 26, 260-265, 266, 273, 280, 295, 298, 305; *Marido hace mujer, El,* 48, 58, 260, 265-273, 279, 280, 285 n. 97, 297, 302, 303, 305, 309; *Más merece quien más ama,* 208 n. 7, 238-243, 244, 249 n. 25, 250, 255, 258-259, 299, 300, 301, 305, 309; *Miser Palomo,* Part One, 23, 42, 207, 209-211, 216, 218-220, 231, 256, 265, 294, 296; *Miser Palomo,* Part Two (or *El Doctor Dieta),* 42, 211-213, 216, 218, 220, 293, 296; *No hay amor donde hay agravio,* 243-248, 288, 292, 302, 305; *Premio de la virtud, El,* 237-238; *Querer por solo querer,* 14, 17 n. 2, 31, 103, 237, 238, 244, 283, 299, 309, Appendix V; *Querer* and *gracioso,* 231-232, 283, 292; and *Más merece,* 238-239; and music, 204; and politics, 44, 49, 300-301; and Villamediana's *Gloria,* 227 n. 17, 228, 235; *Querer,* lyricism of, 52 n. 34, 141, 151-152, 192, 197, 233-235; performance of, 29-30, 48, 222; prologue of, 193; *Quien más miente, medra más,* 48, 275; *Riesgos que tiene un coche, Los* (or *Lo que es un coche en Madrid),* 285-291, 297, 298, 299, 305; C) POEMS: *Décimas,* 132-139; *Romances* and allied forms, 109-132; Sonnets, 139-153; *Vida de Nuestra Señora,* 50, 64, 76, 80, 84, 85, 154-178, 180, 193, 305; D) PROSE: *Aprobación* to E s q u i l a c h e 's *Obras divinas,* 179; *Convocación de las Cortes,* 34-35, 44; *Discurso sobre los Grandes,* 36; *Fiesta que se hizo* ..., 29, 179, 196 nn. 16 and 18, 228; *Relación de los efetos,* 37 n. 71.

Mendoza, Francisco de, 60, 62.

Mendoza, Fray Íñigo de, 162, 163 n. 28, 166, 171 n. 53.

Mendoza Briceño, Jerónimo de, 30 n. 47.

Menéndez Pidal, Ramón, 123.

Mesonero Romanos, Ramón de, 309-310.

Metaphor, 77-80, 84, 85, 104, 136.

Milán, Luis, 88-89.

Mirallo, Marchioness of, 44.

Mocenigo, Alvise, 30.

Molière, Jean-Baptiste Poquelin, 87, 298; his *École des maris* and *El marido hace mujer,* 303, 305.

Montemayor, Jorge de, 93; his *Diana,* 91, 93-94.

Montero, Mateo, 48, 248, 275.

Monterrey, Count of, Alonso de Azevedo y Zúñiga, 48, 60.

Montesino, Ambrosio de, 78, 158, 166.

Montesinos, José F., 125, 126, 150.

Moreto, Agustín, 292, 296; *Desdén con el desdén, El,* 299, 300; *Lindo Don Diego, El,* 256, 295, 298.

Moscoso, Antonio de, Marquis of Villanueva del Fresno, 36 n. 64.

Mourgues, Odette de, 169 n. 48.

Muñoz Cortés, Manuel, 85, 123.

Navarro de Espinosa, Juan, 304 n. 2.

Neo-Platonism. *See* Platonism.

Neo-Stoics and Neo-Stoicism, 51, 86.

Nieto de Molina, Francisco, 307.

Nieva Calvo, Sebastián de, 157.

Nördlingen, Battle of, 37 n. 70, 274, 275.

Nueva Biblioteca de Autores Españoles, 14.

Núñez de Castro, Alonso, 194 n. 8, 304.

Núñez de Reinoso, Alonso, 90.

Ocón Coalla de Pineda, Clara, 33, 36 n. 67, 38, 139.

Olivares, Count-Duke of, Gaspar de Guzmán, 36, 47, 49, 50, 56, 96, 222; and confidants, 30, 36; and Mendoza, 18, 20, 26, 27-28, 29-30, 31-32, 33, 37, 38-39, 40-41, 45, 46, 52-53, 133, 139, 152 n. 94, 302; and music, 196; and Philip IV, 27, 39, 40-42, 134-135, 152, 233; and the arts, 48, 54, 60, 297, 301.

Olivares, Countess of, Inés de Zúñiga, 29, 44, 60, 96, 98, 99.

Orgaz, Count of, 194.

Ortiz de Zárate, Fortún, 17 n. 2.

Osuna, Duke of, Viceroy of Naples, 25, 27.

Ovid, 75-76.

Owen, John, epigrammatist, 73.

Pacheco, Francisco, 186 n. 22, 201
Padilla, Juan de, 77, 162, 166.
Palace decorum and taste, 107-108,
126, 179, 181-183, 184-185, 187-
188, 190, 192, 193-194, 222-225,
226, 228-229, 237, 243, 249, 259,
279, 300.
———— poetasters, 99-101.
Palomares, musician, 196 n. 18.
Palomo, el rey, 207 n. 3.
Pantaleón de Ribera, Anastasio, 70,
92, 146 n. 79.
Papel sellado, invention of, 38.
Paradox, 70, 76-77, 81, 134, 147-148,
170, 175, 185.
Parallelism, 134, 149-150.
Paravicino y Arteaga, Hortensio Félix,
34, 76, 167, 175 n. 65, 180, 181.
Parker, Alexander A., 65.
Parnaso, El, academy. See *Academia
Selvaje.*
Passion, woman of, 228, 241, 259, 287-
289, 292, 299.
Pastoral ballad, 109-117, 132, 184, 185,
197.
———— genre, 93 et` seq., 228, 279,
299, 303.
Pastrana, Duke of, 24.
Paz, Sancho de, *autor de comedias,*
207 n. 4.
Pellegrini, Matteo, 66.
Pellicer y Tovar, José, 41, 61, 76.
Peñafiel, Duke of, 25, 27.
Pérez, Diego, 32 n. 52.
Pérez de Guzmán, Fernán, 92.
Pérez del Barrio Ángulo, Gabriel, 22.
Pérez de Montalbán, Juan, 62, 187 n.
26, 307; *De un castigo dos vengan-
zas,* 273 n. 72; *Para todos,* 48, 155,
250 n. 28.
Persius, 76.
Petimetre, 215, 295, 298.
Petrarch and Petrarchanism, 80, 87,
93, 105, 140, 189.
Pharsalus, 157.
Philip II, King of Spain, 87, 94,·104,
195, 223.
Philip III, King of Spain, 23, 27, 53,
60, 80, 89, 95, 223, 250.

Philip IV, King of Spain *(Fileno),* 27,
42, 46, 47, 56, 95, 110, 141, 149,
250; and academies, 60, 62-63; and
Mendoza, 29-30, 37-39, 40-41, 43,
44, 50, 57, 63, 248, 302; and music,
196-197; and Olivares, 27, 39, 40-42,
134-135, 152, 233; and palace the-
atre, 29, 48, 49, 222, 232, 299-300;
and poetry, 59-60, 110.
Pinheiro da Vega, Tomé, 103, 105.
Pintura (poetic genre), 99-100, 113-
114, 120, 123-125, 127, 132, 151,
168-169, 229, 243, 259.
Place, Edwin B., 294 n. 9, 296.
Platonism, 87, 88, 93, 189.
Pléiade, La, 186.
Poem, identity of a, 195, 202-203.
Poesías varias de grandes ingenios
(Alfay), 56, 120 n. 22, 306.
Poésie galante, La, 93, 186.
Poet, the print-shy, 193-194.
Poeta de bien, El, 11, 187, 212.
Poetry and music, 195-197.
———— and the Nobility, 59-60.
Polo de Medina, Salvador Jacinto, 61,
151 n. 93, 191 n. 37, 182, 184,
187, 188.
Prado, Antonio de, *autor de comedias,*
250 n. 28.
Praz, Mario, 68, 72, 73, 160.
Preciosity, 93, 104, 105-107, 188.
Primavera y flor (Arias Pérez), 20 n.
11, 42, 119, 122, 125, 184, 195, 203,
306, Appendices I and IV.
Pseudo-Bonaventure, The, 166 n. 39,
175, 177.

Quarles, Francis, 68.
Quevedo, Francisco de, 20-21, 65, 72,
85, 118, 120 n. 22, 121, 123, 137,
140, 141, 148, 180, 184, 187, 203
n. 36, 207 n. 3, 220, 307; and González de Salas, 73, 76; and Lipsius,
75; and Mendoza, 48, 50-53, 213,
248, 275; and Olivares, 52-53; and
Silver Age, 75-76; and the theatre,
48, 213; *Buscón, El,* 213; *Culta latiniparla, La,* 105-106; *Epístola censoria, La,* 69, 253; *Isla de los Monopontos, La,* 53.